ArtScroll Series®

Rabbi Nosson Scherman / Rabbi Meir Zlotowitz
General Editors

RAV GIFTER

The Vision, Fire, and Impact of an American-born Gadol

RABBI YECHIEL SPERO

Published by
Mesorah Publications, ltd

FIRST EDITION
First Impression … June 2011
Second Impression … June 2011

Published and Distributed by
MESORAH PUBLICATIONS, LTD.
4401 Second Avenue / Brooklyn, N.Y 11232

Distributed in Europe by
LEHMANNS
Unit E, Viking Business Park
Rolling Mill Road
Jarow, Tyne & Wear, NE32 3DP
England

Distributed in Australia and New Zealand
by **GOLDS WORLDS OF JUDAICA**
3-13 William Street
Balaclava, Melbourne 3183
Victoria, Australia

Distributed in Israel by
SIFRIATI / A. GITLER — BOOKS
6 Hayarkon Street
Bnei Brak 51127

Distributed in South Africa by
KOLLEL BOOKSHOP
Ivy Common
105 William Road
Norwood 2192, Johannesburg, South Africa

ARTSCROLL SERIES®
RAV GIFTER
© Copyright 2011, by MESORAH PUBLICATIONS, Ltd.
4401 Second Avenue / Brooklyn, N.Y. 11232 / (718) 921-9000 / www.artscroll.com

---

ALL RIGHTS RESERVED
The text, prefatory and associated textual contents and introductions
— including the typographic layout, cover artwork and ornamental graphics —
have been designed, edited and revised as to content, form and style.

No part of this book may be reproduced
IN ANY FORM, PHOTOCOPYING, OR COMPUTER RETRIEVAL SYSTEMS
— even for personal use without written permission from
the copyright holder, Mesorah Publications Ltd.
except by a reviewer who wishes to quote brief passages
in connection with a review written for inclusion in magazines or newspapers.

THE RIGHTS OF THE COPYRIGHT HOLDER WILL BE STRICTLY ENFORCED.

ISBN 10: 1-4226-1097-7 / ISBN 13: 978-1-4226-1097-8

Typography by CompuScribe at ArtScroll Studios, Ltd.
Printed in the United States of America by Noble Book Press Corp.
Bound by Sefercraft, Quality Bookbinders, Ltd., Brooklyn N.Y. 11232

RAV GIFTER

לזכר נשמת אבינו

הרב הגאון ר' נחום זאב
בן הרב הגאון אליהו אליעזר זצ"ל

*H*e personified the greatness of Kelm in Torah, Mussar, and responsibility for Klal Yisrael. As one of the pioneers of Torah chinuch in America, he planted seeds that will bear fruit for centuries.

Reuven and Naomi Dessler and Family

לעילוי נשמת

Our father

ר' ישראל ראובן בן ר' צבי יואל ז"ל
Mr. Herbert Freschl ז"ל

*H*e was a man of unimpeachable integrity, kindness and generosity. His word was a deed, without compromise or delay.
His example continues to inspire us all.

Reuven and Naomi Dessler and Family

לעילוי נשמות

Tuvia ben Tzodok Suchard ע"ה
15 Kislev 5763

Miriam bas Shmuel Spivack ע"ה
16 Adar 5770

Mina bas Yitzchok Moshe Suchard ע"ה
27 Sivan 5759

Ilana Zelda bas Tuvia-Elaine Miller ע"ה
11 Nissan 5770

Dedicated by

Dayan Tzodok Shmuel and Rochel Guta Suchard
Rabbi Mordechai Moshe and Yehudis Suchard

In tribute to our parents

Rabbi Shlomo and Bluma Davis שליט"א

*W*ho were pioneers in the establishment of
Telshe Yeshiva in America
and in laying the groundwork for
Cleveland's thriving Torah community.
They had a close and unforgettable relationship with
Harav Gifter זצ"ל, who was their friend and neighbor.

Yosef and Edie Davis

לעילוי נשמת

*O*ur grandfather and great-grandfather

הגאון ר' מרדכי ב"ר ישראל זצ"ל

May his legacy live on for generations.

From his grandchildren and great-grandchild

**Robert and Hinda Rochel Mizrahi
and Matthew**

We pay tribute to the still vibrant memory of

The Rosh HaYeshiva
HaGaon Harav Mordechai Gifter זצ"ל

*H*e was a living Sefer Torah, a wellspring of inspiration
to all who had the privilege of being close to him.
To us personally and to the work of ArtScroll/Mesorah,
he was a father, a mentor, and a friend.
זכותו יגן עלינו

**Rabbi and Mrs. Nosson Scherman
Rabbi and Mrs. Meir Zlotowitz   Rabbi and Mrs. Sheah Brander**

Table of Contents

Publisher's Preface   13
An Author's Reflections   15
Author's Acknowledgments   24

֍ Section 1: Biography — From a Lad to a Lion

1 Humble Beginnings
Baltimore / Early Influences / Yeshivah in New York / A Great Teacher and Correspondence / Lifelong Student   33

2 Journey to Telz — A Life Forever Changed
Adjustments / The Joys of Learning in Telz / A Name for Himself / Disaster Averted / Rav Mottel Pogromansky / The Fire of Torah / Bein Hazmanim / His Bride   43

3 The Journey From Telz
Torah Thoughts / Guarding One's Health / Self-Annulment / The Majesty of Telz / Return to America / Saving His Bride / Martyrs of Telz / Moishele / A Mother's Love / Final Avodah / The Legacy of Telz / Feeling the Destruction / New Beginnings / Waterbury   55

4 Back to Telz ... in America ... and Eretz Yisrael
True Calling / Energizing His Students / Rosh Hayeshivah / Talented Speaker / Telz-Stone / Return to Cleveland   80

5 Final Years in Cleveland
An Impassioned Plea / Twilight / The Will Of Hashem   95

ৼ§ Section 2: Limud HaTorah — Torah Study

6 The Joy of Torah
Torah as a Life Force / Straight From the King's Mouth / The Power of a Torah Scholar / Love of Torah / The Original Text / True Happiness / A Magical Kiss / Dancing With the Torah / Not Taking a Break / More Precious / The Epitome of Joy / Always Fresh — 107

7 Total Immersion
Even in America / Bread and Meat / Total Recall / Total Involvement / The Merit of Total Immersion / Prophecy of Doom — 119

8 Ameilus BaTorah — Toiling in Torah
Like a Business / Learning Without Toil Is Not Learning / Human Nature / The Greatest Delicacy — 128

9 Making the Most of Our Time
Not Wasting a Minute / The Vilna Gaon's Calculation / The Sword of Chizkiyahu / The Timeless Words of the Ramchal — 138

ৼ§ Section 3: Torah Outlook

10 The Torah Approach
Daas Torah / Two Letters / The Letter of April / The Letter of February / One Type of Jew — 145

11 The Supremacy of Torah
University Attendance and Earning a Living / Only Toras Moshe / The Torah as Our Guide / The Spiritual and the Material — 154

12 A Man of Principle
Not Afraid of Any Man / The Cook / The Right Balance / Zealousness in Lithuania / No Personal Agenda / In Pursuit of Kvod HaTorah / The Next Generation — 160

13 The Life and Outlook of a Ben Torah
Learning Mussar / A Ben Torah / Mentchlichkeit / A Monumental Lecture / Kiddush Hashem — 170

14 Deveikus BaHashem — Cleaving to Hashem

The Will of Hashem / Opportunity for Growth / For the Love of Mitzvos / Learning From Our Sages / Guarding One's Eyes / Wonders of Creation / Gratitude to Hashem / Expressing His Closeness / Awaiting Mashiach 177

15 The Torah's Viewpoint

The Holocaust / Current Events / The Yom Kippur War 186

∽§ Section 4: Rebbi — Talmid

16 A True Melamed

Rav Gifter's Monument / No Titles, Please / The Steipler's Opinion / "Melamed" / "Datai Ilavaihu — My Mind Is on Them" / Care and Concern / A Different Kind of Warmth / Strive for Excellence / Following His Teachers' Example 197

17 A Powerful Influence

Keeping His Talmidim in the Yeshivah / A Spontaneous Outburst / Rabbi Azriel Goldfein / Always Guiding 209

18 A Unique Disseminator of Torah

A European Rosh Hayeshivah / Understanding His Shiur / Prolific Writer / Relating to All His Students / Sense of Humor / Baal HaMesorah 217

19 Everlasting Lessons

Three Commitments / An Additional Commitment / The Snooze Button / Three Lessons 231

20 Students of All Stripes

Tailor-made Advice / Future Chassidic Rebbes / Prophetic Advice / An Indelible Impact / A "Talmidah" Remembers 239

21 Connecting With His Students and Encouraging Them to Grow

Living Life to Its Fullest / Keeping Them Close / Your Own Rebbi / "I'm Proud of You!" / Stretching Minds / Learning From Everything Around Us / Learning From Everyone / Spreading the Wealth 252

‿§ Section 5: Emes — Truth

22 Torah of Truth
The Ultimate Truth / Appreciating Other Seekers of Truth / Personal Stringencies/ Be Yourself   271

23 A Life of Truth
Money Matters / The Whole Truth / And Nothing But the Truth   279

‿§ Section 6: Bein Adam LaChaveiro — Interpersonal Relationships

24 A Heart Big Enough for All
Like Family / A Potent Blessing / Personal Involvement / Someone's Livelihood / Sleepless Nights   293

25 With Warmth, Humility, and Respect
Warmth / Humility / Respect / For the Sake of Peace   302

26 Kindness, Appreciation, and Sensitivity
Kindness / Appreciation / Sensitivity / Strong Emotions / Yet Complete Control   316

‿§ Section 7: Family Life

27 Building a Peaceful Home
A Loving Father / Other Family Members / Marital Harmony   329

28 "VeShinantam LeVanecha" — You Shall Teach Them Thoroughly to Your Children
Always a Learning Occasion / Shabbos / Yom Tov   341

‿§ Section 8: Yamim Noraim

29 Preparing for the Days of Awe (Elul)
Always in a State of Teshuvah / The Jewish Heart / Contemplating Tragedy / The Greatness of the Al-Mighty   357

30 A Deeper Understanding of the Yamim Noraim
On a Child's Level / True Desires / My Light and My Salvation / A Time of Closeness   364

31 Appreciating Hashem's Beautiful World
Through the Light of Torah / Limitless Memory / Sincerity That Broke Hearts / Mashiach's Welcoming Committee   370

32 Maximizing the Potential of the Days of Awe
Splitting the Heavens / Crying Out to Hashem / The Shofar   375

Epilogue
Our Rebbi…Forever   383

Afterword   387

Appendix — Family Tree   389

Glossary   395

Index   403

PHOTO CREDITS:

Agudath Israel of America
Artech
Rebbetzen Chaya Ausband
Moshe Benoliel
Rabbi Avrohom Biderman
Bottom Line Marketing
Rabbi Doniel Carlebach
Nesanel Davis
Yosef Davis
Rabbi Simcha Dessler
Rabbi and Mrs. Avrohom Doweck
Rabbi Eliezer Feuer
Gifter Family
Rebbetzin Gifter
R' Tzemach Glenn
Rabbi Dovid Greenwald of Telz Yeshiva
Rabbi Moshe Kolodny
Peninei Chein Collection
Ivan H. Norman
Rav Chaim Nussbaum
R' Eli Oelbaum
Rav Moshe Yaakov Perl
Reisman Family
Yitzchak Saftlas
Siegel family
Telz Yeshiva
Rabbi Dovid Yankelewitz

Publisher's Preface

IT IS A VERY GREAT PRIVILEGE FOR US TO PUBLISH THE biography of Hagaon Harav Mordechai Gifter *zt"l*. When the ArtScroll Series was in its infancy, in 1976, the rosh hayeshivah bestowed upon us and our work the high honor of writing to us and inviting us to meet with him. With trepidation we flew to visit him in Wickliffe, Ohio, not knowing what to expect from one of the *gedolei hador*. The results could not have been more gratifying. The rosh hayeshivah invited us to lunch in his simple home. He said that he was pleased with the recently published Books of Esther and Ruth. He stated emphatically that the times demanded creation of accurate English translations and elucidations of our classics — and, even more, he offered to read and comment on the galleys of future works. Despite his schedule that included no spare minutes, he continued to read and comment for several years, until he founded Yeshivah Telz-Stone in the Judean Hills. The close friendship continued for the rest of his life.

He advised us to embark on the ArtScroll Mishnah Series with the Yad Avraham commentary. And several years later he urged us to embark on the monumental work that became the Schottenstein Editions of Talmud Bavli and Talmud Yerushalmi, in English and Hebrew.

In many ways Rav Gifter was the "father" of ArtScroll/ Mesorah, not only because of the gift of his scholarship and brilliance of his guidance, but because he shared his enthusiasm with the senior roshei yeshivah of the generation, few of whom were fluent in English. It was important to them that a peer of his stature endorsed the initiative as an important contribution to the Torah world.

In this biography, Rabbi Yechiel Spero does justice to his subject. Rabbi Spero is a distinguished *mechanech* in Baltimore and is well known to readers for his very popular "Touched By ... " series of books. He is a native of Cleveland and a *talmid* of the rosh hayeshivah, and knew Rav Gifter and his impact on *talmidim* and the community at large. Writing this biography was a labor of love for Rabbi Spero. He interviewed scores of people, researched the writings and recorded speeches of Rav Gifter, and asked many people to review the manuscript. We are grateful to all those who cooperated with him – especially to Rebbetzin Gifter שתחי׳ and the entire Gifter family, who continually made themselves available throughout his work.

We are confident that this volume will enrich everyone who reads it. Rav Gifter was a man with two primary aspirations: to master as much of the Holy Torah as humanly possible, and to serve Klal Yisrael with every bit of his being. He succeeded in both. Those who knew him in life were incredibly enriched. Through this book, his influence will continue to inspire future generations.

Rabbi Meir Zlotowitz / Rabbi Nosson Scherman

Iyar 5771 / June 2011

An Author's Reflections
The Legacy of Rav Gifter

1FEAR THAT I HAVE FAILED.
Throughout this venture, I was asked many times if I was a *talmid* (student) of Rav Gifter. I learned in the yeshivah for seven years while Rav Gifter was the rosh hayeshivah. Nevertheless, I don't think it would be accurate to call myself a *talmid* — not in the truest sense of the word.

Until now.

This past year, I have been privileged to be Rav Gifter's *talmid*; I have spent six, seven, and sometimes ten hours a day with him. I've listened to many of his *shiurim* and *shmuessen,* as well as recollections of other *talmidim*. Each disciple described his "Rav Gifter moment" — the instant that Rav Gifter, through a brilliant *shiur*, a piercing *shmuess* or a warm smile, made an indelible impact on his life.

And yet, I fear that I have failed.

Rebbetzin Gifter, who read through this manuscript, told me that she was very pleased with the outcome, and that the rosh hayeshivah would have been very pleased with it, as well. Rav Chaim Nussbaum,

Rav Gifter's close *talmid* (for the last 25 years of his life), spent many hours reviewing the fine details of the manuscript. He is hopeful that one day (after 120 years) I will merit to meet Rav Gifter once more, and he will place his hands on my cheeks and give me a kiss for my efforts.

But I fear I have failed.

Because Rav Gifter could not be captured on paper. As my father suggested to me many times, this book should have come with an accompanying CD, because one must hear Rav Gifter's powerful voice — the emotion, the eloquence, the depth — in order to appreciate who he was. Yes, that penetrating, powerful, once-in-a-generation voice that brought out the truth and essence of every word that he spoke. And so, pen on paper cannot do justice. It will not and cannot fully capture Rav Gifter's greatness.

There is another reason: a brutally honest self-assessment. There are so many others who were true *talmidim*, who were much closer than I, who can convey the *mesorah* (tradition), HIS *mesorah*, in a more efficient manner.

On the other hand, two merits work in my favor. The first is *zechus avos* (the merit of my forefathers). My grandfather, Chaim Isaac (Herbert I.) Spero (for whom the *beis midrash* in Telz is named), was a tireless worker for the yeshivah. He was a dear friend of the roshei hayeshivah: Rav Elya Meir Bloch and Rav Mottel Katz and was especially close to Rav Mottel. He was also friendly with Rav Gifter and Rav Boruch Sorotzkin, but unfortunately, passed away a few months before they became the roshei hayeshivah, and did not have the privilege of being as close to them as he had been with their predecessors. He took off a year from work to build the yeshivah. The image of my grandfather standing in his thigh-high boots in the mud of the unpaved roads of Nutwood Farms (that would eventually become the Telz Yeshivah campus) has been described to my family many, many times at *yahrtzeit* gatherings. We can best summarize his contribution to the yeshivah with a compelling story that happened almost 30 years ago.

It was the day of my younger brother Yehudah's *bris*, March 16th, 1983 — a typical wintry, stormy Cleveland day — a day in which most people would have preferred to stay indoors. In fact, that is precisely what Rav Gifter proclaimed as he began to speak at the *seudah*.

"I looked out the window this morning and I figured that I'm not going to the Spero *bris*." It was a 20-minute drive from Telz to the Young Israel on Cedar Road, where the *bris* would take place. With the treacherous driving conditions, it would probably take close to an hour. "But as I was about to make my decision," Rav Gifter continued, "I thought, 'What would Reb Chaim Isaac have done?' He was not one to make excuses; he was one who always managed to find the solution. And that is why I came here today: to show my appreciation to Reb Chaim Isaac for all he did for the yeshivah."

And so, I hope that although there are so many others who are more worthy to write this book, as a manifestation of his appreciation to my grandfather, Rav Gifter would have allowed me to do so.

I also carry the merit of a being a *melamed* (teacher). I am privileged to teach children Torah, the most rewarding profession one can choose. Rav Gifter possessed many talents, yet he took the most pride in his ability to teach: "*Ich bin ah melamed*! [I am a teacher!]" he would proudly declare. While he shunned all other titles, he took great pleasure and satisfaction in his teaching, and invested great love in his *talmidim*. It was a deep connection, anchored in Torah, rooted in *mesorah*: an unbreakable bond of loyalty. He loved, truly loved, his *talmidim*.

These merits gave me the courage to write.

———

Many people have asked what I hope to achieve by writing this book. It is my fervent hope that those who read this book will realize that nothing is impossible.

Every educator who reads this book should bear in mind Reb Peretz Tarshish, a rebbi in a Talmud Torah in Baltimore in the early 1920's, who spent his afternoons teaching children Torah, mostly Tanach. One boy in the class, who originated from Portsmouth, Virginia, would become one of the great Torah giants of his generation. Did Reb Peretz know that he was teaching a future *gadol hador*? Certainly not. This must inspire our teachers of Torah to realize the unlimited potential within every one of our students; perhaps the next *gadol hador* sits among them.

Every child who reads this book can dream of greatness, and can achieve greatness. If you are a bar mitzvah and know one *blatt* of Gemara, even the one you prepared for your entrance exam into a yeshivah, then you stand in good company. Mordechai Gifter knew one *blatt* of Gemara, and didn't make much of an impression on his entrance exam, but it didn't stop him. It motivated him to strive for greatness.

Mordechai hung pictures of Torah giants in his dormitory room. One frame above his bed remained empty; a handwritten note inside it read, "Why not you?"

This book demands that every young person answer that question: "Why not you?"

———•———

A few years ago, Rabbi Boruch Neuberger, assistant to the *menahel* at Yeshivas Ner Yisrael, received a phone call from a woman who wanted to come with her father to visit the yeshivah. They wanted to view a plaque that had been donated many years before (while the yeshivah was at its earlier location, on Garrison Boulevard). Reb Boruch informed the woman that they could come the next day. In the meantime, he walked through the building to find where the plaque had been placed. He located the plaque and arranged to have it cleaned so that he could show it to the visitors.

When the woman arrived with her elderly father, Reb Boruch showed them the plaque, which was located in the basement of the dormitory. The elderly man leaned on his walker toward the plaque and read the commemorative inscription. At the bottom, he read aloud, "Jeanne and Joseph Gifter." The name Gifter elicited a response from Reb Boruch. "Did you say Gifter?"

The old man responded, "Yeah, Joe and Max Gifter were my best friends growing up." The elderly gentleman turned toward Reb Boruch, and he looked pensive for a moment. Suddenly, he called out, "Hey… what ever happened to Max Gifter?"

The dedication plaque

Max, the son of Israel Gifter, became Mordechai, the rosh hayeshivah, one of the *gedolei hador*.

Someone asked Rav Gifter if he had read the biography of Rav Elchanan Wasserman, *Ohr Elchanan*. He responded, *"Der sefer darf men nit leinen, nor mir darf es lernen.* [This is not a *sefer* that we must read, but one that we must learn.]" This book was written with the same intent. Thus, I prefer to call it not a book, but a *sefer*. A "book" could never do Rav Gifter justice. He would have little patience for such a venture, but a "*sefer*" that is worthy of being learned — something that is full of lessons — is definitely a worthwhile endeavor.

This work is not intended to be a comprehensive biography. Although a significant portion of the book concentrates on his history, the focus and purpose of the book is to convey the legacy of Rav Gifter: the lessons and inspiration he handed down to future generations.

One of Rav Gifter's close *talmidim* suggested that if I write about Rav Gifter, I should allow his voice to be heard as much as possible: "Let him talk." I have tried to do just that. Much of the material that has been gathered include Rav Gifter's words, thoughts, and expressions.

Rav Gifter was the embodiment of Torah; it permeated his being, his essence. His *talmidim* witnessed the Torah's truth in his every action. Laymen heard it in his every breath. He implored rabbanim to speak it to their congregants. About 30 years ago, at a *siyum* for the completion of a *masechta*, a small group gathered in my parents' home. Their rebbi was Rav Yeruchem Bensinger, who was moving to Miami; thus the gathering served as a farewell party for him, as well. Rav Gifter's message came across with one fiery statement, "Speak the truth — it hits home!"

Rav Gifter spoke the truth — and it hit home.

Chazal tell us, "*Ashrei mi she'ba le'kan ve'Talmudo be'yado* — Fortunate is he who comes here [the Next World] and his learning is in his hand" (*Bava Basra* 10b). Rav Gifter explained: Praiseworthy is the one whose

Torah study is visible and evident in his actions. If Torah does not permeate his essence and affect his inner being, then even if he knows the entire Torah, he is nothing more than a *"chamor nosei sefarim —* a donkey carrying books." Torah must be *be'yado*, permeating his actions and his being.

Rav Gifter was a brilliant, deep-thinking, and diligent scholar, but that does not paint the entire picture. Torah influenced and dictated his every action and thought; it infused the very fiber of his being; it was *be'yado*.

Although this book contains many words which are not "pure English", we tried to insert 'Yiddishisms' only when necessary, when an English expression would not suffice. Rav Gifter spoke and wrote English impeccably, and he disliked it when people would mix languages, due to their inability to express themselves properly in one language. He stood for the excellence of language. Indeed, he communicated equally well in a magnificent English, Yiddish, and lashon hakodesh.

One time, Rav Gifter ate in the Telz Yeshivah dining room on Rosh Hashanah. He began his speech with a whimsical thought. "I am not sure which language to use to address you. If I speak in Yiddish, 50 percent of the crowd will not understand. But if I speak in English, 75 percent of the crowd will not understand!"

Rav Gifter's mother tongue (*mama lashon*) was Yiddish. He spoke Yiddish growing up in his home, and he felt most comfortable with it. Hearing Rav Gifter's command of the English language, it is hard to imagine him being more comfortable in another language, but he was. When reflecting on the fact that his mother spoke to him Yiddish, he would become emotional and misty eyed.

We have tried to preserve the uniqueness of Rav Gifter in his ability to choose an expression, a vernacular, that captured the soul of his thinking in the most perfect manner. Nevertheless, the standard we have chosen remains English.

Portions of the book have been transcribed (and translated) from lectures or *shiurim* of Rav Gifter. In order to make them clearer to the reader, some of the words were changed, but the overwhelming majority of the message and style remains intact, and true to its origin.

At times, two *talmidim* shared the same thought from Rav Gifter, but had varying opinions as to where the emphasis was placed. Truth be told, over the years, there were times when Rav Gifter repeated the same thought in two different ways. We have tried to maintain that nuance in conveying Rav Gifter's lessons and Torah thoughts.

It is remarkable when one contemplates how many lives Rav Gifter affected. Of course, he had thousands of *talmidim* from the yeshivah, but there were thousands who heard him at a convention or a *shmuess*, and became *talmidim* for life as a result of that one electrifying experience, as was relayed to me in a moving letter:

> *Although I never learned in Cleveland under Rav Gifter, I feel like a true talmid of his. I grew up in a Telzer home and my father, who was very close with Rav Gifter, would quote him all the time. I had the privilege of hearing Rav Gifter speak a few times, and those few speeches made such a powerful impression on me that I still hear his beautiful words ringing in my ears decades later. Every year before the Yamim Noraim, I listen to a tape of Rav Gifter from twenty-five years ago. I heard it live when I was learning in Chicago Telz. His powerful and heartfelt words made me a talmid for life.*
>
> *I named my second son Mordechai Ariel — Mordechai was for Rav Gifter. I would like to share with you what I said at my son Mordechai's bris. The Gemara in Menachos 64b mentions a question that was discussed in the time of the Chashmonaim. The Gemara cites an answer from Mordechai, who Rashi explains is Mordechai HaYehudi, from the days of Achashveirosh. Tosafos ask: How can Rashi say that it was Mordechai, if this conversation took place hundreds of years after the story of Purim? Tosafos explain, this talmid chacham, who lived in the times of the Chashmonaim, was called Mordechai. Men of great intellect [who were appointed in the Beis HaMikdash during those days] were called Mordechai HaYehudi, since they personified a high level of intelligence.*

Rav Gifter was the "Mordechai" of our generation....

This "*talmid*" was not the only one who often hears Rav Gifter's voice. One professional, who attended the yeshivah 40 years ago, told me a powerful story.

Generally, Rav Gifter would daven *Minchah* with the kollel (in a classroom) late in the afternoon. But on the seventh day of Elul, the day that the women and children of Telz in Lita were massacred, Rav Gifter observed the *yahrtzeit*, and he davened earlier in the main *beis midrash*, together with the yeshivah, at the beginning of second *seder*.

After *Minchah*, as Rav Gifter made his way back to his house, he passed some *bachurim* who had missed *Minchah*. He stopped each one and let them know how disappointed he was. That night, Rav Gifter gave a *shmuess*. The room was still as Rav Gifter entered the room. At first, he looked around and suddenly, he thundered, *"Drei vochen far der Yom HaDin!* — Three weeks before the Day of Judgment!"

And then again, *"Drei vochen far der Yom HaDin!* — Three weeks before the Day of Judgment!"

The booming roar of his voice made the room tremble.

Then, Rav Gifter mimicked the *shuckeling* (shaking) of the *bachurim* as they pray, and he continued, "And then you are going to daven…*un der Ribbono Shel Olam vet zuggen* — and the Al-mighty is going to say, *'Vos dreist du Mir ah kup*?! — Why are you bothering Me?! You don't mean it anyway!'"

It is 40 years later, and every year, three weeks before the Day of Judgment, this individual hears his rebbi's voice thunder, *"Drei vochen far der Yom HaDin!* Three weeks before the Day of Judgment!" He sees the image of his rebbi *shuckeling,* and then hears the piercing *mussar,"*And then you are going to daven…but the *Ribbono Shel Olam* is going to say, *'Vos dreist du Mir ah kup?!* — Why are you bothering Me?! You don't mean it anyway!'"

Several months after the passing of Rav Moshe Feinstein and Rav Yaakov Kamenetsky, Rav Gifter spoke at the Agudah Convention, and described the magnitude of the loss that Klal Yisrael had experienced with the passing of these two Torah giants. Rav Gifter quoted the eulogy that the Brisker Rav, Rav Yitzchak Ze'ev Soloveitchik, had delivered after the passing of the Chazon Ish, Rav Avraham Yeshayah Karelitz. The Brisker Rav said that we are now living in a different world. "Before, we were living in a world with the Chazon Ish, and now we are living in a world without the Chazon Ish."

Rav Gifter continued, "Before, we were living in a world with Rav Moshe and Rav Yaakov, and now we are living in a world without Rav Moshe and Rav Yaakov."

And he concluded by exclaiming, *"Un dos iz an andere velt!* [And that is a different world!]"

In a sense, the same can be said about Rav Gifter. As one rav commented to me, "I really miss him…I feel that there is such a void in this world since he passed away." The world is a lesser place.

In the introduction to *Pirkei Emunah* (Volume I), Rav Gifter quotes from the *Nesivos HaMishpat*, who wrote, "*Kedai le'hadfis sefer shaleim im ach davar echad nachon ve'emes yiheyeh bo* — It is worthwhile to print a complete *sefer* if even one correct and true word is in it."

This book has many truths from a man who embodied the truth.

Indeed, *kedai lehadfis* — it is worthwhile to publish.

It is with a considerable measure of satisfaction — and a tinge of sadness — that my work on this book comes to a close. The satisfaction stems from that which I have gained, and the hope that thousands more will develop an appreciation for one of the true Torah giants of our time. But there is sadness, as well. For the past year, I have lived with Rav Gifter on my mind, nearly every moment of the day. I have had the privilege, in a sense, to serve him and learn from our great rebbi every day. And now…it is over.

When Rav Gifter's coffin was taken onto the plane that would transport him from Cleveland to New York and then on to Eretz Yisrael, Rav Abba Zalka Gewirtz, Rav Gifter's friend for almost 60 years, looked at the pilot, and with tears in his eyes, he remarked, "Be careful…you are carrying precious cargo…"

Yes. Very precious indeed…

I end echoing a *berachah*, one that I heard from Rav Gifter countless times. May this book be a source of *nachas* to the Gifter family, to his *talmidim*, but most of all, to the Al-mighty.

Yechiel Spero

Iyar 5771 / June 2011

Author's Acknowledgments

WHEN I WAS FIRST APPROACHED TO WRITE THIS BOOK, I was both flattered and overwhelmed. And with great *siyata d'Shmaya*, everything fell into place. Therefore, I begin by thanking the *Ribbono Shel Olam* for all He has given me and my family. I have written 15 books for ArtScroll, and it is humbling to contemplate how blessed I feel.

Rabbi Meir Zlotowitz was intimately involved in this book from its embryonic stages. He read every word of the manuscript, offering keen insight and direction. When an issue arose, with resolve and great care, he mentored me in how to deal with the challenge. From ArtScroll's inception, Rav Gifter felt a strong connection and close friendship to Rabbi Zlotowitz. This *yedidus* enabled Rebbetzin Gifter and her family to trust that a true picture of Rav Gifter would emerge. I have always thanked Reb Meir at the beginning of each book; never more so than now.

Rabbi Nosson Scherman lent his brilliance as a master wordsmith to almost every page of this book. His many comments sharpened the manuscript immeasurably. Reb Nosson wrote a masterful introduction to the Telz Yeshivah memorial journal. He painted a vivid picture of Rav Gifter, one that I used as a springboard to help develop much material in this book. I have always received great encouragement from Reb Nosson, and this book was no exception. Reb Nosson's gifted pen has enhanced countless volumes of Torah literature. May he continue to have the strength to use his remarkable talent for many years.

Gedaliah Zlotowitz has supported me in this project, as he has in every other. He always finds the right words to bring out the very best of my abilities. His friendship is one of the great benefits that I have acquired along the way.

Avrohom Biderman finds a way to slip under the radar. But his erudition and insight are evident in so many of the scholarly ArtScroll works. Much to his chagrin, in this book, I must publicly recognize the myriad loose ends he has tied together. Thank you for being such a trusted friend.

Mendy Herzberg — you are the calm before, during, and after the storm. I can almost see your smile in our countless communications.

Eli Kroen — a picture tells the story. Your restoration of the many old photos beautifies this volume. The cover is simply magnificent. It always is.

Mrs. Mindy Stern's deft touch lent more shine to the pages.

A special note of thanks to Raizy Ganz for paginating, Devorah Bloch for the scanning of over 430 pictures and documents, Mrs. Toby Goldzweig for entering corrections skillfully, Mrs. Faygie Weinbaum for proofreading, and Mrs. Judi Dick and Mrs. Estie Dicker for the comprehensive index.

When one meets Rebbetzin Shoshana Gifter, there is a sense that you are in the presence of majesty. Indeed, the *malchus* (royalty) of Telz is evident in the rebbetzin's nature. She is elegant and refined, and at the same time, warm, friendly, and approachable — a unique and rare combination. It is an art to be the wife of a rosh hayeshivah. Yet, she mastered it. Of the hundreds of interviews and conversations I had about this book, the meetings I had with the rebbetzin were the most pleasant and revealing of all. The rebbetzin treasured her husband, and cherished every moment with him, even when she became his primary caretaker. With dignity and poise, she perfected her role. I can never thank her enough for entrusting me with the rosh hayeshivah's legacy.

The Gifter family was gracious and helpful throughout the book. Often, in such ventures, it can be draining trying to please everyone. But all of the rosh hayeshivah's children helped bring this project to fruition.

Reb Binyomin and Mrs. Sarah (Subby) Gifter were extremely helpful. Reb Binyomin filled in and clarified many details of stories. He spent hours reviewing small points to ensure accuracy. In addition, he wrote many of the captions. Often, when we would speak, Reb Binyomin would become emotional at the mere mention of his father. This inspired me greatly.

Rebbetzin Shlomis Eisenberg spent many, many hours reviewing the notes I had taken for the manuscript, well before it was ready to be seen. And she did it all as a labor of love. With every word she shared, she further polished her father's legacy. She opened her home for a number of her siblings' interviews, and allowed me to "steal" her most treasured articles and pictures. She acted as a liaison between her family and this author, plodding through many of the minor details. This enhanced the integrity and exactness of the book in countless ways. I am eternally grateful.

Rav Avrohom Chaim and Rebbetzin Luba Feuer met with me in Eretz Yisrael. Although Rav Avrohom Chaim was not well at that time, he spent nearly three hours sharing with me many of the beautiful insights and *divrei Torah* he had gleaned from his rebbi and father-in-law, Rav Gifter. May they both merit good health and strength.

Rav Yaakov and Rebbetzin Chasya Reisman enhanced the book in many ways. Rav Yankel, a close *talmid*, added many insights and stories and inserted many sources to the material in the manuscript. In addition, many of the pictures came from the Reisman family. Although I owe Rav Yankel many more thanks, he prefers that the rest of my words of appreciation remain between the two of us. But the *Yodei'a Machshavos* (One Who knows thoughts) knows it, as well. Thank you!

Rav Zalman and Rebbetzin Miriam Gifter hosted me twice during my visits to Cleveland. Rav Zalman upgraded this volume by obtaining some rare pictures and matching the writings of Rav Gifter to their printed sources. The results can be seen throughout the pages. He also introduced me to *Mili DeIgros* (Volumes I and II), published by Kollel Ateres Mordechai, which proved to be invaluable sources for much of the biographical material in the book.

Rabbi Yisroel and Mrs. Rivka Gifter shared some beautiful anecdotes from their perspective. As the youngest Gifter child, Reb Sroly knew a different Rav Gifter than some of his siblings. And because of that, his viewpoint added much to the book. In addition, he told me two amazing stories that I would not have heard otherwise.

Rabbi Eliezer Feuer is my brother-in-law. From the outset, he encouraged me and guided me as to how to go about this project. Ezzy was extremely close to his grandfather and lived with him for a number of years. Moreover, he disclosed some very personal and unique incidents and material that added to this book in many ways.

Rav Chaim Nussbaum spent countless hours reviewing and adding to the manuscript. I joked with him that I wish I could learn a Rashi with as much attention to detail. Rav Chaim was a *talmid muvhak* of Rav Gifter and inspired me to perfect the manuscript as much as possible. His attention to every word makes this book that much better.

Rav Nachum Velvel Dessler *zt"l* met with me for over an hour a few months before he passed away. Rav Dessler was always princely in his demeanor, and this time was no exception. He regaled me with many stories and anecdotes about Rav Gifter. Many times throughout the interview, his children, who sat in on the discussion, asked him if he wanted to stop; he never hesitated. I felt as though he were transmitting the *mesorah* (tradition). Indeed, he was. He appreciated this book's importance, and how much it would mean to have his perspective. His special relationship with Rav Gifter is clearly evident throughout the pages of the book.

A three-hour eulogy delivered by Rabbi Azriel Goldfein *zt"l* provided great insight into his relationship with his rebbi. Unfortunately, I never merited meeting Rav Azriel, but his recollections enrich this book.

I was privileged to spend two hours on the train together with Rav Avrohom Ausband, a dear *talmid* of Rav Gifter. Rav Ausband shared the unique perspective of a rosh yeshivah, and opened a window into the soul of Rav Gifter to which few others were privy.

My interview with the Munkatcher Rebbe, Rav Moshe Leib Rabinovich, was one of the highlights of my past year. The Rebbe's memories and insights were invaluable. The epilogue of the book is based on that interview. I thank him profusely for his time.

Nearly 35 years ago, when *Pirkei Emunah* (Volume II) was printed, Rav Gifter thanked Rav Shlomo Davis. Rabbi Davis davened in the rear of the high school beis midrash when I was a *bachur*. He personified the Telzer *mesorah* and demanded *mentchlichkeit* from us all. Yet, a smile was never far from his lips. It comes as no surprise that from the very beginning of this project, his son, Reb Yosef Davis, a dear family friend, actively supported and gave encouragement for this project. Following in his father's footsteps, Reb Yosef lent much perspective to an era somewhat forgotten.

Recently, Reb Yosef shared a story that captures the concept of *derech eretz* in Telz. "Once, when I was a small child, I ran ahead of my father as he walked with the rosh hayeshivah, Rav Elya Meir Bloch. When I reached the building, I swung the doors wide open and was about to enter, when suddenly, I felt the grip of the rosh hayeshivah on my shoulder. I looked up at Rav Elya Meir — he looked like a prince — and he said to me, '*Zolst du vissen* [You should know], that you don't ever enter the building before your father. And you don't enter before me, because I am a rosh hayeshivah!'" These timeless Telzer trademarks — *kavod haTorah* and *derech eretz* — would remain seared in Reb Yosef's soul.

Ah! *Derech eretz!*

Rabbi Mordechai Suchard, a close *talmid* of Rav Gifter, provided support, encouragement, and many great memories. His clear recall of many of Rav Gifter's classic Torah thoughts dot the landscape of this book. Reb Mutty's astute suggestions improved this book in many ways. His contributions are a testament to his desire to see honor brought to the memory of Rav Gifter.

In addition, the following people deserve much more than the token mention of their name. Their words and reflections constitute this book; I merely compiled it. Words can never express my gratitude.

They are: Reb Chaim Abraham, Rabbi Avrohom Alter, Rabbi Chaim Amsel, Reb Avrohom Antokol, Artech, Rebbetzin Chaya Ausband, Rabbi Moshe Bamberger, Rabbi Leibel Berger, Rav Meir Zvi Bergman, Rabbi Yaakov Bogart, Mrs. Betzalel Braun, Rabbi and Rebbetzin Chaim Bressler, Rabbi Aharon Brodie, Rabbi and Mrs. Aryeh Burnham, Rabbi Daniel Carlebach, Rabbi Elchanan Ciment, Reb Zev Compton, Rabbi Simcha Cook, Rabbi Simcha Dessler, Rabbi Yitzchak Dinovitzer, Mrs. Chaya Drucker, Rabbi Yaakov Feitman, Rebbetzin Breiny Fried, Rabbi Eli Friedman, Rabbi Reuvein Gerson, Reb Dovid Gewirtz, Rabbi

Jonah Gewirtz, Rabbi Hillel Goldberg, Rabbi Moshe Goldberg, Rabbi Shlomo Goldhaber, Mrs. Toby Klein Greenwald, Reb Moshe Hellman, Rabbi Yehoshua Leib Hill, Reb Michael Hirsch, Reb Shimon Hirsch, Rabbi Boruch Hirschfeld, Rabbi Avrohom Mordechai Isbee, Rabbi Nosson Joseph, Rabbi Chaim Kahan, Rabbi Mordechai Kamenetzky, Rabbi Avrohom Katz, Rebbetzin Esther Katz, Mrs. Mashe Katz, Rabbi Nachman Klein, Reb Shlomo Korry, Rabbi Mordechai Kravitz, Rabbi Ahron Shlomo Lauer, Rabbi Nesanel Lauer, Rabbi Baruch Leff, Rav Zev Leff, Rabbi Dovid Levin, Rabbi Yitzchak Levine, Rabbi Moshe Tuvia Lieff, Mr. Bob Maran, Rabbi Boruch Neuberger, Reb Eli Oelbaum, Rabbi Moshe Yaakov Perl, Rabbi Zelig Pliskin, Reb Asher Rabinsky, Rabbi Eli Reingold, Rabbi Yankel Rosenbaum, Rabbi Kalman Rubinstein, Reb Menachem Rudman, RebYitzchak Saftlas of Bottom Line Marketing, Reb Aharon Sapirman, Rabbi Yisroel Schneider, Rabbi Eli Schulman, Rabbi Tzvi Schur, Rabbi Yitzchak Schwartz, Rabbi Avrohom Shoshana, Reb Shlomo Slonim, Rabbi Aryeh Spero, Reb Chaim Spero, Dr. Moshe Halevi Spero, Reb Sheldon Spirn, Rabbi Reuven Stein, Rabbi Tzodok Suchard, Rabbi Chaim Aharon Weinberg, Rabbi Moshe Weinberger, Dr. Tommy Weiss, Rabbi Dovid Yankelewitz, Rabbi Eli Yelen, and Rabbi Chaim Dovid Zwiebel. I apologize to all those who contributed to this volume, but whose names were inadvertently omitted.

The following publications and their staff were also very helpful: Yated Ne'eman — Rabbi Pinchos Lipschutz and Rabbi Yitzchak Hisiger; Hamodia; Mishpacha magazine and Rabbi Binyomin Rose. Some notes were gleaned from Yeshurun (Volume X) which contains a memorial section commemorating Rav Gifter, edited by Rav Reuvein Gerson and Rav Doniel Neustadt.

A special note of thanks to Mr. Jerry Kadden. Mr. Frank Storch spared no expense in trying to ensure a beautiful cover shot for the book. In the end, another photo was chosen. But his efforts are well noted.

I thank you all.

My editor, Mrs. Susan Leibtag, enables me to express myself, yet somehow makes it sound much better when she is finished. Although she often does that, in this book in particular, my writing was stiff in the very beginning, and she helped to bring out creativity in the writing. Only you know how much you have done. Thank you!

Mrs. Tova Salb joked with me on one occasion that in editing this book, she was somewhat of a housekeeper, as she put everything neatly where it belonged. She knows this book better than I do. At a certain point, it was hard to keep track of everything. Not surprisingly, you did it exceptionally well. What a fantastic job!

My parents, Dr. and Mrs. Abba Spero, and my in-laws, Rabbi and Mrs. Yehuda Lefkovitz, raised Telzer families, as my father and father-in-law both attended Telz. They have been loving and supportive as always. The language of appreciation may be repetitive, but my feelings of gratitude are stronger than ever. In addition, as talmidim of Rav Gifter, my father and father-in-law reveled in the stories I would share, adding poignant and meaningful footnotes. They shared their memories of Telz, often reliving their youth vicariously through this project — and that was thrilling.

At this point, I always thank my family — my children, Tzvi, Avromi, Efraim, Miri, Shmueli, Chana Leah, and Henny — but this time, I must thank you tenfold. You have enabled me to spend nearly a year living with Rav Gifter — sometimes at the expense of family time. My older children loved the Rav Gifter stories I shared with them and they spread them around their yeshivos; their feedback and excitement gave me such *chizuk*. For my younger children, Slurpees and small gifts won't make up for it all, but they had the privilege to have a Torah giant, Rav Gifter, live in their house for a year. One day that will mean a lot to you.

And to my wife, Chumi, more than anyone else, this book is due to your self-sacrifice.

At times, throughout the past year, my wife has lightheartedly answered the phone, "Gifter residence, how can I help you?"

Sadly, though, that will no longer be.

I will miss it; I really will.

May the inspiration Rav Gifter imparted to the world now shine more brilliantly than ever.

Yechiel Spero

Iyar 5771 / June 2011

Section 1
Biography — From a Lad to a Lion

Chapter 1
Humble Beginnings

PORTSMOUTH, VIRGINIA, 1916. WHAT AN UNLIKELY starting place for a future *gadol hador*.

Portsmouth in 1916 was virtually a desert for religious Jews. There were no religious schools; Jewish education had to come from one's parents. This was where Mordechai Gifter was born to Israel (Yisrael) and May (Matla) Gifter, well-meaning, upright, and G-d-fearing people who wanted the best for their children. They named their son Mordechai after Mr. Gifter's father, who had learned in Chavel under Rav Yosef Zecharya Stern, the Zecher Yehoyasaf.

AS THE YEARS WENT BY, THEY REALIZED THAT IF THEY WANTED their children to have a proper Jewish education, they would have to move. Thus, in 1918, when Mordechai was 2 years old, they moved to Baltimore, Maryland, where the spiritual climate promised a stronger, richer environment for their children. Although Israel owned a successful grocery in Portsmouth, he chose to

Baltimore

move in order to provide the proper education for his children. In Baltimore, Israel also owned a grocery store from which he made only a modest living.

During the daytime hours, Mordechai, or Max as he was known at that time, was a student in the Baltimore city public school system. His classmates included children of every type who lived in the large neighborhood of immigrants. His Jewish education began when he attended an after-school religious program; full-time yeshivah education was almost nonexistent outside of New York. Mordechai's siblings, Joe and Rose, attended school with him. At the Hebrew school Mordechai attended, it was Reb Peretz Tarshish, who later in life Rav Gifter desribed as, a "master pedagogue", who served as his rebbi.

Mordechai Gifter

Mordechai showed his propensity for study and deep thought early in his life. His personality, upon reflection after the fact, exhibited the

Mr. Israel Gifter

Mrs. May Gifter

very critical elements for a future leader. A studious young man, he did not like wasting time and filled every available moment with reading and studying.

AS A YOUNG BOY IN BALTIMORE, MORDECHAI WOULD HELP CLEAN the floors in his father's grocery store before going to public school. On the way, he would pass the home of the *shochet*, a great Torah scholar and brother of Rav Yosef Yaakov Marcus (the rabbi of the Mishkan Yisrael shul) and ask his father, "Why is the light on in Rabbi Marcus' home so early in the morning?" When Mordechai heard that the *shochet* was spending his nights learning Torah, Mordechai realized that there was a higher level to strive for.

Early Influences

When he was only 8 years old, he met someone who would have a profound influence on his young soul. As he would retell many times in his life, he was in the Mishkan Yisrael shul with his friend, the son of Rabbi Marcus. At the time, a visitor from overseas was in the synagogue too — the famed Rav Shimon Shkop — who was in town to raise funds for his yeshivah in Grodno, Lithuania. Rav Shimon first gave a blessing to Rabbi Marcus' son. Rabbi Marcus then asked Rav Shimon to give a *berachah* to his son's friend, as well, explaining, "*Er iz ah voille yingele.* [He is a good boy.]" Rav Shkop grasped Mordechai's hand, looked him in the eye, and said something so simple, yet so profound, that Mordechai, even at this young age, knew he should remember it forever: "*Zolst vellen lernen.* [You should (always) want to learn.]"

Perhaps even Mordechai understood that the simplicity of this *berachah* was life altering: not to become a sage, or even one well versed in the intricacies of analytical learning, just to want — to desire — to learn.

When he himself became someone who blessed others, it is this *berachah* that he invoked. "*Zolst vellen lernen.* [You should (always) want to learn.]"

Rav Gifter would later add, "The little bit that I merited to understand in learning is due to the *berachah* I received from Rav Shimon."

Rav Shimon Shkop

Chapter 1: Humble Beginnings ☐ 35

Even at this tender age, Mordechai not only heard the words but understood, somehow, their deepest meaning. He began investing his time in all types of learning: even going to Hebrew school once when snow blanketed the city, because he did not want to lose a day of learning. He even begged his father to trudge through the snow with him; but alas, the Talmud Torah had been closed because of the dangerous weather.

At 13 years of age, Mordechai had but a limited exposure to Gemara. He loved dearly every word that he learned, but most of his learning had been limited to Tanach.

In his later years, he would often quote verses from many of the not so well-known books of Tanach. He would attribute his knowledge of Tanach to his early years of learning (*girsa de'yankusa*).

Yeshivah in New York

BUT HEBREW SCHOOL WAS NOT ENOUGH FOR THE YOUNG scholar. He was eager to enter a real yeshivah, and his parents sent him to New York to take the entrance exam for Yeshivas Rabbeinu Yitzchak Elchanan. His only exposure to Gemara was the single folio he had learned: *Bava Metzia, daf* 26. It is hard to imagine nowadays, with such intensive Gemara education starting in elementary grades, that a boy of bar mitzvah age, knowing only one *blatt* of Gemara, would even be considered for admission to an advanced high school. [1]

This experience remained with him throughout his life. He would often counsel young men, with backgrounds similar to his, to persevere and refuse to give up. He would proudly say, "*Ich shtam fun Portsmouth, Virginia* [I hail from Portsmouth, Virginia], and it never stopped me!" As his son-in-law, Rav Avrohom Chaim Feuer, would later say, "It was because he was so down to earth that he had the power to lift you to the highest of heavens!"

Armed with that one *blatt* of Gemara, he took the entrance exam to Yeshivas Rabbeinu Yitzchak Elchanan. After being tested, he overheard the examiners say that he would be placed in the lowest class because there was none lower! The comment stung, but armed with his usual resolve, Mordechai promised himself that he would do his very best in whatever class he was placed. He made up his mind there and then, "*Ich vell zei vizen.* [I will show them.]"

---

1. Rabbi Nosson Scherman, Introduction – Telz Yeshivah memorial dinner journal, April 14, 2002.

WITHIN SIX MONTHS, MORDECHAI HAD ADVANCED INTO THE *shiur* of Rav Moshe Aharon Poleyeff. Although he would spend only a year and a half in Rav Moshe Aharon's class, his relationship with this rebbi had effects long after Mordechai left the *shiur*. Rav Moshe Aharon had learned in Slutzk in Lithuania and had become one of the close *talmidim* of Rav Isser Zalman Meltzer. In 1920, he came to America and was immediately appointed as one of the Roshei Yeshivah in Yeshivas Rabbeinu Yitzchak Elchanan. A genius in Torah and an innovative thinker, he became well known for his warmth as well as his immense love for his students.

A Great Teacher and Correspondence

Rav Moshe Aharon's Torah thoughts were compiled in the three-volume *Orach Meisharim*. He taught for over 46 years, guiding thousands of students. There is at least one particular student, however, upon whom he left an indelible mark that lasted for decades.

Over the next 28 years, Mordechai and his beloved rebbi corresponded regularly. This communication began in the summer of 1931 and continued through the summer of 1959. During those years, Rav Moshe Aharon watched his dear student grow into one of the most revered Torah scholars of our generation. Their correspondence was compiled into *Mili DeIgros* (Volume II).

The first series of letters was written by Mordechai during his summer vacation in Baltimore. The hot and humid nights made learning so difficult that Mordechai would spend some of the time writing to his rebbi. He would even complain in the letters that due to the stifling heat, he could not learn as much as he wanted to.[2]

One summer night, the heat was so oppressive that he could not learn in his usual manner. But Mordechai would not be denied; he lay flat on his back on the stone patio floor and

Rav Moshe Aharon Poleyeff

---

2. *Mili DeIgros* II 5:15.

Chapter 1: Humble Beginnings ☐ 37

learned from a *Ketzos HaChoshen* he held in his hands.

At first, the letters consisted of basic Torah thoughts. Some of the questions he asked illustrated his misunderstanding of the Gemara and early commentators. Rav Moshe Aharon would gently show him where he was mistaken. Mordechai eagerly awaited each and every response, thrilled with the new insights and happy to receive encouragement and constructive criticism. Rather quickly, Mordechai's level of learning grew. In a relatively short period of time, he became a force to be reckoned with in the yeshivah.

Mordechai Gifter's graduation picture

These letters fueled Mordechai's intellectual development, along with his energy and enthusiasm for learning. His method was to initially learn the subject matter thoroughly and then try to discover the deeper essence of the topic (*sugya*). The original thoughts that resulted were astounding and profound. Best of all, he wrote *everything* down for posterity.

As he would say throughout his life, his pen was his *chavrusa*; that is, as he wrote, his need to express his thoughts helped him to develop his ideas into cogent writings. Later in life, especially when he served as a rabbi in Waterbury, Connecticut, where he had few with whom to share these deep thoughts, he would sometimes talk out loud to inanimate objects just to help himself think through a concept. At times, he would even talk to a Coke bottle![3] During these periods of loneliness, his treasured and cherished pen became his best friend. He would often say that his pen helped him think and helped him navigate his way through the *sugya*.[4]

---

3. Rabbi Eliezer Feuer.
4. Rav Chaim Nussbaum, Rabbi Eliezer Feuer.

THROUGHOUT IT ALL, HE WAS NEVER SATISFIED UNTIL HE REACHED the essence, the truth, in what he was learning. It was that drive and pursuit of the truth of the word of Hashem that enabled Mordechai to develop quickly into a tremendous *talmid chacham*; that, and his ability to concede his own errors. Being shown he was wrong never fazed him; in fact, he relished the arguments and discussions that came with learning.

Lifelong Student

Just as he sought this in himself, he taught it to his students, wherever and whoever they were. Each time he met a student — current or past — he would ask him, "*Avu halt men*? [Where are you holding?]" He expected each one to respond that he was indeed "holding in middle of a *sugya*"[5] — that all of his students were constantly elevating their level of Torah study.

It is rare, if ever, that we are granted a glimpse into the step-by-step growth of a Torah sage. We are fortunate in this case because Mordechai documented all of his lessons and accomplishments. As an example of his unique devotion and discipline in learning, in late summer 1931, he documented his completion of *Maseches Shevuos*. However, like most of his accomplishments, the "end" of something only signaled the beginning of more in-depth work in the area. In this case, after learning through the tractate, he reviewed it, this time with additional *Rishonim*: the Rosh and others.[6]

If he was asked to speak in a shul, even at a relatively young age, he would share his latest Torah thoughts and enter into lively debates with the scholars of the shul. More often than not, the audience would leave knowing that they had been in the presence of future greatness.

During his vacations in Baltimore, Mordechai developed a close relationship with Rav Avrohom Nachman Schwartz, the founder of the Yeshivah Torah Ve'emunah Parochial School in Baltimore. That school would eventually merge with what is now the Talmudical Academy of Baltimore. It was the first Hebrew day school outside of New York City. Some of Mordechai's close childhood friends, among them Rav Avigdor Miller and Rav Yehudah Davis, attended the school.

He enjoyed speaking in learning with Rav Schwartz, who had received *semichah* from Rav Yitzchak Elchanan Spector, among others. On one occasion, Rav Schwartz heard a novel Torah thought from Rav Shmuel Yaakov Meidessar of Bnei Brak, the author of *Amudei Yehonasan*

---
5. Rabbi Mordechai Kravitz and Mr. Moshe Hellman.
6. *Mili Delgros* II 2:9.

Torah novellae by a teen-age Mordechai Gifter were
published in a Torah journal in 1932. He was 16 at the time.

and *Amudei Shmuel*. It says a great deal about the respect in which Rav Schwartz held Mordechai that he repeated this Torah thought to Mordechai for comments.[7] Mordechai was ecstatic to be asked for his insights. In Rav Schwartz's home, he came across many *sefarim* and Torah journals that he would devour. He would learn through them and write down his comments.

In just a few years, from the time he was 13 years old — when he knew only one *blatt* of Gemara — until the age of 24, Mordechai developed novel Torah thoughts on the majority of the Talmud. In his correspondence with his rebbi, Rav Moshe Aharon Poleyeff, one can note the remarkable growth in terms of Torah learning and outlook.

In one letter, written in the late summer of 1932, Mordechai apologized for "burdening" his rebbi with the lengthy correspondence, but felt, he said, that when he writes on Torah topics he has more pleasure *"mei'alfei zahav va'chesef* — than thousands of gold and silver coins"[8] (*Tehillim* 119:72). Rav Moshe Aharon often commented on his own enjoyment of his student's letters and Torah thoughts. He loved Mordechai like a son. In fact, when Mordechai informed him of his impending engagement to Shoshana Bloch (the daughter of Rav Zalman Bloch), Mordechai wrote, "Just as my relationship with [you,]

---

7. *Mili Delgros* II 5:5.
8. Ibid. 5:4.

my dear rebbi, is like two souls bound up together: '*nafsho keshurah be'nafshi* — his soul is so bound up with my soul' [based on *Bereishis* 44:30], so, too, I hope that my rebbi's soul will be bound up with my *kallah*'s soul, as well: '*nafsho keshurah be'nafshah.*' "[9]

Each letter, whether from Rav Moshe Aharon or from Mordechai, begins with a brief greeting, inquiring as to the other's well-being, and then quickly delves into a topic in Torah. Studying these letters, it is amazing to note the breadth and depth of Mordechai's learning and understanding. As time went on, his Torah thoughts changed from the thoughts of a young *talmid chacham* and became deeper and more complex. At first, he would learn one tractate at a time; then, as he gained expertise, he would learn several at a time. Thus, for each tractate there are pages upon pages of Torah thoughts. When he closed the letters, he also wrote beautifully about his service of Hashem (*avodas Hashem*) and imparted other important personal information. Clearly, his rebbi was not only his mentor, but in many ways a father figure.

Rav Moshe Soloveitchik, brother of the Brisker Rav, Rav Yitzchak Ze'ev Soloveitchik

Mordechai quickly catapulted up the ranks to become one of the most respected students of Yeshivas Rabbeinu Yitzchak Elchanan. After a year and a half in Rav Poleyeff's *shiur*, he decided on his own to join the *shiur* of Rav Moshe Soloveitchik, the son of Rav Chaim Soloveitchik and the older brother of Rav Yitzchak Ze'ev, the Brisker Rav. Rav Moshe's incisive and sharp *shiurim* would make an enormous impression on young Mordechai.

Rav Moshe had become a rosh yeshivah a few years earlier, and he appreciated Mordechai's sharp mind. Mordechai emulated the sharpness of Rav Moshe's Torah thoughts and quickly became known as one of the brightest minds and biggest scholars (*lamdanim*) of the yeshivah. He would later attribute his method of learning to the training he had received from Rav Moshe Soloveitchik.

---

9. *Mili Delgros* 26:1.

Years later, in his correspondence with Rav Moshe Aharon Poleyeff, Mordechai would send his novel Torah thoughts to the yeshivah and eagerly wait to hear the reaction of Rav Moshe Soloveitchik, as well. There were times when, later on in life as a rosh yeshivah himself, he would mention Rav Moshe's name and become quite emotional.

Dr. Shmuel Sar

After graduating high school, upon the encouragement and advice of his uncle, Dr. Shmuel Sar, the dean of the yeshivah, Mordechai decided to travel overseas and attend the great Telz Yeshivah in Lithuania. Dr. Sar had learned in Telz under Rav Yosef Leib Bloch, and he told Mordechai that that was the place where he would learn how to learn.

This journey would change his life forever.

Chapter 2
Journey to Telz — A Life Forever Changed

IN 1932, MORDECHAI DECIDED TO TRAVEL TO THE GREAT TELZ Yeshivah in Lithuania. This was the most pivotal move of his life. During the next 70 years, Rav Gifter would become first a student, then a rebbi, and finally the Rosh Hayeshivah of Telz.

His yearning to learn there began in 1928 when he met Rav Avraham Yitzchak Bloch, the rosh hayeshivah and rav in Telz, who was on a fundraising trip in America. Rav Avraham Yitzchak was a third-generation Telzer, the grandson of Rav Leizer Gordon (who had been the rosh hayeshivah and rav of Telz), and the second son of Rav Yosef Leib Bloch (Rav Leizer's son-in-law and successor).

Rav Avraham Yitzchak was brilliant and charismatic. Although he was only 38 years old when they first met, the rav's impact on young Mordechai would last forever. Rav Gifter told his son, Reb Binyomin, *"Lernen hub ich gekent far Telz, uber yiras Shamayim hub ich gekrogen fun rebbi'n.* [I knew how to learn before I went to Telz, but I received my

Rav Yosef Leib Bloch   Rav Leizer Gordon

fear of Heaven from my rebbi, Rav Avraham Yitzchak.]" Remembering him later on — especially after Rav Avraham Yitzchak was killed in the Holocaust — Rav Gifter would always refer to him tearfully as "*Mein rebbi, Hashem yinkom damo* — my rebbi, may G-d avenge his blood."

Although Rav Avraham Yitzchak Bloch was the second son of Rav Yosef Leib, he became the rosh hayeshivah and the rav in the village of Telz, through an incredible act of selflessness on the part of his older brother, Rav Zalman (who would later become Rav Gifter's father-in-law). At the funeral of Rav Yosef Leib, their father, Rav Zalman announced that his younger brother, Rav Avraham Yitzchak, would become the rosh hayeshivah and rav instead of him. Rav Zalman would take on the role of the spiritual leader (*menahel ruchani*) of the yeshivah and *dayan* of the city.

Rav Avraham Yitzchak Bloch so inspired Mordechai (during that visit in 1928) that he told his parents that he wanted to learn in the Telzer Yeshivah. Telz would transform his life. It was the place where Mordechai brought his love of learning and, surrounded by luminaries in Torah and other boys like himself, he would develop that love into a lifelong passion.

Eager though he was to attend the yeshivah, Mordechai knew that it would be very difficult for his parents to help him achieve this dream. First of all, the family had little money; in addition, it was very difficult, especially for his mother, to say goodbye to her precious son, not knowing when she would see him again. In fact, her daughter later said that Mrs. Gifter cried an ocean of tears when Mordechai left.

The financial problem was solved by Mordechai's father, who, in a rare act of self-sacrifice, sold his own life insurance policy. He didn't come close to appreciating what Telz would offer his son, but he saw the fire in Mordechai's heart and knew he had to do whatever he could to make it happen.

The more difficult challenge was for Mrs. Gifter to say goodbye to her son. Her self-sacrifice inspired him throughout his life. Today we see our children off to faraway places and know that we can talk to them often and see them, as well, a few times a year. But when Mordechai set off to learn in faraway Telz, his mother had no idea when he would return. In later years, he would make a point of drawing close to boys who were far from their parents and sympathize fully with what they — and their parents — were going through. As he told one young man who came to Telz from Australia,[1] "My mother went through Gehinnom when I learned in Lita [Lithuania]."

Rav Zalman and Rav Avraham Yitzchak Bloch

In October 1933, Mordechai traveled to Telz on a ship called the Bernengaria.[2]

In order to prepare for yeshivah, Mordechai had taken upon himself a great amount of learning. He had completed the tractates of *Kiddushin, Me'ilah, and Tamid* in less than a year. In addition, he began to learn *Maseches Nedarim* so as not to "waste time" while waiting for the ship to set sail. Even then, he was meticulously writing down his Torah thoughts.[3]

Indeed, Mordechai's growth seems a bit unusual. We must bear in mind that he came from humble origins; nevertheless, he set goals

---

1. Rabbi Moshe Yaakov Perl.
2. *Mili DeIgros* II 8:7.
3. Ibid. 10:3.

Chapter 2: Journey to Telz — A Life Forever Changed □ 45

for himself. And with much assistance from Above, he accomplished and completed one tractate, and then another, and another. We chart his growth for one reason: to show that it can be done. In fact, Rav Gifter would often say, "No one will say that you should have been Moshe Rabbeinu. No one will ask you, 'Why weren't you the Ohr Same'ach [Rav Meir Simchah HaKohen of Dvinsk]?' But you will be asked, 'Why didn't you become all that YOU could have been?' " Rav Gifter would be the first one to tell us that we must try. He did, and he succeeded.

Adjustments

STILL, EVEN WITH ALL OF HIS PREPARATIONS, YOUNG MORDECHAI was a bit overwhelmed upon arriving at his destination. As he would often say, the first time he stepped into the *beis midrash* of Telz, his eyes scanned the many young men learning and lit upon a young man, Moshe Groz, who seemed to be particularly optimistic and happy. Mordechai commented to another Baltimorean, Aharon Paperman, who had already been in the yeshivah for several years, that this boy must be wealthy; what other reason could there be for his joy?

Aharon chuckled at the suggestion. Moshe was one of the poorest boys in the yeshivah; so poor, in fact, that he didn't even own a shirt; he wore only a fake shirt collar. No, there was something else that was making him happy: Torah!

This story became one of Rav Gifter's favorites, illustrating the pure joy of learning Torah.

Rav Gifter (l) with R' Binyamin Bak as young men in Telz

His first *chavrusa* in the yeshivah was a young man named Binyamin Bak. Together, they completed the tractate of *Nedarim* seven times.[4] Soon Mordechai moved on to other *chavrusos*, but the two remained steadfast friends and corresponded for many years thereafter. Rabbi Bak, who later became a rav in Baltimore, would often mention how proud he was that he had learned with Rav Gifter.

The Joys of Learning in Telz

BY THE BEGINNING OF 1934, JUST A FEW MONTHS AFTER HE ARRIVED, Rav Gifter had grown into one of the sharpest minds and finest scholars of the yeshivah. He felt it almost impossible to describe his joy at being in Telz. His level of learning grew by leaps and bounds. When he arrived, the yeshivah was learning *Bava Metzia*. Aside from completing that tractate, he completed *Nedarim* within his first few weeks and moved on to *Maseches Nazir*. In addition, at night he was learning *Maseches Chagigah*!

By the summer of 1934, Mordechai had already finished *Bava Metzia* and *Chagigah*, and he began to learn *Kiddushin*. In addition, he had a special learning group (*chaburah*) in *Maseches Bechoros*. It is nothing less than astonishing to see how quickly young Mordechai had advanced in his learning. He was merely 18 years old and had been learning Gemara for less than five years. Yet nothing was stopping his spectacular progress.

Even though he himself was so happy, Mordechai worried about the friends he had left behind in America. He wrote to many of them, encouraging them to come to Telz, concerned that if they did not spend time in such an intense Torah environment, they might not remain religious. Unfortunately, his letters did not change the minds of his friends, and Mordechai's fears were indeed realized. Two of the friends he had written to moved away from Torah, never to return.

A Name for Himself

AS HE ROSE THROUGH THE RANKS OF THE *BACHURIM* AT TELZ, THE members of the administration and other students took note of him, especially Nachum Zev (Velvel) Dessler, the son of Rav Eliyahu Eliezer Dessler (author of *Michtav MeEliyahu*), future principal of the Hebrew Academy of Cleveland. Nachum Velvel was several years younger than Mordechai.

---
4. Reb Binyomin Gifter.

Rav Gifter (l) and a bachur from France studying together in Telz, Lita

When he first arrived in Telz, he inquired about the boy who was learning so well and with such enthusiasm at the front of the *beis midrash*. From that time on, Mordechai earned the distinction of being known as the *Amerikaner iluy,* the genius from America!

Mordechai took advantage of every moment of learning; any time he was unable to learn he saw as a waste of time. Once, when he had to go to the hospital for a minor procedure, his only concern was that he was unable to learn much during those few days.

ONE DAY, AFTER MORDECHAI HAD BEEN IN TELZ FOR ABOUT TWO or three years, non-Jews began throwing stones into houses. They even threw a stone into the yeshivah, which almost grazed Rav Avraham Yitzchak Bloch's face. The petrified Jews shuttered themselves in their homes while the mob ran through the streets screaming, "Kill the Jews!"

Disaster Averted

Knowing that mortal danger was imminent, Mordechai called the American Consulate in Kovno and said that he was an American citizen, and a pogrom was about to begin in the city where he was studying. The consul told Mordechai to take a train out of the city. However, Mordechai wanted to save everyone in Telz, not just himself. Therefore, he told the consul that it was impossible to get to the train station since the streets were swarming with hysterical peasants. The consul finally agreed to use his influence to have the police intervene. The burly border guards who arrived soon after immediately dispersed the rabble, and the danger subsided. Thus, Mordechai, with his quick thinking, succeeded in saving many lives in Telz.⁵

During those years, Mordechai became close to Rav Azriel Rabinowitz, the son of Rav Chaim Rabinowitz, known as Rav Chaim Telzer. Rav Azriel, who was in his 30's, was the youngest member of the yeshivah's administration. He was responsible to help the younger *bachurim* adjust to the yeshivah, and he also gave *chaburos* on the material the *bachurim* learned in the afternoon, material that the morning *shiurim* did not cover. Mordechai spoke with him in learning for hours. On one occasion, the two discussed Mordechai's thoughts on *Maseches Chagigah* for over two-and-a-half hours!

Rav Chaim (Rabinowitz) Telzer

EARLY IN HIS TELZ YEARS, MORDECHAI WAS INTRODUCED TO RAV Mordechai Pogromansky. Rav Mottel, as he was known, was a brilliant and charismatic young *talmid chacham* who would periodically visit the yeshivah and speak to the *bachurim*. He was especially warm to the boys who came from out of the country, and they flocked to him.

Rav Mottel Pogromansky

Mordechai was mesmerized by Rav Mottel's compelling personality and extraordinary mind. Rav Gifter later recounted how Rav Mottel plumbed the mysteries of a thought from the *Leshem Shevo VeAchlamah* (a Kabbalistic work). After Rav Mottel dazzled him for three hours with his insights, the complex concept he was discussing became crystal clear to Mordechai; Rav Mottel was able to explain and clarify even the most difficult subject matter. Rav Gifter would say that this showed Rav Mottel's unique power of explanation (*koach hasbarah*). But Rav Gifter later said that immediately after leaving the room, he could no longer comprehend the material that had been so understandable not long before.

Still, Rav Gifter felt as though his mind had been stretched, and he would now be able to comprehend things that before would have been incomprehensible to him.

---

5. Rebbetzin Shoshana Gifter, Rebbetzin Shlomis Eisenberg.

When he was rosh hayeshivah in Telz, Rav Gifter would often mention Rav Mottel in his *shmuessen*. He was fond of quoting Rav Mottel: "To feel another's pain, one has to be a *mentch*; but to sense his *simchah*, one needs to be an angel!"

Rav Gifter told a story to illustrate the *emunah* of Rav Mottel: Shortly after World War II, Rav Mottel and a friend were traveling, and planned to reach their destination well before Shabbos. However, they became engrossed in discussion and missed their stop. By the time they disembarked, it was almost Shabbos, and they had no idea where they were!

Rav Mottel's friend was horrified! What would they do? Shabbos was approaching, and they were nowhere near a Jewish community. But Rav Mottel reassured his friend, "A Jew is never lost! If we are here, it is not because we are lost; it is because we are meant to be here!" He proved his point from the story of Hagar. When she was sent away from Avraham's home, the Torah says (*Bereishis* 21:14) that she was lost. Rashi comments that she returned to the house of her father and to a life of idol worship.

Rav Mottel asked, "How do we know that Hagar went back to her life of idol worship? Maybe she was just lost. The answer is that a person who is following the word of Hashem is never lost, because he realizes that wherever he is now is exactly where Hashem wants him to be. Hagar's lamentation showed that she had abandoned her faith in the Al-mighty; she had returned to her ways of idol worship."

Rav Mottel's friend told him, "The *vort* is wonderful, *uber Rav Mottel, mir zennen fort farblundget* — but Rav Mottel, we are still lost!"

Not one to give up hope, Rav Mottel inquired and discovered that there was indeed one Jew in the town. They went to his home. When the man opened the door, he was stunned to find two Jews on his doorstep. He could not believe his eyes.

"Are you Eliyahu HaNavi?" he asked the strangers in shock. Rav

Rav Mottel Pogromansky

Mottel informed the man that he was just a Jew by the name of Mottel Pogromansky and he introduced his friend. The host invited them in and explained that he and his wife had had a baby boy the Shabbos before. They had tried to get a *mohel* to come to the city for Shabbos to perform the *bris*, but they were unable to find anyone willing to come.

"Would either of you happen to be a *mohel*?"

Rav Mottel smiled. He informed their host that indeed his friend was a *mohel* and that he even had his circumcision equipment with him.

Remarkably, the little baby merited to be circumcised on Shabbos, the eighth day!

This vignette was retold by the rosh hayeshivah when he wanted to highlight the *emunah* of Rav Mottel Pogromansky, a man who always felt that he was in the Hands of the Al-mighty.

Rav Gifter always held Rav Mottel in the highest esteem. Many years later, Rav Gifter eulogized Rav Elyah Lopian: a great *mussar* personality, author, and mashgiach in Kfar Chassidim. Included in his many praises about Rav Lopian was that he was the one to discover Rav Mottel!

The Fire of Torah

EXPOSED TO SUCH GREATNESS, MORDECHAI'S ASCENT AT TELZ continued. In his memorable eulogy on Rav Gifter, Rav Moshe Shapiro recounted that his own father had learned in Telz Yeshivah nearly 10 years earlier. He described the atmosphere of Telz as *ris'cha deOraissa*, fire of Torah. When one entered the *beis midrash* with a thought (*sevarah*), he was as passionate as if he were entering the fiery furnace where Nimrod cast Avraham Avinu! In other words, every *bachur* was ready to defend his Torah thought as if he were defending his own life.

In addition to the intense learning environment and the many great *rabbanim* and rebbeim to whom Mordechai was exposed, there were also the many laymen of Telz who made an indelible impression on him. He was astounded by their learning and diligence. Rav Gifter would recount that when Rav Avraham Yitzchak said a *shiur*, many of the laymen would come to listen. But they didn't just listen; they would come and "fight in learning." The rav would say that he had to brace himself to defend his lecture against the *baalebatim* of Telz![6]

---
6. Rabbi Azriel Goldfein.

Baruch Baron Hy"d and Nachum Velvel Dessler standing in front of the yeshivah in Telz, Lithuania

By the summer of 1935, Mordechai was learning *Kesubos, Sanhedrin, and Megillah* with *Turei Even* (an in-depth commentary on *Maseches Megillah*). Soon thereafter, he finished those tractates. Indeed, he was systematically learning all of the Talmud. After his first two years in Telz, Mordechai "spread his wings" and influenced other young men in the yeshivah. He loved Telz. He wrote, "There is not enough paper to hold all the praise I have to write about the yeshivah."[7]

One of his roommates, Rabbi Yitzchak Hertz, remembers that the future rosh hayeshivah did not spend much time in his room or in the house. He was a *masmid* who spent all of his waking hours in the *beis midrash*.

THERE WERE SOME *BEIN HAZMANIM* (INTERCESSIONS) WHEN Mordechai preferred to remain in the yeshivah in Telz. During those times, he would often take a small tractate and learn it in its entirety.

Bein Hazmanim

As a rebbi and then later as a rosh hayeshivah, he drew on this experience and implored the *bachurim* before a vacation, "*Nemt ah kleine masechtala* — Take a small tractate [and learn it]."

Sometimes, after entreating his *talmidim* to learn during *bein hazmanim*, he would conclude his speech by saying, "*Ich hub eich leeb* — I love you." Imagine the impact on *bachurim* hearing such words from

---
7. *Mili DeIgros* II 14:2.

52 □ RAV GIFTER

their beloved rebbi and imagine how much these words made them *want* to please him and do his bidding.

One time, Mordechai traveled through Slabodka and met Rav Isaac Sher, the rosh yeshivah of Slabodka at that time. Rav Isaac asked him, "What have you learned lately?" Rav Gifter responded that he was learning *Maseches Me'ilah*. Rav Sher wondered why a young *bachur* was learning a tractate other than the ones that are commonly learned in yeshivos. He asked Mordechai if he had already completed *Bava Basra* and *Bava Kamma*. But when Rav Gifter reassured him that he was learning *Me'ilah* only during *bein hazmanim*, Rav Sher was highly impressed and blessed him that he should be able to continue this practice.

Vacation also allowed Mordechai to travel to other surrounding villages where he could meet notable *talmidei chachamim*, such as Rav Ezra Altschuler, known as the *Takanas Ezra*. In the summer of 1935, he traveled to Kovno and spent some time speaking to Rav Yosef Zusmanowitz, known as the "Yerushalmi," who was the author of *Teruas HaMelech* and a rav in Vilkomir. He also corresponded during this time with the Rogatchover Gaon, Rav Yosef Rosen, cherishing the responses he received.

Shortly after the Rogatchover Gaon passed away, the Lithuanian *bachurim* wanted to see if Mordechai, as an American, was indeed genuine in his approach to life. They decided to test his authenticity by getting him drunk on Purim, since a drunkard cannot hide his true essence. Sure enough, as soon as the wine began to take effect, he delivered a eulogy on the Rogatchover Gaon.

His Bride

OF HIS GREAT REBBEIM, HE BECAME CLOSEST TO RAV ZALMAN Bloch, the spiritual leader of the yeshivah. He was Rav Zalman's *chavrusa*, and Mordechai lived as a boarder in his home for three years, as well. He felt as though he were not only the student of this great man, but, in a way, one of his children.

Toward the end of his tenure in yeshivah, prior to his returning home to America, a marvelous match was suggested to Mordechai: Shoshana, the daughter of Rav Zalman Bloch!

Mordechai was ecstatic with the proposition, and before long the two were engaged.

Rav Zalman Bloch and family. On Rav Zalman's left is Shoshana Gifter. Mordechai Gifter is standing in the back row.

Chapter 3
The Journey From Telz

ALTHOUGH MORDECHAI'S GROWTH IN TORAH AND DEVOtion to learning in Telz gratified him, it had been a long time since he had seen his beloved parents who had sacrificed so much for him: emotionally and monetarily.

At the same time, he reflected on the last five years. He had left his parents as a young man; by now, he had earned a reputation as a giant in Torah. He was considered to be the lion of the yeshivah, the pride and joy of Telz, and one with whom many sages conversed. Of its 300 *talmidim*, Mordechai had risen to be one of the very best.

Torah Thoughts

MORDECHAI HAD FINISHED LEARNING *MASECHES SHABBOS* AND had developed many novel Torah thoughts. His next hurdle was *Maseches Beitzah* and the rest of *Seder Moed*, with *Seder Kodashim* to follow.[1] It is amazing that he did this while he was learning the tractates in the current cycle of the yeshivah. By the summer of 1937, *Eruvin* and *Succah* were completed

---
1. *Mili DeIgros* II, 17:2.

with, yes ... of course, novel Torah thoughts. *Maseches Rosh Hashanah* would follow, with Mordechai feeling a sense of eagerness and anticipation for the very difficult *Maseches Yevamos*.

Although generally Mordechai felt great pleasure in jotting down every original Torah thought he developed, sometimes he was not satisfied with his ideas and hesitated to record them. Rav Moshe Aharon Poleyeff, however, encouraged him to record everything, telling him that when he became a bit older he would derive much pleasure from the Torah of his youth.[2]

The Steipler Gaon

Mordechai treasured this piece of advice, and many times passed on to his own students the importance of writing down every piece of original Torah.

Later in life, Rav Gifter had a long correspondence with the Steipler Gaon, Rav Yaakov Yisrael Kanievsky. They wrote their Torah thoughts on postcards, and each treasured the other's words. This correspondence continued until Rav Gifter found out that the Steipler personally mailed these letters. Knowing that the Steipler was not well and had trouble walking, he ceased writing to him so as not to burden him.

He also corresponded with Rav Yehoshua Klavan, the rabbi of Washington D.C.

At times, Rav Gifter's correspondents would jot down some notes on the backs of the envelopes that contained the letters. Rav Gifter would send back the envelopes to his correspondents if a few words of a Torah thought had been written on them.[3] This was because all these great men treasured their own Torah thoughts, no matter how minor.

The message was clear: Torah is priceless and thus every word should be treasured, not the least one's own words!

In fact, when Rav Gifter would write small comments (*he'aros*) to others, he would first copy them; he felt accountable to ensure that even

---
2. *Mili Delgros* 22:5.
3. *Pudiyas Toviyah, Sefer HaZikaron* p. 239.

those small pieces of Torah were preserved. We must bear in mind that this was all done by hand, in the days before photocopy machines.

Guarding One's Health

MORDECHAI'S HEALTH SUFFERED AT TIMES FROM HIS INTENSE and driven nature. He often felt weak, and the physician urged him to rest and regain his strength. The rest helped him, and the lesson became an important one.

When he was a rebbi and rosh hayeshivah, he would constantly stress the importance of eating and drinking properly and sleeping eight hours each night. He also felt strongly about the value of *bachurim* exercising and taking walks. Knowing the risks of not taking care of oneself, he did not want the same thing to happen to his *talmidim*.

During his correspondence at this time with Rav Moshe Aharon, Mordechai was distressed to learn that his own illness had worried his rebbi. This proved to Mordechai the strong and meaningful connection the two had: an everlasting personal bond cemented by their mutual love for Torah and the Torah thoughts they shared.[4]

Self-Annulment

THERE HAD BEEN PREVIOUS ATTEMPTS TO ENCOURAGE HIM TO return to the United States, but Mordechai had not yet reached the level in learning to which he aspired. In fact, he had tried to convince many of his rebbeim in America to send their students to Telz in Lithuania, but was not entirely successful.

In response to a family member's letter urging him to leave Telz when he was about 20 years old, he wrote a magnificent response titled *"Chovas HaAdam BaOlamo," Man's Obligation in His World*. Later in life, he would refer to it as the *Michtav HaTachlis* (Letter of Purpose). This manifesto is a gut-check for young *bnei Torah* who are trying to discover who they are and what their future could hold. It shows wisdom beyond his relatively young years, and illustrates the deep thinking he did with regard to his own path in life. Many challenges confronted him, but he never wavered. If anything, the challenges made him stronger, made him think deeper into who he was.

In this letter, Mordechai warns against choosing a purpose (*tachlis*) that contradicts the desired purpose of the Al-mighty. He validates the

---

[4]. *Mili DeIgros* II, 22:4.

(seated l to r) Mordechai Gifter, Rav Avrohom Vessler, and Rav Zalman Bloch

need for outside knowledge but only as it helps one achieve his ultimate purpose. Therefore, he posits, it makes no sense for one to pursue external knowledge before learning the primary wisdom of Torah. He likens it to someone who learns Rashi without ever learning the Gemara, which, he states, is a foolish approach.

In addition, Mordechai warns that the moment we begin to learn general knowledge, we risk empowering the evil inclination to lure us away from Torah study. Toward the end of the letter, he reaffirms his need to continue learning and to strengthen himself in matters of Torah. He knows that his friends in America thought he was foolish to go to Telz. But he cries for them and pities their choice not to lead a life of meaning and closeness to Hashem.[5]

His rebbi, Rav Zalman Bloch, counseled him against sending such a sharply worded letter to his family, so Mordechai reconstructed the letter. Such was Mordechai's self-annulment (*hisbatlus*) to his rebbeim; as brilliant and insightful as he was, he valued their opinions and often changed course based on their input. Later in life, too, Rav Gifter often changed

---

5. *Yeshurun* (Vol. X) pp. 429-431.

course on matters because he thought that others had a better grasp of the situation and he bowed to their greater wisdom. This was especially true when it came to heeding advice from the Steipler Gaon and Rav Shach.

TO FURTHER COMPREHEND THE DEPTH OF LOVE THAT RAV GIFTER felt for Telz, and his reluctance to leave it, one only needs to read a memorable lecture.[6] It is titled,*"Bila Hashem Ve'lo Chamal* [Hashem Destroyed Without Mercy, *Eichah* 2:2]," and was delivered in the yeshivah on the 20th *yahrtzeit* of the destruction of Telz, on the 20th day of Tammuz, 1961. He describes the majesty of the city of Telz:

The Majesty of Telz

The rav, Rav Avraham Yitzchak, the "sar tzeva Hashem [general of the army of Hashem]," would stand before his talmidim as they waged war in the milchamtah shel [the war of] Torah, in the arena of the beis midrash. Mah nora hamareh hazeh! [How awesome this sight was!]

Rav Azriel [Rabinowitz] would come in just a short while before Maariv and would stand in front of me. He did not waste these precious moments. Rather, he would grab a small masechta such as Beitzah or Chagigah and skim through the entire masechta before we began Maariv!

Rav Gifter also reminisced in this piece, with great emotion, about the legendary laymen (*baalebatim*) of Telz. Reb Leib Gertzovitz, or as he was

Telz

---

6. *Pirkei Emunah* I, pp. 182-184.

At dacha (vacation) in Polongin, seated (l-r): Rav Avrohom Vessler, Rav Eliyahu Meir Bloch, Rav Avraham Yitzchak Bloch, Rav Chaim Mordechai Katz, Rav Avner Oklansky, Rebbetzin Miriam Oklansky, Rebbetzin Rassia Bloch, Rebbetzin Rivka Bloch, Rebbetzin Shoshana Vessler, Rebbetzin Chaya Katz and their children

Seated at the head of the table (r-l): Rav Zalman, Rav Avraham Yitzchak and Rav Eliyahu Meir Bloch. Standing behind them are (r-l): then-*bachurim* Mordechai Gifter, Mendel Poliakoff, Chaim Stein; Aizik Ausband is seated fourth from left.

Chapter 3: The Journey From Telz □ 61

known, Reb Leib Minsker, owned a shoe store. But he never missed the afternoon learning session! On the Yamim Tovim, he would come to the home of the rav to hear the rav's lecture. He did not listen politely like a layman, but rather like a young yeshivah *bachur*, fighting to understand and clarify every word.

After finishing his Shabbos *seudah* on Friday night, Reb Leib would go to sleep until 11 o'clock. He would then wake up and go to the *beis midrash* to learn. And he would learn the entire night until *Shacharis*!

In Telz with a Hungarian *bachur*, Miklosh

There was a *tzaddik* in the town, a storeowner, Rav Gifter continued, by the name of Reb Yaakov Dovid Meisels. Reb Yaakov Dovid was a very poor man with a very large family. Mordechai and the other *bachurim* would pass by his store after the afternoon learning session was over. Although it was already late, they would be able to hear the sweet sounds of Reb Yaakov Dovid learning Torah. If they went in during the day to purchase something, he would often suggest that they purchase the item in a bigger store where the item was cheaper! Fittingly, it was Reb Yaakov Dovid who was

Rav Gifter, Rav Moshe Helfan, and Rav Pesach Stein

entrusted with running many of the free-loan organizations (*gemachs*) in the town.

There was Reb Eliyahu Chaim Helfan (whose son, Reb Moshe, a close friend of Rav Gifter's, would later become the financial secretary for the yeshivah in Cleveland), who gave a daily lecture in the *beis midrash*. Imagine, a layman giving a *shiur* in one of the most prestigious yeshivos in the world! In fact, Reb Eliyahu Chaim completed *Shas* seven times, and his *siyumim* were celebrated right in the *beis midrash*; he celebrated the seventh siyum with a "*sheva berachos*"! Rav Chaim Telzer (Rabinowitz) once said about Reb Eliyahu Chaim, "Reb Eliyahu Chaim does not know the power of his *limud haTorah*!"

Reb Eliyahu Chaim Helfan

One Shavuos morning, Reb Eliyahu Chaim noticed Mordechai and a friend taking a walk. Reb Eliyahu Chaim asked them why they were not learning, to which they replied, "*Genug gelernt.* [We learned enough.]" After all, they had been up the whole night learning. Reb Eliyahu Chaim replied, "*Ah shikker zugt kein mohl nit genug bronfin getrunkin.* [A drunkard never says he drank enough whiskey.]" Reb Eliyahu Chaim was pointing out the importance of constant learning and always wanting to learn more!

These were some of the laymen of Telz. In the same lecture, Rav Gifter amplifies our mental picture of Telz by describing the very streets of the town. He reminisces about the time that he was walking down *Navraner Veg* (Navraner Street) with Rav Yitzchak Isaac Hershovitz, the *av beis din* of Virbaln, Lithuania, who commented, "This street is full of Torah, because Rav Leizer Gordon would walk down this street every day, and he never stopped repeating his Torah thoughts as he walked…"

Rav Gifter recounted how the *bachurim* would walk through the fields upon request of the gentile farmers who felt that the land would be blessed by the boys' presence. The sound of Torah reverberated throughout the streets!

This is but a taste of the city of Telz, and the yeshivah of Telz, that Mordechai left behind. It is this atmosphere, this holy environment, that he would strive to rebuild in America — not just a yeshivah, but a life. MORDECHAI KNEW HE COULD NOT REMAIN IN TELZ IN CLOSE proximity to his *kallah,* Shoshana Bloch, during their engagement.

Return to America
Therefore, he traveled back to America in 1939 by ship, for what he thought would be a short period of time. He intended to go back to Europe for his wedding and live there for at least another four, perhaps as many as six, years in order to complete all of *Shas* and *Poskim*, and then become a rav in a small town in Lita. Rav Mottel Pogromansky suggested that he go to Brisk upon his return, to learn under the Brisker Rav, Rav Yitzchak Ze'ev Soloveitchik. But the uneasy and dangerous political climate in Europe prevented any such return.

On his way home, a group of young Romanian Chassidim observed him a bit condescendingly, assuming that he was a "modern" young man, a heretic (*maskil*), since he did not wear the customary Chassidic garb. But this "heretic" piqued their interest. Whenever they saw Mordechai, he was learning. Their initial disapproval turned into curiosity, and eventually, complete reverence. In time, a few of the Chassidic young men introduced themselves to the American and their relationship blossomed.

As Mordechai disembarked in America, he wondered how soon he could return to Europe — but, alas, this was not to be. Europe — and Lita — would soon go up in flames, and Hitler would destroy the yeshivah that Mordechai loved so dearly.

World War II broke out on the first day of *Selichos* 5699 (September 1939). Mordechai immediately traveled to Washington D.C. to try to secure visas for the roshei hayeshivah and students of Telz. For two weeks, he knocked on doors of countless members of Congress and government officials, and succeeded in obtaining hundreds of visas for the roshei hayeshivah and married students, as well as for their families.

Tragically, however, the heads of the yeshivah decided to remain in Telz. Rav Yosef Leib Bloch had dealt with a similar situation during World War I, and had determined not to move deeper inside Russia. They decided again not to move, since they did not sense the imminent danger. When they did, it was already too late.

WHEN MORDECHAI REALIZED HE COULD NOT RETURN TO EUROPE, he sent the necessary documents for his *kallah*, Shoshana, to join him in America. However, she did not make use of them in time, in the hope that her *chassan* would be returning shortly to Europe, and the exit date given on her passport had already passed. In the end, Nachum Velvel Dessler, a fellow student of Mordechai in Telz, helped her. In a dramatic sequence of Providence, Nachum Velvel was able to obtain a visa for Shoshana. It was the last visa from the American consul in Kovno — just a few hours before he himself left the country — the only one given that day to any Lithuanian citizen.

Saving His Bride

Rav Dessler after his arrival in Cleveland

She departed on the same ship as her uncles, Rav Eliyahu Meir Bloch, her father's brother, and Rav Mordechai Katz, the son-in-law of Rav Yosef Leib Bloch, who were traveling abroad to raise funds for the yeshivah. However, her uncles were detained in Japan because their visas had

Rav Eliyahu Meir Bloch

Rav Chaim Mordechai Katz

Chapter 3: The Journey From Telz ☐ 65

expired. Shoshana Bloch docked in Seattle, Washington, on the *Hiwaka Maru*, just before Yom Kippur of 1940.

Her uncles arrived in November 1940. Rav Elya Meir and Rav Mottel, as they were known, traveled with heavy hearts, hoping to be able to return to their homes shortly. No one could have anticipated what was about to happen.

Martyrs of Telz

IN 1940, THE YESHIVAH WAS ABRUPTLY SHUT DOWN BY THE invading Soviets, and the *bachurim* had to scramble to find places to learn and daven. Rav Avraham Yitzchak stressed to the *bachurim* the importance of staying together as much as possible. Maintaining unity was imperative for the dangerous times that lay ahead. The older boys looked after the younger ones and helped them through the turbulent times.

At the end of Sivan 5701 (1941), the Nazis entered the city, and all the men were taken to the city of Rayan for forced labor. Boys who had been taught that they were Jewish royalty were treated like vermin. The Nazis tortured the inhabitants mercilessly. The city was terrorized. People were murdered senselessly in the streets.

Yet the students had been trained to look for deeper meaning in everything around them, and to believe that Hashem is in control of all that takes place in the world, and they drew on that faith now.

A few weeks passed. Then, on the 20th day of Tammuz 5701 (1941), Telz Yeshivah in Lithuania ceased to exist. The entire yeshivah — roshei hayeshivah, rebbeim, and students — as well as the laymen of the city, were brutally murdered, enduring unspeakable horrors and torture. The Nazis tried to dehumanize them, but eyewitnesses testified that these heroic individuals maintained their nobility until the very last breath.

It is impossible for us to understand the self-sacrifice the heroic individuals of Telz displayed. Nevertheless, we will share three incidents that convey the greatness of the families of Rav Zalman and Rav Avraham Yitzchak Bloch.

Moishele

AFTER THE MEN WERE ALL SLAUGHTERED, THE REMAINING people — women and children — mourned. Each family had lost husbands and sons; shuls and yeshivos were now empty; there was no sound of Torah, no praying in the shuls. The silence was deafening.

The fear of what lay ahead was palpable. Over the next few weeks, mothers tried to care for their children, each day speculating if it would be their last. Every time they passed a soldier, they couldn't help but wonder if he might shoot them for no reason at all. Finally, the day they all feared came. On the seventh day of Elul, the women and children were rounded up, and all knew that they would soon be killed. Some of the older girls had managed to escape and would eventually survive, but the younger children all walked to their final destination.

Moishele Bloch (the brother of Rebbetzin Shoshana Gifter) and Malkiel Denis, a cousin, whose mother died in childbirth

Moishele, the 12-year-old brother of Rebbetzin Shoshana Gifter, was among them. Suddenly, he began to grab *siddurim*, *tefillin*, and other sacred articles. He piled them all on top of one another and tried mightily to lift them.

The beautiful child looked as if he were carrying the world on his shoulders. Well … maybe he was. Those who saw him asked him what he was trying to do. Moishele answered, "I am just a young boy. What mitzvos do I have? I haven't managed to learn much of *Chumash*, *Mishnayos*, or Gemara yet. I cannot even be counted with a *minyan*. And I never had a chance to wear *tefillin*. So I just want to take all these mitzvos up to Heaven with me."

Moishele's response is one that speaks of the resiliency and purity that separate a Jewish child from all others.

A SECOND STORY DEMONSTRATES THE ABILITY WE HAVE AS JEWS to transcend all our emotions and elevate our spirits above all else. It

A Mother's Love

also illustrates that there is no love in this world as strong as the love of a mother for her child.

This story is related in the name of Rebbetzin Kleiner, the daughter of Rav Avraham Yitzchak Bloch, about whose aunt the following is told.

Rebbetzin Luba and Rav Zalman Bloch

After all the men had been killed, Rebbetzin Luba Bloch, the wife of Rav Zalman Bloch, the spiritual leader of the yeshivah, was taken with her children. The rebbetzin walked to the area where she knew she would die. It is difficult to imagine how one would act in such a situation. How does one prepare for one's final moments on this earth?

The German guards barked orders and demanded that the Jews prepare for their deaths. At that point, the rebbetzin did something truly amazing. She approached a Nazi and promised to reveal the secret hiding place of all her jewelry and valuables if he would be willing to honor her last request.

The greedy guard wondered what this woman could possibly want in exchange for all her jewelry. Looking defiantly at the wicked man, she said, "Please let me die last." The guard was shocked. He took her for a coward who wanted to delay the inevitable, but he acquiesced to her wishes. What difference did it make to him? And so, all her children were led to the edge of the pit and murdered in cold blood.

Immediately after seeing her children slaughtered in front of her eyes, Rebbetzin Bloch then did one of the most heroic things a mother can ever do. She lowered herself into the pit and tended to the bullet-ridden bodies. Tenderly closing their eyes, she kissed them on their foreheads, and then scooped up a handful of dirt and sprinkled it gently over them. With that, she looked up toward Heaven and declared, "Thank You for giving a *Yiddishe mama* the opportunity to bring her children to *kever Yisrael*."

Reb Binyomin Beinush and Leah (Zeidy and Bubby) Denis — Rebbetzin Shoshana Gifter's grandparents

Then she stood up and faced the Nazi barbarian once more.

"Now you may do what you want to me."

Within moments, she was reunited with her children.

This is the strength of Rebbetzin Luba Bloch, the mother of Rebbetzin Shoshana Gifter. This almost incomprehensible display of courage gives us reason to reflect and to think about what true love means. When the time came for her children to die, Rebbetzin Bloch knew that the only way she could ensure that their bodies would receive a Jewish burial was to do the hardest thing a mother could ever do.

AND NOW, A GLIMPSE INTO THE WORLD OF RAV AVRAHAM Yitzchak Bloch.

Final Avodah Rav Gifter relayed the following (which serves as an introduction to the final story) at an address delivered at a Torah Umesorah teachers' conference in 1974:

The little that I know revealed entire worlds of insight to me ... random incidents that the children of the Telzer Rav [Rav Avraham Yitzchak] related to me.

When the Nazis beat the Telzer Rav upon the head with hammer blows and taunted him: "Where is your G-d, Herr Rabbiner?" the Telzer Rav replied, "He is not only my G-d; He is your G-d. And the world will yet see this."

In a world where some men turned into animals, others became angels.

Chapter 3: The Journey From Telz ☐ 69

Rav Zalman and Rav Avraham Yitzchak Bloch with *talmidim*

Three weeks before the end of Yeshivas Telz in Lithuania, and the murder of all of its faculty and student body, the Nazis took the men to a town called Rayan, where they were forced to perform degrading labor for long hours. The rav, Rav Avraham Yitzchak, tried to continue learning, following the same yeshivah schedule that the yeshivah had kept to when it was in session. The rav even recorded his Torah thoughts at this time of peril!

On the 19th day of Tammuz, a Gestapo officer arrived with a sword in his hand and coldly informed them that their days on earth were numbered. The men were lined up in rows, and the Germans began to beat them.

They were forced to run, but they were weak and the ground was muddy. They kept slipping and falling. And with each fall, they absorbed more and more blows from the Nazis' metal truncheons. The Germans struck at them mercilessly as they tried to shield themselves and maintain their balance.

But for the rav and Rav Zalman, his brother, this degrading exercise was even more challenging. Since Rav Elya Meir Bloch was already in America at the time, they took it upon themselves to help Rav Elya Meir's father-in-law, Rav Aryeh Moshe Kaplan, an elderly man who was unable to run. The two brothers attempted to hold him up and carry him as they ran through the mud.

Bloodied and beaten, covered in mud, they all somehow returned to their hut. Exhausted and in pain, the rav lifted his hands toward

Heaven, and called out, "*Ribbono Shel Olam — grois bist Du, un grois zenen Deine maasim* — Al-mighty G-d, You are great and so are Your actions!"

Then, since he was too weak to read on his own, the rav's daughter (who later became Rebbetzin Chaya Ausband) read to him the section of the laws of *Kiddush Hashem* from the Rambam.

He had to prepare for the final *avodah*: to die *al Kiddush Hashem*.

The following morning would be his last, and he would be ready.

These three vignettes are a small sampling of the unimaginable strength (*gevurah*) of the men, women, and even children of the city of Telz.

RAV GIFTER DESCRIBED THE CITY THAT WAS NO LONGER:

The Legacy of Telz

Telz was the royal realm of Torah, and everything was under the control of the yeshivah. The policy of the Jewish bank, the administration of Yavneh, the girls' school, the elementary school for the boys, the summer camp for poor children were all under control and auspices of the yeshivah. In Telz, everything was Torah law. And the rosh yeshivah directed all the activities of the yeshivah according to the strict dictates of the Torah.

Ultimately, the legacy of Telz and Lita is Torah! The pure study of Torah for its own sake. The willingness to sacrifice and be satisfied with few possessions for the sake of Torah — this was its highest ideal. This is what those generations were like. We lived Torah. It was our life. This was the uniqueness of Telz. It was a town that functioned solely according to the Torah.[7]

Thus, in their desperate anguish for what was lost because of the war, Rav Gifter and others like him were determined to rebuild that world outside of Europe.

RAV GIFTER WAS ONCE ASKED WHERE HE FELT MORE EMOTION, Kever Rachel or the Kosel HaMaaravi. He responded that most people

Feeling the Destruction

would probably answer that they feel more emotion when they are at Kever Rachel, because they can relate to it more. They feel like they can connect to Rachel Imeinu, because who doesn't cry at the grave of a *mama*?

Rav Gifter and Samuel Portnoy were friends from the time they had studied together as children, in the 1920s, at the Western Talmud Torah

---

[7]. Rav Mordechai Gifter, *The World That Was: Lithuania*, pp. 40-42.

on West Lexington Street. When Mr. Portnoy visited Eretz Yisrael in 1988, Rav Gifter wrote him, "Don't fail to shed tears at Kever Rachel in Beis Lechem. I returned about six weeks ago from a three-week visit. I wish everyone to feel what I always experience."

Yet Rav Gifter explained his own feelings regarding these two emotional experiences. "However, I experienced *churban*, as the world I loved was destroyed when Europe went up in flames. And *Churban Europa shtams* [stems] from the *Churban Beis HaMikdash*, as all destruction stems from there. Thus, when I visit the Kosel, I can relate to it even more. Because I feel the *churban*…"

He lived through a *churban* and wanted with all of his being to rebuild what was lost.

New Beginnings

REB MORDECHAI'S FUTURE WIFE JOINED HIM IN BALTIMORE AFTER a long journey across half the world. So on the fifth night of Chanukah, December 19th, 1940, in a small wedding in Baltimore, Reb Mordechai and Shoshana Gifter were married. In Telz, the couple's friends and family also celebrated the wedding, albeit with much heartache that they were unable to participate in person.

After Reb Mordechai's return to Baltimore in 1939, he had begun to give *chaburos* in Yeshivas Ner Yisrael in Baltimore. Before his marriage, Reb Mordechai was appointed the rabbi of the Nusach Ari Shul in Baltimore, and his career in the rabbinate began, even before his rebbetzin arrived. However, with its paltry salary, it was obvious that this particular position would only be a short-term solution. Thus, after his marriage, when the birth of his eldest son was imminent, it was time to move on.

Rebbetzin Shoshana Gifter

AFTER HIS SHORT STINT IN BALTIMORE AS RABBI, HE APPLIED FOR A rabbinic position in Waterbury, Connecticut, a prestigious position at the time. His main competitor was Rav Abba Zalka Gewirtz, a young rabbi in Bradley Beach, New Jersey, who had learned in Yeshivas Chofetz Chaim in New York.

Waterbury

Rabbi Gewirtz had already heard about Rav Gifter and been highly impressed by what he had heard. Rav Henoch Leibowitz, son of Rav Dovid, the Rosh yeshivah of Yeshivas Chofetz Chaim in New York, was sitting in his *beis midrash* when Rav Gifter, freshly back from Europe, entered to sit and learn. Word soon spread in the *beis midrash* that a true *talmid chacham* was among them. Soon many of the *bachurim* gathered around Reb Mordechai to fire questions at him. Reb Abba Zalka remembers hearing from his friends how the young Rav Gifter deflected the questions and quieted his challengers. As one witness described it, it

Rav Gifter's letter accepting the invitation to visit the Waterbury Hebrew Institute

Chapter 3: The Journey From Telz □ 73

From (l) Rabbi Yonah Gewirtz, Rav Gifter, and Rav Abba Zalka Gewirtz in Telz

was like a lion defending his terrain. The others came to contest, argue, and strive with Rav Gifter in learning, but with precision and passion, he silenced them all. They were learning *Yevamos* in the yeshivah and Rav Gifter was not, but it made no difference. At this point, he was completely comfortable in anything he had ever learned. He had mastered the tractates and now he was thirsty for more and more learning. Especially after spending so much time on the boat away from a *beis midrash*, Rav Gifter was hungry for the *ris'cha deOraissa* (fire of Torah) and *pilpul chaveirim* (interaction among colleagues) he had treasured in the yeshivah.

The astonished group of *bachurim* had been exposed to greatness and they would never forget it. Reb Abba Zalka was very impressed upon hearing the story.

When the Waterbury synagogue board voted, their choice was Reb Abba Zalka. When they informed him, he told them they had made the wrong choice. Rav Gifter, he explained, was destined for greatness.[8] As he put it, "He's a better man than I." So the shul hired Rav Gifter, who would always remember Reb Abba Zalka's kindness and generosity.

Eventually, when Rav Gifter finished his tenure in Waterbury, he was succeeded by the same Reb Abba Zalka, based on the recommenda-

---

8. Rebbetzin Shoshana Gifter, Rabbi Yonah Gewirtz.

> XXXXXXXXXXXXXXX
> 56 Woodlawn Terrace
>
> November 18, 1941.
>
> Rabbi Max Gifter
> 2615 Quantico Avenue
> Baltimore, Md.
>
> Dear Rabbi:
>
> It is now my very pleasant task to inform you that the members of both synagogues, at their respective meetings last night, approved, unanimously, the action of the committee in electing you as our Rabbi.
>
> With the formalities thus concluded, let me extend to you a hearty "Birchas Mazol Tov" on both happy occasions, on behalf of our committee and the officers and members of the synagogues, as well as the personal greetings of Mrs. Gelman and myself to you and Mrs. Gifter. May this mark the beginning of a long period of happiness and progress, in the spiritual and material sense, for you as well as the community, individually and collectively.
>
> We are now ready to announce your election officially. To do it properly, I would ask that you be good enough to send me some material for a short biographical sketch in the local newspapers and a good photograph of yourself. I realize the difficulty in writing autobiography, and am, therefore sending a copy of this letter to Mr. Sar, so that he may help us in this respect. But for the photograph we shall need your own help.
>
> The joint committee, appointed last night, is now preparing the agreement, and as soon as the final draft is completed, it will be submitted to you for approval. This, however, is, in a larger sense, mere formality.
>
> An effort is now being made to find a suitable apartment, and we hope to be able to report success in the near future.
>
> With kindest regards and best wishes, I am,
>
> Respectfully yours,
>
> Maurice L. Gelman.
> Chairman of the Committee.
>
> MLG:HS

Letter accepting Rav Gifter as rabbi of the Waterbury Hebrew Institute

tion of Rav Gifter. In fact, Rav Gifter picked him up at the station when he came to replace him, since he was eager to finally see Reb Abba Zalka in person, saying later, "I had to meet the man who praised his competition and gave away his job!" Rabbi Gewirtz remained the rabbi in Waterbury for the next 25 years, until he was invited by Rav Gifter to become the executive vice president of Telzer Yeshivah in 1968.

Not only did Rav Gifter remain connected with Rabbi Gewirtz, but the close relationship between the Gifters and the Gewirtzes carried over to the next generation, as Rabbi Yonah Gewirtz became a close *talmid* of the rosh hayeshivah, and Reb Dovid Gewirtz kept a connection, as well. And then it intensified even more, as the Gewirtz grandchildren came from New Orleans to learn under Rav Gifter.

Rav Gifter's new shul, the Waterbury Hebrew Institute, became his home for the next three-and-a-half years. Although there was less than

Letter from Rav Gifter's uncle Shmuel Sar congratulating the Waterbury community on their selecting Rav Gifter as their rabbi

a *minyan* of Jews who kept Shabbos, the people in the shul had great respect for their rabbi. However, the rabbi had virtually no one to speak to about his Torah learning, so he turned to his trusted pen as his close friend and *chavrusa*.

He wrote to many different *rabbanim*, especially to Rav Yehudah Leib Forer, a rebbi of Rav Elazar Shach, a *talmid* of Rav Chaim Brisker, and the rabbi of Holyoke, Massachusetts. There were times when Rav Gifter would leave his family for a few days to go to Holyoke, because he thirsted to speak with Rav Leib. Their correspondence was compiled into *Mili DeIgros* (Volume I).

In addition, Rav Gifter wrote to Rav Yehoshua Klavan, the rabbi of Washington D.C. Those letters were also printed in a *sefer*, titled *Divrei Yehoshua*.

The Gifters' house in Waterbury   Rav Leib Forer

One of the Waterbury congregants recalled that there was a time when some people had the audacity to stand outside the synagogue and smoke on Shabbos morning. Bob Maran was only 17 at the time and he doesn't remember much from the rabbi's sermons. But he does remember the reaction of Rav Gifter to those who had the chutzpah to smoke in front of the shul. "Let's just put it this way," explained Bob. "After Rabbi Gifter's little pep talk, they never dared to smoke in front of the synagogue again!"[9]

Shortly after Rav Gifter's passing, Yeshiva Ateres Shmuel of Waterbury opened its doors. One day soon after, Rabbi Harold Schuster, one of the old-timers of the community and one of its few Shabbos observers, sat down in the back of the *beis midrash*. He looked around, took in the entire scene, and was clearly moved. He watched the young men learning and sat in silence. Stunned silence. Although he was not dressed in the style of the yeshivah boys, it was not the first time Rabbi Schuster had been in a yeshivah. Many years before, he had been a student of Rav Isser Zalman Meltzer. In addition, at some point, he had learned with Rav Shlomo Zalman Auerbach during *mussar seder*. True, it had

9. Bob Maran, Dunwoody, Georgia.

Chapter 3: The Journey From Telz □ 77

been quite a few years since he had been in those yeshivos, but Rabbi Schuster was not a stranger to Torah study.

A few days later, during the Ten Days of Repentance, the rosh yeshivah, Rabbi Aharon Kaufman, asked Rabbi Schuster if he would be able to speak to the boys of the yeshivah. Rabbi Schuster was extremely emotional as he spoke about the beauty of the yeshivah, and how long he had waited for this dream to come true.

At the end of his moving speech, he shared a magnificent anecdote. Rabbi Schuster did not yet live in Waterbury when Rav Gifter was the rabbi there. However, even years after Rav Gifter became a faculty member in the Telz Yeshivah in Cleveland, Rabbi Schuster realized what was missing. He wanted to live in a city where Torah was learned in a yeshivah; he yearned to see growth in the community.

But for so many years, nothing of the sort occurred. Although Rabbi Gewirtz's valiant efforts enabled the community to continue, the flourishing of Torah that Rabbi Schuster had hoped for had not materialized. Disappointed, he traveled to seek advice from Rav Moshe Feinstein. When he mentioned to Rav Moshe that he felt as if he lived in a desert (*midbar*), Rav Moshe told him that Moshe Rabbeinu was in the desert for 40 years and he did not complain. He then reassured him that there will be Torah in Waterbury. Rav Gifter had planted the seeds for Torah study in the community, and those seeds would one day sprout.

As Rabbi Schuster finished his account and looked around, he wiped away his tears. Indeed, 40 years after the conversation with Rav Moshe Feinstein, Torah had finally sprouted in the desert of Waterbury.

Furthermore, as someone else articulated, "When Rav Gifter walked on Farmington Avenue in Waterbury, and he thought to himself, 'What does this *Tosafos* mean?' he was not only thinking for himself, he was thinking for all of us … the seeds were being planted."[10,11]

---

10. Reb Aharon Sapirman.
11. Rabbi Aryeh Burnham, who came to Telz Yeshivah after serving in the U.S. Navy, was born in

The time Rav Gifter spent learning alone in Waterbury afforded him the opportunity for great diligence and growth in learning. But more than anything, he enjoyed the correspondence with Rav Forer. The two even communicated *about* their letters, debating who was doing whom the bigger favor. At one point, Rav Forer wrote to Rav Gifter and informed him, "Since you do not realize who you are and how important [*chashuv*] you are, I must tell you that there are few like you — not only in America, but also in Europe there are few like you!" [12]

At the time, Rav Gifter was only 24 years old!

When Rav Gifter had come to Yeshivas Rabbeinu Yitzchak Elchanan at the age of 13, he knew only one folio of Gemara. Only 11 years had passed and now Rav Gifter was being heralded as a Torah giant about whom it was said: "*Lo rabim kamohu* — There are not many like him."

His meteoric rise can serve as an inspiration and obligation that it can be done: A typical American boy can become a Torah giant!

The lad had become a lion.

Waterbury, Connecticut. His wife noted that the initial growth of the yeshivah in Waterbury "coincided" with the passing of Rav Gifter.

12. *Mili Delgros, Zecher Binyamin Yosef*, 40.

Chapter 4
Back to Telz ... in America ... and Eretz Yisrael

ALTHOUGH LIFE AS A CONGREGATIONAL RABBI WAS LESS than ideal for Rav Gifter, he was pleased to be earning a living and to be spending a tremendous amount of time learning; this gave him much peace of mind, but when he was needed, he involved himself in communal issues. For example, he worked with the local fish and meat merchants to make their pricing structure more equitable. Once, Rav Gifter closed the butcher shop for two weeks, because the proprietor was overcharging the customers for kosher meat.

True Calling

Nevertheless, when his wife's uncles, Rav Eliyahu Meir Bloch and Rav Mordechai Katz, asked him to join the Telz Yeshivah in Cleveland, he felt he should leave Waterbury. His congregants loved him dearly and wanted him to stay, so much so that they offered to double his salary. Even though his salary in Connecticut would have been a great deal higher than the wages he expected to earn at the yeshivah, he also knew that he was meant to work with students and become a disseminator of Torah (*marbitz Torah*). That was not going to happen in Waterbury, Connecticut.

It is important to note Rav Gifter's mind-set at this point in his life. The world was reeling from the reality of what had happened in Europe; the entire Jewish world was coming to grips with the unthinkable, and the Torah world was mourning the loss of Torah leadership and scholarship at the hands of the Nazis. Utmost in everyone's mind was the need to rebuild the Torah world, perhaps from scratch. And for Rav Gifter, that had to start with rebuilding Telz.

In a riveting letter to Rav Yehoshua Klavan (the rav in Washington D.C. and one of the *rabbanim* with whom Rav Gifter corresponded regularly) he wrote, "*Kibalti ayumos miTelz.* [I have received tragic news from Telz.]"[1] (The letter was written in 1945; it took three-and-a-half years for the tragic news to reach Rav Gifter.)

As Rav Gifter wrote:

In the face of the news we have just received, we must realize what type of responsibility those of us who have survived have to undertake. We must continue the mantra of Telz! This is one of the main reasons I decided to leave the rabbinate and rejoin the yeshivah.[2]

Before we continue, it is important to discuss the way in which we refer to Rav Gifter. Rabbi Hillel Goldberg put it best:[3]

I must dispense with "rabbi." It was not Rabbi Gifter. It was Rav Gifter. The Hebrew conveys infinitely more than the English, just as he conveyed infinitely more than I or anyone shall ever be able to reduce to words. Truly, only G-d Himself can understand this great man; not, however, because Rav Gifter was a hermit or the retiring type. If any person did not live the life of a hermit, did not duck a single issue, did not fear a single person or shy away from an unpleasant confrontation; if anyone personified the verse in the Torah, "Do not fear any man"; if anyone engendered in his disciples a deep sense of sheer love and adoration and openness, it was Rav Gifter.

Rav Gifter would often recount an incident that took place soon after he arrived in Cleveland, while he held the post of part-time rabbi of the Young Israel of Cleveland, along with his duties at the yeshivah. He

---

1. *Divrei Yehoshua,* p. 354.
2. Ibid.
3. "A Lion Arose From Portsmouth," Intermountain Jewish News, 2001.

Chapter 4: Back to Telz … in America … and Eretz Yisrael

Rav Gifter and
Rav Mottel Katz

rarely attended board meetings, but once he did: to inform the members that mixed dancing was prohibited. One of the board members answered defiantly, "Rabbi, quite frankly, that is none of your business."

At that point, Chaim Isaac (Herbert) Spero arose and declared, "If the rabbi says we dasn't [dare not], then we dasn't. [If Rav Gifter says that mixed dancing is not allowed, then it is not allowed.]"[4] Thus, Rav Gifter's presence in the synagogue was felt immediately, as he put an end to a practice that had been accepted as part of the American culture. Indeed, he was not afraid of any man.

Rav Elya Meir Bloch and Rav Mottel Katz had begun the work of establishing the yeshivah in Cleveland in 1941, and they recognized that it was vital to have an American aboard to help lead the *bachurim*; someone who was dynamic, personable, and brilliant. Although he was first brought in as mashgiach in 1945, that was a role that Rav Gifter would soon relinquish for the opportunity to teach the *talmidim* through a daily *shiur*. This was the role he was meant to have.

---

[4]. Dr. Abba Spero, who heard this story many times from Rav Gifter at the *yahrtzeit seudos* held in memory of Dr. Spero's father, Chaim Isaac Spero.

RAV GIFTER ALSO BEGAN TO DELIVER A *VAAD,* AN INFORMAL *SHIUR* given to a small group, in *Shev Shmaatsa,* a classic *sefer* that expounds on various legal principles in the Talmud. Eventually, Rav Gifter would deliver tens of *vaadim* on many different topics, each one unique.

Energizing His Students

The *bachurim* were enamored by the passion with which Rav Gifter learned, and they became energized, as well. He was so passionate that some, throughout their many years in yeshivah, were too intimidated to approach him in the *beis midrash*. If a student had a question to ask the rosh hayeshivah, he knew to make sure that he was prepared and was clear in his thinking. Far from being impatient or angry, Rav Gifter's insistence on the truth was evident in every interaction he had. If he felt that a student's explanation was false *(falsh),* he would react in his unique style and emphatically state the truth.

One *talmid* put it beautifully. "There is no denying that Rav Gifter was fire. But if you allowed yourself to come near to the fire, you realized that his fire did not *burn* you; it *warmed* your soul, and you never wanted to move away from it."[5]

Rav Gifter's concentration in learning was something to behold. He did not merely learn. Rather, he immersed himself completely in the learning — so much so that when you were finally able to get his attention to talk to him about whatever you came to say, he would look up as though he had just lifted his head out of water![6]

(l to r) Yisroel Lapidus, Michoel Kramer, Rav Gifter, and Shimon Hirsch, c. 1951

---
5. Rabbi Aharon Brodie.
6. Rav Avrohom Ausband.

It was not only in the *beis midrash* that Rav Gifter made his mark on the *bachurim*; it was also in his home, where he would deliver various informal classes on many subjects. As mentioned earlier, he gave a *vaad* in *Shev Shmaatsa*. His delivery was not one-sided; he involved the boys and asked questions, wanting them to sharpen their minds at every opportunity.

One student recalls Rav Gifter asking them what seemed a very simple question: What is the most important word in the blessing of *"shehakol nihyeh be'dvaro* — through Whose word everything came to be"?

Each of the young men gave their suggestions. One suggested the Name of Hashem; another thought that it might be *Melech* (King). But Rav Gifter's answer remained with this *talmid* some 65 years later.

"The word *Atah* [You] is the most important word. It shows us that we have a personal relationship with the Al-mighty."

Simple; yet so profound.

Rosh Hayeshivah

RAV GIFTER WAS FIRST THE MASHGIACH, THEN A *MAGGID SHIUR*. Then in 1964, when Rav Mottel Katz passed away, Rav Gifter and Rav Boruch Sorotzkin, a son-in-law of Rav Avraham Yitzchak Bloch, became Roshei Hayeshivah.

Along with his new title came the responsibility of day-to-day administration. This was one part of the job that he truly disliked. Once, when he walked straight from the administrative offices into giving a test, he explained his lateness, "*Ich kum fun Gehinnom*! [I'm coming from Purgatory!]"

Talented Speaker

IN THE MEANTIME, RAV GIFTER HAD BECOME A SPOKESMAN FOR Torah Jewry. His oratorical talent was simply unparalleled. Within a few seconds of his opening his mouth at any event, everyone in the room would be enthralled.

One writer, who knew him well, said, "His oratory and eloquence were the envy of United States senators. If ever there were a book that needs an attached CD, this is it."

When Adolph Beren died in Denver in 1989, Rav Gifter spoke at the funeral. Those who were in attendance reported that within 10 seconds — literally, no more than 10 seconds — he had the entire audience mesmerized. They were awed by Rav Gifter's ability to portray Mr. Beren so vividly that everyone there felt they had known the man personally. Such talent was enough to make others envious![7]

---

7. Rabbi Hillel Goldberg.

Even a simple reading from the *Sefer HaChinuch* (which explains the meaning behind the commandments, and summarizes their laws) could entrance an entire room.

When he would give a lecture in the Young Israel of Cleveland on Chol HaMoed, the entire community would come to hear him; just to hear him speak was a gift.

A *talmid* wrote to me, "To this day, I recall vividly his *mussar shmuess* on Yosef HaTzaddik, in which he repeated — over and over — the two words *'ve'hu naar* — but he was a youth' [*Bereishis* 37:2], drawing out the word *'naar'* to make it sound like *'naaaaar.'* How it struck home the point of the foolishness of youth."[8] By merely enunciating a word, Rav Gifter could bring home a point in a powerful way.

As another *talmid* expressed it:

I might note that Rav Gifter spoke most articulately both in English and Yiddish, but never mixed up the two languages. He never spoke "yeshivah English." He could not stand it. He spoke at various conferences and was always admired for the clarity of his expression and the elegance of his language. His diction was always clear and he presented the Torah viewpoint with outstanding success wherever he appeared.[9]

Rav Gifter attended many conventions for Torah Umesorah and Agudath Yisrael of America, although he was not exactly fond of conventions; he just wanted to learn; he attended only out of a sense of responsibility. Nevertheless, his speeches were the highlight of the conventions for many attendees.

---

8. Michael Hirsch.
9. Reb Shlomo Slonim.

One time, after a particularly captivating speech at an Agudah convention, a listener commented, "Even if Rav Gifter would speak for the janitors, I would make sure not to miss it!"

People wanted to hear him — not just for the way he spoke — but because they appreciated the fact that he spoke the truth, no matter how controversial and politically incorrect.

He wanted to spread truth; if it needed to be said, Rav Gifter was the one to stand up for the honor of the Torah and the honor of the Al-mighty.

According to Reb Chaim Dovid Zwiebel, executive vice president of Agudath Israel of America, Rav Gifter used the Agudah convention podium to convey timely messages to Klal Yisrael. In Reb Chaim Dovid's words:

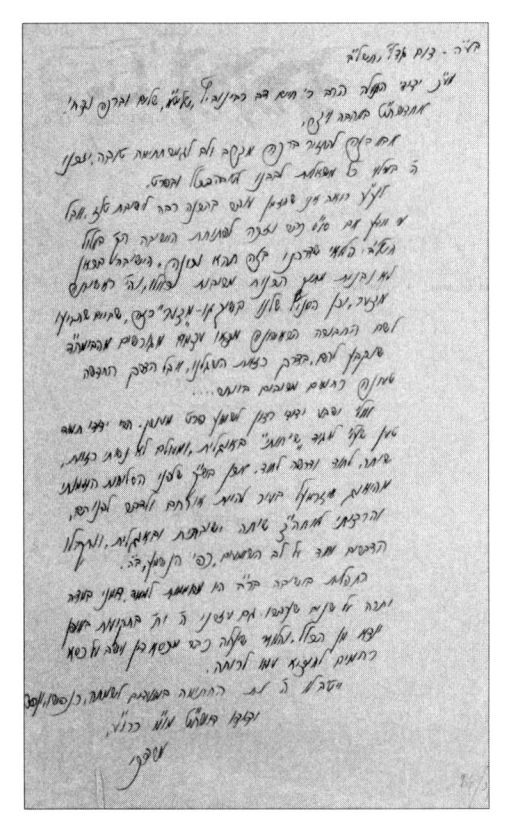

Letter to Rabbi Chaim Dov Rabinowitz, author of *Daas Soferim*, who had advised Rav Gifter to give his *shmuessen* in English, describing the success of his first such *shmuess*

He took his role as melamed seriously, and not only in the classroom. We were all his talmidim.

In addition, Rabbi Zwiebel points out Rav Gifter's substantive engagement on issues of the day:

Whether the issues were halachic (brain death, organ transplantation, efforts to address the agunah problem through secular law) or social (modern Orthodoxy, lifestyle, reform, Conservative), he would take the time to review materials Rabbi[Moshe] Sherer[10] (or others) would send him, make himself knowledgeable, and make his views known whenever he felt strongly about something.

---

10. Former president of Agudath Israel of America.

At the same time, Reb Chaim Dovid points out Rav Gifter's appreciation of people involved in *tzorchei tzibur* and his sensitivity to their emotional needs:

On a personal level, he wrote me several notes, taking interest in my work and offering chizuk and support. I believe Rabbi Sherer, and probably others as well, also benefited from his solicitude.

FOR OVER 30 YEARS, RAV GIFTER LED THE YESHIVAH. IN 1977, HE was given an extraordinary proposal. Mr. Irving Stone, a well-known philanthropist and supporter of the yeshivah, had purchased a piece of land in Eretz Yisrael. Mr. Stone offered the land to the yeshivah, to open a branch of Telz in Eretz Yisrael. The village would be called Telz-Stone.

Telz-Stone

Earlier in life, Rav Gifter's attitude toward living in Eretz Yisrael had been, "*Lernen? Ken mir dah oichet!* — Learning? We can learn here also!" But after one unforgettable visit, in 1977, he came back enamored with the sanctity and beauty of Eretz Yisrael. He simply had to live there.[11]

With 14 *bachurim* and four kollel fellows, Rav Gifter headed to Eretz Yisrael to fulfill his dream.

---

11. Rav Chaim Nussbaum.

Rav Gifter dancing with his *mechutan*, Rav Ahron Yeshaya Shapiro, who came to see him off as he departed Kennedy Airport for Eretz Yisrael

A *talmid* writes:

When Rav Gifter was ready to depart to Telz-Stone from JFK Airport, I went to see the Rosh Hayeshivah off. I shared with him the last thing that I had heard from Rav Mottel Katz, two weeks before his passing. When we were discussing the Telz-Stone project, Rav Mottel said, "Vi kennen mir mekabel zein pnei Mashiach uhn an address in Eretz Yisrael? [How can we greet Mashiach without an address in Eretz Yisrael?] "[12]

Let us take a glimpse at the level of learning and *yiras Shamayim* achieved by Rav Gifter and his *talmidim* during this period:

The first day of the first *zman*, Rav Gifter instituted a half-day fast (*chatzi taanis*), thus conveying the magnitude of establishing a new yeshivah in Eretz Yisrael. He insisted on a subtle day of fasting and prayer, rather than a grandiloquent display through a *chanukas habayis*.

In America, Rav Gifter delivered a general lecture (*shiur klali*) once a week. However, in Telz-Stone, he gave a daily *shiur* on the folio. The *shiur* consisted of Gemara, Rashi, Tosafos, *Rishonim*, and *Acharonim*. Although Rav Gifter had already lectured on these topics several times, he spent eight hours a day preparing each *shiur*! In the winter *zman*, the yeshivah covered 38 folios without compromising on the depth of the *sugya*.

---

12. Rabbi Daniel Carlebach.

Every Friday, Rav Gifter derived great pleasure from a *shiur* he delivered on the *Minchas Chinuch*. Often, Rav Gifter was unavailable on Thursday afternoons because he was so involved in preparing the *shiur*. The *shiur* was attended by many people from outside the yeshivah. Eventually, these lectures were compiled into a *sefer, Pitei Minchah*.

Every other Motza'ei Shabbos, Rav Gifter presented a *shmuess* on the weekly Torah portion. This talk was also attended by those who were thirsty to hear his brilliant insights and gain inspiration. Rav Gifter felt that these talks, although similar in style to those he had given in America, were much deeper. One Sunday morning, he commented that many in the audience had not completely grasped some of the concepts he had wanted to convey. He sensed that this was because this talk was comprised of thoughts he had compiled solely in Eretz Yisrael, and was therefore on an unusually profound level.

On Friday nights, the *bachurim* often joined Rav Gifter in his apartment for an *oneg*. In one *talmid*'s estimation, "The singing split the heavens!" In addition, Rav Gifter regaled the *bachurim* with stories from days gone by. But after all the singing and stories, he always said, "*Yetzt darf men gein lernen* — Now we must go learn." For Rav Gifter, all the externals, however meaningful, led to one road: the road of Torah learning. The singing and stories were all meant to inspire, and inspire they did. But the purpose of it all was to elevate the level of Torah learning.

Inspired by the new heights in Torah for both Rav Gifter and his students, his love for Eretz Yisrael grew; every facet of the land now took on greater meaning. Once, when Rav Gifter met with Rav Nachum Partzovitz of the Mirrer Yeshivah, Rav Nachum mentioned that he was overwhelmed by Rav Gifter's deep appreciation for Eretz Yisrael.

Rav Gifter encouraged the *bachurim* to take a 20-minute walk every day so that they could inhale the air of the land (*avira de'ara*). Rav Gifter would also take a daily walk. A few of the *talmidim* would occasionally join him on his walk in the peaceful, open air and hills of Telz-Stone.

One remarkable incident highlights the serenity and beauty of the rosh hayeshivah's life in Eretz Yisrael. He was taking a walk one day, this time by himself, thinking Torah thoughts. Suddenly, he heard a splendid song. He listened more closely in order to figure out where the tune was coming from. Soon, he discovered the source of this tune: It was coming

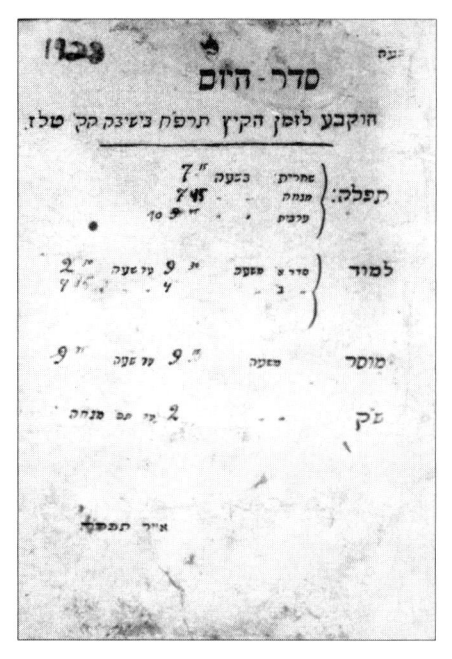

Seder Hayom of Telz Yeshivah, Lita 1928

from him! Incredibly, Rav Gifter was so deep in thought that he didn't realize that he was humming a tune!

His soul was swept up in ecstasy; the combination of Torah and Eretz Yisrael had, in a sense, transformed his soul from the physical to the divine.[13]

On his famed walks, the *bachurim* would love to hear his Torah, and he loved to share it. He would sometimes stop for a moment and point out some of the wonderful wonders of the Creator (*niflaos haBorei*). Every flower taught a lesson.

For example, a wildflower, the *rakefet*, indigenous to Israel, is a veritable feast of color; it rises in all its splendor on a slim and delicate stem. Rav Gifter pointed out that one can learn humility from this exquisite flower. Its most striking feature is its head, and yet, this is the very part that faces downward, not wanting to flaunt its beauty!

(He treasured a framed picture of the *rakefet* given to him by a *talmid* and displayed it prominently in his breakfront.)

Those who were present can never forget how tears of *deveikus* filled his eyes on a Shabbos afternoon when telling of how bright the firmament shines in Eretz Yisrael. "There are places in Eretz Yisrael where one can learn Torah by the light of the moon!"

The emotions stirred inside Rav Gifter on every walk. As he walked through the fields of Telz-Stone, there was one rock in particular that he would stop at: a rock that overlooked Jerusalem. The *bachurim* would leave him alone as he sat at the rock. He would pull out his *Tehillim* and begin to recite the words of King David and he would cry…

As one student, who was privileged to walk with his rebbi on many of these walks, told me with such emotion, "*Oy*…did he cry…."[14]

---

13. Rabbi Eli Yelen.
14. Rabbi Kalman Rubinstein.

In one particularly moving incident, Rav Gifter was walking with his student, Moshe Scheinerman, through the forest of Abu Ghoush. It was the end of winter and the entire forest was barren and lifeless. Suddenly, Rav Gifter stopped and pointed, "Moishe! *Kuk!* — Moishe! Look!" Moshe looked down and saw a tiny flower that had fought its way to the surface and nestled against a rock.

The picture of the *rakefet* which was displayed in the Gifter's home

When Moshe looked back at his rebbi, he was astonished to see that Rav Gifter was crying! Yes, crying! He could not imagine why a small flower was causing such an outburst of emotion.

"You see, Moishe, in a few weeks, this entire forest will be completely covered in green. The trees will be full of leaves; the flowers will have reached full bloom. Yes, there will be life everywhere! And no one will ever remember that the forest was so recently barren and empty. The same is true with the Redemption. One day, soon, there will be Redemption surrounding us all over … and no one will ever remember that there was an Exile. It will all be a distant dream …"

At this point, Rav Gifter became extremely emotional and began to sob even harder.

"But Moishe, where is the flower of the Redemption? Where is the flower?"

Rav Gifter's life in Telz-Stone not only served to deepen his love of Eretz Yisrael, but also his yearning for Mashiach. He wanted the Redemption, not for himself but for the Al-mighty. Rabbi Kalman Rubinstein, one of Rav Gifter's closest *talmidim*,[15] described with great emotion the unforgettable *shalosh seudos* he experienced with Rav Gifter once in Telz-Stone.

---

15. He has called the rosh hayeshivah and/or his rebbetzin every Friday for over 30 years.

It was pitch dark as the *bachurim* sat with their rebbi and sang the regular *shalosh seudos zemiros*. Then they sang emotional and powerful tunes, laced with yearning for the Al-mighty and for the rebuilding of His *Beis HaMikdash*.

Two songs in particular struck a chord with Reb Kalman. And it was these two songs that he would sing to his rebbi, when Rav Gifter reached the point late in his life that he could no longer speak, write, or express himself in any meaningful way.

First, he would sing the haunting song of *Racheim Be'chasdecha* (Have Mercy in Your Kindness), which is sung by Vizhnitzer chassidim. (This song was very meaningful to Kalman, as he was a Vizhnitzer chassid, and Rav Gifter had always encouraged him to pursue his Vizhnitzer background when he was in Israel. In fact, he would encourage him, even push him, to visit Bnei Brak on the off Shabbasos, because of the strong presence of Vizhntizer chassidim in Bnei Brak.) They would conclude with *Ani Maamin* (I Believe). What's more, when Reb Kalman recounted the story to this author and sang the *Ani Maamin*, he described Rav Gifter closing his eyes and singing — with such yearning — the words, *"be'emunah sheleimah* [with complete faith]." These were the songs that Reb Kalman would sing to his beloved rebbi when Rav Gifter could no longer respond.

A rebbi and his *talmid*, forever connected through the yearning for Mashiach ...

RAV GIFTER'S TIME IN ERETZ YISRAEL WITH HIS TREASURED STUdents was to last only two years. When Rav Boruch Sorotzkin died early

Return to Cleveland

in 1979, Rav Gifter was called back to America. When he was hesitant to leave, the Steipler Gaon, Rav Yaakov Yisrael Kanievsky, spoke to Rav Gifter and his rebbetzin (which in itself was a rarity), and convinced them to go, and to consider the move permanent. A firm believer in *daas Torah*, Rav Gifter consented and moved back to America. [16]

---

16. Rebbetzin Shoshana Gifter.

Bris Achim —
"Pact of Brothers"
from Telz-Stone

Nevertheless, he was heartbroken. Indeed, his health would never be the same.

When the Gifters returned to Cleveland, they decided to live in an apartment in the yeshivah dormitory, instead of the house they had left two years earlier. The reason for this is astounding: Rav Gifter said, "I cannot live in a permanent home anymore in *chutz la'Aretz* [out of Israel]! I can't!" He knew that he truly wanted to be in Eretz Yisrael, but was just biding his time until Mashiach arrived. In an extraordinary act of self-sacrifice, the rebbetzin did as she had always done, and followed the wishes of her husband.

As they left the yeshivah in Telz-Stone, Rav Gifter knew that this would be the end of the yeshivah there for all practical purposes. The unimaginable growth that the *bachurim* experienced and the bond that they had formed as a yeshivah were coming to an end. The yeshivah was disbanding. So Rav Gifter wrote a treaty of brothers (*bris achim*) that was signed by every *bachur* in the yeshivah.

This is what it said:

> As we are now ready to take leave from one another, time and space will try to separate us, but we must remain connected. We will do this by committing to three commitments; this is what will keep us united.
>
> (1) We have to commit that wherever we are, whatever we are doing, we will always learn at least one hour a day — preferably the Oral Torah but if we can't, then we may learn the Written Torah.
>
> (2) Wherever we are and in whatever situation we may find ourselves, we must always remember to learn 10 minutes of mussar every day. One may learn whatever sefer is appropriate for him in his particular situation.
>
> And finally,
>
> (3) We must always make the commitment to be mashpia al hazulas, have influence on others. We cannot only live for ourselves. It is through this that we will remain together. [17]

Following the signatures of all of the *bachurim* was one more: Mordechai Gifter.

He did not tell the *bachurim* to stay in touch through person-to-person communication; that would come naturally. Instead, he asked them to commit to learning, refining their character, and sharing their Torah with others — always, forever.

Such was his legacy to the students of Telz-Stone: an eternal connection through Torah.

---

17. Rabbi Eli Shulman, Rav Chaim Nussbaum.

Chapter 5
Final Years in Cleveland

THE FINAL 22 YEARS OF RAV GIFTER'S LIFE WERE SPENT AS the rosh hayeshivah of the Telz Yeshivah in Cleveland.

DURING THOSE YEARS, RAV GIFTER ATTEMPTED TO RESTORE THE method of learning to the way it had been when he was a *bachur*. Committed to covering more topics throughout a tractate, he focused more on the depths of *p'shat*, instead of delivering *pilpul*-style lectures. His comments were penetrating and deep, and he moved quickly through the folio of Gemara and pleaded with the yeshivah to follow suit, saying, "*Men darf uplernen di blettlach Gemara*! — We must learn the pages of the Gemara!" He was anxious to return to the style of the classic European yeshivos, including Telz, where *talmidim* covered much more material than has become common since the war.

An Impassioned Plea

To illustrate his concern, we cite an address he delivered at the yeshivah in 1985. I remember hearing it 25 years ago, during my first winter semester in the yeshivah. Like everyone else who was present, I will never forget it. He described the learning of Yaakov Avinu in the yeshivah of Shem and Ever:

The Sages tell us that Yaakov was "nitman" — he was protected and insulated from the external environment. For that is what a yeshivah is, a place where a person is surrounded by and involved in Torah alone.

Judaism encompasses all of life. But a yeshivah has only one purpose — total immersion and involvement with the Torah, to the point where the person has become one with the Torah. Then after this experience, he is truly able to go out into life and properly face all the challenges the Al-mighty places before him.

Rav Yaakov Emden writes that his father, the Chacham Tzvi, would spend the entire week in the beis midrash, even eating and sleeping there. Only on Erev Shabbos would he and his students go home. To be in yeshivah doesn't necessarily require traveling miles away, but it does demand total immersion in Torah, removed from the world around us, "hidden" in the four cubits of halachah.

At this point, there was a sense that something memorable was about to happen.

How do you hide yourself in Torah? The zman has been going on now for a few weeks. How many blatt should you have learned by now? I'm not referring to a specific yeshivah; every yeshivah in the world, in America and Eretz Yisrael, learns so little. And they call this learning Torah!

The next part of the *shmuess* would send ripples through many yeshivos, not just in America, but worldwide:

The Gemara says, "Ligmar inish ve'hadar lisbor — One should amass knowledge and then develop understanding." I see so many sefarim around — Bircas Shmuel, Chiddushei Reb Reuven. At this stage, such sefarim are far beyond you. Gemara and Rashi is what you need to know. We think Rashi is pashut. The Meiri writes that within one word of Rashi, he found the answers to so many questions that challenged him. Is Rashi pashut? The Rivash writes that without Rashi, Shas would be like a closed book. Gemara means Gemara with Rashi. When you know that well, then start Tosafos! Without it, you won't know what you're talking about!

Rav Gifter referred to such learning as the "*maaseh Satan.*" He saw how much time was being put into learning, and yet he worried: How will Torah grow? Based on these concerns, he demanded a change in the style of learning.

We continue quoting from the aforementioned address:

And if you will tell me that American minds are not up to learning masechtos, I will show you otherwise. We were in Eretz Yisrael for two years. In the second year, I planned to follow the tradition of learning half of Bava Basra in the winter zman and the other half in the summer zman.

At this point, Rav Gifter cited the large number of folios learned by the *bachurim* in Telz-Stone.

And if you will say that they probably didn't remember what they learned, I can tell you that in a casual conversation at a parlor meeting for the yeshivah, when I said over a thought from the Rashba in Kiddushin, one of the students immediately cited a Rashbam on daf 138 to support the same thought. They knew the Gemara, Rashbam, Ran, and Rosh, which is what you must know when you learn a masechta. And they knew it backward and forward!

We must not forget that Rav Gifter was one of the greatest *lamdanim* of our generation, and the first to appreciate the depths of every word and nuance of the Gemara. However, he was pained by the notion that American boys are limited in their ability to master the entire Talmud.

It is noteworthy that through one unforgettable address, we can begin to understand Rav Gifter's entire life. He dreamed of finishing tractates, and he did. When he became older, he feared that others would not do the same, and he was afraid that this way of learning would be lost.

Rav Shach [he continued], *the senior rosh yeshivah in our day, sent a letter telling me how he had seen a number of boys over the bein hazmanim, and each one had said they had learned two or two-and-a-half blatt during Elul. Rav Shach cried. This method is bringing Torah down. I remember what he said at the funeral of Rav Shmuel Rozovsky. He was crying so much, I thought he would fall apart! But he said one thing to the bachurim of the yeshivah: "You don't learn! Why do you need such roshei yeshivos, geniuses in Torah, if you aren't willing to see the breadth of Torah?!"*

Rav Gifter then gave an impassioned plea.

Torah is the greatest merit for Klal Yisrael. "Ki heim chayeinu ve'orech yameinu — *For they are our life and the length of our days." Have pity on yourselves! And have pity on a Jew named Mottel Gifter! I tell you* — *I'm going under from this! I can't take it! People are saying that they are involved in learning Torah, and they say they have learned. It is a disgrace to the Torah!*

With Rav Shach. Among the others are Aron Waldman, Chaim Mordechai Ausband and Sroly Gifter

Finally, Rav Gifter concluded this extraordinary talk:

I hope you appreciate the pain that I feel over this issue. Take heed; if we truly immerse ourselves in the Torah, we can be assured that it will pave the way for the coming of Mashiach!

The *bachurim* sat in stunned silence. His passion was palpable. No one wanted to leave, to stop gazing at his face and feeling his frustration.

This *shmuess* sent out shock waves. American yeshivos had grown accustomed to learning eight to ten *blatt* a year. In Telz, we would learn nearly 30 *blatt*. But Rav Gifter was demanding more.

Rav Gifter once said that a boy proudly reported that he had learned *Maseches Bava Kamma* over the winter. The rosh hayeshivah assumed the boy had finished the tractate. But when Rav Gifter asked him a question on the fifth folio, he stopped the rosh hayeshivah and told him he had only completed up to the fourth folio. Rav Gifter could not believe his ears. Only four *blatt*? He was incredulous!

Soon the word was out; many yeshivos began to place an emphasis on finishing *masechtos*, encouraging learning sessions focused on covering ground (*bekiyus sedarim*) to help finish the *masechta*; the Torah world had heard the voice of Rav Gifter.

Twilight

IN 1995, RAV GIFTER ATTENDED A *SIYUM HASHAS* THAT WAS MADE by a young man named Yehoshua Bressler.

No one thought that Rav Gifter would speak, because illness had begun to rob him of the ability to express Torah thoughts. The twilight of the rosh hayeshivah's magnificent life was setting in. Surprisingly, in fact, nearly miraculously, he attended the *siyum* and spoke for almost half an hour. Those who were present will never forget it.[1]

This was one of his last public addresses.

It pained him tremendously that he did not remember everything, that the precious Torah he knew was not as retrievable as it once was.

A poignant story that occurred in 1987 illustrates the anguish that he felt in his later years when his illness began to rob him of his memory. It was the night of the wedding of his youngest son, Yisroel. On the way to the wedding hall, Yisroel realized that he had forgotten the wedding ring. The family rushed back to retrieve it. Yisroel, or Sroly as he is called, rushed inside, leaving Tzvi, one of Rav Gifter's grandsons, in the car. Suddenly, Tzvi noticed that his grandfather was crying. When the rosh hayeshivah composed himself, he said, "Tzvikele, does it really make a difference if one gives his wife a ring or something else that is worth a *perutah*? Sure, it is preferable to give the ring, but by Torah law both are valid methods of effecting a Jewish marriage. So it's not so bad to forget the ring. But just now I tried to recall a Tosafos ... " At this point, once again, Rav Gifter began to cry. In a trembling, panicky voice, he cried out, "Tzvikele, *gevald, ich hub fargessen di Tosafos!* [Tzvikele, I forgot the Tosafos!] A Tosafos can never be replaced!"

This episode remained embedded in Tzvi's *neshamah*. It had affected him in a very profound manner, so much so that he was unable to repeat the story without being close to tears himself. When the rosh hayeshivah ascended to the Heavenly yeshivah (*yeshivah shel Maalah*), Tzvi was asked to deliver a eulogy on the steps of the Mirrer Yeshivah in Yerushalayim. Broken beyond description, Tzvi began to speak and this telling memory of his grandfather came forth.

This story is an excellent example of the rosh hayeshivah's legacy. He was the embodiment of learning Torah (*limud haTorah*): learning with a relentless, perpetual, unfailing consistency, allowing nothing to impede

---

1. Rabbi Yaakov Bogart, Rav and Rebbetzin Bressler.

his movement forward. He believed in the ability of young men, even in our generation — no, especially in our generation — to maximize their limitless potential and channel it toward becoming as great as they can be. That is what he believed in most, and that is the legacy he left to the world.

A *bachur* once mentioned that there were things he had told the rosh hayeshivah that he had forgotten a short while later. Knowing how sharp Rav Gifter's memory for learning was, he asked the rosh hayeshivah how he was able to remember everything he learned. Rav Gifter responded that it was not because he had such a phenomenal memory. Rather, it was because of a fear he had. When he learned a Gemara, he feared that this may be the last thing he would learn on this world. And he knew that when he appeared before the Master of the World, He would ask him what he was learning. He was afraid he would not remember. This overriding concern motivated him to learn and to know and to remember every piece of Torah he ever studied.

Hence, when he forgot the Tosafos, he simply could not stop crying. Only one with an insatiable love for learning Torah could think in such terms.

It is no wonder that when the rosh hayeshivah would recite his special verse (for his name, Mordechai) at the end of *Shemoneh Esrei* —

"*Mah ahavti sorasecha kol hayom hi sichasi* — O how I love Your Torah! All day long it is my conversation" (*Tehillim* 119:97), he would do so with heartfelt tears.

As he aged and his memory weakened, he would weep, "When I stand before the Heavenly Court, they will ask me what I learned and I will have nothing to show!"

At one point, he gained a measure of comfort. His family brought a specialist to examine him. When the rosh hayeshivah lamented his loss of memory, the doctor said, "Nothing has been lost. The brain is like a computer's hard drive. Everything is still there, even if it can't be accessed."

When he repeated this story, Rav Gifter would smile. Even though his genius was stymied, it had not left him.[2]

The Will Of Hashem

IT IS IMPOSSIBLE TO KNOW THE GREETING THE ROSH HAYESHIVAH received when he ascended to the Heavenly Court, on the 23rd of Teves, 5761 (2001), but we can imagine that he was greeted by his rebbeim — Rav Zalman Bloch, Rav Avraham Yitzchak Bloch, Rav Moshe Aharon Poleyeff, Rav Moshe Soloveitchik, and Rav Yehudah Leib Forer — and Rav Shach and the Steipler Gaon waiting to speak in learning once more.

But no doubt he was also greeted by many of those "*kleine masechtalach*," the small *masechtos* that so many people had never had a chance to learn. He had mastered them and taught others to do so, as well.

Chagigah, Moed Katan, Me'ilah, Horayos ... and so many more.

A young man who was struggling in his learning was present at Rav Gifter's funeral in Yeshiva Darchei Torah, in Far Rockaway, New York, on the way from Cleveland to the flight to Israel for burial. Rav Yaakov Reisman, Rav Gifter's son-in-law, mentioned in his eulogy that Rav Gifter had requested that anyone who wanted to accept something upon himself in his memory should learn one mishnah a day.

Nearly 10 years later, that *bachur* wrote to Rav Reisman that he had made a commitment at the funeral to learn a mishnah a day. And it was the beginning of his own remarkable turnaround. One mishnah led to another, until his entire life was transformed. Eventually, he began to

---

2. Rabbi Nosson Scherman.

Rav Elya Svei being *maspid* at the *levaya* in New York

take all his learning more seriously, and he became a true *ben Torah*. He has now finished all Six Orders of the Mishnah 11 times!

Rav Gifter understood the value of one mishnah a day. What's more, the satisfaction that comes along with one small daily accomplishment can help to transform a person's life.

The tens of thousands whose lives he had changed — sometimes with one speech, one thought, one word — will continue to be inspired, and transmit his legacy.

One summer, one of the counselors at Telz's Camp Kol Torah high school program asked Rav Gifter a question on the Gemara he was learning. Rav Gifter looked at him and shared with him something quite memorable. "I'm so sorry. But I can't help you." The boy was shocked. He did not know that Rav Gifter was not well. He continued to explain, "You see, by the time I reach the bottom of the page, I can't remember what was written at the top of it. *Ich bin ehrger vi ah baalebas* — I am worse off than a simple layman."

Pity must have shown on the young man's face, but Rav Gifter told him one of the most treasured lessons he would ever learn. "I want you to know I am not sad or depressed. I am *malei simchah,* full of joy.

The Novominsker Rebbe being *maspid* at the *levayah* in Eretz Yisrael

Rav Dovid Barkin being *maspid* at the *levayah* in Eretz Yisrael. Rav Nosson Tzvi Finkel is seated at right.

Chapter 5: Final Years in Cleveland □ 103

Veil dos vill di Ribbono Shel Olam fun mir — Because this is what the Al-mighty wants from me."³

And that was his ultimate mission: to fulfill the will of Hashem.

This he did, until his very last breath ... until finally...

The roar of the lion had grown silent.

Throngs fill the streets at the *levayah* in Eretz Yisrael

---
3. Rabbi Shloimie Kohn.

Section 2

Limud HaTorah — Torah Study

Chapter 6
The Joy of Torah

RAV GIFTER WAS THE LIVING EMBODIMENT OF TORAH. Whether he was speaking in learning with his *talmidim* or asking a young child what verse he had learned that day, his interest was Torah. He was completely oblivious to everything else; he was one with the Torah. Every Friday, a young man's father brought him to visit the rosh hayeshivah and his rebbetzin. Rav Gifter would always greet him with a warm smile; the rebbetzin always plied him with candy and treats. And the conversation always turned to which Torah portion and verse he was learning.

Torah as a Life Force

Years later, as he would watch Rav Gifter walk down the path toward the yeshivah, the young man felt that he wasn't looking at the rosh hayeshivah, but at the Rashba himself!

◆

When one entered the *beis midrash*, he would find Rav Gifter pacing back and forth, completely lost in the *sugya* as he prepared his *shiur*. During *mussar seder*, one would be captivated by the melodious sweet

Rav Gifter with the children of Rav Chaim Nussbaum

sounds of *mussar*, as he repeated the words of *Mishlei* (1:8), "*Shema beni mussar avicha* — Hear, my child, the discipline of your father."

He was not learning Torah; he was living it!

Rav Gifter would explain the verse, "*Ve'tzaddik be'emunaso yichyeh* — But the righteous person shall live through his faith" (*Chavakuk* 2:4), the way he heard it from Rav Mottel Pogromansky. A *tzaddik* eats, drinks, walks, talks, and even breathes *emunah*. This is the meaning of "*yichyeh.*" The same must be said of Rav Gifter. He ate, drank, walked, talked, and even breathed Torah.

Rav Gifter expounded on the *Kuzari*'s distinction between the levels of creation: inanimate objects, plant life, animal life, and humans. Yet the Jew is in his own category. Just as each category has its own source of life, the Jew's life source is Torah.

In his *shmuessen*, Rav Gifter would say, "We eat the Rashba, drink the Tosafos, and sleep the Maharsha." His vision for his *bachurim* was to eat, sleep, and breathe Torah.

Rav Gifter did not just learn Torah; it was his life force. It fed him and drove him and infused every fiber of his being. When people would interrupt his learning, Rav Gifter would quip, "They think that they are not letting me learn. They don't realize that they are not letting me live!"

RAV GIFTER USED TO CITE THE MIDRASH THAT DESCRIBES HOW the Al-mighty teaches Torah. The king's son came home from school

Straight From the King's Mouth

and noticed a large tray of food in front of his father. The doting father took the food from the tray and gave a piece to his son. But the son refused. "Father, I do not want to eat from this piece. I want to eat only from the same piece as you; I want to eat from that which you are putting into your own mouth!"

The king, who loved his son very much, shared with him the piece of food he had just bitten into.

The Midrash explains that the same is true of the Jewish nation. The Al-mighty grants knowledge to all the nations of His world. But with His chosen nation, He shares his most intimate wisdom and the deep understanding of the Torah that comes from His own mouth.

Rav Gifter elaborated on this lesson from the Midrash. The king had already distributed food to the members of his court before his son arrived. They were all satisfied with their portions. Why? Because all they wanted was the nourishment from the food. But the king's son was not hungry for the food; he yearned for his father's love to satiate his soul. *"Er hut gevolt oiffessen der tatte alein*!" His desire was to "eat up" his beloved father. The closest he could get to that was to eat the food that came straight from his father's mouth.

For those whose primary goal is to cling to the Al-mighty and become close to Him, Hashem shares true wisdom and deep insight, straight from "His mouth."

ONE OF RAV GIFTER'S FAVORITE STORIES WAS TOLD ABOUT REB Hershel Eisenstadt, a grandson of the Chasam Sofer, Rav Moshe Sofer.

The Power of a Torah Scholar

Reb Hershel once traveled to Vienna to visit a psychologist, to whom he told over a beautiful thought on *Koheles* written by his grandfather. The psychologist had never heard such profound thoughts before. Who is this Moshe Sofer, he asked?

Hershel told him he was a famous rabbi from Pressburg. The professor asked him if the man lived in a stately mansion, but Reb Hershel assured him that the Chasam Sofer lived in a small house with tiny windows. The psychologist was amazed and commented, "It seems to me that from the little window of his house, he can look out and see the entire universe."

Along the same lines, in an article printed in the *Jewish Observer* in 1974, Rav Gifter wrote:

> *We weep at the uprooting of hundreds of years of spiritual growth which was lost with their destruction, at the uprooting of centuries of tradition and scholarship that had found its full flowering in pre-war Europe. The towering personalities who led these spiritual empires had even more than yeshivos and kehillos to their credit. These people were of pivotal importance to the spiritual development of the entire world.*
>
> *The gaon and tzaddik, Rav Daniel Movshovitz of Kelm, once pointed out that at the very same time that the Vilna Gaon was studying Torah in Vilna and illuminating great Divine truths to the world, Emmanuel Kant was in Berlin expounding on the ethical imperative, arriving at truths by human thought. His truth was not developed at parlor discussions and street corner arguments, but as a direct result of the study of Torah of the Gaon in a small dimly lit room secluded from the world.*

RAV GIFTER PERSONIFIED LOVE OF TORAH.

In Lithuania, he was privileged to take a daily walk with his rebbi, Rav Avraham Yitzchak Bloch. The walk began every day at 2 o'clock

Love of Torah

There was one rule: Mordechai was not to speak unless the rav spoke to him first. Otherwise, it was a silent walk, the two of them simply enjoying each other's presence.

During one of these walks, Rav Avraham Yitzchak worried aloud whether he would ever receive reward for learning *Maseches Nedarim*, as he truly enjoyed learning that tractate, and especially derived pleasure from learning the Ran's commentary. "I enjoy it so much," he said, "I just don't know if I can ever learn it *lishmah* [for its sake]."

Mordechai responded, "Perhaps that is what the reward is given for: only when one learns Torah and enjoys it so much, after much toil and effort. Perhaps that is the very definition of *lishmah*." The rav looked at his *talmid*, smiled, and continued walking.

Years later, when the explanation of Rabbeinu Avraham Min HaHar on *Maseches Nedarim* was published, Rav Gifter discovered a Torah thought that he often quoted, *"Ikar mitzvaso hi ha'hanaah ve'hataanug ba'meh she'masig u'meivin be'limudo* — The main mitzvah of learning Torah is the enjoyment and the pleasure that one derives from grasping and understanding what he's learning." In his own words, he would repeat the concept to his *talmidim*, *"Mitzvos lav le'hanos nitnu, uber Teirah — le'hanos nitnah!* — Mitzvos were not given for pleasure, but Torah [pronounced with a Lithuanian accent as *Teirah*] was given so that we can derive pleasure from it!"[1]

I remember hearing this thought from Rav Gifter when I learned *Nedarim* in the summer *zman* of eighth grade, the first year that I came to yeshivah. When he gave us a *bechinah* at the end of the *zman*, he shared this very profound concept with us; young though we were, we still understood and remembered it.

The Original Text

A *TALMID* WRITES: FOR SEVERAL YEARS, I PARTICIPATED IN A weekly chaburah that Rav Gifter conducted for several bachurim in sifrei mussar. One sefer stood out in particular: the Shemonah Perakim of the Rambam. This learning group, with the commentary of Rav Gifter, furnished us with a basic outlook of the duty of a Jew in this world, and has served as a fundamental guide throughout my life. I have taught it to groups many times and am regularly inspired by the emphasis that Rav Gifter supplied on various themes.

An interesting story emerged from our chaburah on the Rambam. On occasion, the translation of Ibn Tibon from the Arabic original was not very clear. Rav Gifter said that everyone knew that the Rambam was famous for his mastery of language and expression. Thus, Rav Gifter very much want-

---

1. The *Iglei Tal*, who lived after Rav Avraham Min HaHar, says a similar thought (in his introduction). Rav Gifter's joy, however, stemmed from the fact that this view was now quoted by a *Rishon*.

ed to read the Arabic original. He was so keen on mastering the original text that he had made plans to take courses in Arabic at Yale University, which was close to Waterbury where he was serving as rav (before he moved to Cleveland to join the yeshivah). This plan, however, never materialized. [2]

WHEN HE RETURNED TO AMERICA, RAV GIFTER CONTINUED TO deliver a *shiur* in *Minchas Chinuch* every Friday. Once, in the middle of the *shiur*, Rav Gifter exclaimed, "Now I understand the simple *p'shat* of a verse that bothered me for many years!"

True Happiness

During the Shabbos that followed, he spoke of that revelation over and over. Each time, the listener could tell by the look on the rosh hayeshivah's face how thrilled he was that he finally understood the verse. He was ecstatic over the clear understanding of a verse — not a Gemara, or a Rambam — but one *pasuk* in the holy Torah.

Other *talmidim* recall the love that he exuded when he spoke of the *Rishonim* and *Acharonim,* the earlier and later commentators on the Gemara, as if he had an actual relationship with them. He called Rashi, *Rashi hakadosh;* the Rashba, the *heilige Rashba;* the *Ketzos HaChoshen* was the *rav;* and Rav Akiva Eiger, his personal favorite, was *Maran.* And the Vilna Gaon? Rav Gifter called him as many others did, *malach Elokim.* [3]

With Rav Yaakov Yitzchok Ruderman

---

2. Reb Shlomo Slonim.
3. Rabbi Azriel Goldfein.

When Rav Moshe Shapiro eulogized Rav Gifter, he said that the Gemara very often uses the term *aliba dideih*, which may be translated as "according to him." But the literal translation of those words reveals much more; *aliba* means "on his heart." This means that when the *Tannaim* or *Amoraim* expressed an idea, it came from their hearts. Rav Moshe said that when Rav Gifter would share a Torah thought, it was always *aliba dideih,* from the deepest recesses of his soul.

A Magical Kiss

AT THE END OF AN AFTERNOON SESSION, A *TALMID* WHO WAS planning to leave the yeshivah waited to speak to Rav Gifter. He stood several feet away from Rav Gifter, who was still learning.

The *talmid* did not want to disturb him. Truthfully, he was less than excited to tell Rav Gifter that he was leaving for good. He knew that the rosh hayeshivah would not be pleased, but he had made up his mind. He was going no matter what. He was leaving because his learning had gone downhill, due to personal problems, including much self-doubt.

After a short while, Rav Gifter closed his Gemara. The young man was about to approach him, when suddenly, the rosh hayeshivah planted a resounding, love-filled kiss on the Gemara. [4]

The kiss seemed magical. There was so much love for the Torah (*ahavas haTorah*) in that gesture that the young man immediately felt invigorated and recharged.

He turned away and never said goodbye. Instead, he stayed on in the yeshivah and completely turned his life around. In fact, 60 years later, he continues to learn and teach Torah.[5]

Dancing With the Torah

RAV GIFTER'S SON, YISROEL, ENTERED HIS PARENTS' APARTMENT late one night and heard tapping sounds from his father's study. To his amazement, he saw his father dancing. Yisroel asked him what the occasion was. His father explained that he had just solved a difficult piece in the *Minchas Chinuch*.

Rav Gifter once told his *talmidim* a story in an attempt to describe this type of joy. Rav Simcha Zissel, the Alter from Kelm, would disappear from the *beis midrash* from time to time. Once, the

---
4. He kissed the page of Gemara and then closed it; he did not kiss the outside.
5. Rabbi Eliezer Feuer.

Learning with Rav Chaim Stein

bachurim followed him and were shocked to discover that he was dancing in the attic of the building! He explained that the dancing came from his sheer joy of understanding a difficult piece in the Rashba. He was so overjoyed that he wanted to "*gei ah tantzel* [do a little dance]!" Since he was a practical man, he knew that if he got up and danced in the *beis midrash*, the *talmidim* would think he had lost his mind.

A few days after telling his *talmidim* this story, Rav Gifter was guiding them through a complex Gemara. At last, they reached a point of sparkling clarity and Rav Gifter declared jubilantly, "Now, this is real joy!"

"Then why don't we get up and dance like Rav Simcha Zissel did?" said Yisroel,[6] one of the students.

Sure enough, the students got up from their benches and started dancing in the *shiur* room. Soon the noise was heard in the *beis midrash,* and all came to see Rav Gifter and his *talmidim* dancing with the joy of Torah.

Rav Avrohom Chaim Feuer, Rav Gifter's son-in-law, served as a rabbi in Miami for many years. One of his congregants, a prominent ophthalmologist, shared with him a magnificent thought.

Why are *tefillin* placed on the forehead instead of between the eyes, as it is stated in the Torah (*Devarim* 6:8): "*bein einecha* — between your eyes"? The doctor explained that the phylacteries are placed on the spot of the forehead that is directly above the optic chiasm, which is the part of the brain where the optic nerves partially cross. Thus, they are actually put between the eyes.

---

6. Rabbi Yisroel Schneider.

Rav Feuer shared this thought with his father-in-law when Rav Gifter and the rebbetzin came for a visit. Rav Gifter was so ecstatic with the explanation that he told his son-in-law that a Torah thought like that warrants a little dance. And so, the two of them proceeded to dance right in the Feuer living room.

IN ORDER TO ACHIEVE TRUE JOY AND LOVE FOR TORAH LEARNING, it must be something that we do every day, never missing a day, cherishing every moment. For if there is a break for even one day, then we have, in essence, proclaimed that our love is not complete.

Not Taking a Break

With this in mind, we recall a memorable *sichah* Rav Gifter delivered before *bein hazemanim*. He cited the famous Gemara (*Nedarim* 50a) that tells of Rabbi Akiva returning home after 12 years of learning. His wife, Rachel, was hounded by a neighbor who challenged her about the fact that her husband had left her for 12 years to go and learn Torah. "What type of a person goes away for so long to learn?"

Rachel's answer is unforgettable. "If I could, I would send him away for another 12 years." At that moment, Rabbi Akiva was right outside the house. He heard what his wife said, turned around, and went away to learn for another 12 years. When he came back after 24 years, he had 24,000 *talmidim*. Rachel, his wife, tried to get through the crowd to see him, but the people would not let her. Rabbi Akiva noticed her and called out, "*Sheli ve'shelachem shelah hu* — What is mine and what is yours is all from her [*Kesubos* 63a]. She is responsible for all of my learning and whatever I have accomplished, and for everything you learned from me."

Rav Gifter would ask, "Where was the *mentchlichkeit* of Rabbi Akiva? Why didn't he at least stop in, say hello, express his appreciation, and then leave?"

He gave an answer in the name of his rebbi, Rav Avraham Yitzchak, "*Tzvei mohl tzvelf is nit ein mohl feer un tzvantzik!* — Two times 12 is not the same as one time 24!"

If one truly loves Torah, then there can be no breaks, no time off.

A *talmid* remembers the happy atmosphere in the yeshivah during the *bein hazmanim* that began after Yom Kippur:

The transformation from dread to joy that followed Ne'ilah would lead into the joyous days of *Succos*. Those who would stay for *bein hazmanim* could feel the joy of Torah and mitzvos that had such a strong presence. You could see that the rosh hayeshivah was the embodiment of Torah on Simchas Torah.

And it didn't end on Simchas Torah. The *zman* in yeshivah would begin on Rosh Chodesh Cheshvan, but he encouraged the *bachurim* to be in yeshivah before Rosh Chodesh. Rav Gifter would stress, "If one is truly joyous with the Torah, then he must start with his toil in Torah right after the simchah." This was how he prepared us for the winter *zman*.

More Precious

IT WAS NOT ONLY THE TORAH AS A WHOLE, BUT ACTUALLY EVERY part of it, every word, that Rav Gifter considered precious. Once, he visited a diamond dealer in New York with his son-in-law, Rav Avrohom Chaim Feuer, as part of a fund-raising mission. Rav Feuer watched the workers poring over tiny baguettes with a microscope: diamonds so small that it takes 400 of them to equal just one carat. Minuscule as these bits were, the workers inspected each one: polishing it, weighing it, treating it carefully. Rav Feuer asked the owner if he, too, could look at the chips through the microscope.

When the diamond dealer noticed Rav Avrohom Chaim's interest in the stones, he said to the rosh hayeshivah, "Rosh hayeshivah, beware! I'm afraid your student may become so dazzled by these baguettes that he may decide to forsake the yeshivah to go into the diamond trade." Rav Gifter said that he was not worried; his son-in-law knew what was really valuable. He had taken to heart the verse (*Tehillim* 19:11): "*Ha'nechemadim mi'zahav u'mi'paz rav* — They [the words of Torah] are even more desirable than gold, than even much fine gold."

However, the rosh hayeshivah continued, a lesson can be learned from the microscope. Every Torah thought and question, no matter how minute, is really a shining diamond. And if every tiny diamond is worth such a great investment of time, then imagine the value of every single word of Torah.

At the end of one *zman*, Rav Gifter was giving *bechinos* to the high school boys on the tractate of *Bava Basra*. Inasmuch as there is quite a lot of *Aggadata* (narrative) in *Bava Basra*, many of Rav Gifter's questions focused on the narrative portions. He was very disappointed when very few of the *bachurim* were able to answer his questions.

Eventually, one frustrated young man piped up, "I don't know what the rosh hayeshivah wants from us; it's only *Aggadata*."

Rav Gifter quickly countered, "There is no such thing as only *Aggadata*! If Ravina and Rav Ashi deemed it necessary to put it between the two covers of the Gemara, you can be sure there is what to learn from it!"[7] In fact, Rav Gifter would read the names of the *Amoraim* with great enthusiasm, explaining, "The names of the *Amoraim* are as important as the halachah itself!"

The Epitome of Joy

HEARING TORAH FROM CHILDREN WAS ONE OF HIS GREATEST JOYS. Once, his *talmid*, Rav Chaim Aharon Weinberg, principal of Yeshivat Ateret Torah in Brooklyn, brought his eighth-grade class on a special class trip to Cleveland to visit the yeshivah. The highlight of the trip was meeting Rav Gifter and receiving a blessing from him. One of the boys in the class had recently learned a piece of Torah by Rav Chaim Brisker and he knew it quite well, so Rav Weinberg decided that this boy should repeat the Torah to Rav Gifter.

Rav Gifter listened carefully as the boy repeated the *vort* with clarity and confidence. When the boy finished, Rav Gifter said tearfully, "Who would have thought that I would merit to see a young American boy say over a Rav Chaim with such a *geshmak*!"

Together with a class from a New York yeshivah. Classes would frequently come to visit the yeshivah and receive a *berachah* from Rav Gifter

---

7. Reb Chaim Abraham.

Chapter 6: The Joy of Torah ☐ 117

In his later years, due to the tremor in his hands, Rav Gifter was no longer able to write while he was seated. He would exert extra effort to stand, since standing on his feet provided him with the extra support he needed to stabilize his tremors. Although this was more difficult, it enabled Rav Gifter to do what he loved most: to write down his Torah thoughts.

At one point, he even obtained a weighted pen to help him write, and he would lean on the hand that shook in order to stabilize it.

ONE FURTHER ASPECT OF RAV GIFTER'S LOVE OF TORAH CAN BE called his "freshness" in learning. He never seemed to tire of the experience. Rabbi Yaakov Feitman, former rav of the Young Israel of Cleveland, shared:

Always Fresh

One of my last memories of being able to speak with the rosh hayeshivah is also the most poignant. The rosh hayeshivah's illness was beginning to take its horrible toll, but that great soul was not allowing it to triumph. He told me, "I am grateful to Hashem, because some get depressed by my disease. I am, however, fully be'simchah. I cannot learn as I once was able to, but I can learn like a young bachur, as if everything is new."

His love for Torah remained fresh, even in the most trying of circumstances.

If someone feels true joy in his Torah study, that joy remains with him throughout his life.

Chapter 7
Total Immersion

Even in America IN 1956, RAV GIFTER WROTE AN ARTICLE THAT APPEARED LATER in Torah Perspectives, a collection of his essays. Titled "A Word to Jewish Parents," it reads:

The Jew, therefore, always combines Torah and mitzvos in the same phrase. Mitzvos are always understood as a direct outcome of Torah, deriving their holiness and internal spiritual power from the utterance and Will of Hashem Yisbarach, which is revealed in the holy letters of our Torah.

Commandments sprout and develop in the rich soil of greatness of Torah. It is true that in Eastern Europe a large percentage of Jews were observant even though they were not great in Torah study. But we always forget the simple fact that the Jewish community — the entire complex of Jewish life — was directed by greatness in Torah.

Hence, he continued, if the level of Torah learning in America was compromised due to our lack of aspiration, then our mitzvah observance would suffer, as well. He was very worried that in America we would raise observant children, but not children who would strive for greatness in their Torah studies.

Keep in mind that this was written in 1956, and at that time in America, raising children to be observant was considered the highest standard. Most children, if they went to yeshivah, ended up attending secular schools of higher education. Rav Gifter was dismayed at this trend and said:

If Jewish parents wish to guarantee a truly Jewish life of mitzvah performance, they must expend the greatest possible effort and they must sacrifice to help create outstanding Torah personalities from among the American youth.

As we have seen elsewhere in this book, this was a recurrent theme of Rav Gifter's speeches — to his students, as well.

Of course, there were many skeptics who reasoned, "America is not Europe," and settled for less. But Rav Gifter pleaded with them:

Let us not make the mistake of thinking that American young people do not possess the raw material of Torah greatness. That is false! Completely false! We have among us the young genius who should become the gaon, the gadol; we lack only the insight and the sense of colossal necessity to create gedolim and geonim.

Rav Gifter's words found their way into the hearts of American Jewry because he spoke the language of the masses. His references to current events were both comforting and energizing to his audiences. For example:

We understand the need for a Jonas Salk to combat the crippling effect of infantile paralysis, but we don't even begin to comprehend our need for the Torah giant who will combat the paralysis caused by superficiality in Jewish life. And because of this, we fail to respond to the most compelling needs of our time.

This was an era in which American parents wanted nothing more than financially and professionally successful children. Most rabbis did not dare address this problem. They felt that if the parents were raising their children to be observant, we can't push them much more than that. But Rav Gifter's passion could not be quieted.

*Our future gedolim often become lost to us because of the narrow-mindedness of parents, **observant** parents, who are so fearful over the material success of their children. We want devout children, but we are blind, **very** blind, to the simple truth that the gaon, the Torah giant, is the only guarantor of mitzvah performance.*

Bread and Meat

IN 1964, RAV GIFTER WROTE AN ARTICLE IN *THE JEWISH PARENT* that discussed the concept of Jewish education as a prerequisite for Jewish survival. This article was based on an address he delivered to the lay leaders of Torah Umesorah. He writes:

In his Yad, the Rambam discusses the profound contemplation of emunah. He devotes to it four chapters which represent the quintessence of religious Jewish philosophy. At the very end of his discussion, he postulates that these profound philosophic considerations can be of value only if they stem from and are based upon the strong foundations of lechem u'basar — the bread and meat of havayos [discussions] de'Abaye ve'Rava — the deep study of Torah in expounding the mitzvos Hashem, because the havayos de'Abaye ve'Rava serve to regulate and discipline the thinking process of the human mind. The strength of mind, the intellectual force necessary for the profound philosophic consideration of emunah, is achieved only through the depths of Torah study.

The inherent qualities of the Jew, with which he is endowed to reach the heights of the Supreme reality of emunah, these qualities are activated to become a practical force through the study of Torah as the prerequisite of shemiras hamitzvos — in the observance and performance of mitzvos.

Torah chinuch then is the "bread and meat" of havayos de'Abaye ve'Rava.

Rav Gifter often spent time at the home of his son-in-law and daughter, Rav and Rebbetzin Ephraim Eisenberg, on Yeshiva Lane in Baltimore. One Friday night, Rav Gifter stepped outside after the meal to get some fresh air. He noticed that a group of *bachurim* from Yeshivas Ner Yisrael was coming toward the apartment to visit with him. He called out, "Go back to the *beis midrash*! Why are you visiting with me when you can be spending time with Abaye and Rava?!"

Rav Gifter himself was a perfect example of a true Torah giant, not only due to his inborn brilliance, but because of his total involvement in his learning.

A *TALMID* REMINISCES:

Total Recall

Rabbi Avishai David told me that once, upon meeting Rav Gifter, he mentioned that he had learned in Yeshivas Rabbeinu Yitzchak Elchanan. Rav Gifter asked him if he remembered the shiur that Rav Yosef Dov Soloveitchik delivered when he first arrived at the yeshivah. Rabbi David replied that he was not even born then. Rav Gifter then proceeded to repeat the entire lecture that Rav Soloveitchik had delivered on that occasion. [1]

At a *sheva berachos* hosted by Rav Gifter and his rebbetzin for one of Rav Pesach Stein's children, Rav Gifter recounted *all* the Torah thoughts that Rav Pesach had shared with him over 25 years earlier when they first met.

Rav Gifter was proficient in the entire Talmud and its commentaries. Once, when he was lecturing on the mitzvah of *korban pesach* in his *Minchas Chinuch shiur* in Telz-Stone, a *yungerman*, who was well versed in *Kodashim*, argued with him about a certain point. To strengthen his argument, the young man cited an obscure Tosafos in *Maseches Zevachim*. Regardless of what Rav Gifter said, the young man would not relent and insisted on citing the Tosafos to refute Rav Gifter's thought, though he did not mention *which* Tosafos. Finally, Rav Gifter smiled and responded in his Lithuanian-accented Yiddish, "*Mein teirer,*

---
1. Reb Shlomo Slonim.

*ich veis der lomdus, uber kuk arein noch amol un ir kent zen az der Taisfes is nit a Taisfes, nor a **piskei** Taisfes.*[My dear one, I know the logic, but look inside again. You will see that the Tosafos that you are quoting is not really the Tosafos, but just a *piskei Tosafos*: a concise summary of Tosafos that cannot be used to prove the point of Tosafos.]"

RAV GIFTER UNDERSTOOD THAT INTENSE TORAH STUDY WAS THE only thing that could rebuild what was lost, and imbue greatness in the next generation.

Total Involvement

In 1953, a young man entered Telz. One could tell from the start that he was less than serious, wasting much of his time in one endeavor or another. One day, he happened to be in the *beis midrash* when it was almost empty, and he heard a compelling sound. The sound came from Rav Gifter, who was learning out loud with tremendous concentration. The *bachur* sat down and stared; he could not pull himself away from the sound and gripping image of Rav Gifter's learning. The learning session began and the room filled, but Rav Gifter did not look out of the Gemara even once. The young man sat there for over five hours, totally transfixed by this sight. He knew that he had just witnessed greatness, and that he would never be the same. Only years later did the former *bachur*, by then a married man, reveal this story to the rebbi who had made such a strong impression on him. And now, 57 years later, that man has dedicated his life to Torah and has written numerous *sefarim*.

That kind of focus is, of course, rare, but makes a huge impression on anyone who witnesses it.

Another disciple, Reb Aharon, remembers the day — when he was a 16-year-old boy — that his heavy, *sefarim*-laden lectern fell with a loud crash, just feet away from where Rav Gifter was learning. Aharon was mortified and frightened. What would Rav Gifter say to him after he disturbed the entire *beis midrash*?

Amazingly, Rav Gifter said nothing; he didn't even flinch, because he literally did not hear the crash. He was immersed in his Gemara and oblivious to everything else. Aharon then realized that he had observed someone who was literally in a different world when he learned Torah.

Reb Aharon has been in Jewish education for over 40 years. He has spoken to hundreds of bar mitzvah boys. And he tells them one story: the story of a man who lived in a different world when he learned.

For that is how one achieves Torah greatness. [2]

Along with the importance of intense study, Rav Gifter always stressed the importance of constant review in order to retain all that one has learned. He would quote "der Uncle," Rav Mottel Katz, "*Ein mohl gelernt iz kein mohl nit gelernt un tzvei mohl gelernt iz ein mohl gelernt* — If you have learned something once, it's as if you haven't learned it at all, and if you have learned it twice, it's as if you have learned it once."

In the Shavuos Almanac for *Dos Yiddishe Vort* from 1956, Rav Gifter wrote:

A discipline whose mystery, whose kernel of truth, is limited, must be studied with limitation. The discipline must be studied according to its nature. But the wisdom of the holy Torah is infinite and unbounded, so its study cannot tolerate limitation. Therefore, a human being who studies it must be engaged with all his strength and be preoccupied with it. Only so can Torah be studied.

Rav Gifter strongly opposed the idea of mixing one's yeshivah studies with a college education. "Harvard Medical School has the greatest respect for Harvard Engineering School, but they don't let you go to both of them, because you can only pursue one at a time. Everyone, on his level, has to learn as much Torah as he can in the yeshivah. But if you want to be a tailor or an accountant, leave the yeshivah to learn the trade."

Examples of his complete engagement in Torah abound.

One time, Rav Gifter was learning with his grandson, Tzvi Feuer, and the phone rang. It was an urgent matter of the Klal, one that demanded his immediate attention. He spent a few moments on the phone. Then, as soon as he hung up, he told Tzvi, as he so often said to his learning partners, "*Kum, lomir tzurik gein tzu der arbit.* [Come, let us get back to work.]" Immediately, he was completely immersed.

---

2. Rabbi Aharon Brodie.

Learning with Rav Chaim Nussbaum

His *talmidim,* Rabbi Azriel Goldfein and Rav Chaim Nussbaum, who were also his learning partners for many years, marveled at Rav Gifter's ability to begin learning the Gemara each day as if he had never left it at all.

Rav Boruch Sorotzkin, his fellow rosh hayeshivah, once commented, "I can't go near Rav Gifter in middle of a learning session. He is literally like a fire!"

He never closed the door to his study when he learned at home. He was able to shut out all distractions, because he was able to focus completely on what he was learning. He didn't even drink or eat while he learned.

Perhaps that is why, before Rav Gifter ascended to the Heavenly Yeshivah, he asked that he be buried with a piece of his desk, the one where he had sat, learned, and written for countless hours.

The Merit of Total Immersion

RABBI HILLEL MANNES, THE GENERAL STUDIES PRINCIPAL IN THE Telz Yeshivah, underwent surgery to separate two nerves in his neck that were pressing together. The pressure had created a short circuit. As a result, his head and neck twitched uncontrollably. The operation succeeded in separating the nerves, but Reb Hillel remained in a coma.

The yeshivah said *Tehillim,* and even changed Rabbi Mannes' name to effect Heavenly mercy, but he remained comatose. (Nevertheless, whenever the rosh hayeshivah entered his hospital room, Rabbi

Mannes sensed it and always struggled to sit.)

After a number of days, the doctors informed the rosh hayeshivah, "We did everything in our power. However, we feel that his body will not be able to take another day of the comatose state. The rest is up to you."

The rosh hayeshivah stormed into the *beis midrash*, pounded on the *bimah*, and called out, "Why are we so complacent? Our friend is struggling with his life, and we go on as if it doesn't concern us. Sure, we spend 10 minutes a day saying *Tehillim,* but then we forget about him. I demand a solid hour of learning without one second wasted!"

Then he ran to the yeshivah office and told everyone there to go into the *beis midrash* and spend an hour learning; even the kitchen workers went! Many remember the sound of that learning. When the hour was up, the public phone in the hall rang. It was the doctor with the incredible news: Reb Hillel had woken up. He had a complete recovery and lived for many years afterward.[3]

Prophecy of Doom

RAV GIFTER'S DETERMINATION TO SHARE THE POWER OF TORAH and intense Torah study was strengthened by so many experiences, especially those connected with other sages. For example, one time (soon after the war was over), he was invited to accompany Rav Elya Meir Bloch on a fundraising trip to New York. During the day, they stopped at a Jewish bookstore, since Rav Elya Meir was interested in buying a volume of *Ketzos HaChoshen*. They introduced themselves to the elderly storeowner and asked him for the *Ketzos HaChoshen*. While the storeowner was searching, they took a quick tour around the store; it was indeed a place to purchase Jewish items, such as candlesticks and *siddurim*, but not necessarily *sefarim*. The old man finally climbed a ladder and retrieved a copy of the *sefer*; it had obviously been sitting there for a long time.

Just as he was about to hand the *sefer* over, the old man pulled it back and looked intensely at Rav Elya Meir. "I will sell you this *sefer* on two conditions," he said. "Number one, I understand that you lost your entire family in the war and that you intend to rebuild what was lost in Europe. Please listen to me. Don't try it! You are committing emotional suicide! You are setting yourself up for failure. There is only so much heartache that one man can take. There is no place for a yeshivah here in America. You'll never succeed."

---

3. Rabbi Shlomo Goldhaber.

Rav Elya Meir Bloch

Rav Elya Meir nodded, not agreeing, but waiting to hear what the second condition was. The man continued, "Second, let's be honest. America is not the type of country where Torah will flourish. What we had in Europe is now gone, and what Hitler destroyed cannot be rebuilt. So treat this relic as a valuable piece of history, because this *sefer* that I'm selling you could be the last *Ketzos* that is ever sold in America."

Rav Elya Meir did not respond. He merely purchased the *sefer* and walked out. Rav Gifter waited for him to explain, and he did, after a few moments of thought. "He's right." At this, Rav Gifter was stunned, but he continued to listen. "*Al pi seichel* [according to logic], there is no chance for Torah to survive in this country. *Al pi seichel*, we are indeed holding in our hands what may very well be the last *Ketzos HaChoshen* ever bought in this country. *Al pi seichel*, there is no place for a yeshivah in America.

"But Torah does not work with logic! The power of Torah is beyond all logic. Torah can cause a yeshivah to blossom and *Ketzos* to be learned. More *Ketzos HaChoshen*s will be printed and bought in America than ever before in history. And you will see, Telz will be rebuilt here in America!"

Indeed, more *Ketzos HaChoshen*s have been produced and purchased in America than ever before.

And Telz, with its intense Torah study, was rebuilt in America.

Chapter 8
Ameilus BaTorah — Toiling in Torah

RAV GIFTER OFTEN ASKED IN THE NAME OF THE TAZ: WHY is it that when one sees a secular scholar, he recites the blessing of *"she'nasan me'chochmaso le'vasar vadam* — Who has given of His knowledge to human beings," while when one sees an outstanding Torah scholar, he recites the blessing of *she'chalak me'chochmaso lirei'av* — Who has apportioned of His knowledge to those Who fear Him"? Why do we change the expression from "giving" to "apportioning"?

Rav Gifter answered that when the Al-mighty gave knowledge to the nations of the world, he gave it as a gift, a *matanah* — "*she'nasan*" — and then disconnected Himself from the gift. But when the Al-mighty gives knowledge to the Torah scholars, He apportions it — "*she'chalak*"; He gives a part, a *cheilek*, of Himself.

"*Kudsha Berich Hu ve'Oraysa ve'Yisrael chad hu* — Hashem, the Torah, and the Jewish nation are one" (*Zohar Vayikra*). We are all connected.

When one learns Torah, he is not merely studying subject matter. He

With Rav Moshe Feinstein

is connecting himself to the Al-mighty.[1] In fact, Rav Gifter would say (in Chassidic style), "When we daven, we speak to the *Ribbono Shel Olam*; when we learn, the *Ribbono Shel Olam* speaks to us."

Learning Torah requires a great deal of *ameilus*, toil. However, many people assume that the work is not so difficult for *gedolim,* because they are blessed with extraordinary minds. Still, when one would watch Rav Gifter learn, one would realize that the concept of *ameilus* does not refer only to brain work (although surely Rav Gifter's mind did toil over many difficult concepts). But rather, Rav Gifter's whole approach to his learning was a model of *ameilus*; his learning was intense and all consuming, comprised of long hours, hard work, and never, ever resting.[2] He deliberately invested his time in the most difficult *sefarim,* and relished the energy and effort it took to understand the texts.

He appreciated *ameilus* in others, as well. One Shavuos in the late

---
1. Rabbi Moshe Goldberg.
2. Rebbetzin Gifter.

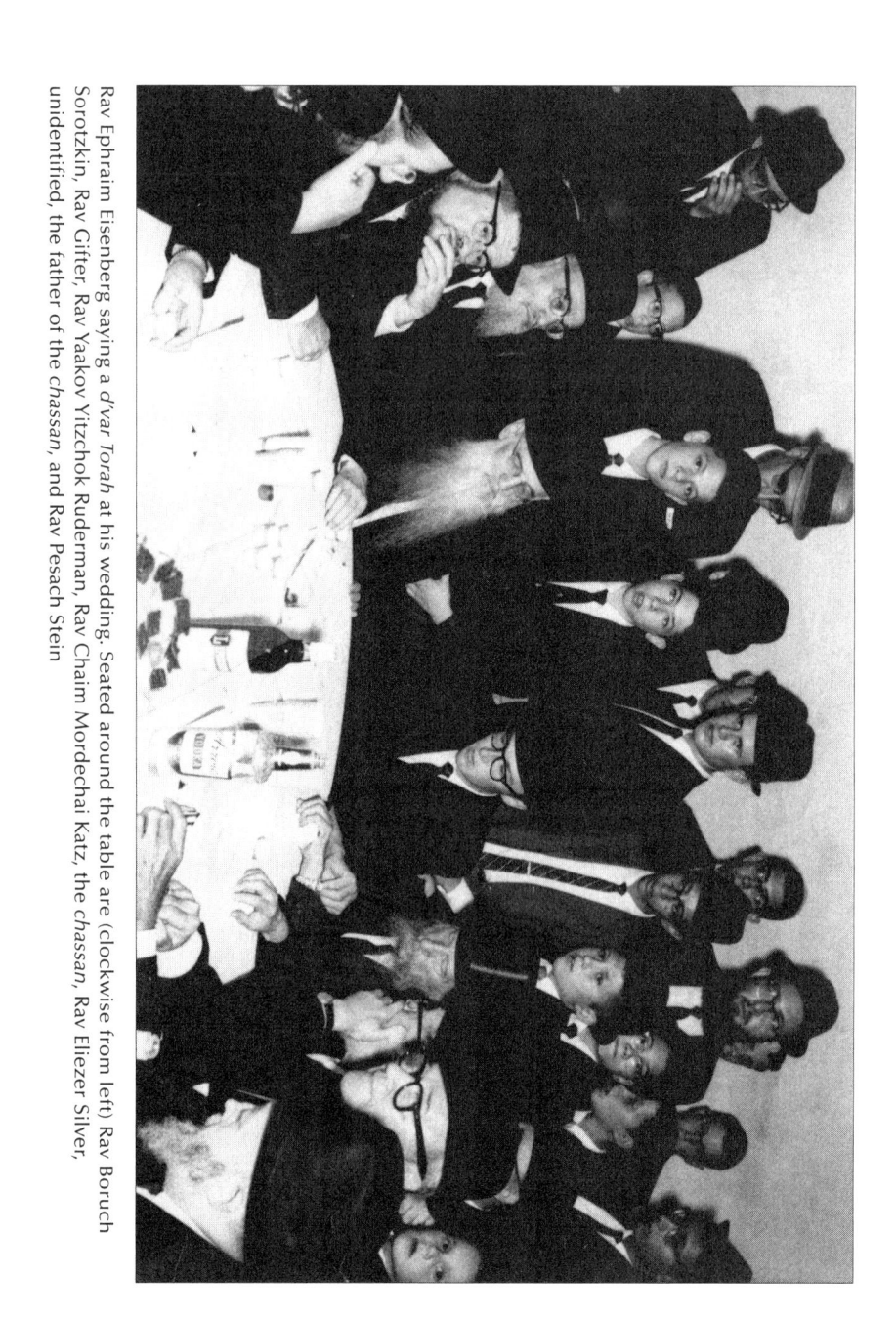

Rav Ephraim Eisenberg saying a *d'var Torah* at his wedding. Seated around the table are (clockwise from left) Rav Boruch Sorotzkin, Rav Gifter, Rav Yaakov Yitzchok Ruderman, Rav Chaim Mordechai Katz, the *chassan*, Rav Eliezer Silver, unidentified, the father of the *chassan*, and Rav Pesach Stein

1950's, Avrohom Mordechai Isbee and some of his friends visited Rav Gifter for an *oneg Yom Tov*. When Rav Gifter began the *oneg*, he seemed ill; one of the *bachurim* asked after his well-being. Rav Gifter responded that he was well, but he was tired, since he had not been able to sleep since the night before Shavuos. He said that after learning on Shavuos night, he had tried to go to sleep. However, the windows to his room were open, and he heard gorgeous sounds coming from the *beis midrash* just behind his apartment; it was a boy learning with a magnificent *niggun* of Torah.

"Imagine that," he said, "a *bachur* learning on Shavuos morning when no one else is in the *beis midrash*. But don't think for a moment that I am upset that I could not sleep. There is no sound in the world more beautiful for a rebbi than the sound of his *talmid* learning."[3]

When Rav Gifter was looking for a husband for his oldest daughter, Shlomis, his interactions with the prospective *chassan*, Rav Ephraim Eisenberg, illustrate his appreciation of *ameilus baTorah* in others. Reb Ephraim spoke to his future father-in-law three times, and each time he discussed the same subject. This was an indication, in Rav Gifter's eyes, of the young man's *ameilus baTorah* (since the young man was so involved in the topic he was learning). Rav Gifter thought that was an admirable trait for a future son-in-law.

Like a Business

ON A FUND-RAISING TRIP TO MEXICO, RAV GIFTER TRIED TO MEET with a particular man who was known to be quite wealthy. After much effort, Rav Gifter was told that the only time available was very early in the morning, before traditional work hours began. Not to be deterred, the rosh hayeshivah agreed to the appointment. When he entered the man's office, he was shocked to see that the man was already doing business on the phone. Seeing his guest, the man apologized, saying, "I'm sorry, I just don't have time to talk to you now."

Rav Gifter replied, "Let's not talk about money. I want to ask you a question. At first, I came to your house to see you there. I saw your beautiful mansion with all the amenities. When do you have time to enjoy it if you are always so taken up with your business?"

---

3. That young man was Reb Zelig Nevis, who still continues to learn with *hasmadah*.

The Jew looked at Rav Gifter, barely comprehending the question. "Rebbi, the house is not for me. I have nothing from it. As you can see, I spend my time in the business. It is for my wife and children. Rebbi," he continued, *"oib mir villen matzliach zein, broch men liggen in gesheft!* [If one wants to succeed, one must be totally immersed in the business!]"

Rav Gifter responded excitedly, "You don't have to give me any money. I have received something much more valuable than money! I have received a lesson that I can convey to my *talmidim*. If you want to succeed, you have to be totally immersed in the business. Our business is Torah!"

The rosh hayeshivah returned from his trip to Mexico with some additional funding for the yeshivah. But more than that, he came back with a lesson that the *bachurim* would hear many times.

"*Oib mir villen matzliach zein, broch men liggen in gesheft* — If one wants to succeed, one must be totally immersed in the business."

Similarly, Rav Gifter often explained that we recite the *berachah* (in *Birchos HaTorah*) every morning, "*laasok be'divrei Sorah* — to engross ourselves in the words of Torah." The use of the word *laasok* (to engross) seems unusual. Perhaps we should recite *lilmod* (to learn); why *laasok*? He explained that an *eisek* is a business; we must treat our learning like it is a business. If we want to be successful in our learning of Torah, then we must live with the Torah.

Rav Gifter took it upon himself to answer questions that others considered impossible. If Rav Akiva Eiger asked a question and *"bleibt shver* — remained with a question," Rav Gifter would spend hours trying to figure out precisely why. (As is mentioned elsewhere in this book, he was not looking for an answer, but just trying to figure out why the great Rav Akiva Eiger had no answer to the question.)

A STUDENT REMINISCED:

Learning Without Toil Is Not Learning

Rav Gifter regularly inquired about my learning schedule. I once told him that I had one spare hour, which I employed to "look around" in various sefarim on the topics we were learning. In response, he said in Yiddish: "From looking around, one doesn't become a lamdan. Get a study partner for the hour and have a fixed learning session."

I duly did so.[4]

At the end of the *zman,* a young *beis midrash bachur* was selected to speak in learning with Rav Gifter at his home. At the time, he was learning the *sugya* of *"Takfa Kohen,"* a difficult topic in *Maseches Bava Metzia,* and he did not have a novel Torah thought. Instead, he decided that he would look up something in a relatively uncommon *sefer,* and he would try to pass it on as his own novel thought.

When the young man shared his "original" thought, Rav Gifter at first listened carefully, but then he exclaimed, "*Dos iz shtusim va'havalim.* [That's foolishness and futility.]"

The *bachur* was taken aback and defended the thought, confessing that he had seen it in the *sefer, Chiddushei HaRim.* Rav Gifter was not persuaded. "I don't know what the *Chiddushei HaRim* says, but what you're saying is silly! You must have misunderstood."

Then, noticing the downtrodden expression on the young man's face, Rav Gifter spoke softly, "I beg you, my dear, don't look in *sefarim* that are filled with big *chiddushim.* Tell me a Rashi that you did not understand at the beginning of the learning session, yet succeeded in understanding by the end of the learning session. And explain to me how you came to comprehend Rashi's explanation."

Today, nearly 40 years later, when this man thinks more deeply into understanding the true meaning of the Gemara, Rashi, or another *Rishon,* he thinks, "This is what my rebbi would like to hear."[5]

A *bachur* sent Rav Gifter a letter in which he attempted to answer one of the difficult questions posed by the *Ketzos HaChoshen* in a very simple manner. Rav Gifter wrote back to the boy that he was amazed that a *bachur* would have the chutzpah to think that he could just answer a question of the *Ketzos HaChoshen.* In fact, he gave a *shmuess* on this topic. As Rav Gifter said in his letter to the boy, the author of the *Ketzos HaChoshen,* Rav Aryeh Leib HaCohen Heller, learned Torah *mi'toch ha'dechak* (under great duress). He had no heat in the winter, and his ink would freeze. He had to defrost the ink in order to write his *sefer.*

"And you," Rav Gifter said, "a *bachur* who eats strawberry shortcake, think that you have an answer that the *Ketzos* didn't think of? You

---
4. Reb Shlomo Slonim.
5. Reb Leibel Berger.

should work hard to try to understand why the *Ketzos* remained with a question, and why your answer is not adequate."[6]

A strong, forceful response, with a timeless message. Torah and toil are an inseparable pair.

One time, a *talmid* who came to visit Rav Gifter noticed that he was not feeling well. When the *talmid* asked his rebbi what was wrong, Rav Gifter gave a sigh as he explained that he was unable to learn.

The *talmid* was puzzled since he saw that Rav Gifter was indeed learning. He asked Rav Gifter about the apparent misunderstanding. His response was, "Yes, I am learning. *Uber ich lern uhn yegiyah, un lernen uhn yegiyah iz nit kein lernen.* — But I am learning without toil, and learning without toil is not learning."

Human Nature

REFLECTING ON HIS OWN LIFE EXPERIENCES, RAV GIFTER WOULD often tell the story of his journey to Europe. Hundreds were on the ship, most of them in a jolly mood, holding party after party during the voyage. In the middle of the trip, a massive thunderstorm erupted and the ship was tossed by the waves and wind. The passengers were panic stricken; Mordechai was sure that once the storm was over, they would become more solemn. Nothing of the sort happened. As soon as the sea calmed down, the people returned to their partying with even greater frivolity. He couldn't believe it!

Later, when he came to Telz, young Mordechai, still affected by the incident, told it to Rav Avraham Yitzchak Bloch; he asked him how such a thing was possible. How could people stare death in the face one moment and then carry on with their lightheartedness in the next moment?

"That is not a question at all!" explained the Telzer Rav. "*Dos iz ah mentch!*"

Rav Gifter understood that this is the true nature of human beings, and it is against this propensity that we must struggle every day. In our Torah study, as well, we must always strive — and toil — for more.

---

6. Rav Yaakov Reisman.

With Rav Yaakov Kamenetsky

IN THE MID-1980'S, THE ROSH YESHIVAH WENT TO FAR ROCKAWAY to participate in the installation of his son-in-law, Rav Yaakov Reisman,

The Greatest Delicacy

as rav of Agudas Yisrael of Long Island. He spent that Shabbos in Far Rockaway, where he addressed packed audiences throughout the weekend.

On Sunday morning, he went to Yeshiva Toras Chaim of South Shore in Hewlett, New York, where he gave a memorable address to the children. The dean of the Yeshiva of South Shore, Rav Binyamin Kamenetzky, had learned in Telz in Europe in his youth. The meeting between Rav Gifter and Rav Kamenetzky brought back a flood of memories from their yeshivah days in Europe.

Rav Gifter decided to share his memories of *p'tcha*. Yes, *p'tcha*, also known as *gala*, is a delicacy made of the congealed liquid formed when cows' feet are cooked in water. In his address to the students, Rav Gifter focused on his memories of his encounter with *p'tcha* in Telz, offering the children and *bachurim* in attendance an everlasting lesson and memory.

As Rav Gifter explained:

P'tcha was a delicacy. But it was a delicacy that I couldn't stand. When my mother would make it back in Baltimore, I made sure to stay away from the house throughout the cooking period. I could barely bring myself to be in the same room as the stuff, let alone at the same table!

As a bachur who had come all the way from America to learn in Yeshivas Telz in Lithuania, I was somewhat of a celebrity. Therefore, I was invited to eat at the home of the principal of the yeshivah. And, just my luck, what

Chapter 8: Ameilus BaTorah — Toiling in Torah   □   135

Listening intently to a *sevarah*

do you think the rebbetzin brought out that first meal on that first Shabbos that I spent in Telz? P'tcha. I don't know how I survived that meal without gagging, but somehow I managed. I was extremely happy when the ordeal was over. After the meal, to my chagrin and horror, the principal informed me that the custom in Telz was for bachurim to eat their Shabbos meals at the same house every week. How would I manage?!

Rav Gifter went on to explain how the second week was also torture. However, as time went on, he learned to enjoy the meal even when the offending *p'tcha* was on the table, as long as he did not have to eat it. After a few months and much prodding from his host, he even gathered the guts to try it — and he found it to be tasty! With time and exposure, he developed a taste for it.

I saw that p'tcha was ah gutte zach [a good thing, treat]. Today, it is the greatest delicacy for me.

Rav Gifter paralleled his encounter with *p'tcha* to learning Torah.

When a person is young, learning Torah is not his favorite pastime. He may not even like it, but if he plugs away — and tenaciously exposes himself to it — he develops a taste for it. Eventually, it becomes the greatest delicacy, a delicacy that he simply cannot live without.

Rav Gifter thundered:

Di p'tcha fun Torah iz di beste zach in di velt. [The p'tcha of Torah is the best thing in the world.] At first, you may not like it, but if you keep on trying, you will see that there is nothing better — and you won't be able to live without it!

His speech made a profound impact on the children. His thundering, emotion-laden voice exclaiming, *"Di p'tcha fun Torah iz di beste zach in di velt,"* still rings in their ears to this day.

Rav Gifter wrote:

The concept of amal haTorah is inherent to the study of Torah. Amal haTorah means being engrossed in Torah to the exclusion of all else. It means a mind completely open to Torah, unburdened with other systems of thought. It means self-denial of material interests and desires. It signifies the power and ability to find in Torah study all the joys and pleasures which one could wish for. It means finding in Torah the joys and benefits "of bread and meat, of wine and oil, of fields and vineyards, of milk and honey, of precious stones and pearls."

Amal haTorah does not mean a life impoverished by complete removal from human joys and pleasures, but rather the sublime contentment of the most intimate contact with the source of all joy and pleasure.

Amal haTorah — this unique characteristic of Torah study — creates a unique world for the Torah student. His greatest sorrow is the kushya — a difficult passage that he cannot master, a difficult Rambam subjected to the critique of the Raavad.

One night, Rav Gifter's grandson, Tzvi Feuer, who often slept in his grandparents' apartment, noticed that his grandfather was awake at a very late hour. He asked his grandfather if everything was all right. Rav Gifter responded in a memorable way, *"Vi ken men shluffen az der Rashba ligt in turmeh* — How can we sleep if the Rashba is trapped in prison?" How could he sleep if he was having difficulty with a Rashba and wanted to "release" it from "prison"?

 The greatest joy of the Torah student is the teirutz [the answer] — he has seen the light, he has felt the truth, and with the Psalmist he sings forth, "Gal einai ve'abitah niflaos miTorasecha — Unveil my eyes and I shall see the sublime wonders of Your Torah" [Tehillim 119:18].

The halachah states that if a student of Torah should have to be sentenced to exile, it is the duty of beis din to exile his rebbi with him. For in reference to galus it is written: "And he shall live." Do all that is necessary to give him life and sustenance and the Rambam comments, "For the students of Torah, *'ki heim chayeinu ve'orech yameinu'* — they are our life and the length of our days."

Only Torah and the *ameilus* of Torah can bring true life to a Torah Jew. Everything else falls short.

Chapter 9
Making the Most of Our Time

IN ONE OF HIS UNFORGETTABLE ELUL *SHMUESSEN* FROM THE 1980's, Rav Gifter discussed the value of time.

What would we do if we saw a person puncturing his life vein, wouldn't we ask him, "What is wrong with you? You are committing suicide!" Or if a person punctured another's life vein and he was losing his blood, wouldn't we say to him, "You're a murderer!"?

What then should we say when we see a Jew wagging his tongue in wasted talk and conversation — let alone lashon hara, forget about that — but just expending the power of speech in wasted talk ... gevalt in der velt ! Why don't we have mercy on him and say, " You're killing yourself. You're committing suicide; 'ki heim chayeinu' — the words of Torah are our life."

Let's say you see a fellow learning, davening, or listening to the Torah reading. Then a good friend walks over to him and disturbs him by wagging his tongue about some "very important matters." Shouldn't we think to say, "What are you doing? Murder! He's engaged in Torah. He's engaged in living! He's engaged in the power and pleasure of what it means to be a *nishmas chaim,* a *ruach memalela* [a living, speaking soul]. And what are you doing to him? You are wasting such a beautiful commodity — the power of speech. You're murdering him!"

Do we think in such terms? When we waste not only minutes, but hours, in empty talk — do we ever stop to think? *Gevalt in der velt!* Do we ever? Never!

IN RAV GIFTER'S DAILY LIFE, NOT A MINUTE WAS WASTED, AND HE was extremely careful about his speech. Indeed, his rebbetzin always

Not Wasting a Minute

said, "My husband is a great speaker, and a small talker."

This author remembers one occasion in which I began talking to someone in the middle of the Torah reading in yeshivah — between *aliyos*. I was so engrossed in the conversation that I did not realize I was being watched. Suddenly, one of my friends walked over and motioned to me that Rav Gifter was staring at me. I looked up and saw his piercing gaze. I felt as though a sword had sliced through me. Without uttering another word, I sheepishly walked back to my seat. It would be a long time before I tried to do anything like that again.

When he saw boys wasting time, Rav Gifter would say to them, "You're not killing time; you're killing yourself."

THE VILNA GAON MADE A CALCULATION ONCE BEFORE ROSH Hashanah. He went through the year and found that for six minutes in the

The Vilna Gaon's Calculation

year, he had not been engaged in Torah. Let's begin to learn from this how the Gaon thought of this commodity called time and how he spent his time, the most precious of commodities. A minute lost is lost forever. You lose a million dollars, you make it back. You lose a diamond, you'll get another one to replace it. You lose one minute, it's gone forever, never to come back. How careful must one be in counting every minute of life. That's how the Gaon lived.

Just make a calculation for yourself: There are 365 days in a year. Every day has 24 hours. Every hour has 60 minutes. *Nu…* count out how many minutes are in a year. And before Rosh Hashanah, the Gaon saw that there were six minutes wasted! And for those six minutes he wept!

Where do we stand when we hear such a thing? Do we know how many minutes we waste? Not in a year, in a month, or in a week. Are we aware of how many minutes we waste in a day?

Chapter 9: Making the Most of Our Time

Before we go to bed, we must figure out: How many minutes were wasted by us, for no purpose whatsoever? Do we have such a calculation?

Time is one of the creations of Hashem Yisbarach, though He Himself is above time, far above time. And he wants it to be used for our benefit. Are we aware of it? Is this the way we have lived throughout our year? When we come to Him on Rosh Hashanah, what are we going to bring to Him? What are we going to tell Him? "Look, Ribbono Shel Olam, look how we took care of this commodity." Is that what we are going to tell Him? And if we do know the truth, we are terribly ashamed.

And I'm not talking to you, gentlemen, I am talking to myself. But I hope you don't mind if you hear what I am telling myself.

If we truly appreciated the value of time, every time we were engaged in something valueless, we would stop immediately and exclaim, "Oy, gevalt! I am taking diamonds and throwing them into the sea!"

In speaking about the mitzvah of shofar, the Rambam writes, "Remez yeish bo — There is something for us to learn from this." And he speaks about those in this world who occupy their time with foolish pursuits. The shofar is a wake-up call. It reminds us to stop wasting our time. We are called by the shofar of Rosh Hashanah to stand before Hashem Yisbarach.

Ford Motor Company had a very catchy slogan, "Ford has a better idea." One of their original ideas was a unique top to the car key that enabled the driver to insert the key in the ignition, without looking which way the key was facing. This would save people the time it would normally take to figure out which way to insert the key. Rav Gifter gave a fiery *shmuess* to the *bachurim* on this matter. "It is a great idea. But what do we do with the time that we have saved? If we waste it, we have gained nothing!"

RAV GIFTER CONCLUDED THE *SHMUESS* WITH A BRILLIANT thought in the name of his great uncle, Rav Zalman Sorotzkin, the Lutzker Rav:

The Sword of Chizkiyahu

The Gemara (Sanhedrin 94b) tells us a most interesting thing about Chizkiyahu. "Na'atz cherev al pesach beis hamidrash — Chizkiyahu stuck a sword by the entrance of the beis midrash." Chizkiyahu HaMelech said, "Sancheirev is here with a powerful army with which he has conquered the entire world. We are the last ones to be attacked. He has a *cherev*, a sword, and we have to be fearful of that *cherev*."

Chizkiyahu took his own sword and put it into the door of the *beis midrash*. And he said, "Whoever shall leave the *beis midrash* and stop the study of Torah shall be killed with this sword." As a result of his actions, when a census was taken of Klal Yisrael, they did not find any man, woman, or child who was not well versed in the laws of purity [a very complex topic].

It is hard to believe; was he really saying that anyone who leaves the *beis midrash* and doesn't study Torah will be killed? There is no such law. Wasting time from Torah study means that a person did not keep a positive commandment. But not keeping a positive commandment does not make one liable to be killed by *beis din*.

I think that our Sages are trying to teach us something very, very deep — something that we have been talking about. We know that if we feel something with our senses it impresses us much more. We know that Torah study is our life, but if someone stands in front of us with a sword — Oy! It's murder!

Chizkiyahu was saying, "You see, Torah is your lifeblood. With that you shall succeed against all the plans of Sancheirev." And the Gemara says that they all left their fields and their vineyards. They had no interest in worldly pursuits. And when they went to the *beis midrash* and they saw the sword,

Learning in the Telz *beis midrash* with Rav Chaim Stein

it reminded them, "If I leave the beis midrash, I am killing myself. If I stay in the beis midrash, there is no sword in the world that can hurt me."

Rav Gifter would punctuate this thought with one sharp caveat, "During war, if a soldier abandons his post, he's a deserter! Therefore, one who does not enter the *beis midrash* during a time of war is also a deserter — and that is why Chizkiyahu said he must be put to death!"

The Timeless Words of the Ramchal

AT THE END OF RAV GIFTER'S LIFE, AS HE SLIPPED AWAY INTO THE twilight, his dear friend, Rav Abba Zalka Gewirtz, came to visit him. As Rabbi Gewirtz later recounted at Rav Gifter's funeral, when he sat down next to the rosh ha-yeshivah, there was no response; the rosh hayeshivah, he learned, was unable to communicate. Therefore, instead of talking, Rabbi Gewirtz decided to sing the classic *mussar niggun* to the words of the great Rav Moshe Chaim Luzzatto, from *Mesillas Yesharim*, "*Adam do'eg al ibud damav, ve'eino do'eg al ibud yamav* — Man worries about the loss of his money, but doesn't worry about the loss of his days. *Damav einam ozrim ve'yamav einam chozrim* — Man's possessions do not help him and his days do not return…"

He repeated these solemn words over and over, as he cried.

Rav Gifter's life was the greatest *mussar sefer* one could learn. He taught with his actions and his deeds. He understood and cherished every moment of life. He valued time as the most precious commodity there is.

And he wanted others to realize how very precious a commodity it is.

Section 3
Torah Outlook

Chapter 10
The Torah Approach

Daas Torah

W E BEGIN THE DISCUSSION OF RAV GIFTER'S OUTLOOK (*hashkafah*) with one of his favorite stories, originally heard from his rebbi, Rav Mottel Pogromansky.
An art connoisseur once brought a friend to the famed Louvre Museum in Paris. He was admiring a Rembrandt painting, noting how the rays of light drew attention to the image, and appreciating the skillful application of the textures and splendrous colors that created the masterpiece. His friend stood there, not impressed in the least. "Aren't you amazed," the man said, "at the sight of this work of art, at the genius that went into its creation?"

The friend stared at the painting, but still showed no emotion. Finally, he looked back toward his friend, and commented, "No, not at all. All I see is *zoir milch* [sour milk]."

As they moved from painting to painting, the same conversation took place. Finally, the connoisseur noticed that his friend's eyeglasses were coated with sour milk! He turned knowingly to his friend and sighed, "When your glasses are smeared with sour milk, all you can see is sour milk!"

Rav Gifter's outlook was based on the concept that we can see Hashem in every single facet of creation and come to love and stand in awe of Him. But in order to be privy to this vision, we must remove the "sour milk" from our lenses, and view all of creation through "Torah *brillen*," Torah spectacles.

———•———

Rav Gifter saw the world through sparklingly clear Torah lenses, and it is with this vision that he developed his *daas Torah*. As he once commented:

*This is what we call daas Torah, meaning that the judgment [daas] of the person who studies is united with the mystery of Torah. It is this daas Torah that the great Torah figures of all generations are privileged to have. By means of this daas Torah, the great men of Torah actually **see** what others, at best, **know** but do not see. The great Torah leaders are granted a "visual sense" from the world of the Torah's mystery, the world of eternity, at a time when smaller people understand and feel everything only according to our small world, the revealed world.*

Woe to those who pose questions in the name of Torah — sincerely or insincerely — to the Torah greats, to the point where they ask, "Who appointed them gedolim that we must obey them?" Such people would reduce Torah authority to the minuscule dimension of an appointment or position.

Not only do the Torah giants understand wisdom, they see deeply in wisdom, as Shlomo HaMelech said, "Velibi ra'ah harbeh chochmah — My heart saw much wisdom" (Koheles 1:16).

Rav Gifter viewed the world as the Al-mighty's canvas through which He sends messages to us; it is our job to decipher these messages. The sages help us to understand the messages and thus improve ourselves and our actions.

———•———

It bothered Rav Gifter greatly when others voiced opinions on some of the great Torah leaders of our time without ever meeting them. These individuals desecrated the honor of Torah. In one of his more memorable addresses, Rav Gifter lambasted a rabbi for spewing vitriol about Rav Elazar Shach, and speaking disparagingly about him. "Rav Shach exudes love!" Rav Gifter thundered. In truth, Rav Gifter had a number of friends (his words) who were not *chareidim*. But he loved them very

Making his way to the funeral of the Steipler Gaon together with Rav Shach

much, as he loved every Jew. Moreover, on one occasion he sent some of those friends to Rav Shach to meet the man who had been vilified by the liberal Jewish media. When they returned from their visit with Rav Shach, they communicated that they were overwhelmed by the unusual softness and warmth with which he greeted them. They had never met such an individual.

Two Letters

THIS PASSION DEVELOPED WITHIN RAV GIFTER AT A YOUNG AGE, as can be seen from his correspondence. While studying in Telz, Rav Gifter corresponded regularly with his father. He also wrote from time to time to Mr. Morris (Yosef Moshe HaLevi) Siegel, a resident of Baltimore with whom Rav Gifter was very close.

Morris Siegel was born in Baltimore in 1902, the fifth of eight children. His parents had come there in the late 1800's from Ponevezh. He was one of a small group of young people who, in 1918, formed a group called Adath Bnei Yisrael, whose members committed to keeping Shabbos, something not very common in those days among young people.

For much of his life, Mr. Siegel ran Shabbos groups for youngsters. These groups encouraged the youth, even those from non-observant homes, to become Shabbos observers. As a boy, Rav Gifter participated

Chapter 10: The Torah Approach ☐ 147

Young Mordechai Gifter

in these gatherings and was influenced by them. He and Mr. Siegel remained lifelong friends, until Mr. Siegel passed away on Rosh Chodesh Elul, 5749 (1989).

Two of the most poignant letters to Mr. Siegel are written primarily in English, and were published decades later in The Jewish Observer. One is dated April 7, 1935. The second is dated (in Hebrew) "Erev Shabbos Kodesh, 2 Rosh Chodesh Adar, 5697, Telz" (February 12, 1937).

One may be shocked at the mention of Zionism in the letter below. It is important to put the letter in its proper historical context. At the time, Zionism was fresh and new to world Jewry and was being led mostly by nonreligious individuals who had a disdain for Torah. In the yeshivah communities in Lithuania and other parts of Eastern Europe, they were leaders of a concerted campaign to undermine Torah values and institutions. This is most likely what Rav Gifter is reacting to, as it reflects the experience of Orthodox community at that time.

RAV GIFTER WAS 18 YEARS OLD WHEN HE WROTE THIS LETTER. WE quote from it in part:

The Letter of April 1935

Dear Mr. Siegel,

It's quite a time since I've left America and haven't once written to you, although we were the best of friends. You may be answered that this is due only to the fact that time is precious in the yeshivah, far more than in the business world where it is said that "time is money." During the year and a half that I've spent in Telz studying our holy Torah, I've progressed quite a bit, B"H. The spiritual enjoyment to be had from study of the Torah is beyond all description. It is only to be felt, and that, only for one who studies in the yeshivah of Telz. At the present time, Telz Yeshivah is the greatest in the world. ... One may think otherwise, but I am thoroughly convinced as to the truth of the statement. You may think that

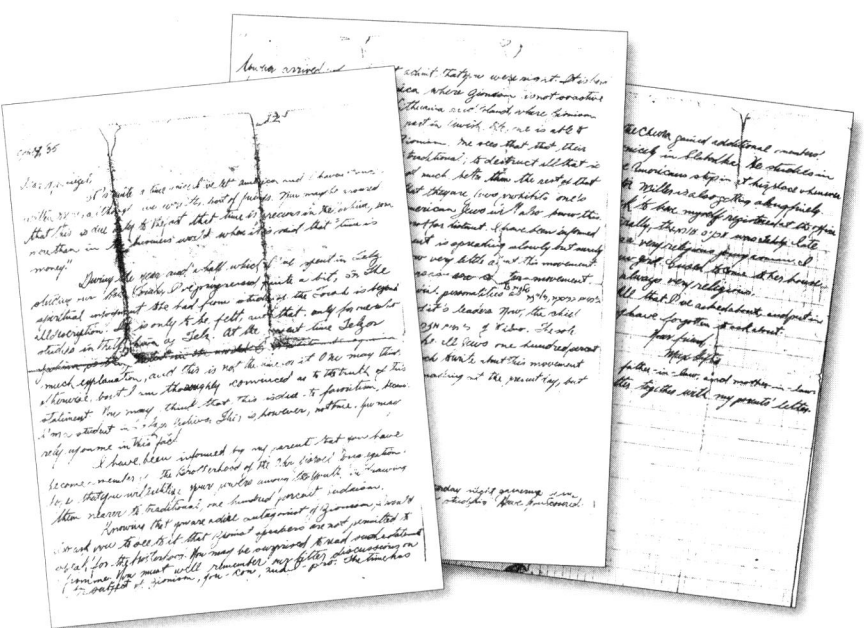

The 1935 letter to Mr. Siegel

this is due to favoritism, because I am a student in the Telzer Yeshivah. This is, however, not true. You may rely on me in this fact.

I have been informed by my parents that you have become a member of the Brotherhood of the Ohr Yisrael Congregation. I hope that you will utilize your powers among the youth in drawing them nearer to traditional, one hundred percent Judaism.

I have been informed that the Agudas Yisrael movement is spreading slowly but surely in America. American Jews know very little about this movement. It was founded about 40 years ago as a counter movement against Zionism by such great Jewish personalities as Rav Chaim Brisker and Rav Leizer Telzer. The Chofetz Chaim was one of its leaders. Now, the chief leader among the rabbis is the gaon, Rav Chaim Ozer of Vilna. The sole purpose of this movement is to make all Jews 100 percent Shulchan Aruch Jews. There is much to write about this movement and the great headway that it is making at the present day, but time does not permit me to do so.

Does the Adath still have its Saturday-night gatherings of the Chevrah Shas? If so, what masechta are you now studying? Have you "covered much ground" since I've left? Has the chevrah gained additional members?

Chapter 10: The Torah Approach ☐ 149

Teddy [Rav Yehudah] Davis is living very nicely in Slabodka. He studies in the Kovno Kollel now, and we Americans stop in at his place whenever we have to be in Kovno. Victor [Rav Avigdor] Miller is also getting along finely. I had to be in Kovno the past week to have myself registered at the office of the American consul. Naturally, the machnis orach was Teddy. I ate and slept at his home. His wife is a very religious young woman. I happen to know her from New York. I used to come to her house to speak with her father. She was always very religious.

Mordechai Gifter and
Mendel Poliakoff

Well, let me know about all that I've asked about and put in any additional news which I may have forgotten to ask about.

Your friend,
Max Gifter

ו' עש״ק ב' דר״ח אדר, תרצ״ז טלז

DEAR MR. SIEGEL,

I have just received your letter and was indeed very happy to hear from you. I was really surprised at your receival [sic] of the letter, but I know that you are continuously busy and can find no time to write. Your ol derech eretz is quite a large one. I always receive your regards through my father, zol gezunt zein, and am indeed very thankful to you. You write quite a bit of interesting news in your letter.

The Letter of February 1937

I knew nothing at all about the fact that Peritzky had left Baltimore but I am happy to hear that you will reorganize the Saturday-night Talmud class. Rabbi Schwartz once studied in Telz, but before I arrived here. From what I have heard about him, he is the only German rabbi that has a Lithuanian look on Judaism and Torah. The Lithuanian "anshauung" is regarded as the real Torah-true "anshauung," so that's quite a lot said about him. I wish you the best of success in your Gemara class.

Happy to hear that you've bought a new home. May you dwell therein in the best of health and happiness.

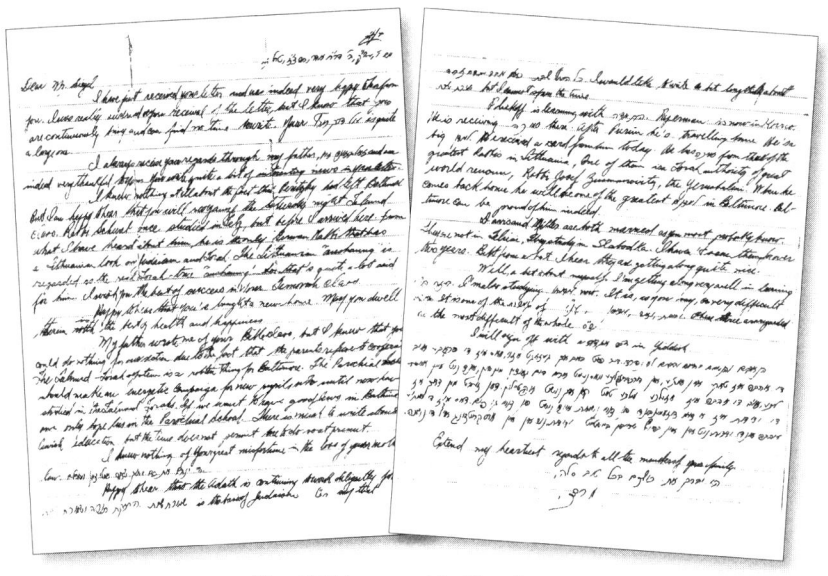

The 1937 letter to Mr. Siegel

My father wrote me of your Bible class, but I know that you could do nothing for our nation due to the fact that parents refuse to cooperate. The Talmud Torah system is a rotten thing for Baltimore. The Parochial School [i.e., Yeshivah] should make an energetic campaign for new pupils who until now have studied in the Talmud Torahs. If we want to have good Jews in Baltimore, our only hope lies in the Parochial School [Yeshivah]. There is much to write about Jewish education but the time does not permit me to do so at present.

I knew nothing of your great misfortune in the loss of your mother-in-law. HaMakom yenachem eschem besoch she'ar aveilei Tzion viYerushalayim…

Happy to hear that the Adath is continuing to work diligently for hachzakas Torah u'shemiras Shabbos. Shemiras Shabbos is the basis of Judaism. Chazal say that "Kol hamechallel Shabbos ke'ilu oveid avodah zarah." I would like to write a bit lengthily about shemiras Shabbos but I cannot spare the time.

[Mendel, Manuel] Poliakoff is learning with hasmadah. [Aharon] Paperman is now in Kovno. He is receiving semichah there. After Purim he's traveling home. He's a big lamdan. I received a card from him today. He has semichah from one of the greatest rabbis in Lithuania. One of them is a Torah authority of great world renown, Rav Yosef Zusmanowitz, the Yerushalmi. When he comes back home

Chapter 10: The Torah Approach ☐ 151

he will be one of the greatest lamdanim in Baltimore. Baltimore can be proud of him indeed.

[Yehudah] Davis and [Avigdor] Miller are both married as you most probably know. They are not in Telz. They study in Slabodka. I haven't seen them for over two years. But from what I hear they are getting along quite nicely.

Well, a bit about myself. I'm getting along very well in learning be'ezras Hashem. I'm also studying Eruvin now. It is, as you say, a very difficult Gemara. It is one of the Gemaras of "**an"i**" — **E**ruvin, **N**iddah, **Y**evamos. These three are regarded as the most difficult of the whole Shas.

 I will sign off with a d'var aggadah in Yiddish [translated]:
"Hane'ehavim v'hane'imim be'chayeihem uve'mosam lo nifradu."
I explained the pasuk as follows:

What is the test if one's love for another is a true love? One that completely encompasses the entire person, rather than just one part. If the love is such that death cannot separate (the parties), then one sees that the friendship is a bond of two souls and not of two bodies. That is the true love and friendship and not in one letter does a friendship matter, but rather "etched in" the soul!

Extend my heartiest regards to all the members of your family.

ה׳ יברך את כולכם בכל טוב סלה,

מרדכי

It is critical for us to remember that the harsh words he writes are not about people; Rav Gifter loved all Jews. Rather, his sometimes harsh critique was directed at what he believed was an attack on the honor of the Al-mighty.

RAV GIFTER ONCE COMMENTED:

One Type of Jew

It is the fundamental affirmation of the Jew of Torah and emunah that there is not such a monstrosity as one tree of Judaism with three branches, or one bird with three wings. Any understanding of Judaism contrary to Torah is not a branch or a wing within Judaism. It is not Judaism!

Rav Gifter would openly question the term Orthodox. "If one keeps the Torah, then he is a Torah Jew! I'm not sure what other type of Jew there can be."

Reb Mutty Schneider was a young married fellow in the kollel in Cleveland, in the early 1980's, who suffered from an illness that would eventually take his life. He had a very close relationship with Rav Gifter. Throughout his illness, he turned to the rosh hayeshivah for guidance, encouragement, and *chizuk*. During one of his treatments, an insensitive and unapologetic individual commented, "Oh, you are a religious Jew? What intolerant people!"

The callous line stung Mutty, but he did not have the strength to fight someone who obviously harbored such ill will for religious Jews. By the time he got home, he was feeling a little better; he decided to tell his rebbi what happened.

Rav Gifter's response was brilliant. Immediately, he said, "Intolerant about ideas, not about people. Unlike [those] Jews who are intolerant of people and not of ideas."[1]

This sharp response reveals the intelligence and insightfulness of Rav Gifter. It also epitomizes Rav Gifter himself:

Intolerant about ideas, not about people.

---

1. Rabbi Reuvein Gerson.

Chapter 11
The Supremacy of Torah

RAV GIFTER SERVED AS THE *SANDAK* FOR RABBI ZELIG Pliskin's son, Yechiel Michel, at his *bris* in 1977, which was held in Aish HaTorah, in Jerusalem. He began his speech with the sentence: "For all the ills of society there is one cure: Torah." As Rabbi Pliskin said, these words made a big impact on the Aish students who heard him speak.

A YOUNG MAN ENTERED HIGH SCHOOL IN TELZ INTENT ON attending university upon graduating. He made his position quite clear,

University Attendance and Earning a Living

and no one could talk him into spending even another year or two in the yeshivah. During his last year in the yeshivah, he asked the rosh hayeshivah to help him choose a more relevant subject matter. He wanted to know why yeshivos concentrate on studying irrelevant topics. If the Talmud is rich with Torah topics that pertain to our daily life, why not study them instead?

To this the rosh hayeshivah replied, "You are laboring under a mistaken notion of the purpose of Torah study. You think that we study

Torah in order to amass information that will enable us to conduct our daily lives. Torah study is much greater and all encompassing. When you devote all your energy to understanding the holy words of the Rashba, you begin to develop and absorb within yourself the thought process of the Rashba. This produces a wondrous effect, for you begin viewing all things in creation through the perspective of the Rashba. It makes no difference if the matter under study is directly relevant or not. Toiling in Torah transforms a person and blesses him with the ability to see all things in the light of truth."

True to his word, the boy continued on to university. Shortly thereafter, though, he left university and returned to the yeshivah. The rosh hayeshivah asked him, "What happened to your resolve? What changed your mind?"

"It's like this, Rebbi," he said. "I was enrolled in a philosophy course. One day, I arrived late. The room was pitch black. In the corner of the room, I saw the professor sitting cross-legged on his desk surrounded by incense and burning candles, and his manner of dress was totally in consonance with his bizarre surroundings. I was then able to see the world clearly through the perspective of the Rashba!"

On the other hand, there were a select few whom Rav Gifter *did* counsel to complete their university studies, but his views on the dangers of college were clear and uncompromising:

Even one who refrains from the study of "treife" philosophy and elects to study mathematics must be aware that a college is an "ohel hameis" [tent housing a dead body]. *When one extends a solitary finger into an "ohel hameis," his entire body is rendered impure!*

One time, a kollel fellow knocked on the door of Rav Gifter's apartment to discuss an important matter with the rosh hayeshivah. By the look on the *talmid*'s face, it was obvious that he was completely broken. When Rav Gifter asked what was bothering him, the young married fellow broke down crying. He told Rav Gifter that he was planning to leave yeshivah to take some computer courses and was afraid that his decision would disappoint Rav Gifter. He was terribly ashamed.

But the rosh hayeshivah lifted him up. He reassured him that he was doing the right thing. He explained to him the responsibility of supporting his family. He told him how proud he was of him that he was going to be making an honest living.

By the time he walked out, the young man's face was glowing. With a few words of encouragement, Rav Gifter had completely transformed his *talmid*'s outlook.

Yes, Rav Gifter's mind was in the clouds, but his feet were always grounded. Thus, he "got" American boys. This was the uniqueness of Rav Gifter. Despite his soul's lofty status, he was always able to relate to his students in a down-to-earth manner. [1]

Only Toras Moshe

WHEN QUESTIONED ON THE RELATIVE PROS AND CONS OF studying within the framework of an institution that elevates secular studies to the level of Torah studies versus studying in a yeshivah during the daytime while attending a secular night school (with all its challenges and disadvantages), he responded that the latter would be preferable over the former. One would at least be assured that the Torah one learns would be "*Toras Moshe Rabbeinu*." Torah study that is not *Toras Moshe*, he felt, does not provide a safeguard even when one is ensconced in an all-Jewish environment.

In an essay that was adapted from a *shiur daas* (*Nishmas HaTorah*), he says:

Someone who studies Torah as if it were another discipline makes of it an ordinary subject, and when it is so relegated it becomes a potion of death, the poison of the human spirit.

The Torah as Our Guide

ONE *TALMID* RECALLED THE WORDS OF HIS REBBI ABOUT HOW THE Torah guides us in every aspect of our lives:

The Torah determines life and death. A pregnant cow is ritually slaughtered and the calf exits the womb post-slaughter. The cow is running and jumping. Is it alive? No. The Torah says that the cow has been slaughtered and explains that an animal sometimes exhibits movement after slaughter. While the cow is still moving, if a limb is severed, most of the world would consider that limb "ever min hachai" [a limb removed from a live animal]. For the Jew, however, there is a separate reality. For him, the limb was severed after death.

The Torah determines how we see the world. The passages in Shir HaShirim extol the beauty of a woman's hair... up until her marriage.

---
1. Rav Chaim Nussbaum.

Once it becomes forbidden to be displayed in public, the same hair is transformed. The Torah deems such exposure utterly disgusting (to anyone other than her husband)...

The Spiritual and the Material

IN AN EPIC TALK TITLED "THE DUAL NATURE OF MAN," RAV GIFTER calls upon us to contemplate whether the *beis midrash* is a cloistered enclave or the life force of the cosmos. This magnificent speech, which was transcribed and printed in the Jewish Observer in 1966, weighed the role of the body (*guf*) versus the soul (*neshamah*).

Obviously, the *guf* needs the *neshamah* and vice versa. But we must ask ourselves, Which one is carrying the other? Rav Gifter defined the two:

Guf is the assertion of one's self. And the human personality finds need to assert itself in matters of personality. This is NOT neshamah, for neshamah is the denial of self in the presence of the Supreme Being.

Guf feels itself as a whole entity. Neshamah recognizes itself as a fragment of the Creator. From neshamah there stems humility, the feeling of human inadequacy which urges, which drives man to the recognition that the only true I is Anochi Hashem Elokecha, I am the Lord your G-d — the commandment of faith.

This eye-opening revelation teaches us that the root of our *neshamah* is humility — complete and total self-nullification (*hisbatlus*) — and this typifies the personality of Rav Gifter.

Even though he possessed such a strong, powerful, and dynamic personality, his self-nullification spoke to the power of his soul and its nullification to His Creator.

In keeping with this theme, Rav Gifter writes poetically:

Guf lives within the present fleeting moment, temporal in nature. Neshamah is eternal, part of an endless past and an endless future.

And, as always, the theme and emphasis return to Torah study.

The study of Torah and the life of mitzvah invest the Jew with the sublimation of neshamah: the mundane and the secular blessed with the spark of Divinity.

The human in his very being is an incomplete entity, part of the whole of Hashem. Torah, the revelation to man of G-d's will, is therefore of necessity given to man in incomplete form, only as a part, as a portion of His Divine wisdom. The greatest act of communion with G-d, therefore, is incomplete man driven to achieve completeness, something which he can find only in the one true and complete entity, the Supreme Being.

Later in this fundamental essay, Rav Gifter writes that it is our very incompleteness that gives us our strength:

This incompleteness of neshamah, which experiences the joy of fullness only in G-d, is the source of strength for Klal Yisrael. Every individual is merely a portion of the whole, and therefore, one Jew is integrally associated with his fellow Jew. **Complete** *entities can be disassociated from one another.* **Incomplete** *entities find themselves in unity with each other, and through their unity [they are united] with the one G-d of Whom their neshamos have been hewn. This is the bedrock of Jewish communal responsibility unique to Klal Yisrael, enunciated in the maxim, "Kol Yisrael areivim zeh la'zeh — All of Israel is responsible one to the other."*

With this theme in place, Rav Gifter gives encouragement to those who are facing difficulties and challenges in their lives.

In realizing that the wholesomeness of a full life is achieved only in G-dly communion, something which is never completed in our mundane life, the Jew develops an attitude toward life which gives him the courage and fortitude to overcome trial and travail ...

Rav Gifter was not one who needed or cared for physical needs (*gashmiyus*). Although he appreciated the simple necessities such as the occasional new frock (*kapota*), and he always carried himself in a very dignified and neat manner, he was not fond of people spending on luxuries.

On one occasion, Rav Gifter attended a wedding, a simple affair. When asked to speak, Rav Gifter used this opportunity to bring home a powerful message that would eventually become the standard regarding spending excessively on weddings, saying tongue in cheek, "Is this a wedding?! Where is the smorgasbord with countless dishes? Where are the fancy flowers and ice sculptures?"

He had used the backdrop of a simple affair to punctuate the importance of not wasting money on frivolous and unimportant items.

The same was true regarding his eating habits. He made it easy for others to cook for him or serve him.

On occasion, the rosh hayeshivah would eat in the yeshivah with the *bachurim* on Friday nights. One time, his waiter asked if the rosh hayeshivah would like to have a top or a bottom piece of the chicken.

In his signature style, Rav Gifter responded, "*Vos iz der chiluk?* [What's the difference?] Tops! Bottoms! *Tzu mir dos iz nit kein nafka mina.* [To me there's no difference.] Chicken is chicken…"[2]

Rav Gifter was satisfied with the barest minimum. As we continue through this essay, we can clearly see why Rav Gifter was conscious of the polar opposites of *guf* and *neshamah*, and he lamented the drives of the *guf* that cause us to ignore the yearnings of our *neshamah*.

Man defaces the glory [of G-d], and degrades His Honor, by attempting to deny the bit of G-d with which he has been invested. However, he becomes thereby pathetic, torn asunder by the never-ceasing drives of the eternal within him which yearns for completeness. Therein lies the tragedy of modern man. Neshamah seeks completion and fulfillment and man feeds the burning desires with more guf. Modern man is disillusioned. With all his success, with all his achievements, even with the conquest of outer space and the drive to dominate the moon and the planets, he lacks peace and knows not why.

Rav Gifter knew and felt quite deeply that we are in exile (*galus*), and we cannot allow ourselves to be trapped in the lure of luxury.

He had moved into the dormitory after he came back from Telz-Stone in order to experience the exile. In fact, he would sign letters written from his home, "*Poh* [Here], *Galus* — Wickliffe [the Cleveland suburb that houses the yeshivah]."[3]

Even his apartment was as plain as the other rooms in the dormitory. One well-meaning *talmid* decided that when Rav Gifter was away, he would carpet the rebbi's rooms. When Rav Gifter returned from *bein hazmanim*, he was upset about the carpeting, feeling that it was installed to feed his *guf*, not his *neshamah*.

One *talmid* observed, "Although Rav Gifter's home was very simple in its décor, whenever anyone entered the dwelling, he felt a sense of royalty. The home was always immaculate, with everything in its place."

---

2. Rabbi Mordechai Kravitz.
3. Rabbi Eli Yelen.

Chapter 12
A Man of Principle

RAV GIFTER WAS NOT INTIMIDATED BY PEOPLE OF POWER and influence.

Once, a number of government officials came to the yeshivah to investigate the visas of several *bachurim* who had come from other countries. When they arrived, Rav Gifter had just begun giving a *shiur*. The officials instructed one of the *bachurim* to let Rav Gifter know that they were waiting to speak with him.

Not Afraid of Any Man

But Rav Gifter was not going to stop for anything short of a dire emergency. "Tell them I will speak to them when I am finished," he told the boy. The officials were clearly unhappy. After about 15 minutes, they sent another messenger to see when Rav Gifter would be available. Once again, the *bachur* came out with the message, "You'll have to wait until I finish my class."

After an hour and a half of constant badgering, Rav Gifter emerged from the room and immediately let the officials know what he thought

With Rav Dessler

of their attempted intrusion. "Where are we living?" he asked them. "Is this Communist Russia or Nazi Germany? I am a professor giving a lecture to my students. How dare you prance in here and demand to speak to me in middle of my lecture?"

Humbled and ashamed, the officials apologized that they had disturbed the rabbi's lecture and accommodated his requests to help his students.

Such was the clarity of Rav Gifter. When he was fulfilling the will of Hashem, no one would stop him from fulfilling this mission.

Rav Gifter was intimately involved with the affairs of the Hebrew Academy of Cleveland. The Academy was led by its renowned principal, Rav Nachum Velvel Dessler, who had known Rav Gifter since they were *bachurim* in Telz. The Telzer roshei hayeshivah cofounded the Academy in 1943, and the Vaad HaChinuch was under the chairmanship of the rosh hayeshivah. For many years, Rav Gifter served as a member and later as chairman (*yosheiv rosh*) of the Vaad HaChinuch. He would come every year to test the students of the Academy.

The Telzer roshei hayeshivah understood that education (*chinuch*) was the cornerstone of Jewish existence, even at the elementary level. Therefore, they always kept abreast of important school matters.

Once, the Federation, which was extremely generous to the school due to the influence of Mr. Irving Stone, attempted to exert influence

At a Hebrew Academy dinner with Rav Dessler. Rabbi Amos Bunim speaking

over the school curriculum. The vast majority of the Federation board were not Torah-observant Jews, and the changes they wanted to implement were contrary to the mission of the school.

It is not easy to turn down a request from a sponsor. This was a delicate situation that had to be handled with "kid gloves." Rav Gifter attended the meeting, along with the board of directors of the Hebrew Academy, the Vaad HaChinuch, and the prestigious and influential members of the Federation. After the Federation leaders expressed their views, the rosh hayeshivah spoke. His remarks were brief.

He said, "You know what we want, and we know what you want. Don't give us a penny, and don't you dare ask us how we are going to survive. We are not changing one thing about our education!"

Those in the room held their breath.

There was a pause of disbelief in the room.

Suddenly, the head of the Federation spoke up. He, too, had only a few words to say.

"Rabbi, that language we understand. This matter is closed for discussion."[1]

The Federation never mentioned another word about the subject.

---

1. Rav Nachum Velvel Dessler.

The Cook

A WIDOW WAS HIRED BY THE YESHIVAH TO SERVE AS THE COOK. Some of the *bachurim* felt that she was not sufficiently observant. They approached Rav Gifter and asked that she be removed, since they were worried that she would compromise the kashrus of the yeshivah's kitchen.

They barely got the words out of their mouths when Rav Gifter threw them out of his office! Unsatisfied, they approached the other roshei hayeshivah, hoping that their concerns would be addressed. The others listened to the concern of these boys and came to Rav Gifter to discuss the matter with him. Rav Gifter said he would handle the kashrus aspect of the issue, but, he added, "I'm not sacrificing my share in the World to Come to remove a widow from her livelihood."

The matter was never discussed again.

The Right Balance

HE ONCE QUIPPED TO A *TALMID*, "MIR DARF ZEIN FRUM, NIT *farfrumt*. [We have to be religious, not fanatically religious.]"[2] His passion for Torah was combined with his incredible common sense and practical view on the world. He learned this outlook (*hashkafah*) in Telz. He saw it in his father-in-law, Rav Zalman Bloch, in Rav Avraham Yitzchak Bloch, and he saw it in Rav Elya Meir Bloch.

As Rav Gifter once commented:

There was a specific characteristic that permeated the work and efforts of the rosh hayeshivah [Rav Elya Meir]. Upon his arrival in this country by way of Siberia and Japan, he met with a group of friends at the Broadway Central Hotel in New York. I recall the gist of what he said ... The rosh hayeshivah was motivated by a deep sense of Divine mission, sent to America by a message couched in the persecution and destruction of European Jewry. It was this sense of mission which brought forth all his endless efforts in the building of Torah in this country ... It was this sense of mission that motivated him in all his indefatigable work for Klal Yisrael ... This sense of mission grows from a realization that life has a purpose and a deep awareness of that purpose ... When one's life is permeated with this consciousness, then all is part of the plan of Divine Providence: All situations and conditions in life represent the various forms in which one must perform the mission for which he has been sent into This World. This was the nature of the rosh hayeshivah's [Rav Elya Meir's] life.

---

2. Rav Chaim Nussbaum.

ALTHOUGH AMERICA WAS VIEWED BY MANY AS A SPIRITUALLY desolate wasteland, it was Lithuania of all places where the spirit of heresy was very strong.[3] Consequently, Rav Gifter began his crusade against those who threaten the authenticity of Torah and the honor of the Al-mighty while he was still a *bachur* in Telz, Lithuania.

Zealousness in Lithuania

As a young man, Mordechai Gifter did not hesitate to express himself when he felt things needed to be said. Once, he spoke in a shul in Shadav on a Shabbos when the *haftarah* of "*Shimu d'var Hashem*" was read. This *haftarah* speaks of the truth of the authentic prophets and the falsehood of others. The young, fearless Mordechai Gifter spoke about how disgraceful it is that there are those who call the poet Bialik a prophet. "Not only is Bialik not a true prophet, he is not even to be considered one of the prophets of the Baal [an idol]!"

The editor of the newspaper Dos Vort, an organ of the Zionist Socialist party, was in the audience and became upset at the chutzpah of this young man. He immediately challenged Mordechai and told him to sit down. But Mordechai would not back off; if anything, the challenge strengthened his resolve. Soon the entire *beis midrash* was in an uproar.

Finally, Mordechai called out, "*Shadaver baalebatim! Ir hut nit dem gehareggen kavod fahr a Torah(dikke) vort. Ir zeit aleh pusta amaratzim! Un deriber, gei ich arop* — People of Shadav! You have no respect for the words of Torah! You are all ignoramuses! And this is why I am stepping down!"

The congregants tried to calm him down, and to convince him to continue his speech, but he refused.

When Mordechai returned to the yeshivah, he worried about what his rebbeim would say when they heard the story. He was pleasantly surprised to find that they had only compliments for him. They assured him that his actions constituted a *Kiddush Hashem* and agreed that more young men like him were needed. Mordechai would not disappoint them.

When he was younger, however, there was one instance where he did go a bit overboard. He tried to disperse crowds that had gathered for anti-Torah meetings in Lithuania by rushing into the room and yelling,

---

3. *Mili DeIgros* II 12:6.

"FIRE!" Needless to say, there was a stampede toward the door. Luckily, no one got hurt.

This time the roshei hayeshivah decided that Mordechai had gone too far. They told him to learn in another *beis midrash* (instead of the yeshivah) for three days as a punishment for his outburst.[4] His rebbi explained to him that his action did not constitute zealotry (*kana'us*); it was wildness and recklessness (*pera'us*). He learned from his mistake and it would never happen again.

The roshei hayeshivah knew that they had a future Torah giant in Mordechai, but they also knew that he had to be taught when and where to use his uniquely powerful and dynamic mode of speech. Endangering people's lives and creating chaos to make a point was not the way of Telz.[5]

No Personal Agenda

A PENETRATING THOUGHT FROM RAV GIFTER EMPHASIZES THIS very important point. The Torah describes Pinchas as a *kanai,* a zealot. People tend to translate the word *kanai* to mean extremist. The Rambam [*Hilchos Dei'os* 1:4] explains that Judaism does not appreciate extremism. The middle path, the *"derech emtza'i,"* is preferred.

On the other hand, Rav Gifter quotes the *Sifrei (Parashas Pinchas)*, which defines *kana'us* as the act of sublimating one's entire self to the wants of G-d, to the extent that the person is willing to give up his life, if necessary. This in no way contradicts the words of the Rambam; one who is on the level to be a zealot when necessary has achieved the middle path in life, as well.

That is why not all of us can assume the mantle of zealotry. Torah-sanctioned zealotry is reserved for those people who are willing to make the ultimate sacrifice for G-d. When a personal agenda does not exist — when all that exists is G-d's honor — then and only then are the person's actions in the category of Torah-sanctioned zealotry. If a person's motives are not completely pure, if there is an admixture of other motives in the act of zealotry, then it ceases to be an approved act of *kana'us*.

It was with this definition of *kana'us* that Rav Gifter acted.

---

4. Rebbetzin Gifter.
5. At a later time, Mordechai was called up to the Torah. Although those who were called up before him had pledged money to a Zionist organization, he pledged money to Telz Yeshivah. When the Telzer Rav heard about this, he praised Mordechai for his actions.

Armed with this selflessness, he guided American Jewry, leading them, and when necessary, admonishing them for veering from the path. Unafraid, he knew what was right, and expressed this truth.

RAV GIFTER SEIZED EVERY OPPORTUNITY TO REACH OUT WITH encouragement to those who brought Torah to Klal Yisrael, no matter who they were. When *Megillas Koheles,* the third *sefer* of Tanach that was elucidated by ArtScroll, was published, he wanted to meet its authors. He invited Rabbi Meir Zlotowitz and Rabbi Nosson Scherman to lunch at his home. The reception, the graciousness, the wisdom, and the guid-

In Pursuit of Kvod HaTorah

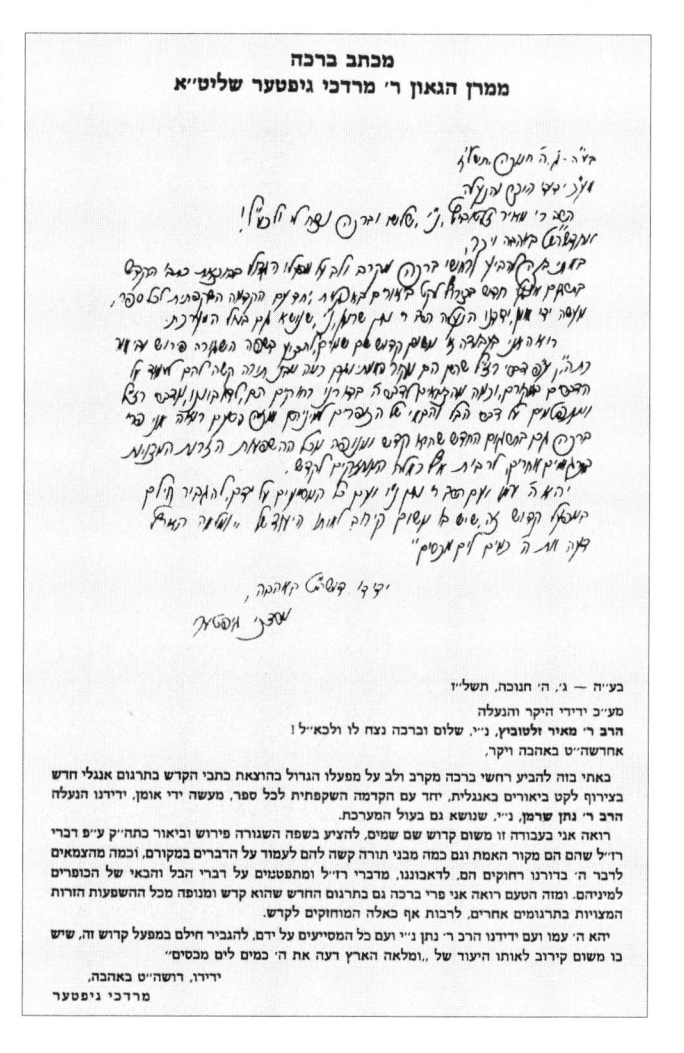

A letter expressing his esteem and conveying his blessings for the ArtScroll Series recently launched

ance were overwhelming to two young men who could not fathom why they deserved it.

Not only did he offer his encouragement, he even offered to read and comment on manuscripts in progress, which he did for several years. He was truly the father of the ArtScroll series, foreseeing its potential when few others did, and providing indispensable support in its fledgling years. At every major new initiative, his guidance and public involvement were essential elements of its success, especially regarding the ArtScroll/Schottenstein Edition of the Talmud, the impact of which he foresaw from the start.[6]

When ArtScroll/Mesorah Publications first undertook the daunting task of translating the Gemara in the Schottenstein Edition of the Talmud, there were those who felt it could not be done properly. As such, there was a disagreement among the giants of Torah Jewry as to whether the project should continue. Rav Elazar Shach, rosh yeshivah of Ponovezh in Israel, was one of those who shared these concerns. But Rav Gifter, who valued Rav Shach's opinion as *the* authority of the Torah world, campaigned avidly for Rav Shach to allow the project to continue.

He felt that he knew American Jewry and understood the importance of such an undertaking. He knew the benefits and understood the concerns. Nevertheless, he felt quite strongly that the project should proceed.

Rav Shach acquiesced; he trusted Rav Gifter's insights and perspectives.

He had no personal agenda, just the pursuit of *kvod haTorah*.

The Next Generation

WHEN YOSEF WAS 9 OR 10 YEARS OLD, HIS FATHER BROUGHT HIM and his younger brother to an Agudah convention. On Thursday evening, Yosef's father noticed Rav Gifter walking in the lobby. Yosef's father explained to his sons who Rav Gifter was, and said that he would bring them over to greet Rav Gifter and ask for a *berachah*.

Yosef's father greeted the rosh hayeshivah and introduced Yosef as his eldest son. On cue, Yosef extended his hand and said, "*Shalom aleichem*, Rebbi," as his father had instructed. Rav Gifter then asked Yosef his name in Yiddish. Although at the time Yosef's understanding

---

6. Rabbi Nosson Scherman.

of Yiddish was limited, he knew enough to understand what the rosh hayeshivah had asked, and proudly answered, "Yosef Aharon."

Rav Gifter continued to speak in Yiddish as he asked Yosef which yeshivah he attended. When Yosef was able to answer that question, as well, he felt proud of himself that he was able to converse with a great man in Yiddish.

But then the problems started.

Rav Gifter asked Yosef something else in Yiddish. This time, since Yosef's understanding of the language was limited, he finally conceded, "I don't speak Yiddish well." He hoped that would be the end of the matter. But it wasn't.

He can still hear it today. Ringing in his ears. In a loud, powerful tone, Rav Gifter indignantly demanded, "And why NOT?!"

Yosef was shocked at the intensity of Rav Gifter's question, but blurted out a response, "Because I'm an American!"

Yosef can still envision Rav Gifter's penetrating gaze, as his voice grew even louder, and a few notes shriller. "I'M ALSO AN AMERICAN AND I WENT TO PUBLIC SCHOOL, AND I SPEAK YIDDISH!"

At this point, Yosef tried to hide behind his father, looking beyond the trees in the lobby for the nearest exit. Rav Gifter pressed his hand a bit firmer (he had not let go) and said to Yosef, "I want you to promise me that when you get older you will speak in Yiddish."

Yosef gave Rav Gifter his word, and Rav Gifter gave him a beautiful *berachah* — in Yiddish — that his father later translated for him.

Because of this incident, Yosef made sure to learn Yiddish well.

―•―

Many years later, during Pesach vacation, 1998, Yosef attended a wedding in Cleveland. Since the wedding took place on a Thursday night, most of the *bachurim* who came for the wedding stayed for Shabbos.

On Friday, along with one of the rosh hayeshivah's grandsons with whom they were acquainted, four of the boys went to visit Rav Gifter. When he first caught sight of Rav Gifter sitting in a wheelchair in the small hallway, a mere shell of his former self, Yosef was so shaken that he stood rooted to the spot and his eyes filled with tears. Although he had known that Rav Gifter was not well, it did not hit home until that moment. The last time Yosef had seen him, in the early 1990's in Camp Agudah, Rav Gifter was still relatively fine.

One of the *bachurim* initiated a conversation with the rebbetzin. Glancing at the rosh hayeshivah, Yosef felt that it was not proper not to include the rosh hayeshivah in the conversation, so he recounted the entire incident — mostly in Yiddish — that had taken place with Rav Gifter at the Agudah convention when he was about 9 or 10. He concluded by telling Rav Gifter, "*Yetz ken ich gut farshtein un redden Yiddish.* [Now I can understand and speak Yiddish well.]"

Rav Gifter's eyes seemed happy.

At this point, Yosef decided to ask the rosh hayeshivah a question. He was not sure whether he should go back to Eretz Yisrael for a fourth year or go to Beth Medrash Govoha in Lakewood, New Jersey, as he was turning 22 shortly.

As soon as Yosef said, "Should I go back to Eretz Yisrael for another *zman?*" Rav Gifter vigorously nodded his head. His eyes were closed and appeared to be tearing a bit. The rebbetzin assured Yosef that the rosh hayeshivah felt that he should return to Israel.

From the hallway where they had originally stood conversing, the boys were then ushered into the dining room, where the rebbetzin gave each young man a can of Pepsi and a cup, and told each one to make a *berachah* so that the rosh hayeshivah could answer *amen*.

Then each *bachur* said a *d'var Torah* on the *parashah*. Yosef can vividly recall how content and even relaxed Rav Gifter seemed as he turned his head to listen to every *d'var Torah*. When one fellow mixed up what he was saying, though, Yosef noticed Rav Gifter's eyes become big and round.

As they left, they each wished Rav Gifter a good Shabbos and a complete recovery. That was the last time Yosef saw Rav Gifter.

But today, every time Yosef hears a *shmuess* or *shiur* in Yiddish, he thinks back to the charge Rav Gifter gave him and the lesson that remained with him to this day.

Rav Gifter — a man of principle, whose goals were:
Kvod Shamayim.
Kvod haTorah.
With no excuses, and no apologies.
Just the truth.

Chapter 13
The Life and Outlook of a Ben Torah

ONE OF THE UNIQUE ELEMENTS OF TELZ YESHIVAH WAS the *shiur daas*, an especially profound *mussar shmuess*. Rav Gifter used to refer to his own *shiurei daas* as "talks" (*sichos*), using a much more humble description. His humility notwithstanding, these talks were incredibly deep, not in any way a typical talk.

RAV GIFTER DEVELOPED HIS APPRECIATION FOR *MUSSAR* FROM A memorable incident that occurred when he was a young man in Lithuania. When Rav Avraham Yitzchak Bloch delivered a *mussar* talk, he would speak in a venue outside of the yeshivah, so that the entire community could attend. One yeshivah *bachur*, however, was missing: Mordechai Gifter. Instead of attending the *shmuess*, Mordechai used that time to learn in the *beis midrash*. He rationalized that hearing a *mussar shmuess* outside the *beis midrash* was not necessary. Not only that, he surmised that such a talk may even be considered wasting learning time (*bittul Torah*).

Learning Mussar

In the old *beis midrash* on the Telz campus. Aron Stein is standing at the *shtender*, Reb Chaim Tzvi Katz is seated

Rav Avraham Yitzchak noticed that Mordechai was not present at the *shmuess* and asked him why. Mordechai explained that he believed that the *mussar shmuessen* not delivered *in* the yeshivah were not directed at the students of the yeshivah, and he could use his time better by learning.

The rav listened to Mordechai and then quoted the Gemara in *Shabbos* that states that Rav Chisda was willing to give a great reward to one who shared with him a Torah thought of Rav that he, Rav Chisda, had never heard before. When Rava bar Me'chasia did this, Rav Chisda was very pleased. Then Rava bar Me'chasia asked Rav Chisda, "Is Rav's Torah very dear to you?"

When Rav Chisda answered in the affirmative, Rava bar Me'chasia exclaimed, *"Milsa a'levishaihu yakira* — Silk is dear to those who wear it and know its value." He meant to say that one who is used to hearing the Torah of Rav appreciates its great worth.

Chapter 13: The Life and Outlook of a Ben Torah □ 171

Rav Avraham Yitzchak looked at his *talmid* and shared with him an important lesson. "One day, may you merit wearing [the] silk [of *mussar*; then you will appreciate its value]."

Mordechai felt those words penetrate him like a dagger. "Without raising his voice," he explained later, "my rebbi admonished me in a way that changed my whole perspective on learning *mussar*." And from that day on, he never missed the rav's *shmuess*.

In fact, after that day, whenever Rav Avraham Yitzchak said a *mussar shmuess*, Mordechai would don his Shabbos clothing (perhaps trying to sense the precious silk that *mussar* is, for it shapes and molds men).

A Ben Torah

IN THE LATE 1980'S, ELI FISHMAN WAS A COUNSELOR IN A RUSSIAN boys' summer camp that was located in a former KGB training camp in Zalinigrad, a small Russian village. The facilities were crude; the water was nearly undrinkable.

As such, the camp purchased bottled water for the use of the campers. But with the heat as it was, the bottled water was quickly consumed. One day, a boy suddenly appeared with a case of cold Pepsi bottles. The boys were ecstatic, grabbing the drinks and guzzling them to quench their thirst.

However, Eli did not immediately drink; instead, he ran into the building, and reappeared a few minutes later with a cup. Intrigued, his friends asked him what all this was about. "Let me explain," he said. "One time, when I was 9 years old, I had just finished playing basketball on the Telz Yeshivah campus, and was sweating terribly. I was quenching my thirst from a can of soda in my hand as I walked back into the yeshivah. Then I saw Rav Gifter. He came over to me with a warm smile and told me something I would always remember. 'I consider you a *ben Torah*. And it is not befitting a *ben Torah* to drink from a can.' He asked me right then and there to make a commitment that I would always drink from a cup."

Eli held out his bottle. In his other hand, he held his cup. He smiled and poured his soda into his cup. Nothing was going to stop him from keeping the promise he had made to the rosh hayeshivah. In that small moment of interaction with Rav Gifter, Eli had learned an important lesson about what it means to be a *ben Torah*.

Mentchlichkeit

MENTCHLICHKEIT WAS SO IMPORTANT TO RAV GIFTER. IF ONE'S learning did not make him a better person, then what was the learning for? He would often cite the *pasuk*, *"Ve'chazakta ve'hayisa le'ish* — Be strong and become a man" (*Melachim I* 2:2), which was David's dying message to his son and successor, Shlomo.

The rosh hayeshivah would say, "It doesn't say, *'Ve'chazakta ve'hayisa le'gaon'* [Be strong and become a genius], or *'Ve'chazakta ve'hayisa le'lamdan'* [analytical learner]. Or *'Ve'chazakta ve'hayisa le'philosof '* [philosopher]. It says, *'Ve'chazakta ve'hayisa le'ish.'*

"*Mir darf zein ah mentch* — One has to be a *mentch*!"

A Monumental Lecture

IN A PRECEDENT-SETTING AND WARMLY RECEIVED INITIATIVE, CASE Western Reserve University in Cleveland, Ohio invited the rosh hayeshivah to lecture on "Talmudic Jurisprudence and How It Relates to Society." This monumental lecture was published in *Law in a Troubled World*.

Michael Hirsch, who learned in Telz during this time, recalled, "The rav [Rav Gifter] asked me to join him when he was invited to lecture at Case Western Reserve Law School on Talmudic Jurisprudence. It was awe inspiring to hear his erudition as he lectured in English (with a vocabulary equal to that of a William Buckley, *le'havdil*, who also used words that most people need a dictionary for)."[1]

The Law Journal of Western Reserve University 1957, which includes Rav Gifter's monumental lecture on Talmudic Jurisprudence

LAW IN A TROUBLED WORLD

TALMUDIC JURISPRUDENCE
Mordecai Gifter

ROMAN LAW AND ROMAN CITIZENSHIP
Francis Bliss

THE NAPOLEONIC CODE
Melvin Kranzberg

THE ANGLO-AMERICAN COMMON LAW
Oliver Schroeder, Jr.

LAW IN THE FUTURE
Robert N. Wilkin

THE PRESS OF WESTERN RESERVE UNIVERSITY
CLEVELAND 6   OHIO

1. After his lecture, Rav Gifter was offered a position as a professor in Western Reserve University. Rav Gifter responded, "I don't have the time."

In this talk, Rav Gifter posits:

Where order exists in society, humankind can develop to the fullest extent its capacities for progress under freedom and liberty. A society governed by the law is therefore given a guarantee against anarchy, against chaos and disintegration …

Talmudic Jurisprudence is unique in that the very purpose of the law itself is the development of man's moral and ethical personality.

At the end of his dynamic presentation, Rav Gifter concluded:

I think we have made some points, though of necessity quite superficial, that if digested and taken to heart will be found to have great bearing upon the problems besetting us in these troubled times. Freedom and liberty under law rather than violence under tyranny; this is the great problem of our day. The further the advance of science in developing nuclear energy and in conquering outer space, the greater is the poignancy of this problem. The law, Divine in essence, was given to all the people to lead and guide them to the heights of human nobility and dignity; therein lie our strength and security as free men.

THE FOLLOWING LETTER HIGHLIGHTS THE IMPACT RAV GIFTER'S exemplary behavior had on non-Jews.

Kiddush Hashem *Many years ago, around the late 70's or early 80's, my husband and I were visiting from Israel. We were traveling with our little ones in the Cleveland-Pennsylvania area. One night, we ended up in a small motel in Conneaut, Ohio — a modest, no-frills place that just happened to be on the road on which we were traveling.*

Lo and behold, whom did we meet outside as we were checking in? Rav and Rebbetzin Gifter. (She was, by the way, one of my first teachers in YABI, Yeshivath Adath B'nai Israel.) Naturally, we were thrilled to see them; they were happy, too, to see a young, religious family whom they knew. We spoke for a while, and they told us that they had come to that motel a number of years earlier, and ever since then, they came back every summer for a few days to relax. I remember saying to myself, "That's what I want to look like with my husband, some day, when we reach that age. They don't need frills. They don't need a five star-hotel. All they need is each other."

Then, while we were checking in, the proprietor asked, "You know that rabbi?" When we replied in the affirmative, he told us how much he liked "the rabbi and his wife," what special people they were, and how happy he was that they came back to his motel.

> Many years later, while I was in Cleveland at my mother's bedside in Hillcrest Hospital, I spent some time with a Catholic nurse who had taken care of my father three years earlier, when he was in the hospital. She was a very religious woman, a paragon of kindness in the purest sense of the word.
>
> She asked me if I knew the Gifters, as she had attended to Rav Gifter when he was in the ICU in Hillcrest. She had spent time with them and had gotten to know them well. She told me how much she respected Rav and Rebbetzin Gifter and how much she enjoyed spending time with them. I told her it was a great zechus (and I explained what "zechus" means) for her to have had the chance to take care of Rav Gifter. She said, "I could tell that. I could see that they are very special people." [2]

One time, a non-Jew was standing and conversing with Rabbi Moshe Sherer. They were working together on the AARTS program. After Rav Gifter walked into the room, the non-Jew commented, "I felt as though someone from the Bible walked in."

In an article published in Coalition in March 1988, Reb Chaim Dovid Zwiebel, who was then the director of communal affairs for Agudath Israel of America, wrote the following "letter" to a victim of euthanasia:

Dear Debbie,
> I did not know you in your lifetime. I learned about you only a few weeks ago, when the Journal of the American Medical Association (JAMA) published an article written by your murderer.

Rabbi Zwiebel details the dosage of morphine that was administered, and the opinions of the various segments of society on the issue.

But then he mentions a medical symposium that was sponsored by Agudath Israel of America and explains the Torah perspective on these issues. And he discusses the high point of the symposium:

> Suddenly, all activity stopped. Total silence fell over the entire room. As if by pre-arranged signal, every one of the doctors stood up from their seats. For, at that moment, the venerable member of the Moetzes Gedolei HaTorah, Telzer Rosh HaYeshivah Rabbi Mordechai Gifter, had entered the room.

---

2. Mrs. Toby Klein Greenwald.

A Letter To Debbie
BY CHAIM DOVID ZWIEBEL

(COALITION ADAR - NISAN 5748/MARCH 1988)

Dear Debbie:

I did not know you in your lifetime. I learned about you only a few weeks ago, when the Journal of the American Medical Association (JAMA) published an article written by your murderer.

Reading that article, I learned that when your killer met you, you were in great pain: a 20 year old woman lying in a hospital bed, suffering from terminal cancer, body emaciated, hooked up to an I-V machine, receiving nasal oxygen. I learned that the man who took your life (actually, it may have been a woman; JAMA acceded to the murderer's request that his or her name be withheld from publication) was a hospital resident who had never seen you before that fateful night.

I learned that when the resident came to your hospital bed, you said all of five words: "Let's get this over with." I learned that your killer decided that since he could not give you your health, he would give you your rest. I learned that he injected you with a lethal dosage of morphine, and that four minutes later when you died, the older woman who had been your companion in the hospital room stood erect and seemed relieved.

It would be presumptuous of me, and disrespectful, were I to ask you whether you really wanted this resident to take your life. I can only hope and pray that the *Ribono Shel Olam* will never place me in a position where I will experience the type of pain and suffering you obviously felt — or the type of *nisayon* you obviously faced.

But I wonder about your murderer. Did you sense that he felt remorseful when he took your life? Nervous? Humble? Heroic? Did the resident say anything to you as he administered the fatal injection? Did he tell you that in a recent survey of California doctors conducted by the Los Angeles-based Hemlock Society, a self-styled "right to die" organization, 79 of the 588 doctors who responded to the survey admitted that they had practiced euthanasia at least once, and 29 more than three times?

Did your killer mention that in the Netherlands it is legal for a physician to kill a patient who requests that his suffering be put to an end? Or that the voters in California will soon have an opportunity to adopt "The Humane and Dignified Death Act," which would legalize active euthanasia in cases similar to yours?

Did he tell you that in a 1986 Roper Poll of some 2,000 Americans, 62% of those surveyed agreed that "when a person has a painful and distressing terminal disease, doctors should be allowed by law to end the patient's life if there is no hope of recovery and the patient requests it"? Or that only 27% felt that the law should not permit euthanasia under those circumstances?

I am ashamed to tell you that American Jews responding to the Roper Poll sent an even more overwhelming message of support for "mercy killing": 71% supported

---
79 of 588 doctors admitted they had practiced euthanasia
---

euthanasia, while only 18% opposed it. One would have thought that the horrible lessons of recent history would be fresher in the collective memory of the Jewish people.

I would like to think, though, that the pollsters missed at least one segment of the Jewish community, those whose adherence to Torah gives them literally a different perspective on life.

Debbie, I want to tell you about a day-long symposium I recently attended in New York. It was sponsored by the Conference of Branch Rabbonim of Agudath Israel, and focused on the theme "The Medical Profession Today: A Torah Perspective." Nearly 250 doctors and other health care providers from all across the country came to hear some of our generation's leading rabbinic scholars and thinkers expound on a number of burning issues of contemporary medical concern as viewed through the prism of Torah values. The presentations were thought-provoking and inspiring.

But perhaps the high moment of the symposium came when the speaking stopped. It was during lunch. The main course had just been served. The chairman of the lunch program began his remarks. Doctors continued eating; chairs continued rustling; forks and knives continued clanking.

Suddenly, all activity stopped. Total silence fell over the entire room. As if by pre-arranged signal, every one of the doctors stood up from their seats. For, at that moment, the venerable member of the Moetzes Gedolei HaTorah, Telshe Rosh HaYeshiva Rabbi Mordechai Gifter *shlita*, had entered the room.

The hush was palpable. For a full 30 seconds, as the Rosh HaYeshiva made his way to his seat, not a sound could be heard. Only when the Rosh HaYeshiva took his place at the dais, and the luncheon chairman continued his remarks, was the spell broken.

I do not know who your killer is. But of one thing I am virtually certain: he was not in the audience on that day. He did not experience the awesome power of *kvod haTorah* displayed by nearly 250 health care professionals during that luncheon event.

The doctors who stood up that day were not merely standing for a man they admired. They were standing out of respect for a person who represented for them what human life's meaning can be, a meaning that is connected with the definition even of lives like yours and mine. And they were standing up for the principles of Torah that teach us how to respect this meaning.

The resident who snuffed out your *tzelem Elokim* did so in the name of "human dignity." The doctors who stood with such reverence before a senior Rosh HaYeshiva displayed a different understanding of human dignity. Which of these two competing views will mankind ultimately embrace?

May you rest in peace. And may your murder bring us all to our senses.

Respectfully,
Chaim Dovid Zwiebel

Chaim Dovid Zwiebel is Director of Government Affairs for Agudath Israel of America

The letter from Chaim Dovid Zwiebel published in Coalition

The hush was palpable. For a full 30 seconds, as the rosh hayeshivah made his way to his seat, not a sound could be heard. Only when the rosh hayeshivah took his place on the dais, and the luncheon chairman continued his remarks, was the spell broken.

I do not know who your killer is. But of one thing I am certain: he was not in the audience on that day. He did not experience the awesome power of kvod haTorah displayed by nearly 250 health-care professionals during that luncheon event.

The doctors who stood up that day were not merely standing for a man they admired. They were standing out of respect for a person who represented for them what a human life's meaning can be, a meaning that is connected with the definition even of lives like yours and mine. And they were standing up for the principles of Torah that teach us how to respect this meaning ...

Chapter 14
Deveikus BaHashem — Cleaving to Hashem

IN *HILCHOS GERUSHIN* (2:20), THE RAMBAM DISCUSSES WHAT IS done when a husband refuses to give his wife a *get* (divorce). The Rambam states, "*Makkin oso ad sheyomar rotzeh ani* — We beat him until he says, '*Rotzeh ani* — I want [to give the divorce].'" This unusual halachic ruling dictates the use of force; we use all necessary methods to coerce the husband into giving his wife a divorce. When the Rambam authorizes forcing the husband to say, "*rotzeh ani,*" it is because we are trying to get to the part of him that really wants to do the right thing.

Rav Gifter, in a *shiur daas* (*Shirah*), saw in this halachah the unbreakable bond between man and his Creator. Of course, there are times when the evil inclination threatens that relationship. Nevertheless, our will remains pure. In fact, that is man's challenge: to remove the separations so that he can reconnect with the Al-mighty.

This is the *deveikus* we are meant to feel with our Father in Heaven.

Rav Gifter viewed all that happened to him and all that happened around him as a means to drawing closer to Hashem.

Our Sages tell us that Chizkiyahu hid the *Book of Remedies*. How could Chizkiyahu have done that. It's *pikuach nefesh*. There are so many people who have suffered and died from illness, and the *Book of Remedies* could have helped them all. So why did he hide it?

Rav Gifter answered that if we would have a book with all the remedies, then we would have no reason to cry out to Hashem. And that would constitute a greater danger, one that affects Klal Yisrael's soul: "It would be a life without the Master of the World. And that is not life!"

IT SAYS IN *TEHILLIM* (16:8), "*SHIVISI HASHEM LE'NEGDI SAMID* — I have set Hashem before me always." Rav Gifter explained that every

The Will of Hashem

action, speech, and thought of an individual should be guided and dictated by the will of Hashem.

The Torah, which is itself the very will of Hashem, should be so internalized that one should not even have to think about or decide what to do. In every situation, the will of Hashem that is planted in his heart and mind will instinctively guide him to do what is expected of him.[1] As he would say, "The one and only thing that counts is that you are a Torah Jew and live as dictated by *Toras Hashem*."

When Rav Gifter was already walking with a walker, and people would ask him how he was doing, he would respond, "*Vi der Ribbono Shel Olam vill* — As the Al-mighty wills it."

Just as a violin or piano, when finely tuned, plays the most pleasing melodies, the rosh hayeshivah was the instrument through which the Torah, the word of Hashem, constantly played. The music that came forth from this holy instrument was filled with love of Torah, fear of Heaven, and faith.

Rav Gifter held his uncles, Rav Elya Meir Bloch and Rav Mottel Katz, in the highest regard. Rav Mottel had been married to the daughter of Rav Yosef Leib Bloch. Although she died tragically at a very young age, Rav Mottel was always known to the Bloch family as "*der* Uncle," even after he remarried. In fact, in *Pirkei Emunah*, Rav Gifter, who was very careful about the excessive use of titles, referred to Rav Mottel as a "*sar ve'gadol*" (prince and great sage).

---

1. Rav Chaim Nussbaum.

(l to r) Rav Chaim Stein, Rav Mottel Katz, and Rav Gifter. In the background is Rav Elazar Levi, the rosh mechinah

Rav Mottel was well known and respected throughout the Torah world for his wisdom and sage advice. One time, Rav Gifter came to Rav Mottel's house in Cleveland to discuss a specific matter with "*der* Uncle." While waiting for him, Rav Gifter sat in the kitchen and observed Rebbetzin Katz as she swept the kitchen floor. Rav Gifter commented that she should continue sweeping. When the rebbetzin seemed puzzled by his remark, Rav Gifter explained, "You were sweeping toward the middle of the room. During the times of the Spanish Inquisition, one of the ways the Jews maintained their identity was by sweeping the dirt away from the doorposts, which house the *mezuzos*. So I said that you should continue sweeping, because you were doing it the correct way, the way a Jewish woman should sweep."

Many years later, "the *Tante*" still fondly recalls this important lesson.[2] Indeed, it is another example of how Rav Gifter was always aware that Hashem was in front of him, and thus every action of his was guided by the Torah.

RAV GIFTER USED TO SAY THAT ONE OF THE GREAT KINDNESSES OF Hashem is that He causes time to change, so that we always have an opportunity to improve.[3] Imagine what our lives would be like if there were no such thing as a "next day." If we were to start the day on the wrong foot, we would never have an opportunity to restart!

Opportunity for Growth

---

2. Rebbetzen Esther Katz, Rav Mottel Katz's wife.
3. Based on *Pirkei Moed* I: *Moadim U'Zmanim*.

Hashem created our world so that we always have a chance to start a new day, with new vigor and new goals. If we had a bad week, then there is always Shabbos to help us recover. Bad month? There is always Rosh Chodesh to start fresh.[4] The year was difficult? Rosh Hashanah is here for us to pray for a sweet new year. The various holidays reenergize us with their varied rays of mitzvos, lessons, and holiness.

For the Love of Mitzvos

THE LONG-AWAITED DAY OF *BIRCAS HACHAMAH*, A ONCE-IN-28-year event, finally arrived and the weather was unpredictable; everybody at Telz was concerned whether or not they would be able to see the sun, a prerequisite for reciting the blessing. After davening, all the men walked out of the yeshivah's *beis midrash*, still wearing their *tallis* and *tefillin*. Everyone stood watching Rav Gifter. The sky was cloudy and the sun was nowhere to be found. Rav Gifter looked to the heavens, pointed his right arm upward, and screamed, *"Nu!"* Within moments, the clouds dissipated and the sun shone brightly. In a loud, unified voice, the congregation recited the blessing, "Who makes the work of Creation."

———◆———

Whenever Rav Gifter pledged money for charity, he was careful to immediately follow through on that pledge. In fact, even on Chol HaMoed, Rav Gifter would write out a check, stressing that he did not want to possibly transgress the commandment of *"Lo se'acher le'shalmo — You shall not be late in paying it"* (*Devarim* 23:22).

Due to the tremors that Rav Gifter experienced later in his life, he was unable to put on his *tefillin*. Rebbetzin Gifter, in her devoted fashion, would drive her husband to the yeshivah so she could help him put on his *tefillin*. Although at times it took over half an hour to wind up his *tefillin* (after taking them off), Rav Gifter insisted on doing that action himself. He had such love for mitzvos that he did not want to give up the opportunity.[5]

Learning From Our Sages

RAV GIFTER LOVED TO SHARE STORIES OF OUR SAGES WITH HIS students, to illustrate how these lofty men conducted their lives, and how they constantly worked on drawing closer to Hashem. For example, he once related that the Telzer Rav, Rav Yosef Leib Bloch, would not

---

4. *Pirkei Torah, Bo* 12:2.
5. Rabbi Eliezer Feuer.

move during *Shemoneh Esrei*. He would stand like a soldier, silently mouthing the words of the prayer. The butcher of the town, Reb Itzele Ratzkofsky (also known as "*Der Roite,* the Redhead"), entered the back of the *beis midrash* and heard the rav sigh as he prayed. He exclaimed, "*Oy, er redt doch mit Ehm alein*! [Oy, he's actually conversing with Hashem.]" (Rav Gifter noted that it was due to Reb Itzele's uncomplicated, simple nature that he noticed something that had eluded the *talmidim* of the yeshivah.)

Rav Gifter also related that the Ponovezher Rav, Rav Yosef Shlomo Kahaneman, was taking a walk in Eretz Yisrael during a Shemittah year. At one point, he bent down, kissed a tree, and lovingly said, "*Gut Shabbos* to you!" The connection between Shabbos and Shemittah was not an abstract concept to this Torah giant; it was as real as going over to a fellow Jew in shul and wishing him *"gut Shabbos."*

In the same vein, fighting the *yetzer hara* was not an abstract concept to Rav Gifter. Rav Gifter was walking in Telz-Stone with a few married *talmidim* who had come to visit him. When they passed the yeshivah, they noticed a distraught-looking young man. Rav Gifter seemed to know what was bothering the *bachur,* who still stood a few feet away from him. Suddenly, Rav Gifter began to make boxing motions with his hands. "Punch him!" he exclaimed. "Punch out that *yetzer hara*!" And as he spoke, he continued swinging his arms. Many years later, those students who were walking with Rav Gifter can still picture their rebbi "punching out the *yetzer hara*," and the powerful lesson it taught them: We must fight the *yetzer hara* with all of our strength.

Guarding One's Eyes

ON JUNE 2, 1978, THERE WAS A HORRIFIC BUS EXPLOSION IN Jerusalem, and a number of innocent people were killed or injured. Among the victims were two young men, Aharon Yosef Sheinfeld and Aharon Meir Auerbach. Rav Gifter, who was living in Telz-Stone at the time, went to be *menachem avel* the broken families. After he returned to the yeshivah, he was completely overwhelmed with emotion. He said, "I went to strengthen these families, but they strengthened me."

One of the young men who was killed was extremely careful to guard his eyes. When he would travel on buses, he would remove his glasses to prevent him from seeing any type of immodesty. Rav Gifter cried with deep emotion over the loss of such a saintly person.[6]

In another episode, which dovetails beautifully, we get a glimpse of Rav Gifter's piety. One time, Rav Gifter traveled to one of the most beautiful parts of Eretz Yisrael, called Rosh Hanikra, a picturesque area located in the northwest corner of the land. Rosh Hanikra is famous for its mountains that meet the Mediterranean Sea, with many areas where the water enters caves within the mountains. Rav Gifter traveled with a *talmid* named Moshe Turk for many hours, and they eagerly anticipated viewing the breathtaking scenery and reveling in Hashem's Creation. However, when he stepped out of the car, Rav Gifter noticed that the other tourists were not dressed properly. Immediately, he got back into the car, and they went home.

True, he loved the wonders of Hashem's Creation. But even more than that, he loved the Creator.[7]

Wonders of Creation

PERHAPS BECAUSE OF HIS UNUSUAL APPRECIATION OF THE wonders of Creation and his admiration for them, one of his favorite discourses followed this theme:

The mishnah in *Avos* (3:9) states, "*Hamehaleich baderech veshoneh, umafsik mimishnaso ve'omer mah na'eh ilan zeh, umah na'eh nir zeh, maaleh alav hakasuv ke'ilu mischayeiv be'nafsho* — One who walks on the road while reviewing [a Torah lesson] but interrupts his review and exclaims, 'How beautiful is this tree! How beautiful is this plowed field!' — Scripture considers it as if he bears guilt for his soul."

Rav Gifter wondered about this mishnah. The beauty of the world was given to us as a gift to behold and enjoy. We even make a blessing during the month of Nissan on the exquisite flowering fruit trees. We thank Hashem "*shelo chisar be'olamo davar u'vara vo beriyos tovos ve'ilanos tovim le'hanos bahem bnei adam* — for nothing is lacking in His universe, and He created in it good creatures and good trees, to cause

---

6. Reb Eli Oelbaum.
7. Reb Eli Oelbaum.

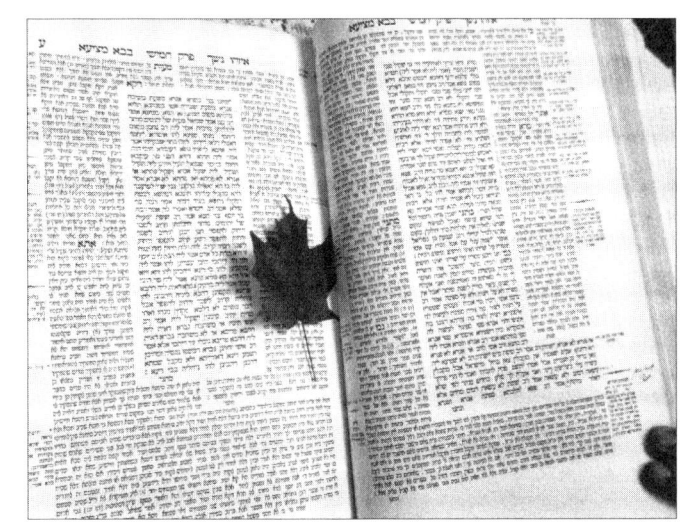

Rav Gifter would frequently pick up a leaf and place it inside his Gemara.

mankind pleasure with them." What could be wrong with admiring the beauty of the physical world?

Rav Gifter explained that if one has to be *mafsik mimishnaso*, to leave the vista of Torah, in order to appreciate the beauty of the world that Hashem has gifted us, *"ke'ilu mischayeiv be'nafsho,"* then he is guilty, for he is missing the whole point of his learning.

Through proper Torah learning, we come to appreciate all facets of creation.

Rav Gifter saw Hashem's utter greatness in the wonders of Creation. He often told the story of one of the first *baalei teshuvah* in our times, Nathan Birnbaum, who looked into many "isms" before discovering the truth of Torah. (He actually coined the term "Zionism" while influencing Theodore Herzl to turn his efforts toward founding a Jewish homeland in Eretz Yisrael rather than in Uganda.) His moment of truth arrived when, upon finding himself on an ocean liner, he gazed at his surroundings and exclaimed, "The wonders of the heavens above, the vast expanse of sea, *es muz doch zein a G-t!* [There must be a G-d!]"

The prophet Yeshayah (40:26) proclaims, "*Se'u marom eineichem ur'u Mi vara eileh* — Raise your eyes on high and see Who created these." As the rosh hayeshivah explained, modern science focuses on "the what" while ignoring "the Who." The verse in *Yeshayah* stresses "the Who." This is the foolishness of astronomers, who see so much yet understand so little.

Chapter 14: Deveikus BaHashem — Cleaving to Hashem ☐ 183

Rav Gifter once shared a science article with his students. Based on certain evidence, a scientist was convinced of the existence of a yet-undiscovered constellation. The discovery of this constellation would wreak havoc upon decades of scientific calculations (and on the theories based upon the calculations) regarding the interworkings of the heavenly bodies. The scientist spent six months with the Mount Palomar telescope in California, at the time the most powerful telescope in the world, gazing up at the heavens. As the article explained, eventually he found his constellation. When the rosh hayeshivah read this, he was overjoyed. Now, he thought, scientists will finally understand that they should not be so haughty, and they will recognize the Greater Force at work. Alas, he was sorely disappointed. In a follow-up article on the subject, six new theories filled with heresy popped up, one of them advanced by a Jesuit priest!

His son said, "Every year, we would go on a trip to a beautiful orchard a half-hour away from our home. The orchard had 100 species of apples, among other fruits. As we would walk through, my father would drink in the beauty of our surroundings. He would mention the miracles of nature in his *shmuessen,* as well. Years later, when he was no longer well, my mother would take him for drives to see the wonders of nature."

Gratitude to Hashem

WHEN RAV YITZCHAK HUTNER, ROSH YESHIVAH OF YESHIVA Rabbi Chaim Berlin, was on a plane that was hijacked in 1970, Jews all over the world recited *Tehillim* for the release of Rav Hutner and his fellow passengers. One Friday, word spread that the hostages were going to be freed. Rav Gifter instructed Boruch Hirschfeld to gather 10 *bachurim* so they could recite *Tehillim* for Rav Hutner. When 10 boys had assembled, one of them asked Rav Gifter why they were reciting *Tehillim* if Rav Hutner was going to be set free.

Rav Gifter answered, "Until now, we were saying *Tehillim* so that Hashem should bring a salvation; now, we must recite *Tehillim* to thank the Al-mighty for bringing the salvation."

Rav Gifter elaborated that many have a tendency to say *Tehillim* only during a tragedy. Once the tragedy has passed, they cease their *Tehillim*. In truth, we must also recite *Tehillim* after the salvation comes, out of gratitude to Hashem.

Rav Gifter chose to recite Chapter 30 in *Tehillim* ("*Mizmor shir cha-*

nukas habayis"). Boruch was struck by the many verses in this particular chapter that referred to a person in captivity.

Years later, Boruch, now known as Rabbi Hirschfield, became the rav of Ahavas Yisroel, "Berger's shul," in Cleveland. He was so moved by that particular incident that when he wanted to inspire the members of his congregation to really appreciate the daily miracles that the residents of Eretz Yisrael are living with, he chose to institute the recital of that chapter every Motza'ei Shabbos as a chapter of gratitude.

And when he recites the words, Rabbi Hirschfeld still thinks about the emotion-laden psalms of gratitude that Rav Gifter recited over 40 years before.

RAV GIFTER LOVED TO EXPRESS HIS *DEVEIKUS BAHASHEM* IN song. A number of songs were particularly meaningful to him. He would sing the famous tunes of Rav Levi Yitzchak of Berditchev, especially one that calls out to the Presence of Hashem and laments how far away It is from us. He was also very fond of the *Kaddish* of Rav Levi Yitzchak.

Expressing His Closeness

TO RAV GIFTER, MASHIACH'S ARRIVAL WAS A REAL AND TRUE possibility. One time, when he was sitting with some *bachurim*, he suddenly burst out crying, "*Oy, ich hub geshpeert in meine beiner az Mashiach geit kummen heintige yahr* — Oy, I felt in my bones that Mashiach would come this year."[8]

Awaiting Mashiach

He would often say, "Mashiach is right around the corner; we just have to open the door for him!"

---

8. Rabbi Eli Yelen.

Chapter 15
The Torah's Viewpoint

RAV GIFTER WAS ALWAYS ABLE TO LOOK AT EVENTS IN history and current world affairs through his Torah lenses, and to give us the proper outlook and approach.

OF THE MANY EVENTS HE SPOKE ABOUT, NONE WAS EXPRESSED IN a more heartfelt way than his speeches on the Holocaust (*Churban Europa*). At a Torah Umesorah teachers' conference, Rav Gifter spoke about the Torah's directive for teaching about the Holocaust.

The Holocaust

This speech took place nearly 40 years after the Holocaust. He lamented:

We are late in dealing with the Holocaust. Our Sages explain the corrosive effect time has on the experiential quality of an occurrence. Midrash Eichah [2:5] comments on the verse "Bila Hashem ve'lo chamal — Hashem destroyed without mercy" [Eichah 2:2].[1] Our Sages say that many years

---
1. Based on *Pirkei Emunah: Bila Hashem ve'lo Chamal.*

after the destruction of the Beis HaMikdash, Rabbi Yochanan was able to explain this verse in 60 different ways, whereas Rabbi Yehudah HaNasi, who lived one generation before him, was able to explain it in 24 different ways. The Sages tell us that Rabbi Yehudah HaNasi was one generation closer to the destruction of the Beis HaMikdash, even though he did not live in the time of the actual Destruction. Thus, he and his colleagues felt the intensity of the lamentation and the sorrow that much more deeply. After explaining the verse in 24 different ways, Rabbi Yehudah would break down and weep; he did not have the emotional stamina to continue. Rabbi Yochanan and his companions, who lived one generation later, were that much more removed from the destruction of the Beis HaMikdash and could therefore deal with it differently.

We are only one generation removed from the destruction of European Jewry, and yet the memory fades from our minds. Our emotional bankruptcy permits us to speak about it casually in a detached manner and even forget about it ...

And yet, merely listening to Rav Gifter pronounce the names of the concentration camps when he spoke at the *siyum HaShas* in 1975 made those in attendance shudder with horror. One could hear his powerful voice crack with emotion.

He would often repeat a thought that he had heard from his rebbi, Rav Avraham Yitzchak Bloch, that describes Tishah B'Av. Yirmiyahu HaNavi refers to the day as a *moed*, which is normally translated as a festival. Could it be that Tishah B'Av is a *moed*?

His rebbi explained that the term *moed* stems from the root word *vaad*, which means appointment.

It is a time of appointment of Hashem with the world, when His greatness is manifested. The greatness can be seen from two aspects: the redemption from Egypt or through destruction so great that it could have been administered only by Divine plan. Two separate moments in the history of Klal Yisrael: Geulah and Churban, Redemption and Destruction. From the time the Second Temple was destroyed through the present, and on until the Final Redemption, we are caught in one long moment of "going out of Jerusalem — be'tzeisi mi'Yerushalayim," punctuated by harrowing experiences such as the Holocaust.

It bothers some that the Jewish nation seems to have suffered more than others. But Rav Gifter teaches us:

History is not impressed by insignificant individuals; only great Klal Yisrael occupies a central position in history as the chosen nation. An orphan grows up wild and uncared for ... he has no one to reprimand him and chastise him for his errant ways. Not so the child with parents. The Holocaust should become a source of inspiration and encouragement for us. We are assured that we have a Father in Heaven Who cares for us and is concerned enough with our spiritual status to demonstrate His disfavor.

In a riveting talk that he gave on Erev Tishah B'Av in Camp Agudah in the early 80's, he spoke about this theme and the idea that Al-mighty joins Judgment and Mercy (*Din* and *Rachamim*):

Our Sages say that the Holy One wanted to create the world with the Attribute of Judgment, but He saw that mankind would not be able to live through it. Therefore, He joined it with the Attribute of Mercy. Not that Judgment is not Mercy, but if it is given in its full power, we human beings do not understand and do not see, "Dos iz der Tatte Alein! — It's Daddy Himself! Er shmaist unz! — We think that He is just beating us!"

We don't realize that He is hitting us for a constructive purpose; we think he is merely being cruel, so to speak.

The rosh hayeshivah once said that if one sees someone kissing a child in the street, this is not a sure sign that he is kissing his own child. But if one sees someone striking a child in the street, then he can be sure that it is a father hitting his son.

By quoting one penetrating sentence, Rav Gifter put it best for those who doubt the Al-mighty's Presence in the Holocaust. "The Nitra Rav [Rav Michoel Ber Weissmandl], in a telegram to the Vaad Hatzalah of the Agudas HaRabbanim during World War II, remarked: 'For those who doubt and ask, there are no answers. For those who do not doubt, there are no questions.'"

Rav Gifter once made an important comment at the end of a talk on how to teach children the proper view of the Holocaust.

There is so much to be researched. And when this is done and collated, it must be taught through the perspective of emunah. Then, out of the destruction, children will emerge fortified, understanding the significance of Tishah B'Av: Moed as an encounter with God ... they will emerge forti-

fied, understanding that the vow, "He will not forsake us," is indeed binding forever.

After all, we are dealing with but a moment in history, and all moments together lead us gradually to that final moment for which we all wait longingly — when Mashiach will come!

Current Events

THE ROSH HAYESHIVAH TAUGHT HIS *TALMIDIM* HOW TO VIEW world affairs and deal with life's challenges, all from the Torah's point of view. One Erev Rosh Hashanah, after the massacre at the Munich Olympics in 1972, Rav Gifter gave a *shmuess* about the event. The *bachurim* were somewhat uninformed about the episode, since they did not pay a great deal of attention to international news. Therefore, when Rav Gifter began to speak, they had no idea what this topic had to do with the upcoming Day of Judgment. By the time he was finished, though, they clearly understood that Hashem orchestrates both world events and our personal lives. They realized that his *shmuess* was not only a primer for Rosh Hashanah, but something that they would remember always.[2]

When Secretariat, a prize racehorse, won the Belmont Stakes, the final leg of the Triple Crown, the world became enamored with the horse and the story grabbed world attention. Rav Gifter gave a memorable talk speaking about the absurdity of the matter and focused his discourse on the difference between real honor and imaginary honor (*kavod ha'medumeh*).

The Yom Kippur War

IN A MEMORABLE ESSAY, WRITTEN SHORTLY AFTER THE YOM Kippur War in 1973 for the Jewish Observer, Rav Gifter describes our relationship with the Al-mighty.

Hashem said through the prophet Yeshayah [62:1], *"Lemaan Zion lo echesheh u'lemaan Yerushalayim lo eshkot* — For the sake of Zion I will not be silent and for Jerusalem's sake I will not be still ..." As Rav Gifter explained:

The Targum's interpretation of this verse casts a brilliant light on the current world situation. Hashem pledges that until Zion and Jerusalem are peaceful and secure, He will allow no rest for the nations of the earth. Thus, the situation of the nations of the world cannot be viewed in a vacuum, separate and apart from the world order.

---

2. Rav Yaakov Reisman.

We are in the habit of scanning the long list of international crises and feeling that the situation of our beleaguered brothers in Eretz Yisrael would matter precious little to anyone except fellow Jews were it not for the ever-present danger of a superpower confrontation. Energy crises, floundering Great Britain, Watergate and its threat to the American political system, French recalcitrance in Europe, Russo-Chinese hostility, the sanguinary "ceasefire" in Vietnam; the list goes on and on. People who put things in "perspective" are well aware that in terms of "the big picture," a few pieces of real estate in Sinai and Golan are of little significance on the larger landscape. So on the one hand, we are grateful that the physical survival of three million Jews in Israel is interwoven in the fabric of American-Russian relations; hence, it is important enough to demand the notice of the White House and the Kremlin. But on the other hand, we tremble in anticipation of possible Jewish sacrifices on the altar of détente and increased petroleum production.

Isaiah tells us we are wrong. Eretz Yisrael is not simply one problem in isolation of myriad world problems; it is a major source of world problems. Hashem has made a pledge that as long as Zion and Jerusalem live in crisis and fear, the world will have no rest.

Japan will falter and suffer loss of face. Great Britain will rock with domestic instability and a trade imbalance that boggles the mind. The United States will be told that it must curb its energy appetite and change its lifestyle. Why? Because the Supreme Being will allow rest and security to no nation as long as His most favored nation is threatened!

It was no coincidence that Vietnam threatened to erupt again shortly after the Yom Kippur War, or that Europe, France, and the United States descended to levels of petty squabbling unmatched since the trade wars of two generations ago; that political upheaval has threatened almost every major power these past months. Hashem will not be silent to others as long as they look with apathy or antipathy upon the tribulations of Zion and Jerusalem.

Aside from the remarkable grasp Rav Gifter had on the political world situation, one can also see the manner in which he viewed the Al-mighty's relationship with us, His children, as He protects us and hovers over us like a mother.

Rav Gifter continued:

When we agonize over Eretz Yisrael, we are contemplating not only the Holy Land, but the entire universe, just as the heart surgeon knows that his area of specialization controls life itself.

Indeed, the stakes are even higher than that. The prophetess Devorah curses those who did not come to the aid of her forces as they battled the hordes of Sisera "because they did not come to the help of the L-rd, to the help of the L-rd against the mighty men" [Shoftim 5:23]. Rashi explains that if someone helps the Jews it is as though he had helped G-d Himself. Our Sages comment on this same verse that whoever attacks the Jewish people wages war against the Creator, as it were; hence, whoever defends Jews defends the Creator [Sifrei, Be'haaloscha].

This then is the true perspective with which we must view not only the Yom Kippur War, but the entire pattern of world history. The Chofetz Chaim said when the Russo-Japanese War broke out, "This war is a message to Jews. We may not know what it is telling us, but there is no doubt that we must learn something from it, because Chazal taught us 'Ein puranus ba'ah le'olam ella bishvil Yisrael — No world catastrophe strikes but for Israel.' By the same token, whenever there is a major catastrophe in India, a bloodbath in Russia, we must always see in it a Divine message to Jews — a call for improvement and repentance. Surely when the cataclysmic events center on Eretz Yisrael itself, we must see in them a Heavenly call.

In the immediate aftermath of the Yom Kippur War, there had been an uncontrollable tendency to sigh with relief, even to applaud a military victory that in many ways dwarfed the triumph of the Six Day War. The superficial reaction was quickly overshaken with grief and a wave of fault-fixing. Over 2,000 lives were taken from a nation which has been taught since its inception that "saving a Jewish life is the equivalent of saving the whole world." The wounded number in the thousands — precious Jewish souls who will never see again, never walk again — whose bodies, sometimes even minds, will never be whole again. Sadat takes his losses with equanimity; he invests freely many thousands more to win the right to hold his head high. Lives may matter precious little to others; but for us, the loss of each ... is a catastrophe.

Citing the aforementioned thought from Rav Avraham Yitzchak Bloch, Rav Gifter writes that Yom Kippur is a *moed* (meeting time), in its own way. Hashem is calling us, making demands upon us. It is for us to decipher its message and act upon it.

Many are quick to blame the nonreligious for our woes. "Their sins caused the tragedy and still they refuse to learn their lesson from G-d's anger at them!" Let us stop looking at others and peer deep into ourselves. Let there be no mistake. The Heavenly call comes not to nonbelievers; it is coming to those of the Am Hashem who know that our mission on earth is embodied in the Torah.

After the Deluge, Hashem showed Noach the rainbow and told him that the rainbow would serve forever as a sign of the Divine covenant that such a flood would never again take place. The Sforno explains that from then on, the rainbow would be a Heavenly sign to the righteous people that their generation has sinned and that it is their duty to teach and chastise their straying generation. He goes on to explain that when the righteous have perceived G-d's signal and done what is expected of them, G-d will take notice of the prayers of the righteous and withdraw His wrath from the human race.

Let us mark the illuminating words of the Sforno: The Heavenly call is to the righteous of the generation, not to the sinners. The sinners cannot hear the call; they look at the rainbow and see but a colorful spectrum. Their spiritual senses are deadened. But the righteous of the generation can hear and see, and they can interpret the Heavenly sign. It is to them that G-d calls and it is for them to respond by praying, coming closer to Torah, and trying to bring others along with them.

Rav Gifter continues to encourage us to rise to the challenge in times of crisis as that is the true test of one's character. Our sense of closeness to Hashem needs to guide our every step.

A mishnah in the tractate Keilim [Chapter 17:13] says: "All items made from fish and other sea life cannot be rendered ritually impure." The Torah ordains that only land animals and fowl are subject to impurity. "There is one exception to this rule; it is the kelev she'beyam, the sea lion." Why is the sea lion different? Because when it is in danger, it flees to dry land, proving that, despite its habitation of the seas, it is basically a land animal.

Rav Tzadok HaKohen of Lublin (introduction to Ohr Zarua) draws an incisive moral lesson from this mishnah. If we want to determine someone's true character, we must observe him in the time of crisis. People may preach loyalty to Torah and absolute belief in Hashem, but even they cannot know how sincere their preachments are until they are challenged by events.

What happens to the truth of a businessman if he perceives truth as costing him dearly? Does he put Torah imperatives above expediency and profit?

What happens to the faith of the observant Jew when a dear one is deathly ill? Does he hang onto his doctor's word or does he know that his Tehillim is more potent than a prescription pad? And where was each of us when our brothers and sisters were in mortal danger, and where are we now when the danger is less obvious, but still present? It is now that we are being tested.

Whatever other lessons the Yom Kippur War may hold, it certainly cries out to us that we are a people in danger and that we must choose our refuge. If we expect to find it by seeing what the political pundits have to say, where the Gallup Polls point, what Dr. Kissinger is saying between the lines, and so on, then we are demonstrating that, when the chips are down, we are as secular and materialistic as those whom we so often decry. If, on the other hand, we turn to the beis midrash and the beis haknesses when we are endangered, then we are showing that we are truly worthy of being called the Nation of Hashem.

Rav Gifter concluded this memorable essay by imploring us to heed the prophetess Devorah's call.

When we look at a faraway war through Torah binoculars, then it truly becomes part of an immediate experience. Every one of us has the responsibility to be at the front in the Torah's terms. Devorah mercilessly castigated those tribes and individuals who did not come to help. Devorah, mother of her people, can find no justification for her wayward children.

But there were others who likewise were not to be found in the infantry. For them, Devorah had only praise, because they joined the battle in their own way, in an enormously significant way. "My heart goes out to the lawgivers of Israel, who offered themselves willingly among the people. Bless the L-rd!" The Targum beautifully illuminates her gratitude to the lawgivers: Devorah said that she was G-d's agent to praise the Torah sages. During the years of alien oppression, they never stopped teaching the Torah, so it is fitting that they should now sit in a place of honor in the study halls expounding the Torah, blessing and thanking G-d. They sacrificed their personal interests to go about the land, teaching and joining to form courts when the law had to be decided [Shoftim 5:9,10].

Her words are directed at our generation as much as her own. When Jews are in danger, the mobilization must be complete, all inclusive. Everyone who can help must help. But ultimately, the forces of evil are attacking G-d Himself when they bare their fangs at Israel.

In a battle against G-d, our most powerful weapons are Torah and mitzvos. The sages who ignored odds, public opinion, and inconvenience to study and spread Torah were also part of the army; and Devorah, who knew the reasons for her miraculous victory, gave her heart to them.

The world will continue to be turbulent as long as Eretz Yisrael is threatened, and Eretz Yisrael will continue to be menaced until every single one of us heeds the call to mobilize in the only meaningful way.

Rav Gifter taught us to heed the calls all around us and come closer to Hashem.

Rav Gifter taught his students *"vi a Yid darf kuken"* — how a Jew must view the world. He showed them that world events are merely instances of the Al-mighty talking to us, delivering messages; those in tune with the Torah outlook can understand these messages and learn from them.

Section 4
Rebbi — Talmid

Chapter 16
A True Melamed

Rav Gifter's Monument

WHILE STILL IN HIS 40'S, RAV GIFTER DICTATED WHAT he wanted inscribed on his monument:
Limeid Torah ve'he'emid talmidim baalei maalah u'madreigah be'Torah ve'yirah.
He taught Torah and raised students of stature and high caliber in Torah and fear of the Al-mighty.
This is how he wanted to be known. There are no great titles listed before his name; it merely says "HaRav." On the other hand, he described his students as *"baalei maalah u'madreigah be'Torah ve'yirah,"* attributing much praise to them.

In his will, he said that he be eulogized only to give inspiration to his students. And he requested that it be said at his funeral that many of his students are great scholars: *"shelo lefi maasai* — [although] not according to my own deeds."

Rav Gitfer's *tzava'ah*, expressing his wishes for how he should be eulogized, asking that his *talmidim* study for the benefit of his *neshamah*, and directing that his *matzeivah* give him no titles

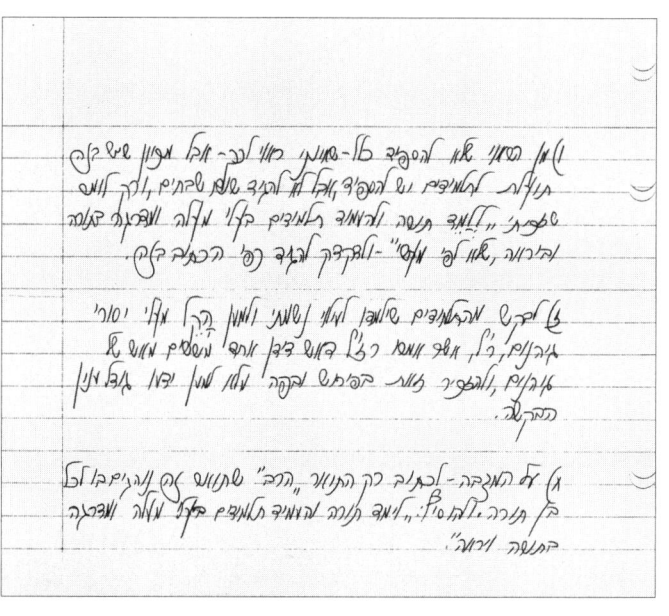

The *matzeivah*, with the inscription respecting his wishes

AT AN AGUDAH CONVENTION, HE WAS ONCE INTRODUCED AS the "*sar haTorah*" (prince of Torah). Rav Gifter spent the first 10 minutes of his speech dispelling the notion that he was worthy of such a title. "*Her uf mit di titelin* — Enough of the titles!"

No Titles, Please

198 □ RAV GIFTER

The Steipler's Opinion

IN 1965, THE NINTH GRADE OF HEBREW ACADEMY OF CLEVELAND went on a class trip to Eretz Yisrael. The trip was led by Rabbi Herschel Baron, the principal of the high school.

Prior to the students leaving Cleveland, Rav Gifter gave them a letter and asked them to hand-deliver it to the Steipler Gaon, with whom Rav Gifter had corresponded for many years.

The boys arrived in Eretz Yisrael and made the trip to Bnei Brak, eager and excited to meet the Steipler. After receiving a blessing from the Steipler, one boy, Aryeh, was chosen to hand over Rav Gifter's letter. When the Steipler looked at the letter, he said to Aryeh, "*Er iz der gadol hador*. [He is the *gadol hador*.]"

Aryeh knew that Rav Gifter was a great rosh hayeshivah, but he was only 50 years old at the time. Yet, the Steipler Gaon felt he was the *gadol hador*![1]

The Steipler would begin his letters with elaborate titles befitting Rav Gifter's stature. But Rav Gifter, in his humility, was uncomfortable with all the acclaim, and he asked the Steipler to abstain from praising him, explaining that the Steipler did not really know him. The Steipler responded, "It is not true that I do not know you, since I have read your comments on the lectures given by the Telzer Rav [Rav Yosef Leib Bloch], and from there I can see your greatness. Still, *retzono shel adam zehu kevodo* — fulfilling the will of a person is honoring him."

"Melamed"

BUT THERE WAS ONE TITLE THAT HE YEARNED FOR, ONE THAT HE was proud of: "*melamed*" (teacher). He wanted only to spend his life teaching Torah.

He preferred the title *melamed* to all others because the Master of the World is described in the *Birchos HaTorah* as "*HaMelamed Torah le'amo Yisrael* — He Who teaches Torah to His nation, Israel. "And if that title is good enough for the Al-mighty," he would say, "it's good enough for me!"

For 55 years, from the time he came to Telz Yeshivah in Cleveland in the mid-40's, at the age of 29, he was the quintessential *melamed*. He taught both the students in his classroom and those he never met, but who had read or heard about his teachings. As an orator, he was truly gifted. Able to captivate audiences of all ages and backgrounds, he kept them spellbound with rich content and powerful messages.

---

1. Rabbi Aryeh Spero.

In my research for this book, many, many people shared with me their "Rav Gifter story." Those who had the good fortune to encounter him rarely forgot the moment: the words, the intensity, the kindness.

He taught by his own example how to be a rebbi: with one key ingredient: care.

HE OFTEN QUOTED THE GEMARA IN *BAVA BASRA* (8B) THAT describes the master *melamed*, Rav Shmuel bar Shilas, the paradigm of

"*Datai Ilavaihu* — My Mind Is on Them" teachers of young children. His rebbi was Rav, the greatest scholar of that generation. One time, Rav was shocked to find his student, Rav Shmuel, in his garden while the yeshivah was in session. Rav asked him why he was not with his students; he wanted to know if he had stopped teaching. Rav Shmuel answered, "Rebbi, I have not been in this garden for 13 years! And even now, *datai ilavaihu* — my mind is on them. I am constantly thinking about my students."

Rav Gifter would use this Gemara to bring out his point. "Over the ages, countless volumes have been written attempting to teach the science of education. Believe me, everything that can be said on this subject can be summed up in the pithy, two-word statement of Rav Shmuel bar Shilas, '*Datai ilavaihu!*' My mind is on them. Any rebbi who sincerely cares about his students and gives them serious thought will be blessed to find the proper approach to influence and educate them."

Rav Gifter's care and concern for his *bachurim* can best be summed up as "*datai ilavaihu*"; he thought about them constantly.

A *bachur* from Australia once confided to Rav Gifter that he had not been home for over five years. His parents missed him very much and wanted him to come home permanently, but the boy did not want to remain in Australia. He expressed his feelings that he would prefer not to go home at all than to go and not come back to Cleveland.

Rav Gifter instructed the boy to compose a letter to his parents stating his feelings and to bring it to him for review. The rosh hayeshivah read the letter and made comments, and even wrote the last few paragraphs himself. The letter was mailed.

With Rabbi Moshe Yaakov Perl

Speaking at the *vort* of Dovid Lipins

Being *mesader kiddushin* at the wedding of Rabbi Getzel and Breiny Fried. Rav Moshe Helfan is standing, center.

A few months later, the *bachur* did leave the yeshivah to return home.

His time in Australia was frustrating for the boy; he truly wanted to spend more time learning before he had to start earning a livelihood. During that year at home, he continually corresponded with Rav Gifter.

One of the letters he received from the rosh hayeshivah left a major impact. Rav Gifter wrote that he missed him and needed him back in Cleveland. If necessary, he was prepared to pay for the ticket! Once the young man's parents read that, they were convinced that their son should return to Telz.

They knew that they had nothing to worry about. He would be loved and cared for by Rav Gifter as if he were his own.

"Datai ilavaihu!"

Rav Gifter felt a tremendous sense of responsibility for his *talmidim* and their families. After he received word about the fatal car crash that killed Rabbi Chaim Tzvi Anemer and two of his children, Rav Gifter insisted on going (together with Reb Chaim Tzvi Katz, a cousin of the deceased) to tell Mrs. Anemer, who lived in Cleveland, the devastating news about the death of her son and his children.[2]

---
2. Mrs. Mashe (Anemer) Katz.

A draft of a letter written by a *bachur* to his parents in Australia, pleading that they allow him to stay in yeshivah. Rav Gifter edited the letter.

Care and Concern

RAV GIFTER ONCE CALLED IN HIS *TALMID*, BORUCH HIRSCHFELD, and asked him how he was learning. He answered that he was learning well. "And how are you eating?" Boruch responded that he liked the food in the yeshivah. Still, Boruch was quite thin, and Rav Gifter was concerned. He smiled at Boruch and said, "I want you to learn like Yaakov and eat like Esav!"

When Rav Gifter left to set up the yeshivah in Telz-Stone, he brought along a group of *bachurim* who he felt would learn well there, and who constituted a cohesive group.

One *talmid*, Nechemia Sutton,* very much wanted to join the group. However, Rav Gifter dissuaded him; although Nechemia was a brilliant boy, he was a bit introverted, and Rav Gifter did not think that he would blend well with the group.

---

*Name has been changed.

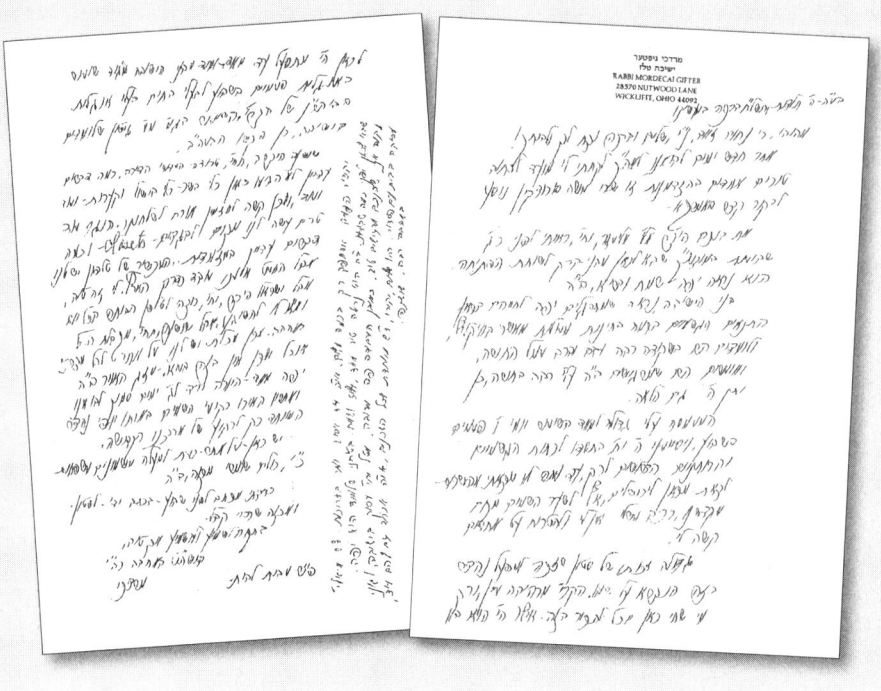

A historical correspondence between Rav Gifter and Rav Nachum Velvel Dessler. Rav Gifter wrote this letter one month after his arrival in Telz-Stone. In it, he describes his schedule, how wonderful life is in Telz-Stone, the beauty of Eretz Yisrael, and the great *zechus* of Irving Stone. The letter also mentions some of the challenges in getting settled, as the *fleishige* dishes had not yet arrived and the closets were not yet in place.

One day, Nechemia appeared at Rav Gifter's door in Telz-Stone. Once again, Rav Gifter repeated that he did not think that Telz-Stone was the best place for him. Instead, he arranged for him to learn in the Chevron Yeshivah in Jerusalem.

That night, Nechemia suffered an appendicitis attack. Since he was alone in the country, he asked that the hospital contact Rav Gifter. Rav Gifter got in touch with Rav Eliezer Sorotzkin and arranged a good doctor for Nechemia. Rav Gifter and the rebbetzin went to visit him in the hospital and assured him that they would take care of him when he was discharged. Sure enough, he recuperated at the Gifters' home for a few weeks.

In the end, he did join the yeshivah in Telz-Stone. Knowing his diligence and drive to learn, Rav Gifter would ask Nechemia from time to time if he had finished learning *Shas*. With his characteristic humility, Nechemia always demurred. When he became engaged, Rav Gifter asked him again, "Tell me the truth. Did you finish *Shas* already?" Although Nechemia was very humble, he eventually admitted to Rav Gifter that he had completed all of *Shas*. Rav Gifter said to him, "Now that you are married to the Torah, you can get married to your *kallah*."

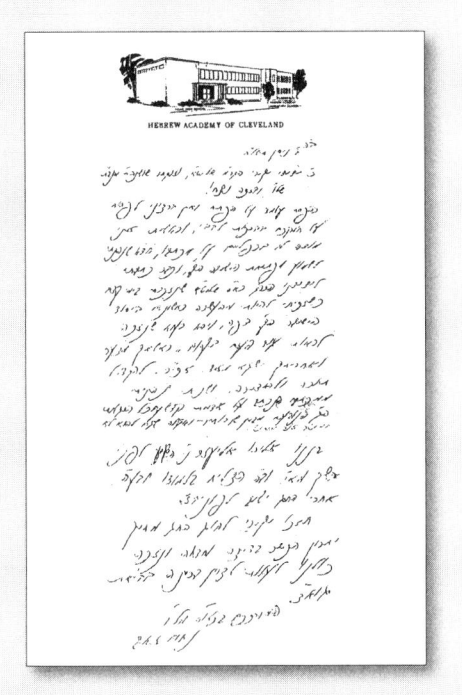

Rav Dessler responds that the enthusiasm is reminiscent of the excitement 40 years earlier, when he was among the first 10 involved in Telz, Cleveland. He concludes with the *berachah*, "*V'hayah reishis'cha mitzar v'acharischa yisgeh me'od* ... Though your beginning will be painful, your end will flourish greatly (*Iyov* 8:7)!"

Once, a *talmid* from a poor family confided that he was worried about his future: about earning enough money to support a family. Although it was time for the afternoon learning session, Rav Gifter sat with the boy for four hours and gave him a practical lesson on effort (*hishtadlus*) and trust (*bitachon*). Rav Gifter told him his own life story, including the difficulties he had in supporting his family. He said, "Without trust in Hashem, I would not even have a loaf of bread on my table."

He told him how he had been offered a position in the yeshivah at a far smaller salary than he was earning as a congregational rabbi in Connecticut. He worried about supporting his family, but he knew that if he was going to teach Torah, he had to trust in Hashem that things would work out.

This unforgettable conversation, which began during daylight hours and ended well after the room had grown dark, changed the *talmid*'s life. It taught him how to have faith, but more importantly, it taught him how a rebbi cares for his student.

Chapter 16: A True Melamed ☐ 205

ONCE, SOME *BACHURIM* ASKED A CLOSE *TALMID* OF RAV GIFTER TO ask him to adapt a warmer approach to his students. When the *talmid* shared the *bachurim*'s concerns, Rav Gifter responded, "I don't know what they want from me. *Bei dem heilige rebbi* [By my holy rebbi], the 'door' was closed. If you wanted to get in, you had to climb through the window. But my 'door' is always open. There is nothing more I can do." Rav Gifter could not and would not be a pal or friend of his *talmidim*. Although they would not have to climb through windows, they would have to walk through the door in order to reach him.

A Different Kind of Warmth

His care and genuine love for his *talmidim* was sensed in a real way. He would not put his arm around you, but if he ever held your arm and explained something to you, the warmth was electric.

HIS LOVE AND CONCERN DID NOT OVERSHADOW THE DEMANDS he made of his students to continuously strive for excellence in their Torah learning. He chastised those who wasted time and praised those who learned with diligence. He would often say, "*Men darf hor'even, matteren, mutchen zich tzu farshtein di d'var Hashem!* — One has to toil, wear himself out, and pressure himself to understand the word of Hashem!"

Strive for Excellence

He drove the boys hard, always challenging them to dig deeper. If someone asked a good question, he was rewarded with a "*gingold!*" — an expression that describes something made of pure gold.

He gave his *bachurim* latitude, yet demanded that they live up to the unspoken expectations he had of them. Through this, he forced them to grow, to act in a responsible manner. This method of pedagogy brought

Gift certificate — a reward from Rav Gifter for excelling in learning out the strength and character of his *talmidim*; this is how he molded them.

As Rav Avrohom Ausband, rosh hayeshivah of Telz in Riverdale, related in his eulogy for Rav Gifter, his *mussar* could cut as sharp as a knife. However, since everyone knew it emanated from love, it penetrated deeply and profoundly into the listener's soul.

At the high-school graduation in Telz, the valedictorian traditionally gave an academic talk, while the salutatorian's speech was more entertaining. One year, the salutatorian began his speech with a few jokes, and the overall content of the speech was lacking in meaning.

Rav Gifter remarked, "I expected more of you." The words cut sharply into the young man's soul. He was devastated that he had disappointed his rebbi, and he was determined to make up for it.

Many years later … he is a *talmid chacham* — and a well-known rav and rebbi.

He wouldn't want to disappoint his rebbi.

At test (*bechinah*) time, the high-school boys were especially nervous, since Rav Gifter would occasionally come to the high-school classes to test the boys. At first, he would sit quietly as the boys answered questions, most of them very direct; he would also pay attention as they would say a Gemara, a Rashi, or a Tosafos.

But Rav Gifter wanted to see more. He wanted to see if the boys could think. He would often ask questions on the topic in the Gemara (*sugya*) that had bothered him. Obviously, for this type of test, there was no way to prepare. And quite often, there were many who would fail to even suggest an answer to Rav Gifter's question.

One boy who did well at this type of grilling was Yossi Marcovich, a *bachur* from Mexico. Rav Gifter asked a deep question and Yossi responded very well. Rav Gifter could hardly control his excitement. He went on and on in his praise for Yossi, praise that would never be forgotten.

At the end of the *zman*, a *bachur* was assigned to speak in learning with Rav Gifter. He was bubbling with excitement to share a great question on a piece of Torah of Rav Chaim Brisker. He was even told by some kollel fellows that Rav Gifter would love the question. But when his turn finally came, before he even had a chance to finish his point, Rav Gifter interrupted, "But maybe there is another way to explain the *p'shat*?" And just like that, the session was over. The *bachur* was very disappointed.

One week later, when he was already home for vacation, a letter arrived in the mail for the *bachur*'s father. It was from Rav Gifter, and it described the excellent impression the young man had made on Rav Gifter at the *bechinah*, and how it was evident that his son had a clear understanding of the Gemara. Rav Gifter wished the parents much *nachas*.

The *bachur* never felt so good.

Following His Teachers' Example

NO DOUBT, RAV GIFTER'S GREATNESS AS A REBBI STEMS FROM THE magnificent relationship he had with his own rebbeim, Rav Moshe Aharon Poleyeff, Rav Zalman Bloch, Rav Avraham Yitzchak Bloch, and Rav Azriel Rabinowitz. No matter how brilliant they were, their minds (*daas*) were constantly *ilavaihu* (on their students). He tasted what it meant to be cared for and loved. He had the privilege to be a *talmid* of some of the "Rav Shmuel bar Shilases" of his own day. And he intended to pass that on to the next generation.

I spoke with one *talmid* who broke down crying upon thinking about his rebbi.

"Write that in your book," he told me. "Tell them that a *talmid* couldn't even speak about his rosh hayeshivah without breaking down." Overcome with emotion, he managed through his tears, "*Oy* … I miss him so much …."

Betzalel awoke in a cold sweat. His face was pale, and he was visibly shaken. His wife was concerned that perhaps he was in shock. When he finally calmed down, he described to her his vivid dream.

Rav Gifter had appeared to him and had involved him in a discussion, in which Rav Gifter had expressed his concern that Betzalel was not learning enough. Betzalel tried to explain to his rebbi that he did not have enough time to learn, but Rav Gifter voiced disappointment. And that is when Betzalel awoke. The image of his rebbi, along with his concern about his spiritual welfare, was still very much a part of his life.

His mind was always on them, and they grew to love him and learn from his ways.

Chapter 17
A Powerful Influence

Rav Gifter tried to encourage *bachurim* to learn as long as possible before leaving the *beis midrash* to earn a living. In those days, many of the boys went to college, and it was very rare for young married men to learn in kollel.

Keeping His Talmidim in the Yeshivah
In response to parents who worried about their children earning a livelihood, Rav Gifter would often say, "We don't make a living; we take a living. Don't worry about your source of revenue; it comes from the Al-mighty. He makes it; we take it."

If a boy from a less-observant background expressed interest in remaining in yeshivah, Rav Gifter would frequently invite the boy's parents for a visit. Just seeing the *beis midrash* and the joy on the faces of the *bachurim* would often convince the parents to allow their son to remain a while longer in this lofty environment. Many times, as their visits would draw to a close, the parents could be heard advising their sons to stay in the yeshivah for "as long as Rabbi Gifter will watch over you."

A story from many years ago illustrates the length to which Rav Gifter would go to help *bachurim* remain in yeshivah. Shimon and Naftali Hirsch, brothers from Chicago, were learning in Telz in 1950. That year, their father, Dr. Marcus Hirsch, passed away. Rav Gifter was not in the yeshivah at the time; he was in Baltimore fund-raising for the yeshivah. As soon as he returned, he learned of Dr. Hirsch's passing and heard that the boys had decided to stay in Chicago after the *shivah* and go to work to help support the family.

As soon as he heard this, Rav Gifter went to the rosh hayeshivah, Rav Elya Meir Bloch, to speak about the tragedy. When Rav Elya Meir noticed that Rav Gifter was crying, he asked Rav Gifter how he had known Dr. Hirsch. Surprisingly, Rav Gifter responded that he had not known him. Rather, he was crying because two of the *bachurim* who had been in the yeshivah had left, since they had to support their family now that their father had passed away. And in his opinion, yes, this was a terrible tragedy. He asked Rav Elya Meir for permission to go to Chicago to try to bring them back.

Rav Elya Meir gave his consent, and Rav Gifter traveled to Chicago at once to see if he could find support for the family so that the boys would be able to return to yeshivah. He met with two men who were active in community affairs, Mr. Isidore Kaplan and Mr. Helberg, along with Mrs. Hirsch. The men promised the widow that they would help her with whatever she needed, and they requested that she allow her sons to return to Telz. The meeting was successful, and the boys returned to their beloved yeshivah.

Over 60 years later, Shimon Hirsch related this story and insists that what Rav Gifter did that day — traveling to Chicago immediately after a tiring trip to Baltimore — changed his life forever.

Aryeh Burnham, whose interest in Judaism was sparked during his time in boot camp, and continued through his service in the Navy, came to Telz in 1973. His father, who was acquainted with Rav Abba Zalka Gewirtz, the executive vice president of Telz, convinced Rabbi Gewirtz to invite Aryeh to Cleveland. When Aryeh arrived in Telz, he did not resemble your typical young man; he was tall, well built, and he had a full beard. (When he first became interested in the Torah, he had read in the Bible that a man must not shave, and he understood it literally.) In Aryeh's words:

I had my interview with Rav Gifter on a Friday morning. He asked me a few questions about my background, and I mentioned that I had recently attended a speech given by Rav Yosef Dov Soloveitchik in the Maimonides school in Boston [where I had begun law school]. Rav Gifter asked me to say over what the Rav Soloveitchik had said. I began repeating as much as I remembered, until Rav Gifter stopped me in the middle. When we spoke about Telz, he saw that I was quite hesitant about joining the yeshivah. At first, I didn't want to tell him what the problem was.

Rabbi Aryeh Burnham

However, when I looked at him, he looked so great and pure, that I felt I had to be honest with him and say what was bothering me. I explained to him that I felt that Lithuanian Jews were not as loving and spiritual as Chassidim. (I had had contact with Chassidim in my recent past.)

When he heard that, Rav Gifter was momentarily taken aback. Then he said, "I can assure you that yeshivish Jews are very loving." He paused for a moment and then asked me, "Do you want to see angels?"

I hadn't really thought about it before, but it sounded like a good idea, so I said, "Yes, I would like to see angels." Rav Gifter said, "Stay here, and you will see angels."

Rav Gifter arranged for the best *bachurim* in the yeshivah to be Aryeh's learning partners, and instructed them to stay away from all other conversations, even *hashkafah*, and just learn Torah with Aryeh: "*Nor lernen* — Only learning." And, as Aryeh sums it up:

A few days later, I called my friends in Boston and asked them to pack up all my things and send them. I totally loved it in Telz, angels or not.

Nearly 40 years later, Rabbi Aryeh Burnham lives in Eretz Yisrael where he disseminates Torah.[1]

---
1. Rabbi Aryeh Burnham, Rabbi Nosson Scherman.

Chapter 17: A Powerful Influence ☐ 211

SOMETIMES, RAV GIFTER INFLUENCED HIS *TALMIDIM* IN THE MOST profound ways without even planning to. Important lessons could even be learned from a spontaneous outburst in the middle of a *shiur*.

A Spontaneous Outburst

One such incident occurred in the mid-1950's, when Rav Gifter was still a young rebbi. The yeshivah was learning *Maseches Yevamos* (16a), and the class was learning the story of a young man whose name was Yonasan, who brought 300 proofs to permit a *tzaras habas* (a case in the Gemara) to marry. Rav Gifter stopped and said, "Let us try to imagine what that means. Three hundred proofs! We can barely manage to squeeze out one or two. Yet, this great Torah personality was able to bring 300 proofs. Do you know why he was able to and we cannot? It is because we are so far removed from the truth and essence of Torah!" And suddenly, he broke down crying.

Imagine sitting in that classroom and seeing your rebbi burst into tears over the pain of his distance from the truth of Torah. What a major impact such an outburst would have!

RAV GIFTER WAS EXTREMELY CLOSE TO RABBI AZRIEL GOLDFEIN. Reb Azriel's relationship with the rosh hayeshivah began when Azriel had come from Minneapolis to the yeshivah as a young man. He had met Rav Gifter once when the rosh hayeshivah had come to Minneapolis, and it had changed young Azriel's view of Torah and of life. He had never met anyone so brilliant and so full of life. The spirit of life (*ruach chaim*) that suffused Rav Gifter was like none Azriel had ever before experienced, and he decided to become a student of Telz.

Rabbi Azriel Goldfein

When Rav Gifter passed away, Reb Azriel delivered a three-hour eulogy in Johannesburg, South Africa, where he served as rosh yeshivah and led the community for many years. He reflected on the most important day of his life: the day that he asked Rav Gifter to learn with him.

It came with little fanfare. In 1956, when he needed a *chavrusa* for the winter session, Azriel built up the courage to ask Rav Gifter if he would learn with him, and waited with bated breath for a reply.

"When?" was the reply.

Azriel was stunned by the quick response.

"In the morning," was all he could muster.

Rabbi Azriel Goldfein *zt"l*, rosh yeshivah in South Africa

"Fine."

And with this brief conversation, a relationship that would span over 50 years began. The first *zman*, they learned 50 *blatt* of Gemara. The next *zman*, they learned another 50. First *Pesachim*, then *Yevamos*. It was incredible. They learned for four hours straight every day. Azriel had never experienced such power of mind, such enormous depth in learning. The clarity was like a bright light illuminating the clouded *sugya*. The sheer energy lifted him to places he had never thought possible.

They were learning partners for a few years, but the bond that was formed lasted a lifetime. Even after Reb Azriel had left the yeshivah, a month would not go by without an exchange of letters between the *talmid* and rebbi. Often, Reb Azriel would fly in to seek guidance, and sometimes just to say hello.

One incident, which occurred while Azriel was still in yeshivah, provided a lifetime of guidance for Reb Azriel. Although he was learning exceptionally well in Telz, he began to consider leaving the yeshivah so that he could learn in Eretz Yisrael. He decided that he would bring the question to his rebbi.

Rav Gifter asked him, "Are you learning well?"

Azriel responded that he was learning well.

Rav Gifter looked at him. "So then why would you go?"

Azriel responded, "Because maybe I can learn better."

Rav Gifter told him something that he would never forget. "*A kranke darf zuchen far eitzos. Ah gezunte durch eitzos vet er krank veren!* — A sick person needs to look for a cure. But a healthy person who looks for cures will become sick from them!"

Reb Azriel concluded his eulogy of Rav Gifter with beautiful imagery, about how he pictured Rav Gifter receiving his eternal reward:

When I picture my great rebbi in Gan Eden, I see him in two ways.

At first I see him as a young man, a prince, saying a shiur with great clarity and depth.

But more than as a teacher, I see our rebbi as a student, wanting to learn more and more. I see him sitting in the shiur of Rabbi Akiva. He sits in the beis midrash and is listening to the shiur, when suddenly he cries out, "Rebbi! Ba'er devarecha! — Explain your words!" And immediately, an explosive argument erupts in the beis midrash. This is my rebbi's Gan Eden!

Rav Zev Leff, the rav of Moshav Mattisyahu and a *talmid* of Rav Gifter, once said, "My rosh hayeshivah, Rav Mordechai Gifter, has observed that our Sages are not called *chachamim* (wise) but *talmidei chachamim* (students of the wise). They do not merely possess wisdom but are guided by it; they are its students. In fact, the Rambam refers to *talmidei chachamim* as *mevakshei hachochmah* (those who seek wisdom)."

Always learning. Always yearning.

Always Guiding

FROM TIME TO TIME, THE YESHIVAH WOULD HOST A GROUP OF DAY-school youngsters for a Shabbaton. Every *bachur* was assigned two children to care for over Shabbos. The goal was to develop a connection with the boys so they could have an ongoing relationship. One of the boys, Richie, was really inspired over Shabbos and remained connected to his mentor, Leibel. He began to daven and put on *tzitzis* every day.

One evening, Leibel received a call from Richie's irate father. He warned him, in no uncertain terms, that if Leibel ever spoke to Richie again, he would come and break every bone in his body!

Terrified and nervous, Leibel went to Rav Gifter to seek his advice. Rav Gifter told him something profound. "I want to tell you something important. If you understand it, you belong in this business of outreach, and if you don't, then it's best if you get out now. Even if you must cut off ties right now with Richie, in 25 years, he will have a son who attends a day school. He, too, will go to a Shabbaton in a yeshivah, and his son will meet a different *bachur*. Once more, this child will become interested in growing in his Yiddishkeit. But this time, his father will not be so opposed to his son becoming observant (because his father, Richie, had a connection many years ago with you, Leibel). If you understand this, good! However, if you are looking for instant gratification, you don't belong in this business!"[2]

In 1983, Rabbi Hillel Goldberg of Denver, the editor of The Intermountain Jewish News, denounced the Joint Conversion Group, a group of liberal rabbis who had converted hundreds of families under their auspices. The sham was described by the Intermountain Jewish News in a 12-page exposé. This episode earned Rabbi Goldberg great respect in Rav Gifter's eyes, and he felt he could trust him.

A number of years later, Rabbi Goldberg called Rav Gifter to ask him if he would be allowed speak to a large gathering of Jews from all backgrounds, as part of a roundtable discussion with a Conservative and a Reform rabbi.

Rav Gifter told him he could participate on two conditions: First, he could attend the meeting only if it is not held in the sanctuary of the synagogue; second, while each of the other rabbis is fighting for position and trying to get the first word in and the last word out, Rabbi Goldberg must remain silent. In fact, he should not utter one word during the first 45 minutes of the session. When the moderator asks for his opinion during that time, he must decline and pass.

"Finally," Rav Gifter said, "after 45 minutes, you will ask to speak. At this point, those present will be anxious to hear what you have to say, and they will allow you to speak for as long as you want. Once you

---

2. Reb Leibel Berger.

have the floor, you will deliver a well-prepared statement about Torah Judaism."

Rabbi Goldberg followed Rav Gifter's wise counsel, and it worked precisely as he had predicted.

Rabbi Goldberg wrote the following shortly after Rav Gifter passed away.[3]

Here I use the word "disciples" advisedly, quite deliberately. Rare today is the teacher of Torah who has many genuine disciples. If stricken or perplexed, who today turns to a teacher of Torah for authoritative guidance? Who surrenders his autonomy and accepts someone else's perspective on critical, personal issues? Many people today consult a rabbi or a yeshivah dean in order to gain insight, to trade ideas, to share pain or to ask for blessing; but who asks for authoritative guidance — indeed, yearns for it, relishes it, feels privileged to receive it? Even fights for the opportunity to receive it?

Banish one thought from the mind: that Rav Gifter, in dispensing guidance, was controlling or manipulative. Such are the adjectives that come to mind in 2001 when the term "authoritative guidance" is used. How debased our understanding of Torah authority has become that so many associate it with genuflection or absence of critical thinking.

Rav Gifter's guidance was sought not because he demanded allegiance, but because he commanded respect. Rav Gifter's persona was appreciated not because he played with other people's psyches, but because he consistently and successfully worked to straighten his own. He listened. He discerned. He perceived. He cut below the surface. He read beyond a person's words into his real message. Needless to say, it is no less important that Rav Gifter brought all these qualities to his study of Torah. When one sought counsel from Rav Gifter, one received two gifts: a finely calibrated reading of one's heart, and a finely etched application of the pertinent Torah teaching. This is authoritative guidance.

It is not always what one wants to hear, or expects to hear. Conversations with Rav Gifter could leave the questioner struggling with the truths that Rav Gifter enunciated — this, amidst an overwhelming sense of gratitude to G-d for bestowing such a mind and soul on the Jewish people — and for access to it.

One *talmid* echoed the sentiment he had heard from Rav Gifter about his own relationship with his rebbi. "I would not dare to call myself a *talmid*, but I treasured having him as my rebbi."[4]

---

3. Rabbi Hilel Goldberg, Intermountain Jewish News, "A Lion Arose From Portsmouth."
4. Rabbi Yitzchak Schwartz.

Chapter 18
A Unique Disseminator of Torah

T O SIT IN RAV GIFTER'S CLASS WAS TO BE IN THE PRESENCE of an awe-inspiring mind and spirit. While some of his students became great roshei yeshivah, chassidic rebbes, and community leaders, each student felt the warmth of his soul, and the fire and brilliance of the man.

RAV ZEV LEFF, RAV OF MOSHAV MATTISYAHU, EXPLAINED WHAT kind of rosh hayeshivah Rav Gifter was :

A European Rosh Hayeshivah *Some say that Rav Gifter was an American rosh hayeshivah. Sheker! The halachah is that if the ladle is completely immersed in the soup, it is no longer a kli sheini — a secondary utensil with diminished heat. It takes on the status of a kli rishon; it is like the pot itself.*

Rav Gifter was so completely immersed in Lita, he was a Litvishe rosh hayeshivah; he was like the pot itself.

Understanding His Shiur

ATTENDING HIS *SHIUR* WAS ONE THING; KEEPING UP WITH THE mind and thinking of Rav Gifter was quite another. He spent hours preparing, following the method of his rebbi, Rav Avraham Yitzchak. And the delivery was fast paced and intense, and did not always end with a flawless solution. Instead, it opened up avenues of new approaches in the *sugya*. But it was perfectly, astonishingly clear! Rav Gifter was seeking the truth, and in his pursuit of it, he was unforgiving. The shape and texture of the *shiur* would change as he wound his way through it, and it was not easy for anyone to keep up.

One *talmid* recalls, in a humorous manner, that having the stamina to sit through the class became something of a competition the students had with themselves, if not with one another. Most became confused early on, while only some could follow the entire *shiur*.[1]

For Rav Shalom Shapiro, who has served as the mashgiach of the yeshivah for the past 40 years, the *shiur* was a lesson in humility.

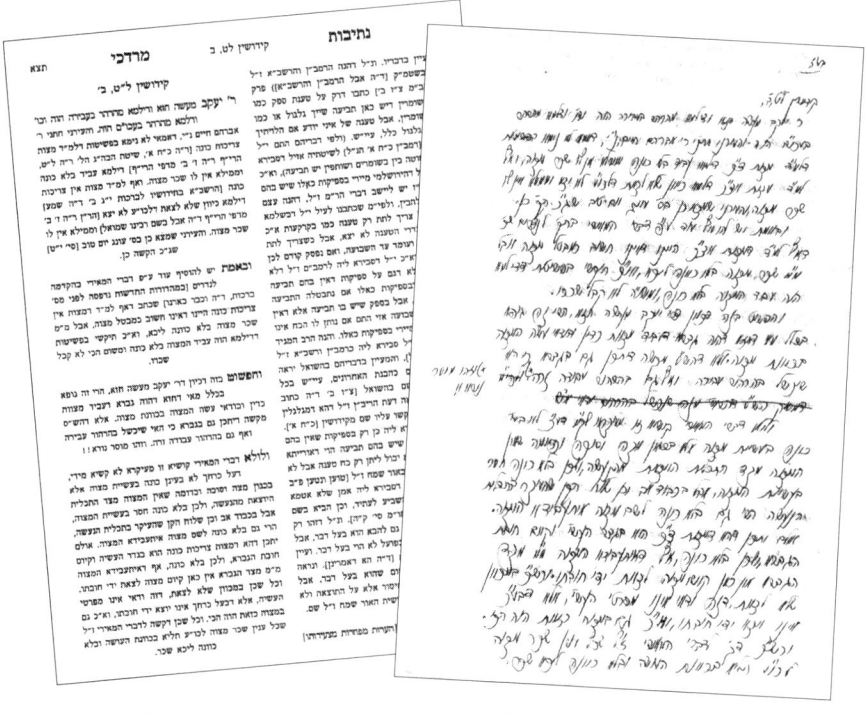

Nesivos Mordechai, Kiddushin 39a, where Rav Gifter cites his son-in-law, Reb Avrohom Chaim (Feuer)

---

1. Rabbi Yisroel Schneider.

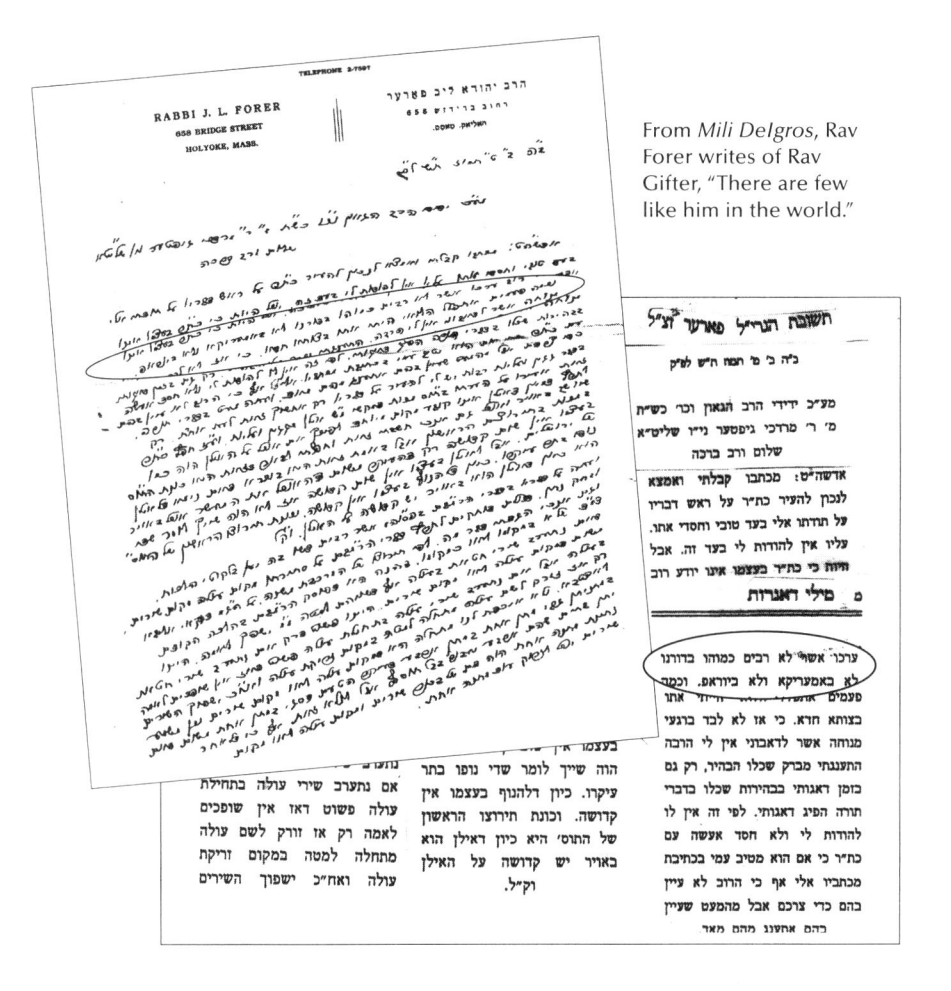

From *Mili DeIgros*, Rav Forer writes of Rav Gifter, "There are few like him in the world."

Rabbi Yisroel Schneider commented, "We went into the *shiur* thinking that we understood the topic in Gemara perfectly well. By the time we walked out of the class, we realized how infinitesimal our understanding was."

Rav Dovid Barkin was a close *talmid* of the rosh hayeshivah. In fact, Rav Gifter wrote in his will that Rav Dovid should be one of the men who learn in his memory. Rav Dovid recalled that he had once written 24 pages of notes for one *shiur*!

Another close *talmid*, Rabbi Azriel Goldfein, related that he had learned a Tosafos 15 times before hearing it from Rav Gifter, and he had still not understood it the way Rav Gifter explained it. Once he heard the rosh hayeshivah's explanation, however, it seemed like it had been there all along.

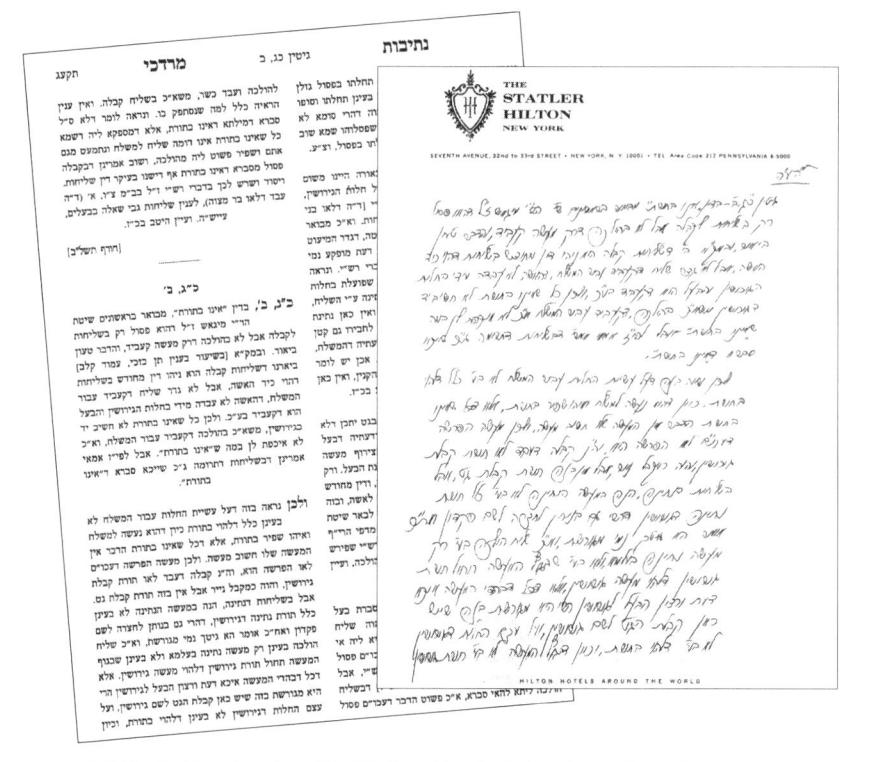

Chiddushei Torah, printed in *Nesivos Mordechai* on *Maseches Gittin*, written during a trip to New York, while staying at the Statler Hotel. Every minute was precious.

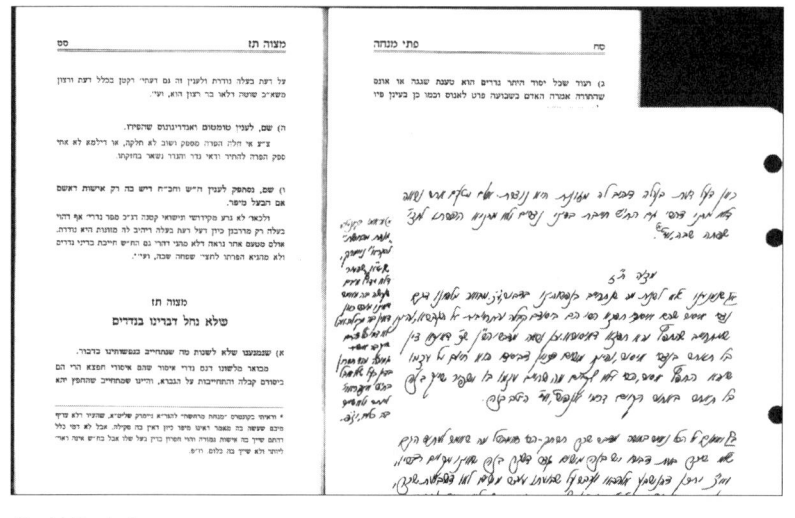

Pitei Minchah

Pirkei Torah

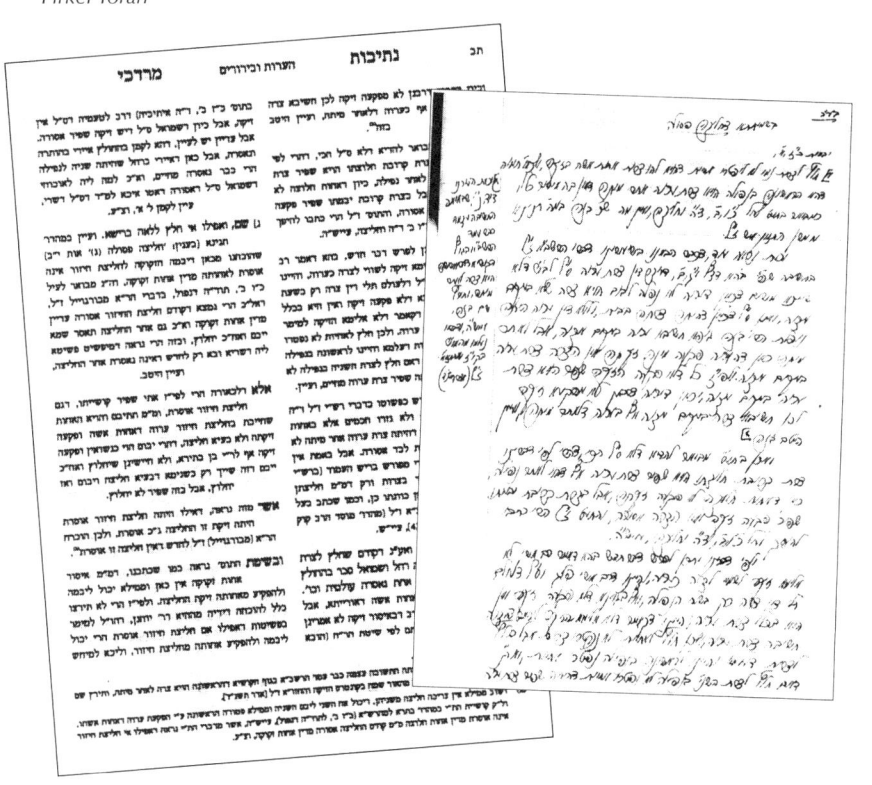

Nesivos Mordechai, Yevamos, where Rav Gifter cites Rav Dovid Barkin

Sitting with his *chavrusa*: his pen

When it came to learning, time had no meaning to Rav Gifter. He never looked at the clock, and if a *talmid* did not understand the *shiur*, he would invite him to stay after class and discuss it. One *bachur* came from abroad and only spoke Hebrew. Rav Gifter spent hours with him, saying over the entire *shiur* in Hebrew.

THE ROSH HAYESHIVAH WAS A PROLIFIC WRITER AND WROTE many *sefarim* (*Pirkei Emunah, Pirkei Moed, Pirkei Iyun, Pitei Minchah, Nesivos Mordechai*, among others). In addition, since his love for Torah did not find its borders in his own soul, and he yearned to share his joy with others, he wrote extensively in many Torah journals: *Hapardes, Talpios, Hadarom, Am HaTorah, Moriah, Pri Eitz Chaim,* and many others. Of course, many of his *talmidim* had already retained those discussions and *shiurim* in their memories. Thus, some would say, "I can still hear his *shmuessen* ringing in my ears!"[2] when they would read his words cited in an article.

Prolific Writer

---

2. Rav Yaakov Reisman, Rav Chaim Aharon Weinberg.

IN HIS LATER YEARS, WHEN RAV GIFTER ALTERED THE STYLE OF HIS *shiur*, it allowed more of an opportunity for the *bachurim* to ask questions and to engage in discussion. Many remember that the discussions would become quite heated, which gave Rav Gifter much pleasure.

Relating to All His Students

After one particularly heated exchange with a student about the Gemara, the student approached Rav Gifter and apologized for his behavior. Rav Gifter responded, "I haven't had such pleasure since I was a young man in Telz and I would fight with my *chavrusa*."

Rav Gifter once gave a masterful *shiur daas* on the importance of "*Asei lecha rav* — Accept a teacher upon yourself" (*Avos* 1:6). In that talk, he documented his educational approach. One of the points he mentioned was the importance of speaking in a way that the *talmidim* could understand, using the language of the times.

Even though Rav Gifter was so brilliant and had many characteristics that were similar to European roshei yeshivos, he was able to relate to American boys.

He loved watching the younger boys play ball, and encouraged them to do so. As a sign of respect, the high-school boys would stop playing baseball when any of the roshei hayeshivah came by. But when they would stop for Rav Gifter, he would stop, watch, and then in a loud and jovial voice, cry out, "Play ball!!!" What a moment for those young boys; what love they felt as they saw him smiling at the boys and encouraging them to play!

Once, his grandson, Tzvi(ki) Feuer, was at the plate. As Rav Gifter walked by, the game came to a halt until he passed. However, he was interested in seeing how his grandson would play, so he stopped to watch the game. Thus, the game continued as Tzviki hit a deep line drive over an outfielder's head. He raced around the bases, and when he finally rounded third, he looked at his grandfather, who was standing and watching. In his inimitable voice, he called out, "Tzvikele! A home run! *Gevaldig*!"

Rav Gifter spoke the language of the times.

Sense of Humor

WHEN RAV ABBA ZALKA GEWIRTZ'S GRANDSON, RABBI YONAH Gewirtz's son, Danny (Doniel), was learning in the yeshivah, Rav Gifter challenged him to finish the tractate he was learning, and then to take a test on the material. Rav Gifter promised Danny $100 if he passed the *bechinah*. Danny had grown up in New Orleans and had made tremendous progress since he came to the yeshivah. But finishing *Bava Kamma* was a much greater challenge than anything he had ever attempted before.

At the time, he was in Rav Dovid Barkin's *shiur*, learning with the son of Rav Shaul Dolinger, another second-generation Telzer. Danny knew that his father was a *talmid* of the rosh hayeshivah and that his grandfather was a close friend. Danny felt that he wanted to excel in order to please everyone. Therefore, in order to finish, the learning partners decided to learn one *blatt* a day of *Maseches Bava Kamma*. Soon, though, they encountered some difficult topics, and realized that they were not going to finish.

After a brief talk with his son, Danny's father gave Rav Gifter the update. When Rav Gifter encountered Danny, he said, "Dan, I spoke with your dad, and he says you are close to finishing. Are you ready for the *bechinah*?" Danny said he was not yet ready. So Rav Gifter assured him that he would only be asked questions on the material he had learned.

When the time came for the test, Rav Chaim Stein and Rav Dovid Barkin were also in the room. Rav Chaim asked Danny a question on the Tosafos, even though the *bechinah* was supposed to be only on Gemara and Rashi. Fortunately, Danny happened to know that particular Tosafos. But then Rav Gifter asked Danny a question about something at the very end of the tractate. Danny looked at the rosh hayeshivah and reminded him that he had not finished the tractate. Nevertheless, Rav Gifter told him, "I will tell you the Gemara, and then I will ask you a question on it. Let's see how you think. Let me hear your explanation [*sevarah*]. I want to see how your mind works."

Although Danny was nervous, he answered Rav Gifter to the best of his ability. Nevertheless, to his surprise, Rav Gifter said, "I'm sorry, but you did not earn the $100 reward. And I have to call your father to tell him." Danny was devastated. He had worked for an entire year to finish, but he had just fallen short. And furthermore, Rav Gifter had assured him that he would test him only on what he had learned. It seemed to him that the only question he had not answered correctly was the one on the part of the tractate he had not learned. Still, he waited and listened as Rav Gifter picked up the phone to call his father.

"Reb Yonah," Rav Gifter said into the phone, "I just finished testing Danny. And he did not earn the $100 for the *bechinah*." There was silence on the phone that seemed to last a lot longer than the five seconds it actually was. Then, a wry smile appeared on Rav Gifter's face. "Instead, I am going to give him 100 and 50 dollars! That is what he deserves for such a wonderful accomplishment and such a great *sevarah*!"

Rav Gifter removed his personal checkbook from his pocket and wrote out a check for $150 and handed it to Danny. Danny took the check home with him, framed it, and proudly displayed it on his wall.

This story provides great insight into the kind of teacher Rav Gifter was. First, he wanted the students to know that he expected a great deal from them, pushing them to do more than they thought they could. Second, he knew that a feeling of accomplishment was critical in education. Even when Danny didn't finish what he had promised, he knew Danny's mind could handle independent thinking "on the spot" and wanted to prove to Danny that he could do it. In addition, he also knew that sometimes it's more important to think on your feet than to recite memorized texts.

And of course, this story also shows what a wonderful sense of humor Rav Gifter had. Although he was a serious and intense man, he appreciated a good joke and knew when it was needed to help lighten a mood or make someone feel good.

A *talmid* recalls that Rav Gifter had a lively sense of humor that spiced his remarks, and he was quick to spot the mirth in a given situation:

Rav Gifter regularly selected one bachur who read very quickly to read the Aggadah [narrative] portion of the Gemara. While the reader was rac-

ing, some members of the shiur said that they had lost the place and asked where he was holding. In reply, Rav Gifter said that he had lost him, too. When asked what he was up to, the reader admitted that he himself had lost the place. Rav Gifter joined the entire class in laughing heartily at their predicament.

On another occasion, during a bechinah on the Mishnah Berurah, Rav Eliyahu Meir Bloch posed a question in Yiddish to a bachur: "What blessing does one recite upon eating the [edible] shollachts [bark] of a tree?" This American bachur did not know what shollachts was, so the other boys explained to him that it meant the bark of a tree. The bachur responded, "Rebbi, you're barking up the wrong tree." Rav Eliyahu Meir, who did not speak English, did not know what the bachur meant, but Rav Gifter, who was present at the bechinah, as well, was doubled over with laughter.[3]

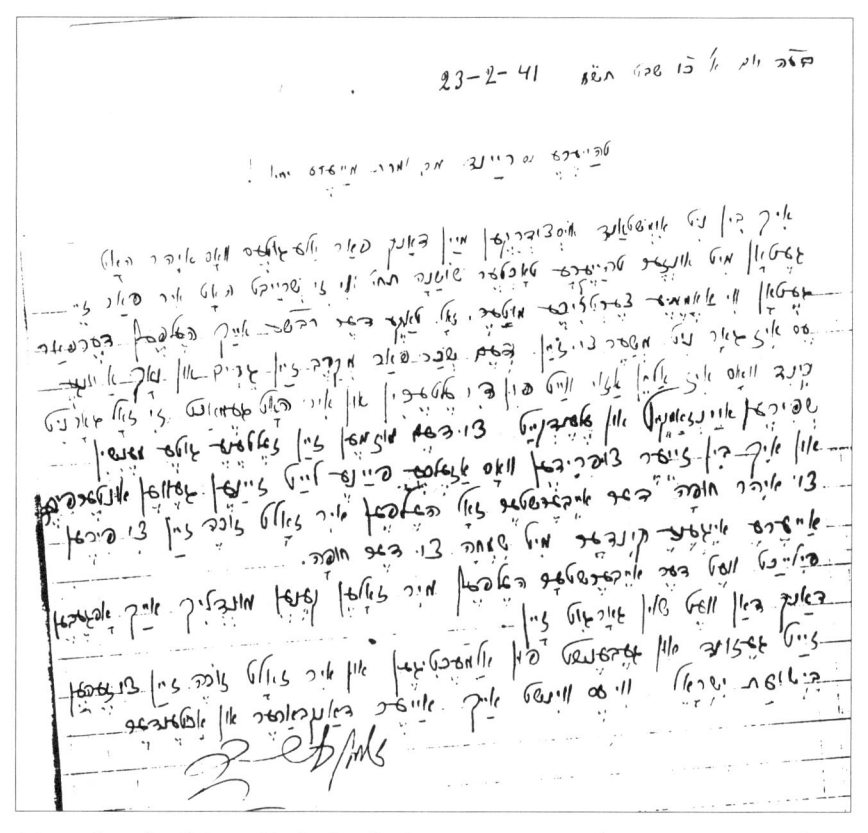

A letter from Rav Zalman Bloch, dated February 23, 1941 / 26 Shevat 5701, to Mr. and Mrs. Myers. He thanks them for escorting his daughter Shoshana to the *Chuppah*.

---

3. Reb Shlomo Slonim.

Rav Zalman Bloch with Rav Avner Oklansky

Baal HaMesorah

RAV GIFTER WOULD OFTEN TELL THE FOLLOWING STORY THAT illustrates the unique clarity of the *Rishonim*. Rav Meshulem Igra, who was the rav of Pressburg prior to Rav Moshe Schreiber, the Chasam Sofer (about 200 years ago), was universally regarded as one of the geniuses of his generation. His student, Rav Yaakov Lorberbaum, the author of the *Nesivos HaMishpat* and the rav of Lisa, asked a very serious question to his rebbi. "I don't understand something, Rebbi. There are times when I will diligently toil over your *shiurim* for many, many hours. And still I cannot understand them. Yet, when I learn the words of the Rashba [one of the famous *Rishonim* who lived over 700 years ago in Spain], I do understand what he is saying. How can that be? Rebbi, you are standing right before me and you speak the same language I do."

Rav Meshulem answered him in a cryptic manner. "Indeed, that is the greatness of the *Rishonim*. They knew how to wrap their words in well-fitting garments."

Rav Gifter explained:

The Al-mighty gave the Rishonim the ability to clothe their words and thoughts in a manner that every individual — from the entire intellectual

Rav Pinchos Helfan and his family *Hy"d*. Rav Gifter stayed in their home when he first arrived in Telz.

spectrum — *can understand on his level. For example, even though the Ramban would toil to comprehend a Rashi, a 7-year-old will be satisfied with the way he understands the Rashi. And that gift was given only until the era of the Rishonim; after that, it no longer existed.*

Although he was not on the plane of the *Rishonim*, perhaps in a certain way we can say the same about Rav Gifter. He had a keen ability to convey his thoughts in a lucid manner; every listener comprehended the rosh hayeshivah's words on his own level.

Rav Gifter would often mention that Hillel entrusted Rabban Yochanan ben Zakkai to transmit the *mesorah*, tradition, from his generation to the next. The Rambam, in his *Mishneh Torah*, describes how Torah was transmitted through 40 generations: From Moshe at Har Sinai until Rav Ashi and the completion of Talmud Bavli, each generation would carefully transmit it to the next. But the Gemara in *Succah* (28a) mentions that the smallest of Hillel's *talmidim* was Rabban Yochanan ben Zakkai. This begs the question. Why did he entrust the *mesorah* to the smallest of his *talmidim*, and not his greatest *talmid*, Yonasan ben Uziel?

The answer is:

The baal hamesorah, who is designated to transmit the tradition from one generation to the next, is not necessarily the greatest talmid chacham and genius. Rather, it is the one who best makes the transition from the previous generation to the present one. [4]

This, more than anything else, made Rav Gifter a unique transmitter of Torah. Of course, he was extremely learned, but so were others. But he was different; he was someone who understood our culture.

In yeshivah on Purim with Aron Waldman (l) and Pesach Siegel (r)

It says in *Koheles* (1:5), *"Ve'zarach hashemesh u'va hashamesh* — And the sun rises and the sun sets." The Midrash sees deep meaning in this phrase. Rav Berachiah said in the name of Rav Abba bar Kahana: Don't we know that the sun rises and the sun sets? Rather, the verse is telling us that before the "sun" of one righteous man sets, the "sun" of another righteous man begins to rise.

Before the sun of Sarah Imeinu set, the sun of Rivkah began to rise. Prior to the setting of Moshe's sun, Hashem caused the sun of Yehoshua to rise. On the day of the death of Rabbi Akiva, Rabbi Yehudah HaNasi was born.

This is the pattern of Jewish death and life. In fact, Rashi was born on the day that Rabbeinu Gershom Me'or HaGolah died.

Rav Gifter emphasized the importance of this concept in Jewish life, citing the rising of the sun in America as the sun of Europe came to its tragic sunset. G-d had prepared for the continuity of Torah in America.

And there is no better representation of the rising American sun than the dazzling rays of Torah that emanated from Rav Gifter.

After the Holocaust, how would we be able to recover the glory

---
4. Rav Avrohom Chaim Feuer.

Rav Yosef Leib Bloch

Rav Avraham Yitzchak Bloch

and grandeur of Lithuania that Hitler had destroyed? Was it possible to recover? Who would be able to convey, in a picture-perfect manner, what the world of European Torah was like? Who would be able to transplant the traditions of Klal Yisrael into a country and land that was so completely foreign to these concepts and ideas? Who would be able to get American boys to dream about greatness in Torah, and one day, perhaps achieve that same level of *ameilus baTorah*?

There was one man who had the ability. He was born in America, trained in Europe, and was a firebrand saved from the fire (*ud mutzal me'eish*); a man who could speak the language of the boys and the language of the land, who would love and care for *talmidim* without pampering them.

And it was he whose words and ideas would forever be etched in the souls of thousands.

Chapter 19
Everlasting Lessons

ASIDE FROM THE TRADITIONAL ENVIRONMENT OF THE *shiur*, Rav Gifter educated his students in other ways, too. He held special *vaadim*, informal classes, in his home on ethics (*mussar*), analytical learning (*lomdus*), and philosophy (*machshavah*), and even coached *talmidim* on current events and public speaking. In addition, he taught many lessons in his *shmuessen*, and many lessons were learned from his actions, as well.

IN ONE PARTICULARLY SPECIAL GROUP (*CHABURAH*) TITLED "*Chaveirim*" (Friends), a group of *bachurim* had to accept upon themselves three special conditions in order to gain admission.[1] If any member transgressed any of these commitments (*kabbalos*), he had to place a penny in the middle of the table and commit to improving the next time. Although a penny seems like an insignificant amount, the *bachurim* accepted upon themselves to be men of growth (*bnei aliyah*),

Three Commitments

---
1. Rav Avrohom Ausband.

Rav Yisroel and Chasia
(nee Bloch) Ordman Hy"d

Walking with Rav Chaim Nussbaum

and that "punishment" encouraged them to keep to their commitments.

The three commitments were:

(1) Arrive at least three minutes early to every study and prayer session. Rav Gifter was very particular about punctuality. He wanted them to come a bit earlier than expected, just to make sure that they were on time.

One time, he spoke in the high school, and was disturbed that some of the boys walked in late. When boys continued to roll in late, Rav Gifter stopped and walked out in the middle of the speech. He felt that coming late is not *kvod haTorah* and shows disrespect to the individual speaking and the subject matter at hand.

Rav Gifter insisted that punctuality was a Telzer trait. In fact, he recounted that Rav Yosef Leib Bloch (the father of his father-in-law, Rav Zalman Bloch, and his rebbi, Rav Avraham Yitzchak) used to give a *shiur* at precisely 4 o'clock in the afternoon at his home. Once, Rav Gifter's brother-in-law, Rav Ordman, appeared at the home of Rav Yosef Leib five minutes early, at 3:55. Rav Yosef Leib told him, "Four o'clock means 4 o'clock, not a minute before and not a minute after." In fact, people could set their clocks by watching when Rav Yosef Leib took his daily walk; they knew that he passed by each house in the neighborhood at exactly the same time every day.

(2) Never lean on a lectern when learning or davening. *Chaveirim* are meant to be soldiers in the army of Hashem, and therefore need to

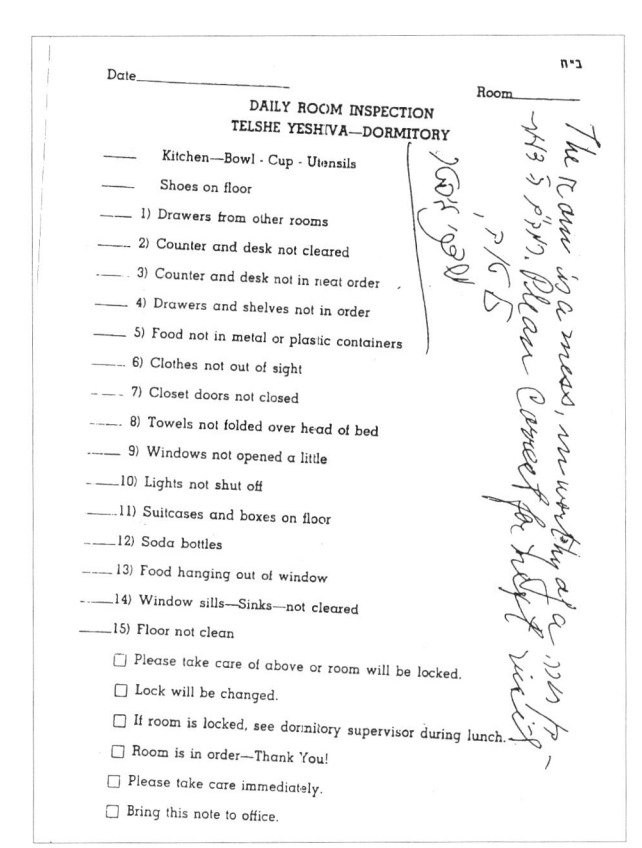

| DAILY ROOM INSPECTION |
| TELSHE YESHIVA—DORMITORY |

Date_____   Room_____

____ Kitchen—Bowl - Cup - Utensils
____ Shoes on floor
____ 1) Drawers from other rooms
____ 2) Counter and desk not cleared
____ 3) Counter and desk not in neat order
____ 4) Drawers and shelves not in order
____ 5) Food not in metal or plastic containers
____ 6) Clothes not out of sight
____ 7) Closet doors not closed
____ 8) Towels not folded over head of bed
____ 9) Windows not opened a little
____ 10) Lights not shut off
____ 11) Suitcases and boxes on floor
____ 12) Soda bottles
____ 13) Food hanging out of window
____ 14) Window sills—Sinks—not cleared
____ 15) Floor not clean

☐ Please take care of above or room will be locked.
☐ Lock will be changed.
☐ If room is locked, see dormitory supervisor during lunch.
☐ Room is in order—Thank You!
☐ Please take care immediately.
☐ Bring this note to office.

Clean-up chart with note from Rav Gifter, who had that day checked the dormitory for cleanliness

Rav Gifter wrote: The room is a mess, unworthy of a ben Torah — Rambam, *Hilchos Dei'os*. Please correct for next week. Kol Tuv, Mordechai Gifter

sit upright whenever they are in the midst of "battle." One of the students in the group asked Rav Gifter why he would be permitted to lean on Pesach night, as is required. Surprisingly, Rav Gifter kept quiet. Years later, the *talmid* would find that one earlier commentator wrote that one must lean only at the time of the actual drinking of the four cups of wine, but at the time of the blessing he should sit upright, in awe of the Al-mighty (*be'eimah*).[2]

(3) Each *talmid* must commit to taking a 20-minute walk every day. It wasn't required that the students "talk in learning" during the walk, although most did anyway.

The third commitment seems to be different from the other two. Rav Gifter knew the importance of not pushing oneself too hard and always clearing one's mind.

---

[2]. Rabbi Avrohom Shoshanah; Yeshurun X.

He wanted the young men, who were so focused and driven, to understand the importance of being healthy.

Rav Gifter would always encourage the *bachurim* to accept upon themselves something small and doable for Elul and would, in fact, accept something upon himself, as well.[3]

An Additional Commitment

LATER ON, THE MEMBERS ACCEPTED UPON THEMSELVES AN additional commitment. They decided that they would not sit in the yeshivah dining room and schmooze after they were finished eating. Instead, immediately following their meal, they would go to wherever they were supposed to go.

The Snooze Button

RAV GIFTER DESPISED LAZINESS. ONE PARTICULAR INCIDENT THAT revolved around this trait occurred with his grandson, Eliezer Feuer, who served him for a number of years. This occurred during the time that Rav and Rebbetzin Gifter were living in the dormitory. Eliezer's room and the rosh hayeshivah's apartment were in the same wing of the dormitory. Early one morning, Eliezer heard the rebbetzin getting ready to drive Rav Gifter to the yeshivah. Afterward, she would go to her teaching job.

With his grandson Eliezer Feuer, Rebbetzin Gifter is at left.

---

3. Rabbi Boruch Hirschfeld.

Eliezer jumped out of bed and called out, "Bubby, I need an alarm clock. Please make sure to get one with a snooze on it."

Rav Gifter turned around. He was stunned. "A snooze?!"

It was everything that Rav Gifter was opposed to. He let his grandson know, in no uncertain terms, exactly what he felt about snooze alarms. Not only that, but the next *shmuess* in yeshivah was dedicated to how contrary a snooze button is to the concept of alacrity (*zerizus*) and the way a yeshivah student should arise in the morning. If one is accustomed to pushing off his awakening by pushing the snooze button, this is a sign of laziness.

Rav Gifter once commented incredulously, "An alarm clock was meant to wake us up, and we are using it to put us to sleep!"

THERE WERE MANY OTHER LESSONS HE CONVEYED TO THE *bachurim* outside of the classroom, but three in particular stand out.

Three Lessons

(1) Maximizing Potential

He always stressed the importance of each person striving to maximize his potential. Rav Gifter would often lament that in Europe, people blessed each other that their children should grow up to become *gedolei Yisrael*, Torah giants, while in America, they are satisfied that they should become upright, honest Jews. And while that is certainly admirable, it falls short of greatness (*gadlus*).

He told his *talmidim* how in Lithuania, there had been great "cedars of Torah [*gedolim*] in the shadow of which the smaller trees [*baalebatim*] were able to grow." But he worried how those smaller trees will grow in America if we do not encourage greatness among American Jewry. Rav Gifter dismissed the notion that American boys just didn't have it in them.

In 1964, Rav Gifter spoke to the lay leaders of Torah Umesorah:

We must measure success or failure in the light of purity of the soul [zakus hanefesh]. How far have we gone in changing the consciousness of our generation? How far have we gone toward making toiling in Torah the generating force of Jewish living? How far have we gone toward creating elders [zekeinim], gedolei Torah? Ours is a day of specialization. How far have we gone toward implanting into the young minds and hearts of many of them the dream of becoming a Chofetz Chaim, a Rav Chaim Brisker, a Rav Meir Simchah [Ohr Same'ach], a Chazon Ish?

Much indeed has been achieved in the past two decades. But with the great change that has been wrought, we have not yet brought this generation to Sinai. We have not made this generation see what was seen and what was heard.

The challenge of Torah chinuch is that we "come close to the mountain" and that we take our children with us to see and hear what our forefathers saw and heard. We must become witness to the great reality of emunah, with renewed intensive efforts of consolidating positions already won, and in the continued conquest of new horizons for Torah.

He believed deeply in the goodness of people and the potential greatness they had within them. But it could not come from coddling and pampering an entire generation. He saw the capabilities in all people and yearned for them to see what they could accomplish, as well.

(2) Appreciating What We Have Lost

The second important lesson he conveyed was the richness of the life that had but recently flourished in Lithuania and the rest of Europe. At the *siyum haShas* in 1975, in one of his most memorable addresses, Rav Gifter pleaded with the crowd *"tzu hubben geduld"* (to have patience) while we let out *"ah krechtz"* (a sigh). Rav Gifter then transported the entire crowd back to pre-war Europe. *"Ah krechtz far Telz, un Pressburg, Varsha [Warsaw], un Lemberg, Cracow, Berlin, un Frankfurt,"* and wherever Jews had lived. After he loudly proclaimed the name of each city, he paused to allow everyone to contemplate the magnitude of what was lost.

The sigh was heard around the world, and it pierced the hearts of Klal Yisrael. It truly gave pause to those who had no idea what that life was, to think for a moment about the magnitude of what was lost during World War II.

As a matter of fact, at the most recent *siyum haShas* in 2005, a tribute was paid to the *gedolim* who had passed away since the previous event. And they played this clip from 30 years before.

(3) Incorporating Torah Into All of Our Actions

The third lesson he taught was that Torah must bring us to a love of the Al-mighty and to mitzvah observance; that it is not to be learned simply for the intellectual exercise. He lamented how there were those who were lax in business dealings and honesty. Rav Gifter suggested that the holidays that we generally take to heart stem from the tractates of *Rosh Hashanah, Yoma* (which is about Yom Kippur), *Pesachim,* and

The world that was ...

"A krechtz
far Varsha ...
Cracow ...
Frankurt."

Succah. But he warned that when people are lax in their business dealings, it is because they have disconnected themselves from *Bava Kamma*, *Bava Metzia*, and *Bava Basra* (which deal with money matters). [4]

Torah is a complete way of life.

Rav Gifter often surprised the *bachurim* with his controlled reactions to difficult situations. A group of *bachurim* in Telz, some coming from Chassidic backgrounds, were fond of holding a *Melaveh Malkah* every week, complete with eating, singing, and dancing. After they would get the food, they would hide in a corner of the campus so as not to attract the attention of those who did not feel that their particular type of *Melaveh Malkah* was appropriate. Finally fed up with hiding, though, the *Melaveh Malkah* group decided to hold their celebration right in their rooms. This irritated some boys, who began banging on the dormitory room door, insisting that they stop the event.

---

4. Rabbi Azriel Goldfein.

Ignoring the protestors, the *Melaveh Malkah* group continued to celebrate, getting louder and eventually beginning to dance. It was a lively event. When the protestors' knocking stopped, the partyers felt vindicated; it seemed that the rest of the boys were going to let them be. A moment later, though, another knock was heard.

One of the boys in the room noticed that the banging sounded different and called out, "Who's there?" The voice from the other side of the door replied, "You'll be surprised!" There was no mistaking that voice; it obviously belonged to Rav Gifter! (At that time, he and the rebbetzin resided in the dormitory.) It was, after all, 11:30 at night, and they were sure they would be reprimanded. One brave young man opened the door, and sure enough, there was Rav Gifter in his shirtsleeves. "Well," he said, "are you surprised?"

"I sure am …" was all the terrified young man could muster. He was embarrassed and nervous as he waited for the tongue-lashing he was sure they would all receive.

"Well, I must tell you," Rav Gifter continued, "the rebbetzin and I enjoyed the beautiful singing so much. It was really quite special. But what can I say… *Di tantzen iz mamesh iber dem kup.* [The dancing is literally right over my head.] Continue to enjoy your *Melaveh Malkah*, but please do it without the dancing."

And that was it.

No rebuke. No admonishment. No *mussar*.

Now, 25 years later, when one of those involved told me the story, he still could not get over the incredible self-control and patience the rosh hayeshivah displayed on that Motza'ei Shabbos. He was still in awe of the fact that Rav Gifter had not yelled at them, but had just asked them to stop dancing. He had even made it a point to praise the singing!

It was a lesson in character that he would never forget.

It was a perfect example of how Rav Gifter taught about the Torah way of life through his actions.

Chapter 20
Students of All Stripes

MANY YOUNG MARRIED MEN, WHETHER THEY HAD learned in Telz or not, came to Rav Gifter for advice on their careers in *chinuch*. This was always a fascinating experience for these young men, since Rav Gifter's responses were often different from what they had expected to hear.

Tailor-made Advice

One *talmid*, who had come to the yeshivah only after he married, was encouraged by Rav Gifter to begin teaching in the local high school. In addition, he instructed him to accept an offer to give a class once a week in Columbus, Ohio, which was about 140 miles away! The reason for the strange response? Rav Gifter believed that every Jew should feel a sense of responsibility toward other Jews. Therefore, not only should he strengthen his own learning, but he should use his talents to help the general Klal. The young man, he felt, should share his Torah as widely as possible, no matter how long the drive between jobs.[1]

---
1. Rabbi Moshe Tuvia Lieff.

Rav Gifter was often consulted on matters pertaining to the *chinuch* careers of people whom he did not even know.

A young American couple who had learned in Eretz Yisrael, and planned to stay there, had to return to America for family reasons. The man ended up teaching in Miami and doing very well there. When the family problems were resolved, and it was time for them to go back to Eretz Yisrael, the man told the school's principal that he was leaving. The principal, who saw that the young man had been successful as a teacher, wondered aloud if the rebbi should ask a *gadol* about returning to Israel. Thus, the young man turned to Rav Gifter for advice.

Just a short while before, Rav Gifter had returned from Eretz Yisrael; he was heartbroken that his dream had to be cut short. The rebbi and his wife went to Rav Gifter, when the rosh hayeshivah was visiting his daughter in Baltimore, and explained their situation, emphasizing their love for, and heartfelt desire, to return to Eretz Yisrael. Surely, they thought, someone like Rav Gifter would understand how important it was for them to live in Eretz Yisrael, and would encourage them to return.

But Rav Gifter didn't.

Instead, Rav Gifter asked the man if he was successful as a rebbi. When the rebbi assured Rav Gifter that he was indeed successful, there was nothing left to discuss. With much emotion, Rav Gifter told him to continue to live in America. He cried as he told him to serve in the greatest profession anyone could hope for; he should continue to be a rebbi.

Now, 25 years later, this "*talmid*" has a picture of Rav Gifter hanging in his dining room. He never learned under Rav Gifter, never attended the yeshivah there, and was certainly not a *talmid* in the traditional sense of the word. But the community in Florida has been enriched by the dedication of this outstanding rebbi, who followed Rav Gifter's advice like a loyal *talmid*.[2]

As one rebbi, who was not a Telzer *talmid*, wrote to me:

…. I was learning in Ner Yisrael, and Rav Gifter was visiting his children, the Eisenbergs. Around Minchah time, I went up to him and asked

---

2. Rabbi Dovid Levin.

him, "Rosh Hayeshivah, what is the *chiyuv talmud Torah* [obligation of learning Torah]? There's so much to learn. What is the proper Torah curriculum? What exactly should I learn to fulfill the mitzvah of *talmud Torah* properly?"

He answered, "The *chiyuv talmud Torah* is to learn whatever you want to learn, but to learn it because the Al-mighty told you that He wants you to learn in order to attach yourself to Him." [3]

Rav Yosef Granofsky always dreamed of starting a yeshivah. However, he was often discouraged by those who felt he would be better off returning to America and not concerning himself with the money worries that come along with running a yeshivah.

Close to 30 years ago, Rav Granofsky met Rav Gifter in the Hotel Reich in Jerusalem, and related his lifelong dream to Rav Gifter. He also shared the pessimistic views of those who had discouraged him.

Rav Gifter responded by citing the verse in *Devarim* (8:18) that urges us to remember that Hashem is the One Who gives us the strength to make *chayil* (wealth). The *Targum* translates this to mean that Hashem provides us with the inspiration so that we can acquire capital. "Don't give up on your dream; Hashem will provide you with the funds and the *bachurim*."

Fortified with Rav Gifter's encouragement and advice, Rav Granofsky founded Yeshiva Ohr David, a yeshivah for American boys in Jerusalem. Indeed, 27 years later, the yeshivah continues to flourish. Rav Granofsky has always given credit to Rav Gifter for being one of the "founders" of the yeshivah.

The year after Rav Gifter passed away, Rav Granofsky had a dream. In it, Rav Gifter appeared to him and thanked him for giving him credit for being a founder of the yeshivah. Rav Granofsky was shocked that a 15-minute encounter had enabled him to see Rav Gifter in a dream.

Rav Gifter explained to him, "Gan Eden is like a hotel. There are three-, four-, and five-star hotels. The difference between them is just a few little extras. Whenever you say good things about the deceased, it enhances his Gan Eden and adds another star to his hotel. So thank you for upgrading my hotel!"

---

3. Rabbi Baruch Leff.

THERE WERE SOME FAMOUS REBBES WHO LEARNED IN TELZ WHEN they were young.

Future Chassidic Rebbes

The Munkatcher Rebbe, Rav Moshe Leib Rabinovich, came to Telz as a young *bachur*. Although he was from a Chassidic dynasty, he became quite close with Rav Gifter. Although Telz was not a Chassidic yeshivah by any means, Rav Gifter would quote from Chassidic *sefarim* and rebbeim in his *shiurei daas*. Some of his personal favorites were the writings of the Baal HaTanya, the *Avodas Yisrael* of the Kozhnitzer Maggid, and the *Sheim MiShmuel*, If it was the truth, it did not make a difference who said it, and Rav Gifter was eager to learn it and to teach it.

But Rav Moshe Leib appreciated much more about his rebbi. In fact, we can see from the following quote that he attributes his method of learning (*derech halimud*) to Rav Gifter:

While other roshei yeshivah would concentrate on the **conclusion** *when teaching the Gemara, Rav Gifter took the talmidim on the same journey he took, until he reached his conclusions about the sugya. He gave us a path of learning that we could follow. The conclusion was never as important as the route that took him there.*

He would often say that a talmid who listens to a shiur of a rosh yeshivah is not like a layman who listens to a discourse of a rabbi in the shul. That layman is only interested in the conclusion [maskanah]. But a talmid must receive a method from his rebbi. Therefore, if you do not understand how the rosh hayeshivah came to his conclusion, then you cannot consider yourself a talmid.

One of the Munkatcher Rebbe's most unforgettable moments was when Rav Gifter came to give a *bechinah* to the *talmidim* of the Munkatcher Yeshivah. In his unmatched style, Rav Gifter asked the class a difficult question, and offered a reward to anyone who gave the proper answer. When one boy answered cor-

The Munkatcher Rebbe being *maspid* Rav Gifter at the *levayah* in New York

rectly, Rav Gifter took out his checkbook and wrote out a $10 check to the boy! The *bachurim* had never seen such a rosh hayeshivah before, and they would certainly never forget this encounter.

Prophetic Advice

TO EVERY STUDENT, RAV GIFTER DROVE HOME THE SAME BASIC points: It doesn't matter what you do in life, but always sanctify the Name of Heaven in whatever you do.

Tommy Weiss first came to Telz on a school trip led by the famed educator, Rabbi Shmuel Kaufman. He was in ninth grade at the time at Yeshivas Bais Yehuda in Detroit. Although he was from a more modern background, he had just switched from a more modern school. However, Tommy, along with some of the other boys, still sported very long hair.

That Friday night, Rav Gifter ate in Telz Yeshivah's dining room with his rebbetzin. When he first began his speech, he spoke in Yiddish. Even though the boys from Detroit were unable to understand the language, they were impressed with Rav Gifter's commanding presence. But then suddenly, Rav Gifter switched to English and said, "And what do the boys from Detroit come to tell us? That there's a barber strike?"

The vast majority of the boys slunk down a bit lower in their seats. Still, something struck a chord inside of Tommy; he realized that something was different and special about Rav Gifter. And he wanted to experience it firsthand. The next year, he transferred to Telz and stayed there for five years.

One time, Rabbi Hillel Mannes, the general studies principal, expressed concern over the manner in which the high-school boys were behaving and performing in their secular studies. He shared his concerns with Rav Gifter. The rosh hayeshivah delivered a special *shmuess* to the high school.

When Rav Gifter spoke to the boys about the situation, he seemed genuinely upset. The *bachurim* cowered behind their lecterns as Rav Gifter demanded better behavior and improved performance. "If one is capable of excellence and gets less than an A, it is a *chillul Hashem*!" Since Tommy took his secular studies seriously, he felt validated.

As the years passed, Tommy excelled in Torah learning and general studies. Thus, he was chosen to be the class valedictorian. His parents were very proud of Tommy's achievements but insisted that he leave yeshivah to go to college. However, the rule in the yeshivah was that a boy could deliver the valedictory address only if he was committed to stay for one year of post-high-school learning in the yeshivah. As such, they had little choice but to let him stay.

The next year, though, his parents were adamant that it was time to move on, and Tommy felt that he needed Rav Gifter's guidance. He went to the rosh hayeshivah and shared his concerns. Thus began a series of many hours of discussion between the rosh hayeshivah and Tommy. Rav Gifter shared his own experiences as a teenager and many of his struggles.

The underlying message was that a *ben Torah* must follow his heart and there will be sacrifices one has to make. In Tommy's case, those sacrifices came in the form of terrible friction between him and his parents.

Indeed, Tommy stayed in yeshivah one more year. At that point, after two years of learning full-time beyond high school, Rav Gifter gave him permission to attend Yeshiva University.

Tommy felt that Rav Gifter understood the different aspects of his personality, as well as his capabilities. In fact, during the course of the many conversations between the two, Rav Gifter told Tommy that he envisioned him one day as the president of his shul. In addition, he assured him that one never knows where an individual is heading, commenting that perhaps his *chavrusa* would some day not be Torah observant. At the time, Tommy was learning with a boy who was very focused on his learning and appeared to be very dedicated.

Indeed, many years later, when presented with the opportunity to become the president of his shul, Tommy heard the echo of Rav Gifter's voice in his ears. "I envision you one day becoming the president of your shul." He took the position and enjoys a reputation of being a layman who is involved in Torah pursuits.

And sadly, Rav Gifter was correct about his *chavrusa*. He has tragically strayed from the path of Torah.

ANOTHER MAN WHO WAS NOT OFFICIALLY A *TALMID* TOLD ME:

An Indelible Impact

In the summer of 1987, I was learning in Kol Torah in Bayit VeGan. Rav Gifter, who was in Eretz Yisrael with his rebbetzin for a wedding, was staying near the yeshivah. My rebbi encouraged me and two of my friends to visit him. He greeted us warmly, and, although he did not know us, spoke with us for over an hour about life in Lithuania.

Rav Gifter and Rav Shach, at the *chasunah* of Chaim Mordechai Ausband. At far left is Rav Aizik Ausband; at far right is Rav Avrohom Ausband

One story was particularly memorable. He described, with tears, how mussar seder looked in Telz. At times, it would take place at sunset. One would begin the seder reading a passage of the mussar sefer over and over by the light of day, and as the sun set and darkness fell in the beis midrash [these were days before electricity was available in such areas], the talmidim cried out loud, uninhibited, repeating again and again the lines of mussar, engraving them in their hearts. One would hear wails in the absolute darkness that pierced one's heart and soul.

During another visit, while we were listening to Rav Gifter, there was a knock at the door. At the entrance stood none other than the gadol hador, Rav Elazar Menachem Man Shach! He had come from Bnei Brak to Yerushalayim to visit Rav Gifter. They kissed and spoke to each other for a while with great affection. After escorting Rav Shach out the door, Rav Gifter told us, "I always tell Rav Shach that I am going to come to him when I am in Eretz Yisrael, but he always manages to beat me to it!" Those extraordinary moments made an indelible impact on me, a 19-year-old yeshivah bachur.[4]

---

4. Rabbi Moshe Bamberger.

Chapter 20: Students of All Stripes ☐ 245

A "*Talmidah*" Remembers

I FIRST MET RAV GIFTER AS A COLLEGE SOPHOMORE ON ROSH Hashanah in 1969. I had committed to keeping Shabbos and davening daily as a result of some reading I had done about Judaism while a counselor at a traditional Jewish sleepaway camp in 1968, before traveling to Ohio to attend college. Since the college had no High Holy Days services, interested students were hosted by families at a Reform congregation in a nearby town. My experience there as a freshman was rather disappointing: The "rabbi" was very welcoming but announced in his sermon that the congregation drew inspiration by the presence of the visiting college students. Before returning to Ohio for my sophomore year, I asked the "rabbi" of my own Conservative synagogue (who, unbeknownst to me, had learned in an Orthodox yeshivah), "Isn't there any place I can go to this Rosh Hashanah where the people want to daven with kavanah?" (as described in the books I had read and as I aspired to daily.) I explained to my rabbi that I yearned for a High Holy Days service that would provide inspiration. He wrote down the word "Telshe" (an alternate spelling of Telz) on a piece of paper and advised me to see if I could make arrangements to spend Rosh Hashanah there.

Of course, having never heard of a yeshivah, I was merely hoping for a more spiritual synagogue. (In fact, I had never met a religious person other than my Conservative rabbi,) and I was the only person I knew who cared about Shabbos, davening, and connecting with G-d. When I located Telshe through directory assistance, the non-Jewish bookkeeper was dubious about my request, asking if I realized I was calling a boys' boarding school. However, she offered to see what she could do for me, inviting me to call back in a few days. At that time, she told me I could come and that I had been invited to stay at the home of a widow and would be hosted by a few families. She then cautioned me to wear a skirt.

When I arrived at Telz on Erev Rosh Hashanah, it was immediately apparent I had entered a different world: Numerous slight, black-suited young men with strange black hats were scurrying about (like ants) with an air of palpable excitement and anxiety. The classmate who had driven me asked if I was sure I wanted to get out of the car; otherwise, he would be perfectly happy to drive me back to our familiar campus (only an hour or so away by car, but clearly light-years away from this sober scene, which seemed to be taking place on a different planet and in a different generation, perhaps even a different century!). I bravely assured him I wanted to stay.

If I had any qualms, they evaporated once the Rosh Hashanah davening started. Then I was totally transported, instantly recognizing that I had stumbled into my own personal Shangri-la. It was incredible to discover that I was not the only one in the world aspiring to fulfill the relationship with G-d that I had read about. Rav Gifter and Rav Boruch Sorotzkin had each invited me for a Yom Tov meal. Since Rav Gifter was American and spoke English (unlike the Sorotzkins who were very kind, but spoke Yiddish at the table), I found it possible to connect with him immediately. Rav Gifter was warm, friendly, and took an interest in me. At my request, I was invited back for Yom Kippur.

After Yom Kippur, I arranged to meet with Rav Gifter. I told him that Telz was exactly what I'd been looking for, without knowing it existed, and that this was the life I meant to lead. Over Yom Kippur, I had decided I wanted to drop out of college to attend Gateshead (since I was sharing a room at the home of Rebbetzin Bloch with an alumna of Gateshead and she had told me all about it). I wanted to become well educated like her and study Torah with a chavrusa; I didn't want the tremendous inspiration of the High Holy Days to dissipate back on campus. I asked Rav Gifter's opinion. He shared my enthusiasm, but cautioned me that he was not an expert on girls' education. He told me he'd connect me with another rabbi in New York who could advise me better.

I made arrangements to fly home for a few days and meet with the rabbi suggested by Rav Gifter, Rabbi Borchardt. He questioned me about my desire to leave college for Gateshead, asking why I couldn't keep Shabbos at college. I remember telling him that while that would be theoretically possible, "I want to be on a higher level [madreigah], and I don't see that happening if I'm on a campus without any religious people at all for the next three years." When he learned that I needed three more years of college to enter the two-year graduate school program in my intended field (for this was decades before on-line programs, CLEPs, or other shortcuts), Rabbi Borchardt advised that since Gateshead would be an additional three-year commitment and also a huge adjustment and academic challenge for someone of my background, he didn't recommend it. He recommended that I return to school and spend Shabbos at Telz, as often as I could, and arrange to study Torah there informally. I was disappointed, but I took his advice, which he relayed to Rav Gifter on my behalf. (This plan required that I find a part-time job in order to cover the weekly cost of the campus limo service as well as the public transportation needed for the hour-and-a-half trip to and from the yeshivah.)

Rav Gifter arranged for me to be hosted by kollel families at the yeshivah, and I quickly developed close relationships with them, as well as a yearning for kollel life for my own future family. As I became a regular at Telz for Shabbos, I also became close to several other families among the administration, but Rav Gifter remained my guide in what I should be reading and learning, and how I could lead a Torah observant life on my college campus, which had no kosher meal plan or other basics of Jewish life.

He generously gave me his time and related to me in such a warm, natural manner, that I found in him not only a respected mentor, but also a friend. Of course, I had no inkling of his tremendous stature, and in any case, I was totally unacquainted with the concept of kvod haTorah for gedolei Torah. I remember my surprise when I witnessed the extreme deference accorded him by the students I observed at Rav Gifter's Shabbos table. The next time we met privately, I expressed my concern that this deference could create a social barrier in his relationships and wondered if he found his position socially isolating. (If I recall correctly, Rav Gifter acknowledged that this could indeed be an issue.)

I was able to spend that January at Telz during my college's independent study program, boarding right near Rav Gifter. In addition to pursuing my Jewish studies, I had much more exposure to the rosh hayeshivah and Rebbetzin Gifter and their family. I remember being struck by his humility

Purim scenes at the Telzer Yeshivah

and commitment to truth when I learned (perhaps from Rebbetzin Gifter) that he and the other rosh hayeshivah, Rav Baruch Sorotzkin, paskened all personal shailos for each other, instead of relying on themselves in areas in which there could be any personal negios. When I was troubled by learning of mitzvos that were incomprehensible from my limited background (such as killing innocent children in an ir hanidachas[5]), Rav Gifter reassured me that all my questions had satisfactory answers.

I continued to spend Shabbos and Yom Tov at Telz during the school year until the following winter (when I was able to spend the semester before my

---

5. A "condemned city"; see *Devarim* 13:13-19.

Chapter 20: Students of All Stripes □ 249

wedding in another state with an established Torah community). During that time, I continued to enjoy a close relationship with Rav and Rebbetzin Gifter and their family, sharing in Yisroel's bar mitzvah, etc.

My husband and I elected to return to Telz for our Shabbos sheva berachos, because we felt this symbolized the central role we wanted the yeshivah to play in our marriage. Rav and Rebbetzin Gifter attended the sheva berachos of course, and we received encouragement and warm berachos from the rosh hayeshivah. The yeshivah itself made us sheva berachos in the dining hall for shalosh seudos, at which time Rav Boruch spoke. He stated that sheva berachos were held in the dining hall only for talmidim of the yeshivah. He then said that in view of the fact that in this unique case it was the kallah rather than the chassan who had learned in Telz, he was bestowing upon me "an honorary sheepskin as a graduate of the yeshivah."

(Decades later, when my husband and I flew to Cleveland to be menachem avel after Rav Gifter's passing, the airport was teeming with alumni of the yeshivah, who renewed old relationships and introduced themselves to talmidim from different eras in the yeshivah, sharing and comparing their reminiscences of Rav Gifter. They were taken aback to learn from my husband, "Actually, it was not me but my wife who learned at Telz!")

My dream came true when my husband agreed to defer grad school after our college graduation, a year after our wedding, so he could learn in kollel for a year at Ner Yisrael in Baltimore. We were able to maintain our connection with Rav Gifter as he visited his son-in-law who was a rebbi at the yeshivah. As my husband's one-year commitment extended to eleven-and-a-half years in the kollel and our family grew, I looked forward to Rav Gifter's visits, knowing I could meet with him for daas Torah and the chizuk of our ongoing relationship. Rav Gifter continued to demonstrate warmth and caring, going so far as to visit me one Yom Tov when he learned that my husband was away at the hospital with one of our children who needed surgery.

As the years went by, not only we, but also our children, relished our special connection with Rav Gifter and his family. They have special memories, for example, of visiting Rav and Rebbetzin Gifter in the Telz dormitory apartment in which they lived upon their return from Telz-Stone.

The rosh hayeshivah passed away the week of our oldest son's wedding, and we had just received a beautiful letter of berachos from Rebbetzin Gifter for the chassan and kallah, as the rosh hayeshivah's health had not permitted him to respond to the invitation.

Rav Gifter took pleasure in our family's growth and progress throughout the decades of our relationship and expressed his satisfaction at witnessing the positive results of the time and caring he lavished on me. Nevertheless, I couldn't help but be disappointed that he was no longer alive when I learned several years ago from a report of genealogical research written on the occasion of a family reunion, that both my maternal great-grandmother and great-grandfather and their extended families had actually come from Telz in Europe, and that one of my relatives had actually taught in the yeshivah! No wonder that I had experienced the yeshivah as my personal Shangri-la almost 40 years earlier and had sensed that in coming to Telz for Rosh Hashanah that I had actually "come home." On the other hand, perhaps Rav Gifter would not have been at all surprised ....

Yes, an indelible impact ... on so many different types of Jews: in Eretz Yisrael, in Telz, in Columbus, in Baltimore, in Miami, in Munkatch, in Detroit.

All of them were his students.

Chapter 21
Connecting With His Students and Encouraging Them to Grow

RAV GIFTER CHERISHED LIFE; HE SAW EACH MOMENT AS precious, as a gift to be used properly. He loved productive people,[1] and constantly encouraged goal-setting. One time, when Rav Gifter was already confined to a wheelchair, a young man stopped his baseball playing to wait for the rebbetzin to wheel her husband by. Rav Gifter called out to the *bachur*, "What are you looking at: an old man? Play ball, and if you aren't playing ball, then go the *beis midrash* and learn something! Be productive!"

Living Life to Its Fullest

He was merely echoing a sentiment of his from 40 years before, when he would say to a group of boys playing baseball, "Hit a home run!"

He would often shout something encouraging to the boys as they played ball. When they would look at him in surprise, wondering why

---
1. Rabbi Azriel Goldfein.

The rebbetzin taking Rav Gifter across the yeshivah's campus after he injured his foot

he was cheering them on, he would say, "*Ah mentch darf tun altz mit zeine gantze koach. Azoi darf zein in leben.* [A person must do everything he does with his entire strength. This is the way it must be in life.] Otherwise, the tendency of not doing so will insinuate itself into everything you do."

A famous line of his was, "If you fool around [*batel*] in the afternoon [during secular studies], you will end up being one who wastes learning time [a *batlan*] in the morning [during Torah studies], as well."

Once, when a *bachur* who was leaving yeshivah to further his secular education came to say goodbye to Rav Gifter, he instructed the young man, "Make sure to sanctify the Name of Hashem. Do you know what that means? It means getting A's and not B's!"

Keeping Them Close

HIS ABILITY TO ENCOURAGE AND SUPPORT ENDEARED HIM TO many, but especially to those who made an effort to become close to him. One *talmid*, who felt extremely close to Rav Gifter, was devastated to find out that his beloved rebbi could not attend his wedding. The *talmid* was so upset that he did not contact the rosh hayeshivah for many months. Then one day, it hit him, "Who am I hurting by not being in touch with my rebbi? I am hurting myself." From that day on, he began to call and contact the rosh hayeshivah weekly, and the relationship lasted for over 30 years.

With Rav Shimon Schwab

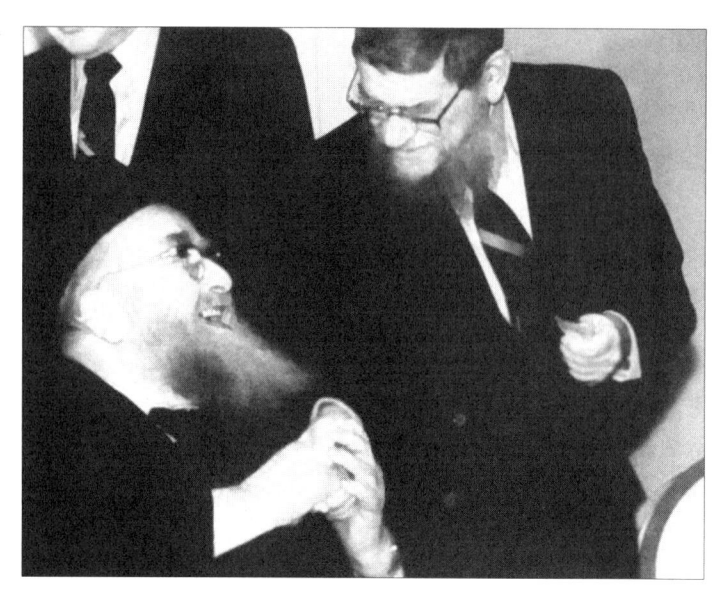

On a number of occasions, when *bachurim* needed to talk to him, they would escort Rav Gifter to his home while they schmoozed. More often than not, he would invite the boy into his home for a meal. If the rebbetzin was not home, he would fry an egg, or make a tuna sandwich (with a tomato included!) for the *talmid*, insisting that the boy eat first and then they would discuss the matter at hand. [2]

As dear as learning Torah was to him, if someone needed to speak to him, Rav Gifter would make himself immediately available. This is how he dealt with personal matters as well as matters of the Klal.

One *talmid* wrote:

Rav Gifter was my rebbi, my mentor, my guide, and my inspiration. I learned in his shiur for one year — two zmanim — but they were memorable days. I remember when we presented him with a sefer, and it was inscribed: "Venafsheinu keshurah be'nafsho [Our soul is bound up with his soul]," and all of us signed. He was deeply moved. He proceeded to deliver a mussar shmuess on what it means that the souls of a rebbi and his talmidim are bound together in a combined commitment to Torah study and love of Torah.[3]

As is the case with many prominent figures, many of the students were shy about approaching him. But he was wonderful at putting

---

2. Rabbi Yehuda Lefkovitz, Rabbi Eli Friedman.
3. Reb Shlomo Slonim.

Befriending a youngster

everyone at ease. Sometimes, just doing something very out of character would show them his lighter side and give them the courage to come closer.

That rare balance of being approachable, yet inspiring a healthy sense of awe for a rebbi, was part of what endeared him to his students.

One *bachur*, Eli, very much wanted to ask Rav Gifter a question on the *sefer, Avnei Miluim,* but thought that it would be dismissed as being silly. Remembering the rule that one may approach him if there is a light on in his home, the boy gathered his courage and asked.

The two of them went through the *sefer* together. By the time Eli left, it was nearly midnight. Eli thought he had never been so happy; the feeling was something he would never forget. It charged him up and gave him a newfound pleasure in learning. Soon Eli became one of the better boys in the yeshivah. He used this incident as an impetus to always speak to Rav Gifter in learning, even long after he had left the yeshivah. The bond had been formed. Remarkably, this closeness lasted for nearly 50 years.

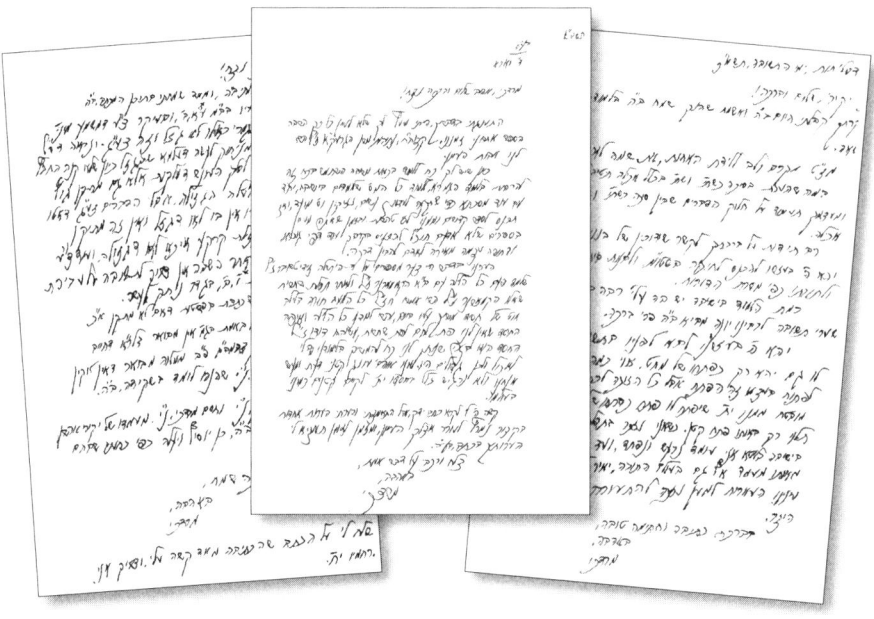

Rav Gifter's letters to Rabbi Mordechai Moshe Suchard undertaken despite the fact that his tremors made it very difficult for him to write

Mutty Suchard, a young *bachur* from South Africa, planned to stay in yeshivah for Succos. He was looking forward to the opportunity, but he was slightly apprehensive and a bit homesick.

In the days leading up to Yom Tov, Mutty was learning a small tractate, *Maseches Horayos*, as Rav Gifter would encourage the *bachurim* to do during *bein hazmanim*. He came to *daf* 6, which he found perplexing. He asked some of the older kollel fellows for help and one man suggested he ask Rav Gifter.

Unabashedly, Mutty went to the dormitory to Rav Gifter. He knocked and the rebbetzin took him to the rosh hayeshivah. After thinking about it, Rav Gifter was intrigued with the question. He invited Mutty to search through the personal notebook that he had written as a *bachur* in Telz on the same tractate.

Amazingly, Mutty found that very question there. Although Rav Gifter had written an answer in his notebook, he wrote that the answer was a *dochek* (a forced explanation), and left it at that, concluding that it would remain a *dochek* until Mashiach would supply a better answer. Mutty was thrilled that he had had the same difficulty as Rav Gifter, and he was prepared to leave.

However, the rosh hayeshivah was not finished. He and Mutty consulted the *Sefer Birkei Yosef* from the Chida on *Maseches Horayos.* Indeed, they discovered that the Chida had also asked this question!

Mutty was excited that he had shared these meaningful moments with Rav Gifter and was ready to leave once again, but Rav Gifter asked the rebbetzin to bring cake and tea. For the next four hours, Rav Gifter took his new *talmid* on a virtual journey through Lithuania, and regaled him with Torah, *hashkafah,* and stories.

Mutty realized then and there that Succos would not be so lonely after all.

About 50 years separated the rebbi and *talmid,* but one question on the Gemara had brought them together. And for the remainder of his tenure in yeshivah, Mutty became practically a member of the Gifter family. Even after he officially left the yeshivah, Mutty kept a close connection with Rav Gifter.

As mentioned, Rav Gifter was a committed correspondent. He didn't write only to *gedolei hador,* on Torah topics, he also wrote to former students, long after they left the yeshivah, offering guidance or just inquiring about their well-being. He even corresponded with individuals with whom he had never learned but had developed a relationship. In fact, anyone who wrote to him would receive a reply.

Your Own Rebbi

ALTHOUGH THERE WERE TIMES THAT RAV GIFTER ADVISED PEOPLE who were not his *talmidim,* usually he would strongly encourage people to seek guidance from their rebbi, rav, or rosh yeshivah, rather than give his own advice.

One morning, while Rav Gifter was visiting his son, Reb Binyomin, in Brooklyn, Reb Binyomin had an early morning appointment in the Bronx, so he asked Rabbi Chaim Kahan to give Rav Gifter a ride back to Reb Binyomin's home after davening.

As he waited for Rav Gifter, Reb Chaim could not help but notice an animated conversation between a young married fellow and the rosh hayeshivah. The young man was clearly disappointed by what Rav Gifter was saying, but he did not relent. Finally, the two parted and both seemed frustrated.

A minute or so after entering the car, Rav Gifter said to Reb Chaim, "I imagine you think I'm a cruel person." Reb Chaim did not know how to respond. He knew nothing of the incident, and he assured Rav Gifter of that fact. Rav Gifter then shared what the argument was about.

With Rav Ruderman

"This fellow wanted me to give him advice on a specific matter. But he is a *talmid* of Rav Ruderman [rosh yeshivah of Ner Yisrael in Baltimore]. And I told him to seek counsel from his rosh yeshivah.

"He told me that Rav Ruderman had instructed him that if he saw me in New York, he should ask me the question."

Rav Gifter paused for a moment as he mulled over the incident. And then he continued.

"You know, when I say *Viduy* on Yom Kippur, I have the most *kavanah* when I say the words, '*ya'atznu ra* — we have given bad advice.' I tell the Al-mighty that I am not the Steipler Gaon, and I cannot give the proper advice to the entire Klal Yisrael. But I ask Hashem to give me the Heavenly assistance to at least be able to guide my own *talmidim* in the proper path."

Still exasperated and broken, he concluded, "I wish I could have helped him. But I could not advise him; he is not my *talmid*!"

"I'm Proud of You!"

ONCE, A *BACHUR* WAS TRAVELING TO ISRAEL FOR SUCCOS, AND needed to take his oral *bechinah* privately prior to his leaving. The next day, the boy arrived in the room to be tested. Sitting in front of him were Rav Gifter, Rav Chaim Stein, and Rav Dovid Barkin. Rav Chaim asked the *bachur* the question on a difficult Rambam that they had discussed in *shiur*. The young man began to answer the question; he knew it well. But suddenly, his mind went blank. He tried to recall any of the five different answers that had been cited in class, but none came to mind.

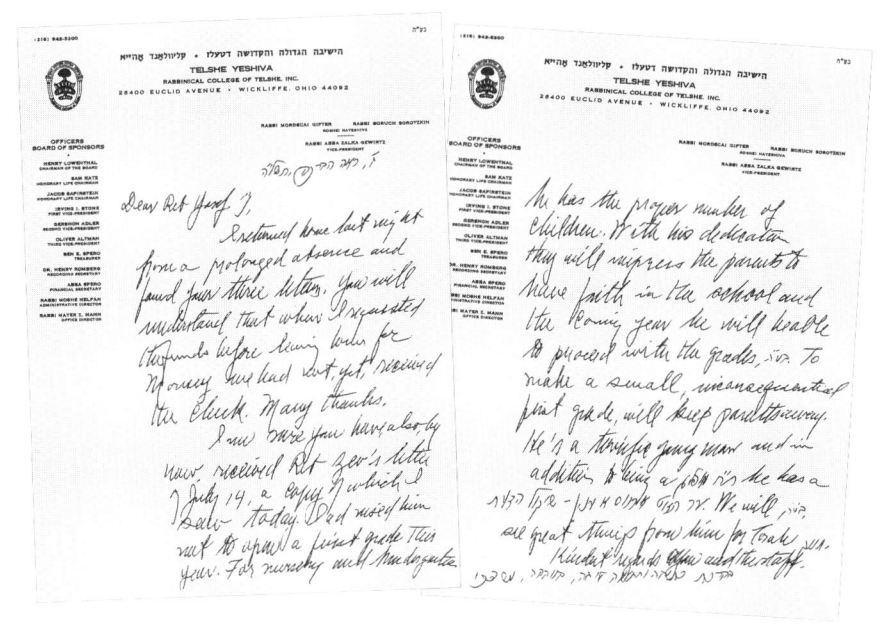

A letter from Rav Gifter to Torah Umesorah, praising Rav Zev Leff and encouraging the organization to support him.

Rav Gifter encouraged him to think. He did, and he managed to answer the question. But it was not any of the five answers mentioned in *shiur*. It was his own original answer, and he feared it was just not good enough.

To his complete shock, Rav Gifter began to cry, and said, "That is the answer that my rebbi gave to this difficulty in the Rambam."

The boy smiled — no, he was *beaming* with pride.

When the *bechinah* was over, Rav Gifter put his arm around the young man. "You did well today. I'm very proud of you!"

My older brother Chaim told me this story. It happened nearly 30 years ago, but he smiles when telling it as though it happened yesterday.

Rav Dovid Barkin

Chapter 21: Connecting With His Students and Encouraging Them ☐ 259

When Rav Zev Leff spoke about how Rav Gifter had made him who he is, he quoted the words of our Sages, "*Kol ha'melamed es ben chaveiro Torah maaleh alav ha'kasuv ke'ilu yelado* — Whoever teaches his friend's son Torah, Scripture views him as if he had fathered him" (*Rashi, Bamidbar* 3:1; *Sanhedrin* 19b). It was considered as if Aharon's children were Moshe's own, although they surely learned from Aharon, as well. On the other hand, Avraham Avinu and Sarah Imeinu were the only ones who taught Torah to many souls — "*ve'es hanefesh asher asu ve'Charan* — and the souls that they made in Charan" (*Bereishis* 12:5).

Rav Leff described his relationship with Rav Gifter as similar to the relationship of Avraham Avinu and those he brought close to Hashem, since he felt that Rav Gifter alone was responsible for his accomplishments. To accentuate his point, Rav Leff recounted an incident that occurred soon after he first came to Telz Yeshivah. He was on the second-year *beis midrash* level and was assigned to Rav Gavriel Ginsberg's *shiur*. The class was learning *Bava Kamma* at the time, and Rav Gavriel explained a commentary from the *Nesivos HaMishpat* (commonly referred to as the *Nesivos*) in the lecture. Zev looked up the commentary, but he couldn't find any mention of *Bava Kamma*-related topics in the *Nesivos*. When he posed his question to Rav Gavriel, Rav Gavriel smiled and said, "*Tzaddik*, you are holding a *Nesivos* **Olam** from the Maharal in your hands." Such was the elementary level of young Zev when he first came to the yeshivah.

Nevertheless, Zev wrote copious notes on every word he heard in the *shiur*. One day, Rav Gifter, as he would often do, stopped at a lectern and opened up the notebook that was on it. Zev watched from a short distance away. After a few moments of perusing through the notes, Rav Gifter looked up, noticed Zev, and asked, "Are these yours?"

Zev nodded that indeed they were. Rav Gifter responded, "You keep writing and one day we will print them; you'll see."

And one day, Rav Zev Leff, as a rav and rosh yeshivah, would remember those words — that completely changed his vision and goals in life — with tremendous emotion and gratitude. As Rav Leff expressed it, "You have no idea what that did for me. It gave me such motivation …"

Soon after Reb Zev was married, he contributed a Torah thought to the Telz Kollel's Torah publication, *Pe'er Mordechai*. After Rav Gifter read it, he told the rebbetzin to call Reb Zev's wife and to tell her how much the rosh hayeshivah enjoyed reading her husband's piece. He wanted her to value her husband and to feel proud of him.

BY OPENING UP THEIR EYES IN VARIOUS WAYS, RAV GIFTER stretched the minds of his students.[4] Just like Rav Mottel Pogromansky,

Stretching Minds

Rav Gifter influenced the boys to stretch their minds and aim higher.

Rav Gifter learned this lesson from his own rebbeim and inculcated it into his personal method of learning (*derech halimud*). For example, Rav Yosef Leib Bloch (the father of Rav Zalman, Rav Avraham Yitzchak, and Rav Elya Meir Bloch), was a brilliant and deep thinker. He would walk around with notes on the classic Kabbalah writings of the Baal HaLeshem, Rav Shlomo Elyashiv (grandfather of Rav Yosef Shalom Elyashiv of Jerusalem). When asked why he spoke over the heads of the laymen in the city, Rav Yosef Leib responded that he was not speaking to their minds; he was speaking to their hearts and to their souls.

When a kollel fellow decided to leave kollel to go to work, he went to ask Rav Gifter for a blessing. Rav Gifter smiled and responded, "I give you a *berachah* that you should grow to be just like the Rashash." (The Rashash, Rav Shmuel Shtrashun of Vilna, was a Torah giant who was a businessman, too.) Seconds later, he corrected himself, "No … you should grow to be better than the Rashash!"

RAV GIFTER TAUGHT HIS STUDENTS TO LEARN FROM EVERYTHING they experienced. He would often cite lessons from the world of science

Learning From Everything Around Us

and physics that helped him to understand various portions of the Torah. He once read an article to a *vaad* about Albert Einstein's life and lessons. He cited Einstein's explanation of the unique physical properties of water molecules that form an exceptionally strong bond with one another on the surface of any body of water. This is known as "molecular bonding-surface adhesion"; the bond at the surface is actually stronger than the bond of molecules beneath the surface. He was overjoyed about this concept, as it had helped him understand a distinction found in the laws of *mikvaos*.

Personal experiences became his greatest teachers and teaching tools. He collected leaves and enjoyed breathtaking views and cloud formations as well as brilliant sunsets. Blossoming flowers and rushing waters became his mentors for life's lessons. He would often warn

---

4. Rav Avrohom Chaim Feuer.

against becoming "*ah kalter lung un leber* — a cold piece of meat."⁵

He would frequently recall his trip from Lithuania back to America aboard a rickety old ship. He was traveling with his future father-in-law, Rav Zalman, who had come for fund-raising purposes, and they had brought just barely enough food to last them the trip.

Rav Gifter greeting the Veitzner Rav at the dinner of the Chicago branch of Telz. Rav Chaim Dov Keller in the background

In fact, on the second to last day, all we had was the remaining three drops of Slivovitz and a kreichtikel harte broit [a dried-up crust of bread]. We knew that this would be our last meal before landing; we wouldn't taste anything else for another day or so. Never did I enjoy a bite of food or a drink like that kreichtikel broit or troppele [drop of] Slivovitz!

But the story didn't end there. There was always a lesson that would follow.

This is the way I try to learn Gemara, like it is my last shtikel broit [piece of bread], the letzte troppele trunken [last drop of drink]. That is how much I relish it!

Rav Gifter speaking with Rav Yaakov Reisman and Rav Avrohom Ausband

---

5. Rav Avrohom Chaim Feuer.

Rav Gifter visting Yeshiva of the Telshe Alumni, then in Westwood, New Jersey, and now in Riverdale, New York. At center is the rosh yeshivah, Rav Avrohom Ausband

RAV GIFTER, IN HIS *SHIUR DAAS* ON *"ASEI LECHA RAV,"* MENTIONS that one of the reasons it is important to have a rebbi is because having a rebbi makes you realize that you are learning something that is bigger than you, from someone who is holier than you. For this reason, even if the rebbi seems smaller in stature than you are, you will still accept (*mekabel*) his words, because the Torah you are learning is so great. If we are learning Torah for its own sake (*lishmah*), then we must train ourselves how to learn from anyone. This is an important part of our tradition (*mesorah*).

Learning From Everyone

Rav Gifter had many rebbeim. Some were greater, but some were much less known, but he learned from everyone he met. Students who offered good answers to questions became his rebbeim. He was eager and anxious to hear what each person said; he was always happy to hear and learn something new. Thus, as great as he was, he was always encouraging his students to share their insights with him.

Because he built up his students and connected to them, Rav Gifter also succeeded in teaching them how to maximize their potential and learn from everything and everyone around them. It is no wonder that many of his students have become Torah scholars and laymen who bring light to the world.

Chapter 21: Connecting With His Students and Encouraging Them □ 263

With Rav Chaim Schmelczer

Rav Avrohom Chaim Levin at the dinner inaugurating the dormitory building in Telz, Chicago

LIKE THE FIRST TELZER RAV, RAV ELIEZER GORDON, RAV GIFTER had an insatiable drive to spread the word of Hashem. He therefore established the Yeshiva of the Telshe Alumni, originally located in Westwood, New Jersey. He recruited his *talmidim*, Rav Avrohom Ausband, son of Rav Aizik Ausband (one of the roshei hayeshivah in Cleveland), and Rav Yaakov Reisman (Rav Gifter's son-in-law), to lead the yeshivah. A few

Spreading the Wealth

Nachas report letter

years later, the yeshivah relocated to Riverdale, and Rav Ausband continued on as the rosh yeshivah. Although a branch of Telz in the New York area would cause some of the New York "Telzers" to stop coming to learn in Cleveland, nevertheless, Rav Gifter founded the yeshivah; his goal was the dissemination of Torah. Rav Gifter was so selfless that he agreed to be the guest of honor at the yeshivah's first dinner. Although he detested honors, he was willing to forgo his preferences if being honored would bring money to the new yeshivah.

Following in the footsteps of Rav Gifter, the roshei hayeshivah of Yeshiva of the Telshe Alumni have developed a close connection with their *talmidim*, and continue to watch as the *bachurim* earn themselves a name for their diligence and depth of understanding. The yeshivah, now over 30 years old, has a stellar reputation among the yeshivos in America.

Announcing Rav Gifter's lecture in Northwestern University

PUBLIC LECTURE

Announcing . . . . .

THURSDAY EVENING, MARCH 25, 8:00 O'CLOCK

"JEWISH LAW: A THING OF THE PAST OR A GUIDE TO THE FUTURE?"

A PUBLIC LECTURE ON TALMUDIC CIVIL LAW OF SPECIAL IMPORTANCE TO LAWYERS AND OF EXTREME INTEREST TO THE GENERAL PUBLIC

by

ONE OF THE WORLD'S FOREMOST TALMUDIC AUTHORITIES

RABBI MORDECAI GIFTER

HEAD OF TELSHE YESHIVA, WICKLIFFE, OHIO

at NORTHWESTERN UNIVERSITY SCHOOL OF LAW

LINCOLN HALL, 357 E. CHICAGO AVENUE (Superior Street Entrance)

SPONSORING COMMITTEE

JUDGE ABRAHAM W. BRUSSEL, Chairman

JUDGE JACOB M. BRAUDE	JUDGE IRVING EISERMAN	JUDGE HARRY A. ISEBERG
JUDGE DAVID A. CANEL	JUDGE SAMUEL B. EPSTEIN	JUDGE IRVING LANDESMAN
JUDGE IRWIN N. COHEN	JUDGE HUGO M. FRIEND	JUDGE DAVID LEFKOVITZ
JUDGE NATHAN M. COHEN	JUDGE HYMAN FELDMAN	JUDGE BENJAMIN NELSON
JUDGE JOSEPH J. DRUCKER	JUDGE IRVING GOLDSTEIN	JUDGE BEN SCHWARTZ
JUDGE NORMAN N. EIGER	JUDGE HARRY G. HERSHENSON	JUDGE PHILIP A. SHAPIRO

ADMISSION FREE   NO SOLICITATION OF FUNDS

A Public Service of THE FRIENDS OF TELSHE YESHIVA

Rav Gifter gave support and guidance to the Telz branch in Chicago. Telshe Yeshiva Chicago was founded in 1961, when Rav Mottel Katz, the Telzer rosh hayeshivah, sent two outstanding *talmidim*, Rav Avrohom Chaim Levin and Rav Chaim Schmelczer, to establish the yeshivah. Shortly thereafter, they were joined by Rav Chaim Dov Keller. The yeshivah flourished from the outset.

In 1962, Rav Gifter visited the yeshivah and wrote a *"nachas* report," describing the signs of greatness in Torah among the *talmidim.* In 1965, when the yeshivah celebrated its fifth anniversary with a two-day celebration, Rav Gifter traveled to Chicago to speak for the affair. Shortly thereafter, the yeshivah arranged for Rav Gifter to give a lecture in Northwestern University (in Evanston, Illinois) on the topic of "Jewish Law: A Thing of the Past or a Guide to the Future," a standing-room-only event. In 1967, at the seventh annual dinner, Rav Gifter was the guest speaker, once again. The yeshivah continued to glean from Rav Gifter's fiery inspiration with each subsequent visit. In 1979, as the yeshivah launched its dormitory-building celebration dinner, Rav Gifter, as guest speaker, graced the banquet with his presence and encouraging words. With parental pride, he watched as the yeshivah continued to grow.

This past year, the yeshivah, which continues to flourish, celebrated its 50th anniversary with a gala dinner.

Section 5
Emes — Truth

Chapter 22
Torah of Truth

URING THE PREPARATORY STAGES OF THIS BOOK, I ASKED the rebbetzin what is the most important attribute to mention about the rosh hayeshivah. The answer was clear to her. "He was an *ish emes*, a man of truth."

Throughout the tractate *Avos*, the sayings of the various Sages are introduced with the words: *"Hu hayah omer… —* He used to say…" Rav Gifter explained that it was not necessary for the *Tanna* mentioned to express his lesson verbally; rather, "he used to say…"; i.e., his actions and way of living articulated more than words to all who observed him.

The same can be said about Rav Gifter, whose entire life was a symphony of *emes*. Every facet of his life was dictated by truth.

The Ultimate Truth

SHIMON HAAMSONI HAD AN EXPLANATION (*DERASHAH*) FOR every time it says the word *"es"* in the Torah. For example, when the Torah says, *"Kabeid es avicha … —* Honor your father…" (*Shemos* 20:12, *Devarim* 5:16), he derived that *"es"* includes the obligation to honor one's older brother. When he reached the verse, *"Es Hashem Elokecha tira —*

Hashem, your G-d, you shall fear" (*Devarim* 6:13, 10:20), he found it impossible to explain the word "*es*," for who can be compared to G-d in terms of awe and fear?

His students asked him, "Rebbi, if you can't find an explanation for this '*es*,' what will happen to all of the other times it says '*es*' in the Torah?" He told them, "Since this '*es*' cannot include anything, so, too, I concede that the other '*esim*' have no special meaning. And just as I received reward for explaining the '*esim*,' I will now receive reward for withdrawing from them." Then Rabbi Akiva came along and derived from the "*es*" in "*Es Hashem Elokecha tira*" that just as we must be in awe of Hashem, we must be in awe of *talmidei chachamim* (*Pesachim* 22b; *Rashi*).

Rav Gifter used to relate how the Veinuter Rav, Rav Ezra Altschuler, elucidates the above Gemara. What did Rabbi Akiva see that enabled him to explain this "*es*," one that even the expert on the subject was unable to explain? The answer is: He saw Shimon HaAmsoni. A lesser person who had an explanation for every "*es*" in the Torah, but was missing just one, would have found some explanation for it, even if it wasn't exactly perfect. For if not, he would have said, "What will become of all my other interpretations? I can't let them fall by the wayside." Yet, here was Shimon HaAmsoni, who was interested in one thing and one thing only: the undiluted truth. If the explanation was not applicable in one place, then even if it meant admitting that his thesis on all the "*esim*" was wrong, he was willing to do so. For this wasn't about him; it was about the true meaning of the Torah.

When Rabbi Akiva saw that for the pursuit of truth, this Torah scholar was willing to sacrifice all of the teachings he had worked on so diligently, he came to the conclusion that this "*es*" must include the fear of a *talmid chacham*.

Once, when Rav Gifter was already the rosh hayeshivah and was delivering a *shiur*, a student asked a particularly penetrating question, which in essence disproved what Rav Gifter was trying to say. The rosh hayeshivah closed his Gemara and walked out. The class was over.[1] He was not angry or insulted, but rather satisfied that the truth had been discovered, so the class could end.

---

1. Rabbi Eli Friedman.

Rav Gifter giving *shiur*

This was his method of learning (*derech halimud*). Each question and answer moved one to another level of understanding the truth of Torah.

Rav Gifter's *shiurim* always centered on *p'shat*, and he spent his energy searching for the truth in the Gemara. His incisive mind cut through the topic (*sugya*), seeking out that truth, and he would not stop searching — ever.

As one *talmid* noted, "Our rebbi never said, '*Efsher ken mir zuggen* — Perhaps we can say…,' as that would indicate that it was also possible that we not say this explanation. And that was not true. If the rosh hayeshivah said it, *ess **muz** zein emes!* — it **had** to be the truth!"

However, he could be unrelenting with himself in his search for truth. One time, while learning with Rabbi Azriel Goldfein, the two of them came across a question that was asked by Rav Akiva Eiger, who had written that he could not resolve this difficulty. Rav Gifter suggested an answer for Rav Akiva's question on the Gemara. But then he said, "How can it be that Rav Akiva Eiger could not think of this answer, while *I* could?" Thereupon, he sat down and learned through the Gemara for *three* hours until he found the flaw in his own logic, so that the original difficulty still remained.

Since he was always trying to discover the ultimate truth, Rav Gifter never looked at his *shiurim* from the previous cycle of learning while preparing for the present cycle. He did not want those *shiurim* to "influ-

Speaking in learning with Rav Boruch Sorotzkin

ence" his way of thinking in preparing his *shiur*. In fact, Rav Gifter would daven that the Al-mighty should help him to forget his previous *shiurim* while he was preparing his new *shiurim*. This way, he would be able to prepare with a complete freshness. After he finished preparing the lectures, he would look at the previous ones so that he could jot down some comments.

(Nevertheless, he would give out his notes freely for others to look at and learn from, and he would comment, *"Dos iz nit mein Torah; dos iz der Ribbono shel Olam's Torah* — This is not my Torah; it is the Al-mighty's Torah.")

Once, when he was ill, he refused to give his *shiur* since he felt that he had not prepared enough and the *shiur* would not be thorough enough.

Rav Gifter would convey the importance of constantly searching for the truth through a story about Rav Shimon Shkop, who was a *maggid shiur* in pre-war Telz for nearly 20 years. After Rav Shimon's first *shiur*, he was walking down the street, when he met the nephew of Rav Yisrael Salanter (the founder of the *mussar* movement). Rav Shimon told him that he had just given his first lecture in the yeshivah and went on to detail some of its elements. As he was taking leave of Rav Shimon, Rav Yisrael's nephew gave him an unusual blessing. "May you merit to *never* say the 'truth' in your *shiurim*." The "blessing" stunned Rav Shimon. It sounded more like a curse than a blessing!

The man explained to Rav Shimon that if he ever felt that he found the truth, then perhaps he would stop seeking it, and that must never happen. Man must constantly be searching and yearning to find the truth, but one must never feel as though he has discovered it.

Another powerful lesson learned, and lived.

Rabbi Hillel Goldberg described Rav Gifter's uncompromising honesty as follows:

> The enunciations of Rav Gifter emerged from a certainty of being, a loftiness of knowledge, a fearless and uncompromising honesty derived from his innate integrity and from complete absorption of the very letters of the Torah. Rav Gifter could unravel uncertainties with a straightforwardness that astonished and satisfied. "There is no joy like the unraveling of uncertainties," says the Rambam. Every conversation with Rav Gifter was, in this sense, a genuine joy. Like the prodigiously talented lawyer he could have chosen to become, Rav Gifter cut through nonsense, obfuscation, arguments, and conflicts to reach the truth. When I read in Exodus of G-d thundering at Mount Sinai, the only human voice I can summon that meets the requirements of the imagination is the voice of Rav Gifter.

Appreciating Other Seekers of Truth

RAV GIFTER RECOGNIZED AND APPRECIATED PEOPLE WHO WERE seekers of truth. Avi was a lifeguard in Camp Kol Rinah in the summer of 1962. He attended a modern high school, and was a particularly bright boy. He was having a fantastic summer, one of great fun, but more importantly, great spiritual growth. The director of the camp, Rabbi Dr. Yaakov Greenwald, suggested to him that he attend Yeshivas Telz. Avi was hesitant at first; he knew virtually nothing about the yeshivah. In addition, the school he currently attended was light-years away from Telz in its Torah outlook. Nevertheless, after much thought, he decided to write a letter to the yeshivah to explain why he wanted to go there and why he should be accepted.

Avi wrote a 12-page manifesto and sent it off to the yeshivah. A few days later, Avi was lifeguarding at the pool when the phone rang in the camp office. He was summoned to the office, and was told that Rav Gifter was on the phone!

Rav Gifter explained that he appreciated Avi's letter, but there there were no beds available in the yeshivah. Avi was terribly disappointed; he begged that he at least be granted an interview. After more discus-

Rav Pesach Stein

sion, Avi offered something bizarre. "What if I were to sleep on the roof of the yeshivah?"

Rav Gifter was astounded that a young man had such a strong desire to come to yeshivah that he was willing to sleep on the roof. Rav Gifter responded that Avi's strong desire had earned him the chance to take an entrance examination (*bechinah*).

When he arrived at the yeshivah, Rav Gifter assigned him to prepare a page of Gemara. Even though Avi was very bright, he had never learned Gemara in depth. Fortunately, Rav Gifter assigned a *talmid* to learn with him and help him prepare. Avi performed admirably on the examination, and was accepted to the yeshivah, to Rav Pesach Stein's *shiur*.

There was only one problem. Rav Pesach gave his *shiur* in Yiddish and Avi didn't speak Yiddish, not one word of it. Determined to overcome that obstacle, Avi made himself a makeshift dictionary in his Gemara, and jotted down every new Yiddish word he heard.

He worked and toiled and reviewed. And reviewed. And reviewed. In fact, nearly 50 years later, when he told this story to this author, he cried as he recalled the effort and review he had put into mastering his rebbi's *shiur*.

Rav Avrohom Chaim Feuer being *maspid* his father-in-law, Rav Gifter at the *levayah* in Yerushalayim. Rav Nosson Tzvi Finkel is seated at right.

Avi would eventually outgrow his nickname and become Avrohom Chaim — Rav Avrohom Chaim Feuer — a noted *talmid chacham*, rav, author, and disseminator of Torah ... and the son-in-law of Rav Gifter.

RAV GIFTER WAS NOT INTERESTED IN REPRESENTING HIMSELF AS greater than he felt he was. For example, he only grew *payos* later in life, as it was only then that he felt he was "holding there." And it was at that age, that his rebbi, Rav Avraham Yitzchak, grew his *payos*.

Personal Stringencies

Soon after joining the family, his son-in-law, Rav Yaakov Reisman, entered the home of Rav Gifter and was shocked to discover Rav Gifter in his shirtsleeves. Puzzled, he asked his father-in-law about the tradition that Rav Yosef Leib Bloch (Telzer Rav and rosh hayeshivah in the early 1900's) had never walked around without his frock; if so, why had Rav Gifter not adhered to that custom?

Rav Gifter answered, "I am not on that level; I do not conduct myself that way."

His sense of truth dictated which stringencies he took upon himself, and which he did not. In addition, as careful as Rav Gifter was about his own personal stringencies (*chumros*), he never imposed them upon his family.

Rav Chaim Nussbaum, one of Rav Gifter's closest *talmidim*, related that prior to his wedding, he asked the rosh hayeshivah for advice.

With Rav Ruderman

With Rav Chaim Nussbaum at his *chasunah*

His rebbi said two things. First, he should not shake (*shuckel*) or hold any papers while standing under the *chuppah*. "A young *chassan* shouldn't act as though he is so important." He then smiled and added, "I was recently at a wedding and the *kallah* was shaking so hard, I was afraid she might hit her face on the floor."

The second recommendation was something that would affect Reb Chaim well beyond his wedding. "I have seen many beautiful marriages destroyed because of stringencies. Use your common sense." And with that, he kissed his dear student and said goodbye.

When it came to kashrus, he was quick to say, in the name of Rav Breuer, "*Ah mentch in leben darf zein nit kein glatt kosherdike Yid, nar a glatt yosherdike Yid.* [In life, one need not be a glatt kosher Jew, but more importantly, a straight, honest, and upright Jew.]

Be Yourself

RABBI ZELIG PLISKIN RECALLS THAT RAV GIFTER WOULD INSIST, "BE yourself, but be certain to utilize your full potential." He emphasized this point from the Torah. Yeast and honey were not permitted in the offerings on the altar, but salt was. Rav Gifter taught that yeast makes the dough rise higher and honey makes things sweeter, but both are external additives. Salt, however, only brings out the food's existing flavor.

When serving Hashem, we should follow the model of salt: We should be ourselves, but bring out the best flavor in ourselves, and make every effort to be all that we can be.[2]

This is the true path of the Torah.

---

2. *Pirkei Torah, Vayikra* 2:11.

Chapter 23
A Life of Truth

RAV GIFTER DEMANDED *EMES* FROM HIMSELF AND FROM his *talmidim*. He wanted their internal behavior to match their external conduct.

A good example of this happened just after the Six Day War, in 1967. At that time, the feeling of euphoria and Jewish pride was at a high level. However, there were concerns regarding the spreading of a boastful and haughty feeling that it was we, not the Hand of G-d, who had defeated the enemy.

One of the younger rebbeim in the yeshivah, Rabbi Tzodok Suchard, wrote a beautiful piece regarding the war in the Telz Alumni Bulletin. He concluded it with a poignant poem that depicted how he felt for the Israeli soldiers who had fought so bravely in battle.

One prominent Torah personality wrote Rav Gifter a letter challenging the outlook of this rebbi, since he felt it was written with questionable allegiance to the Israeli Army. He underlined in red ink the parts that he felt were problematic. He strongly suggested that Rav Gifter take this rebbi to task, as he wondered, "What type of rebbeim do they have in Telz Yeshivah?"

At a Melaveh Malkah in Eretz Yisrael with Rabbi Tzodok Shmuel Suchard, Rav Leizer Sorotzkin, and Reb Yosef Sorotzkin

Rav Gifter took the letter very much to heart, and he told Reb Tzadok about it. Reb Tzadok was taken aback by the challenge. In his heart, though, he felt very strongly about what he had written and that it was in accordance with Torah *hashkafah*. On the other hand, Rav Gifter apparently was displeased and was waiting for his response.

Reb Tzadok told Rav Gifter that he would have to take the letter home, read it, think about it, and give him an answer the next day. He came home completely shaken and at a total loss about what his next step should be. He knew what was at stake — his position as a rebbi in the yeshivah — but he was troubled by the fact that he really believed what he wrote. Although he reviewed his article over and over, with the utmost respect to the letter Rav Gifter had received, he still maintained that he was right; he stood by what he said.

The next day, after little sleep, Reb Tzadok visited Rav Gifter and said, "Rebbi, I thought it through many times, and I ... stand by what I wrote."

Reb Tzadok waited for an argument but instead, Rav Gifter responded, "If that is the way you feel, then write that back to him." He did not question him any further on the subject matter; he just wanted to ensure that he held strong to his own convictions and beliefs.

Money Matters

JUST LIKE RAV GIFTER INSISTED THAT EVERY PERSON BE COMPLETEly honest with himself and his beliefs, Rav Gifter was extremely scrupulous with himself about money matters, as well.

When Rav Gifter was a student in Telz in Lithuania, his parents were not always able to send him money for his needs. As a result, he was forced to take a *chalukah* (stipend) from the yeshivah. As soon as he was able to, he sent the money back to Lithuania to repay the yeshivah for the money they had laid out for him.

Every year before Rosh Hashanah, Rav Gifter would give a check to the yeshivah to pay for any food he may have eaten from the yeshivah kitchen that he was not entitled to.

Rav Gifter often visited the ArtScroll offices in Brooklyn, when he was in New York. On one such visit, he asked Rabbi Meir Zlotowitz, general editor of ArtScroll, for some *sefarim* and books. Reb Meir was extremely honored; he gladly gave the items to Rav Gifter free of charge. But Rav Gifter insisted on paying for them on the spot. At first, Reb Meir refused to accept any money. However, Rav Gifter remained firm. Finally, seeing that he had no choice, Reb Meir agreed to "charge" Rav Gifter a total of $1.75 for the several books he purchased. Without hesitating — and in all seriousness — Rav Gifter wrote out a check for that sum and forced Reb Meir to take it. Of course, Reb Meir never cashed the check; he gave it to his daughter, Estie Dicker, who worked there at the time. And since that day, she has kept the check in her wallet.

A copy of the $1.75 check Rav Gifter forced Rabbi Meir Zlotowitz to accept for the *sefarim* he "purchased"

As a man of truth, he neither demanded nor would accept frills or favors.

※

A *talmid's* parents sent airline tickets for Rav and Rebbetzin Gifter so they could attend the *talmid's* wedding in New York. Soon after the wedding, the *talmid's* parents received a check in the mail for exactly half of the ticket. The rosh hayeshivah explained that while he was in New York, he had attended to something for the sake of the yeshivah. It was therefore only proper that the yeshivah share the cost of the ticket.

He taught his students to be honest and upright in all their dealings, too.

※

One *talmid* told the following story:

I came home one bein hazmanim to find that we had a water leak from a second-floor bathroom that had caused very minor damage. The insurance company was called, and an adjuster came down to report the claim. The entire repair job cost us about $150, so we were surprised to see a check from the insurance company for $1,650. When I went back to yeshivah, I asked Rav Gifter what to do with the money.

Rav Gifter said that a similar thing had happened to him when he had bought a home. When he moved in, the electricity wasn't working. He submitted a claim to the insurance company, and he received a check for a large amount of money, enough to rewire the house. He subsequently found a second fuse box in a first-floor closet; after tinkering with the fuse box a bit, the electricity in the house worked well. The insurance company told him to keep the check, since it would cost them more [in paperwork] to take the money back.

The rosh hayeshivah told me that I should send the insurance company a check for the difference and, he said, "They will probably send it back to you." I did just that and soon received a phone call. "We have a rule that once a claim is settled, the file is closed and the money belongs to you." Thus, they sent the check back.

Rav Gifter said, "You never know what a little falsehood [sheker] can cause, and you never know all the benefits being honest can bring."

※

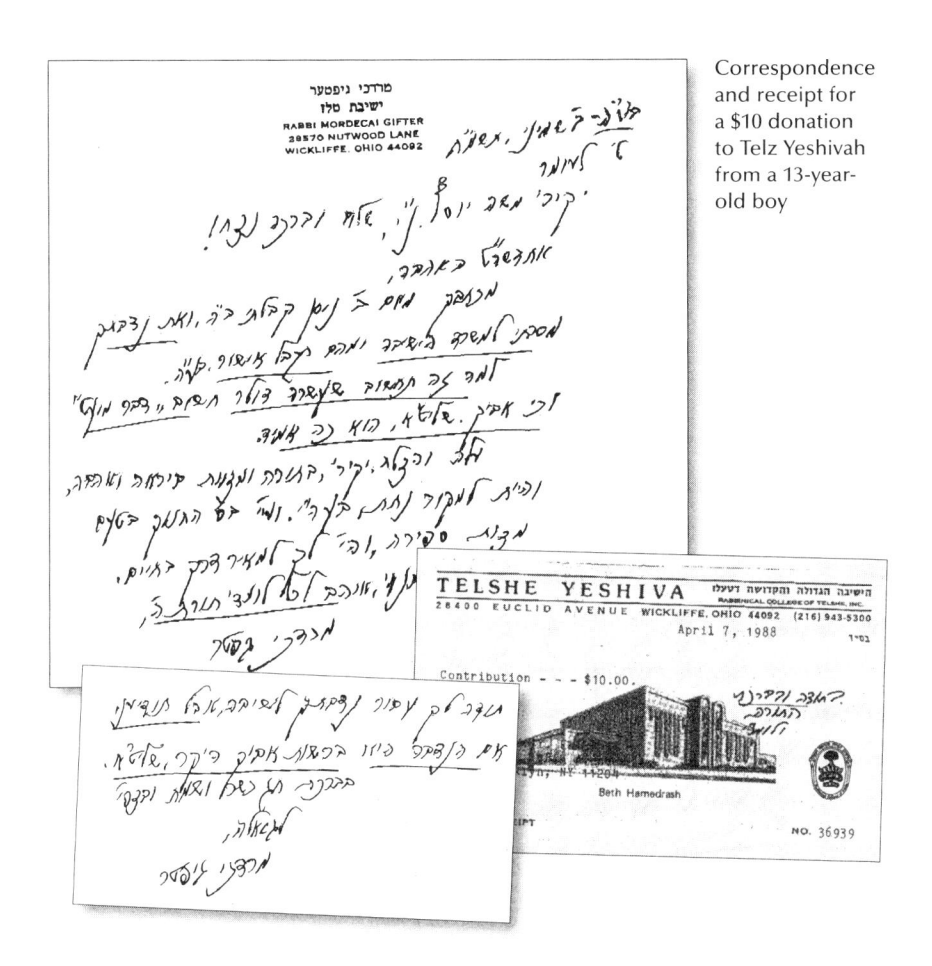

Correspondence and receipt for a $10 donation to Telz Yeshivah from a 13-year-old boy

When Reb Shlomo Feldman's son, Moshe Yosef, was about to become a bar mitzvah, his father advised him to send letters to various Torah sages to ask for guidance on becoming a bar mitzvah. In addition, Reb Shlomo instructed his son to send a donation of $10 to a few yeshivos, including Telz. Although the Feldmans were not men of means, Reb Shlomo felt it was important to educate Moshe Yosef to donate money to Torah institutions.

The young man sent $10 checks to the suggested yeshivos. A few days later, he was shocked to discover that Rav Gifter had written him a letter thanking him for his donation, but wondered if his father knew that he had sent the money. Moshe Yosef was very surprised that a rosh hayeshivah had taken the time to be concerned with such an issue. But if it was a matter of honesty, it was not a small matter for Rav Gifter.

Chapter 23: A Life of Truth □ 283

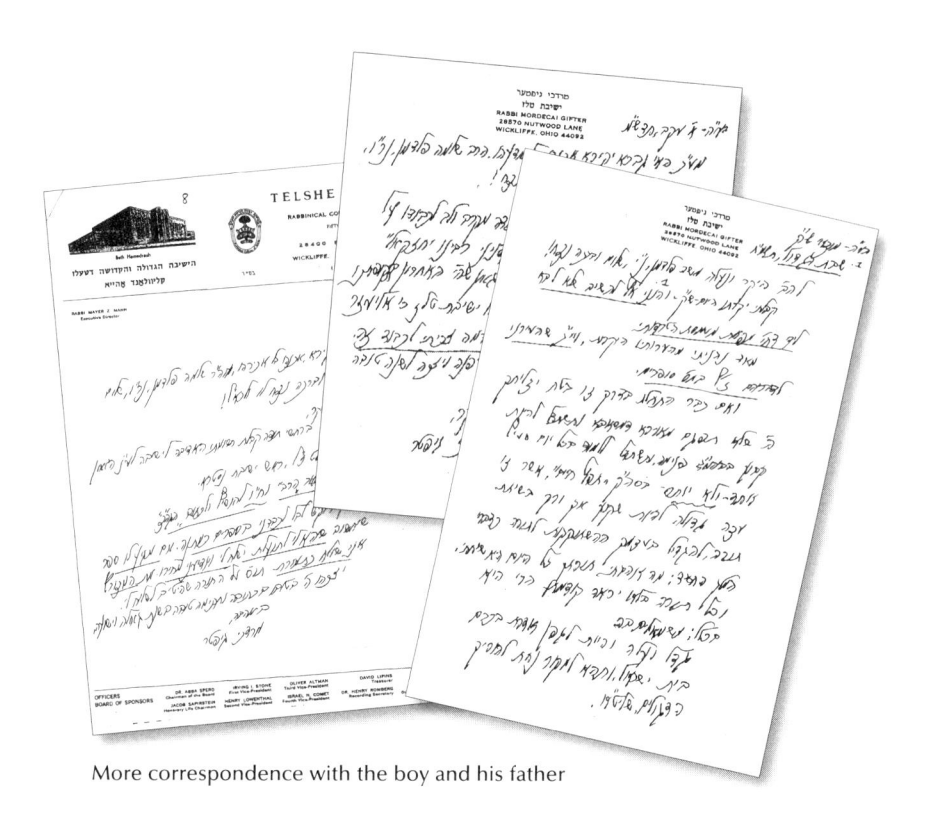

More correspondence with the boy and his father

The bar mitzvah boy responded that his father was aware that he had sent in the money. He also mentioned that since it was only a small amount of money, he did not feel it was necessary for his father to know about it. He cited the law in the *Shulchan Aruch* (*YD* 248:4) that specifies that a child need not have permission to give away a small amount of money.

Rav Gifter responded a second time to Moshe Yosef, acknowledging receiving his letter and informing him that the yeshivah would send him a receipt. But he added one line, "Why do you consider $10 to be a 'small amount'? Is your father so rich that the amount of $10 means nothing to you?"

This lesson remained indelibly etched in the impressionable young man's mind. He learned how important it is not to take money matters lightly, even if the money is from one's own father. And 30 years later, this message continues to resonate in his heart.

It is truly amazing that a rosh hayeshivah would correspond with a 13-year-old boy to teach him to appreciate the importance of honesty and the value of money.

Rav Gifter was once notified that boys were stealing money from the pay phones. He gave a special *shmuess* in which he threatened that if this type of behavior continued, the yeshivah would close. He remarked quite forcefully, "If the yeshivah is producing dishonesty, then there is no reason to have a yeshivah."

The Whole Truth

RAV GIFTER APPRECIATED *EMES* IN EVERY FORM, AND BECAME distressed when he sensed that something did not portray the complete truth.

The yeshivah's official letterhead originally bore the name Rabbinical College of Telshe. However, the name was officially changed to Telshe Yeshiva because the term "rabbinical," according to Rav Gifter, implied that its purpose was only to develop rabbis.

And in Rav Gifter's estimation, that was not true. He felt that the purpose of a yeshivah was to produce the next generation of Klal Yisrael.

Hence, the original title was misleading.

When Rabbi Shlomo Mandel was offered a position in the yeshivah, the administration highlighted all the benefits of the appointment and detailed the opportunities to which it could lead. As is often the case when making a job offer, the *hanhalah* made it sound as though they were doing Reb Shlomo a favor. Suddenly, Rav Gifter interrupted, "Tell him the truth! Tell him that the yeshivah needs him!"

When Rav Gifter was sick with shingles, he was in tremendous pain. One night, the pain was so awful that he was unable to sleep. However, although he was awake, he would not leave the light on. He was concerned that people would think that he was up learning, and he did not want to mislead them.

And Nothing But the Truth

RAV GIFTER'S INSISTENCE ON THE TRUTH WAS ALWAYS EVIDENT, but perhaps never in a more emphatic fashion than in the following incident.

When Binyomin, Rav Gifter's eldest child, was 10 years old, he had a life-altering interaction with his father. One day, he walked into the house smelling of smoke; indeed, he had been smoking cigarettes. The very strong odor of smoke made it clear to Rav Gifter what his son had been doing. However, he wanted to hear the truth from Binyomin.

Therefore, he asked Binyomin if he had been smoking. Binyomin started to cry but denied that he had committed the "crime." Again, Rav Gifter asked his son if he had been smoking, and again, Binyomin denied it emphatically. Once more, Rav Gifter posed the question, and for the third and final time, Binyomin maintained his innocence.

Rav Gifter looked at his son and told him the following. "To smoke or not to smoke is a choice that you will make when you become an adult. If you're smart, you won't; if you're not so smart, you will. But telling a lie as a 10-year-old is something that is not your choice." And Rav Gifter gave his son a smack. Then, following the educational method instituted by Rav Yosef Leib Bloch, Binyomin was told to kiss the hand that had hit him: to demonstrate his awareness that the punishment had not come from anger, but only from love.

This incident made such an impression on Binyomin that honesty became his trademark. In fact, as an insurance salesman, he earned the nickname "Honest Ben."

Rav Yaakov Feitman recalled a noteworthy incident:

A woman in Cleveland was named "Jewish Woman of the Year," and her story was published in the following issue of the Cleveland Jewish News. She was a supporter of Israel, a member of the upper leadership of the Federation, and a Reform convert. Rav Gifter wrote her the following note:

"Dear Mrs. P,

You are to be commended for your good works and efforts. However, it is my duty to inform you that you are not Jewish. You may find fulfillment of your obvious concern for morality and ethics by adhering to the Seven Noahide Laws. They are ... [he listed the seven laws]. Should you be sincerely interested in converting properly according to Jewish Law, please call Rabbi Feitman."

One day, I received a call from this well-known woman requesting a meeting to discuss conversion. I was politely trying to dissuade her when she protested, "But Rabbi Gifter told me to call!" On realizing the situation, I was certain I would be dealing with an annoyed and furious woman. Instead, it became obvious that she recognized the

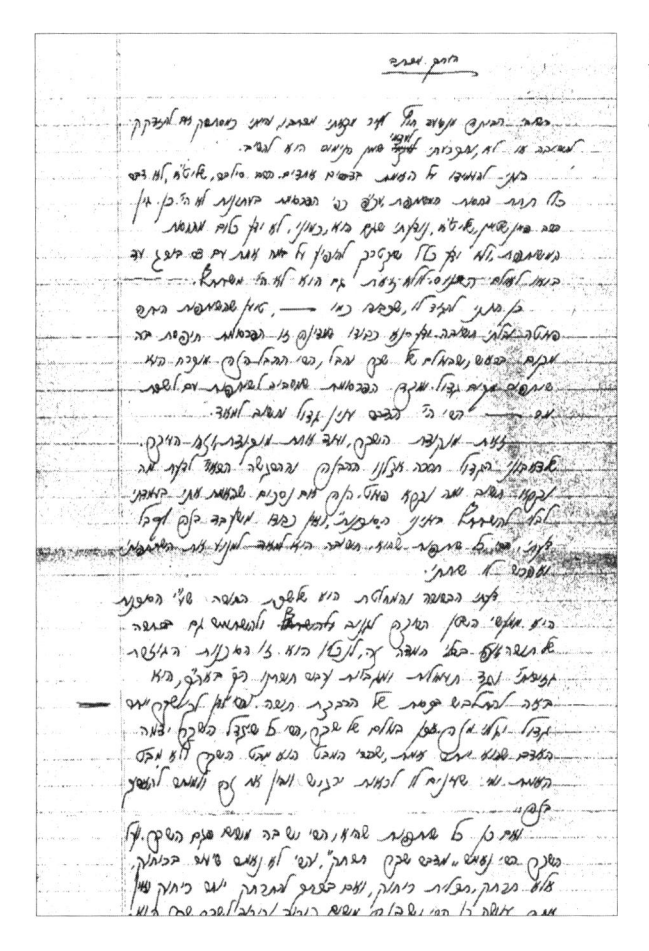

Letter from Rav Gifter to a member of the Histadrus HaRabbanim about emes

voice of truth and integrity. The rosh hayeshivah had asked her for no donation, wanted nothing for himself. He was simply and candidly conveying the truth, and thereby showing tremendous care and concern for the woman.

Rav Gifter had many encounters with Jews who were not Torah-observant, whom he respected as individuals. Once, an elderly man came into the *beis midrash* and was having difficulty putting on his *tefillin*. Rav Gifter walked over to help. After davening, they began talking. They spoke about a number of *hashkafah* issues, about which they obviously had different opinions. While respectful, the conversation became a bit heated. Of course, Rav Gifter would not budge an inch in his view.

The man was tremendously impressed with Rav Gifter's patience in explaining his standpoint, and with his intelligent and articulate arguments. Soon after, he gave the yeshivah a very generous donation.

In public settings, Rav Gifter was looked to as someone who would speak on topics that others would not dare broach. Sometimes after he spoke, the organizations who had invited him would be asked to retract his unpopular or controversial messages. Nevertheless, this did not stop him from continuing to speak the truth.

His sense of *emes* influenced all his interactions with others. Flattery was something he did not indulge in. At one high-school graduation, there were only a few boys who hadn't achieved National Honor awards for accomplishments in their secular studies. One of the speakers attempted to console them, saying something along the lines of, "Well, they're focused on their Torah studies."

Rav Gifter immediately got up and said, "We teach general studies, and they should be studied properly. One should try to excel at whatever he does."

Rav Gifter once wrote a letter to a respected member of the Histadrus HaRabbanim. He felt that the rav was misguided in his association with those rabbis who had less-than-perfect Torah integrity. In the letter, Rav Gifter highlighted the fact that the Torah says, "*Mid'var sheker tirchak* — Distance yourself from a false word" (*Shemos* 23:7). Yet, the Torah does not give a measurement as to how far one should stay. This teaches us that there is no limit to the distance one must maintain from falsehood. Rav Gifter then admonished the rav for relaxing the standards of truth and integrity in upholding the Word of G-d. He felt that anything less than total distance in these situations constitutes falsehood.

When Rav Gifter served as a rabbi in Waterbury, he had a cordial relationship with the local Catholic priest. This priest once invited Stephen Wise, the powerful Reform leader, to a reception. Rav Gifter was not invited to attend. A few days after the event, Rav Gifter met the priest, who approached the rosh hayeshivah somewhat hesitantly. "Rabbi, I hope you weren't offended," the cleric said softly, "that I didn't invite you to the reception." The rosh hayeshivah responded with a smile, saying that he would not have attended anyway. With a sigh of relief, the priest revealed, "I told the committee you were a different kind of rabbi and we should not even bother you."

Rav Gifter would always conclude this story with a wry comment, *"Nor yenner galach hut farshtannen* — only that priest truly understood."

Yes … a different kind of rabbi.

Section 6

Bein Adam LaChaveiro — Interpersonal Relationships

Chapter 24
A Heart Big Enough for All

RAV GIFTER WAS A BUSY PERSON. HE SPENT THE MAJOR portion of his day learning and teaching. In addition, he shouldered a lot of communal responsibility. And yet, he always had time for others. It didn't matter who the needy person was, where he came from, or what he wanted; if someone came to him, he made the time.

Although he was often seen as an intimidating figure, Rav Gifter's powerful personality softened when he was dealing with someone in need. As tough as he was while defending a point of learning, he was equally soft when helping the downtrodden.

WHEN A YOUNG WOMAN LOST HER HUSBAND, SHE FOUND HERself harassed by creditors from all sides. Rav Gifter defended her as if she were his own child.

Like Family

Sometime later, when she fell ill, Rav Gifter was contacted immediately. Again, as he would do for a family member, he called the doctor and hurried to the hospital to be with her and her family. She was diagnosed with a brain tumor that called for surgery to reveal whether the tumor was benign or malignant.

Rav Gifter recited *Tehillim* in the *beis midrash* before the procedure. Those who were present recall how the walls reverberated with his cries. Following the *Tehillim*, Rav Gifter delivered his *shiur*. When he concluded the *shiur*, he was approached with the news that the tumor was indeed benign. Overjoyed and overwhelmed with emotion, Rav Gifter proclaimed that the yeshivah should recite *Tehillim* once more, but this time out of gratitude.

When he came to the words *"ve'harbei imo fedus* –and with Him is abundant redemption" (*Tehillim* 130:7), Rav Gifter broke into tears![1]

After all, it was a "member of his family" who had been redeemed!

A student who had a close connection to Rav Gifter recalled:

I was close to Rav Gifter, not only as a talmid to his rebbi, but as a frequent guest in the Gifter home. Quite often, he would invite me for a Shabbos or Yom Tov meal; I need not say how warmly he and the rebbetzin greeted me. Moreover, since I was from Australia and did not go home even once during the six-and-a-half years of my sojourn in the yeshivah, I needed a place to eat all eight days of Pesach, when the yeshivah kitchen was closed. On more than one occasion, I ate at the Gifter home, three

---

1. Reb Yankel Rosenbaum.

times a day right through the eight days of Pesach. I cannot even begin to acknowledge the enormous debt that I owe Rav Gifter, and especially the rebbetzin, for all their kindnesses. Those visits were rich in flavor [taam] and spirit [ruach].

One year, during the last days of Pesach, a bachur who was sleeping in the yeshivah with me woke me up and complained that he had terrible stomach pain and felt like he was dying. I dressed immediately and took him by taxi to the hospital, where he was diagnosed with a gallbladder attack and had to be operated on immediately. Since I knew that I would not be able to see him for hours, I walked back to the Gifter house, where the family was in the middle of their Yom Tov meal.

As soon as I told them that the bachur was being operated upon, Rav Gifter arose and began reciting Tehillim with very great concentration. The scene of Rav Gifter's immediate reaction is stamped on my memory forever; it made a deeper impression on me than 10 mussar shmuessen. [2]

A Potent Blessing

AS A KOLLEL FELLOW IN THE YESHIVAH WALKED RAV GIFTER home, he lamented that he and his wife had not yet merited having children. As they walked into the apartment, Rav Gifter commented, *"Ich bin nit kein rebbe.* [I am not a Chassidic rebbe.] Therefore, I do not have the ability to assure you a child." But the rebbetzin, hearing the young man's story, prodded the Rosh Yeshiva to tell the man something to make him feel better.

Rav Gifter then reassured the fellow, *"Heint, iber ah yahr…* [Next year at this time …]" Remarkably, the couple's prayers were answered and the next year they had a child.

While Rav Gifter would have been upset if someone would have referred to this event as a "miracle," his *talmidim* often felt that his efforts on their behalf, and on the behalf of others, yielded amazing results. His empathy for those in

---
2. Reb Shlomo Slonim.

pain was unparalleled; as mentioned, the way he poured out his soul when praying for someone else's recovery was enough to make the entire room weep.

In the early 1970's, Rav Gifter traveled to Monsey for a full week to deliver many classes. One day, while he was speaking, a fellow ran into the *beis midrash* to tell Rav Gifter that a young girl in the community was undergoing a serious operation. Rav Gifter immediately announced that he was donating the reward of their Torah study as a merit for the young girl, to bring about a complete recovery.

Her father recounted how special the family felt, knowing that Rav Gifter had made such a meaningful declaration.

MR. ASHER RABINSKY, A WELL-KNOWN GENTLEMAN IN CLEVELAND, shared the follow incident with me.

Personal Involvement In 1967, Rav Gifter spent a large amount of his time in matters of the Klal. He and Mr. Rabinsky received phone calls about a 19-year-old Israeli boy, whose last name was Sassoon. Until that time, he had been learning in Yeshivat Porat Yosef in Jerusalem. Now, however, his kidneys were failing and he needed to receive dialysis followed by a kidney transplant, something unavailable in Israel at the time. He would be coming with his mother to the world-renowned Cleveland Clinic. Both men were told that money was not an issue.

Reb Asher had some contacts in the clinic and worked hard to get the boy admitted into the hospital. He even went to the airport to pick them up.

The plan was for the boy to receive dialysis and gain enough strength for a kidney transplant, which would be donated by his mother. Until he was strong enough for the transplant, though, he needed dialysis often, which was very expensive.

After a few phone calls, Reb Asher was dumbfounded to learn that he had misunderstood the phrase "money is not an issue" regarding this family. Money was not an issue, because there was none; the family was penniless. Now the funds for the huge medical expenses would have to be raised.

Then the situation became more complicated when the family's *chacham* (Sephardic rabbi) contacted Mrs. Sassoon when he heard what she planned to do, and he told her that under no circumstances was she to donate her kidney to her son. Now they had to prepare for an even longer haul: dialysis, while waiting for an available kidney from a stranger.

The first order of business was to find the woman a place to stay for a while. Nothing in the immediate vicinity was appropriate, as the hospital was in a neighborhood that was less than safe. Rav Gifter made many calls and finally procured an apartment for the boy's mother. Then he proceeded to go shopping for pots and pans for the woman. Once these items were purchased, Rav Gifter went to the supermarket in order to stock the apartment with food. He did not leave this to one of his assistants; he did it himself.

During the next few weeks, the boy underwent dialysis in the hospital. After a while, the hospital decided he should no longer remain an in-patient. Without hesitation, the rosh hayeshivah decided that the boy would reside in the yeshivah. Three times a week, an ambulance brought him from the yeshivah to the hospital for his treatment. Eventually, the boy gained much strength, but a kidney had not become available.

It was obviously time for the boy and his mother to return to Israel. Providentially, during these months, the chief of Hadassah Hospital came to visit the Cleveland Clinic. He met the boy and his mother, and guaranteed that the boy would be given dialysis in Israel on one condition: The clinic would have to provide a dialysis machine, since it was a rarity in Israel in those days. Incredibly, the clinic agreed and the complicated arrangements were made.

The boy was flown back with his mother to receive the treatments at Hadassah Hospital. Because of that boy, and the efforts of Rav Gifter and Mr. Rabinsky, Hadassah Hospital gained a vital piece of equipment that helped countless others over the years.

It is not known what happened to the boy and his mother after that. But one thing is clear. The efforts of Rav Gifter and Mr. Rabinsky enabled a lost woman and her son to feel that someone cared. And no doubt their efforts prolonged the boy's life.

Rav Gifter saw these acts as simply what one does and no more. As he wrote in 1950 in The Jewish Parent magazine:

Every human being is part of the great family of Mankind; and if one is really to enjoy life, he must share with others that which has been granted to him.

Rav Gifter continues, in reference to Avraham Avinu:

It was not merely a question of sharing with others. No, it was indeed far more than that. Avraham felt that all that had been bestowed upon him, physically and spiritually, was of value to him only insofar as it was given and imparted to others. If the occasion for acts of kindness did not arise, Avraham felt a deep and personal loss. His riches became atrophied within him for lack of activation.

Therefore, Rav Gifter wrote:

The teacher should never fail to have the idea of chesed occupy an important place in classroom decoration. If we have honor rolls for perfection in studies and attendance, we should have the same for perfection of character development.

And, as always, the lessons Rav Gifter taught return to our relationship with the Al-mighty.

A very important lesson that must be taught to the child is chesed Hashem: the fact that we are constantly enjoying the lovingkindness of Hashem Yisbarach. And from this vantage point, the child should be impressed with the importance of performing acts of kindness to others.

Someone's Livelihood

FOR AS LONG AS I CAN REMEMBER, UNGER'S KOSHER BAKERY IN Cleveland has been one of the main sources for kosher food and baked goods. In the early years, Unger's was owned by the Davis family. However, over 30 years ago, a young man by the name of Moshe Rosenberg and his brother bought the business.

Not many people knew these young men, who had recently moved to town. Nevertheless, the people assumed that they would be able to rely on them to continue the high standard of kashrus that the previous owners had maintained. The first few weeks went by uneventfully. People came, bought their baked goods, and were satisfied. One Shabbos, though, everything changed.

Unger's is located right in the middle of the Orthodox community, directly across from the Hebrew Academy building where the Young Israel is housed, and a block away from the Torah U'Tefillah shul in one direction, and the Shomer Shabbos and Khal Yereim shuls in the other direction. Therefore, virtually anyone who goes to shul on Shabbos is bound to pass Unger's. On this particular Shabbos, as people walked by, a man pulled up in a truck and began to work on the air-conditioning system that was located on the roof of the bakery.

The passersby were appalled. How could a religious Jew hire someone to fix something in his store on a Shabbos? This was particularly risky for merchants who were new to the area and were trying to build a good reputation. No one knew much about these fellows, just that their name was Rosenberg and that they had obviously emigrated from another country. And now they were apparently desecrating Shabbos! Everyone was talking about it around the Shabbos table, though no one tried to find out the truth about what had happened. Instead, the next morning, signs went up all over town encouraging people to take their business elsewhere. The signs demanded that the community stop supporting those who do not keep Shabbos to the letter of the law. The next week, business at Unger's plummeted. Those who had seen the man working on the roof of Unger's had their own suspicions, while the others read the signs and assumed it was better to play it safe than to be sorry.

Moshe did not know what to do. He and his brother, Tibor, had never called the fellow to come on Shabbos. The man had come on his own, to follow up on a call from a few weeks before. But how could they prove it? Who would help them? They spoke to some of the community activists in town who directed them to discuss the problem with Rav Gifter.

Rav Gifter had heard about the incident and was asked to speak with the brothers. He greeted them warmly and listened carefully as they told their story. He asked for the name of the worker who had worked on the roof. He called him and confirmed that indeed he had not been asked to work on Shabbos, as the brothers claimed. Now all they needed was a letter from the rosh hayeshivah stating that the community could rely on the brothers' word and could resume shopping there. But when they asked for the letter, the rosh hayeshivah simply replied that they would not need one. They could not imagine what he meant.

However, soon they would find out.

The next day, early in the morning, Rav Gifter walked into Unger's to make a purchase. Many people saw him as he walked in and out of the store, since school was about to start and *minyanim* had just ended. The next day, the same scene repeated itself. Once again, Rav Gifter made the 25-minute trek from the yeshivah to the "Heights," as it is called, to buy something from the bakery.

Day after day, the rosh hayeshivah came to buy baked goods. By the end of the month, business was better than ever before. And since that day, it is hard to imagine the landscape of Cleveland kosher-shopping without Moshe and Tibor Rosenberg as the proprietors of Unger's Bakery.

There are many things to be learned from this story. Obviously, we must never be quick to make assumptions. In addition, when someone needs the help of a friend to clarify why something happened, we cannot simply stand by and hope that someone will read a letter that we wrote on his behalf. Instead, we must take the initiative and show our support through our actions. Not just words.

It can save someone's livelihood, even his life.

And it did.

Rav Gifter expected nothing in return for his staunch defense of these men. Moreover, many years later, Moshe reflected that he was never able to extend his own hand in welcome to Rav Gifter, for Rav Gifter

A letter to a talmid concerning another talmid in need of money

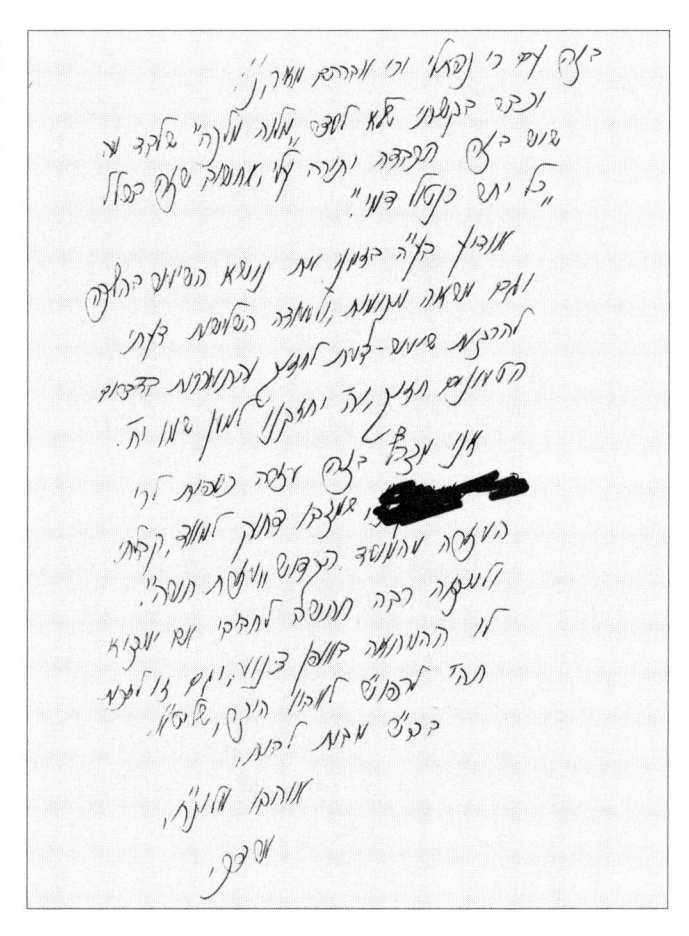

always beat him to it, asking, "How are you, Mr. Rosenberg?" Not "Moshe," but "Mr. Rosenberg."

We see the respect he showed a simple shop owner, not only by his courageous purchase in the store, but by extending a hand and giving a warm smile.

Sleepless Nights

ONCE, A CLOSE *TALMID* APPROACHED THE ROSH HAYESHIVAH THE morning after he returned from a trip to New York. The rosh hayeshivah looked pale, wan, and very troubled. The disciple, one of the rosh hayeshivah's closest *talmidim* who learned for decades in Telz, was worried about Rav Gifter. Finally, he mustered the courage to ask Rav Gifter, "Is everything all right? Did something happen to the rosh hayeshivah on his trip?"

The rosh hayeshivah responded, "I just cannot calm down. While I was in New York, two people approached me with difficult problems and I could not help them. I could not sleep the entire night just thinking of their pain, and I still cannot come to myself.

"*Vi ken men shluffen ven ah Yid hut tzaros* — How can one sleep when a Jew is having troubles?"[3]

Indeed, this is a question we should all be asking ourselves.

---

3. Rav Chaim Nussbaum.

Chapter 24: A Heart Big Enough for All ☐ 301

Chapter 25
With Warmth, Humility, and Respect

RAV GIFTER KNEW HOW TO MAKE OTHERS FEEL WELCOME and special. It is hard to describe how one feels when approaching a *gadol* of his stature only to realize that he is truly interested in what you have to say and how you feel.

ONE ROSH HASHANAH, AS RAV GIFTER WAS WALKING HOME FROM shul after the shofar blowing and *Mussaf*, a close *talmid* approached him, holding the hands of his two young daughters. With great reverence, he greeted his rebbi and said, *"Gut Yom Tov."* The rosh hayeshivah, looking worn from the strenuous davening, smiled warmly at his beloved disciple, and responded in kind. He then turned to the two little girls and, with a loving smile on his face, said, "You have such beautiful outfits!"

Warmth

At first, the young father was astounded at the remark. Soon, though, he realized that Rav Gifter understood young children's understand-

Joining the first grade of Mosdos Ohr HaTorah as the boys celebrate receiving their first *Chumash*. Looking on are the *menahel*, Rabbi Avrohom Fishman *zt"l* (r) and *ybl"cht*, their Rebbi, Rabbi Shlomo Elbaum

ing of Yom Tov, which is wrapped up in the externals, the tangibles that they can comprehend. He knew that complimenting them on their clothing was appropriate for them, since it helped them appreciate the specialness of Yom Tov.

He had a way of using words and emotions to remove barriers, break down walls, and connect *neshamos*. The following vignette, witnessed by Rabbi Yaakov Feitman, who was the rabbi of the Young Israel of Cleveland at the time, is quite revealing:

A glimpse into greatness. Rav Gifter is about to leave the house of mourning. The mourners are mostly not Telzers. Some are even antagonistic toward the yeshivah … The rosh hayeshivah begins to recite the time-honored words, indeed for most others just words. He says, "HaMakom yenachem eschem besoch" — and his voice begins to break. "She'ar aveilei"… tears begin to flow. "Tzion vi'Yerushalayim"… and he is sobbing uncontrollably. He leaves, I stay behind, and it is obvious that something important has happened. An attitude has changed. People have witnessed emes. True emotion, true yearning, true sadness. Truth itself. They may not yet be Telzers. But they will never again be anti-Telzers.

Chapter 25: With Warmth, Humility, and Respect □ 303

They have been touched by Rav Mordechai Gifter and they will never be the same.

Rav Zelig Pliskin tells the following anecdote:

When I came to the yeshivah for my entrance bechinah, all of the roshei hayeshivah were there. Rav Gifter already knew me, since he had eaten at my home in Baltimore. In a friendly and cheerful voice, he said, "Good morning, Zelig. How are you today?"

I will always remember that "good morning." He had such a powerful voice. I was a young boy, 13, and nervous about my bechinah. His friendly and cheerful "good morning" put me at ease. Every morning, when I wake up and say Modeh Ani, I hear my rebbi saying, "Good morning, Zelig. How are you today?" And that was in 1959!

An older *bachur*, Yitzchak* was going through a very difficult period. He was feeling dejected, very much in need of a "pick-me-up." When he learned that Rav Gifter would be visiting his town, he decided to set up a time to talk with him, since Rav Gifter had helped lift his spirits in the past.

First, though, he planned to attend a lecture that Rav Gifter was giving for the community. Rav Gifter was about to begin his discourse to a packed crowd when he noticed the older *bachur* sitting in the audience. Suddenly, Rav Gifter called out, "Yitzchak! How are you? How is everything? I haven't seen you in a while." Everyone looked to see whom Rav Gifter was addressing. Yitzchak sat up tall and proud.

Without saying more than a greeting, his rebbi had lifted his spirits in an incalculable way.

Rebbetzin Breiny Helfan Fried, the principal of Cleveland's Mosdos Ohr HaTorah's girls' division, grew up next door to the Gifters. She was often privy to Rav Gifter's sensitive and caring side. When she was a teenager, nearing high-school graduation, she was occupied with writing a speech she was to give at the ceremony. At the same time, her family was involved with another *simchah*, an orphan cousin's bar mitzvah.

---

*Name has been changed.

The house was in a state of tumult as the family prepared for the bar mitzvah of their cousin, who had lost his father in a tragic plane crash. The only place Breiny could practice her speech in peace was on top of the stack of folding chairs that had been rented for the affair. On the Thursday night before the bar mitzvah, Rav Gifter came into the house to wish the family mazel tov. When he saw Breiny practically reaching the ceiling, he asked her why she was sitting there. Breiny told the rosh hayeshivah that she was practicing her valedictory address in the only private place in the house at the time. Rav Gifter didn't hesitate for a moment. "I will listen to your speech," he said. He listened carefully and corrected some of her grammatical errors.

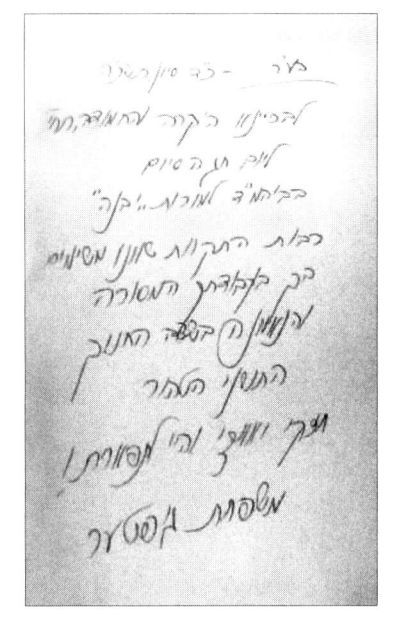

Inscription in the Tanach Rav Gifter gave Breiny Helfan (now Rebbetzin Breiny Fried) upon her graduation from Yavneh

---

Shmuel,* a young man who was learning in Yeshivas Ohr Somayach in Eretz Yisrael, heard a *shmuess* from Rav Gifter and was really anxious to learn in Rav Gifter's yeshivah in Telz-Stone. When he visited Rav Gifter to discuss the matter, Rav Gifter explained that as a beginner, Shmuel needed to spend more time with the basics, perhaps moving on to a more advanced learning environment later. The young man, however, wouldn't take no for an answer. When Rav Gifter saw how determined Shmuel was, he told him he would think it over. When Shmuel came back again to discuss the matter, Rav Gifter was in middle of writing something with much intensity. However, as soon as he noticed him, Rav Gifter dropped his pen and greeted Shmuel warmly, with a smile; he made him feel so important. Rav Gifter then told Shmuel, "Since you have such a strong desire, I cannot just push you away." In the end, although the rosh hayeshivah felt that Shmuel was still not ready to learn in Telz, he knew that the wonderful Rav Gifter had truly listened to him, and he never forgot those encounters.

---

*Name has been changed.

A young woman came to Rav Gifter with horrific news. She had been diagnosed with a life-threatening illness, and the doctors gave her little hope for survival. She was frightened and in great need of support and encouragement.

Rav Gifter voiced a heartening thought, which is all the more powerful for its simplicity: Doctors in every field are constantly quoting statistics in an attempt to predict an individual's chances of recovery. They quote medical journals that give patients a very slight chance of attaining their goal of healing. Yet although they can quote figures offhand, they are powerless to actually peg a patient's chances on their graphs.

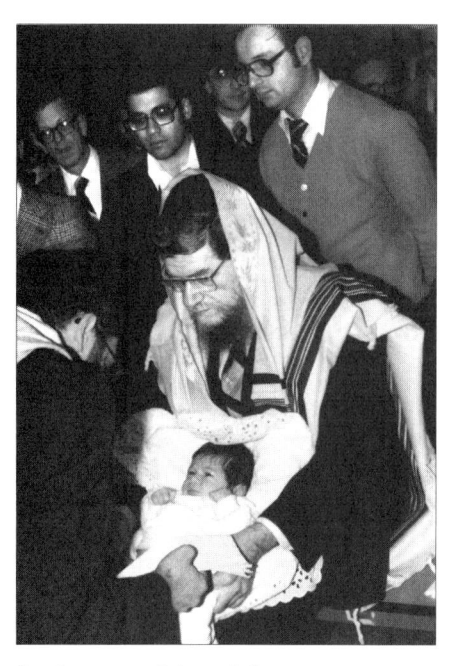

Serving as *sandek* at a *bris*

As Rav Gifter explained, statistics can tell you about the past, but they cannot predict the future. Only the Al-mighty can control the future.

Throughout her difficult odyssey, this young woman held onto the incredible *chizuk* that Rav Gifter had given her, which imbued her with faith in Hashem Alone.

Today, she is a grandmother.

———

In a similar case, a *talmid*'s son was born during a three-day Yom Tov. Just before Shabbos, as the *shalom zachar* was being prepared, the couple found out that the child had Down Syndrome. Several days before the *bris*, the Clevelander Rebbe of Ranaana, Israel suggested a name for the child: Eliyahu Noach. The portion of the week was *Parashas Noach*, and the prophet Eliyahu is said to attend every circumcision, and bring healing.

Rav Gifter was there for the family during this challenging time, with comfort and support. He said the following at Eli's *bris*, "What did

Noach HaTzaddik and Eliyahu HaNavi have in common? They both had enemies from their own generation. The enemies of our generation are some of the people in the medical profession, who cause despair and lack of *bitachon* [trust] and offer little or no hope. But we still have belief and trust that Hashem will watch over another *neshamah* in Klal Yisrael. '*V'chol banayich limudei Hashem* — All your children will be students of Hashem'" (*Yeshayah* 54:13).[1]

One small speech gave this family support for the difficult years ahead.

Dancing with his lifelong friend, Rabbi Aharon Paperman

(He would often quote the verse (*Shemos* 21:19), "*ve'rapo ye'rapei* — and he shall provide for healing."

"From here we learn," Rav Gifter said, "that the Al-mighty gives permission for doctors to heal. But that is all doctors have permission to do. A doctor has no license to tell someone how long he is going to live. If he does, he is not a doctor!")

The Gewirtzes are more than just close friends of the Gifters; they are family. About 70 years ago, Rav Abba Zalka Gewirtz suggested that the community of Waterbury accept Rav Gifter as their rabbi, even though Rabbi Gewirtz was their first choice. From that moment on, Rav Gifter had great respect for Reb Abba Zalka, and eventually brought him to Cleveland in 1968 to become the executive vice president of Yeshivas Telz.

Reb Yonah and Reb Dovid, Reb Abba Zalka's children, both had a special relationship with Rav Gifter. On the last Rosh Hashanah of Rav Gifter's life, when he was already quite ill and nonresponsive, Reb

---
1. Reb Zev Compton.

Dovid came by with his family, to wish the rosh hayeshivah and the rebbetzin a *gut yahr*, as they always did.

When Reb Dovid entered the house, he was overcome by a strange feeling. He had always been somewhat intimidated by Rav Gifter, and yet, in many ways, he viewed the rosh yeshivah as his grandfather. In fact, as a young child, Rav Gifter had bounced him up and down on his lap. He even sang to him a special ditty, titled, *"Reb Dovidel fun Vasselkof"* (Reb Dovidel, Reb Dovidel fun Vasselkof, itzter er iz in Tahrnoff…). When Dovid was young, Rav Gifter would sometimes call him *Reb Dovidel fun Vasselkof.*

When Dovid had gone away to yeshivah, Rav Gifter had demanded that he send him his Torah thoughts. Rav Gifter would return them with his comments and sign the letters, "With love, Mordechai." As Dovid explained to me, the Torah thoughts were not always up to par, and Rav Gifter would let Dovid know that he expected more of him. Consequently, the next letter that Dovid would send would usually contain a sharper Torah thought.

But now, Reb Dovid felt strange because he saw that Rav Gifter was a shell of his former self. Although he had been placed by the table, he was unresponsive. When Reb Dovid walked into the room, he wished the rebbetzin a *gut Yom Tov* and a *gut yahr*, and then turned his eyes to Rav Gifter. Although Reb Dovid was overcome with emotion, he still wanted his yearly blessing. That was what kept him going from year to year. And now, it seemed a distant dream.

Ignoring the reality, Reb Dovid called out, "Rebbi, *gut yahr*! Can I have a *berachah*?" When no response was forthcoming, Reb Dovid continued, "Doesn't the rosh hayeshivah remember me? Please rebbi, give me a *berachah* …"

Reb Dovid was becoming quite emotional as he sat down right next to his rebbi. "Rebbi, please … it's *Dovidel fun Vasselkof*." And, through his tears, Reb Dovid began to sing the lullaby that Rav Gifter had sung to him when he was a young child. Amazingly, tears began to roll down the rosh hayeshivah's face, too. Then once more, Reb Dovid begged the rosh hayeshivah for a blessing he was unable to deliver. Finally, Reb Dovid asked for one *amen*, as he slowly repeated the *berachah* he had heard from the rosh hayeshivah so many times in his life.

Shockingly, Rav Gifter suddenly responded, *"Amen ve'amen!"*

Reb Dovid's tears blinded his vision, but it was this blessing that he would remember more than any other.

The *berachah* for *Reb Dovidel fun Vasselkof.*

Humility

RAV GIFTER ONCE EXPLAINED:

When the Torah discusses Hashem's summons to Moshe, it uses the term "Vayikra — And He called." However, when it mentions Bilaam's prophecy, it says "Vayikar Elokim el Bilaam — Hashem happened upon Bilaam" [Bamidbar 23:4]. Rashi explains that the word "vayikra" is an affectionate term; "vayikar," however, is not. It denotes impurity and transitoriness. In the Torah, the first word of Parashas Vayikra is written with a small aleph. Baal HaTurim explains that Moshe did not want to write the word vayikra, but instead the word vayikar. Moshe did not want to write vayikra because he did not consider himself worthy enough that the Torah should say of him that "Hashem called him." Nevertheless, Hashem commanded him to write the full word, vayikra, but in a final attempt to make the word appear like vayikar, Moshe wrote it with a small aleph.

These two terms are more than just two different ways that Hashem addresses a prophet; they actually describe the essence of prophecy itself. Rambam [Yesodei HaTorah 7:1] writes that a Jew can receive prophecy only if he is suitably prepared. He must possess elevated character traits and have absolute control over himself. Once he has achieved this, Hashem calls to him in an act of final preparation. Other nations' prophets do not require the same preparation to receive prophecy. For example, Bilaam was vile and corrupt, yet he was the greatest non-Jewish prophet of all time. His prophecy was not attained through his righteousness, but solely because Hashem desired that the nations have a prophet equal to Moshe. Since Bilaam's prophecy was not the result of self-elevation and preparation, there was no need for Hashem to call him and further prepare him. Instead, "He happened upon Bilaam." Thus, whereas vayikra denotes great self-discipline, vayikar does not.

Even after Hashem told him to write vayikra — that he was indeed a prophet worthy of the calling — Moshe, in his humility, still tried to avoid expressing this and wrote the word with a small aleph.

In light of this explanation, we now can understand something else. When Moshe descended Har Sinai with a second pair of Tablets, his face radiated light. What caused the light?

Midrash Tanchuma [Ki Sisa 20:20] explains that it emanated from the extra ink that remained after Moshe had finished writing the Torah. The Veinuter Rav, Rav Ezra Altschuler, explains that there was extra ink only

With Rav Shach at the *chasunah* of Reb Chaim Mordechai Ausband

because Moshe wrote a small letter aleph in the word vayikra instead of writing a full-sized one. The light that radiated from Moshe's face was thus the light of his humility. True anivus, humility, does not cause one to lose out. On the contrary, it is the very cause of actual elevation and glorification. [2]

This beautiful thought best describes the manner in which Rav Gifter acted. The light that radiated from his face was also the light of his humility.

Letter from Rav Shach

When Rav Shach came to Telz-Stone to give a *shiur* for the first time, Reb Yudi Sova walked behind Rav Gifter as he escorted Rav Shach into the *beis midrash*. They did not know anyone was behind them.

As they were about to enter the narrow door of the *beis midrash*, Rav Gifter turned to Rav Shach and said, "*Nu, der rosh yeshivah iz mechubed* [the rosh yeshivah gets the honor]," indicating that Rav Shach should go in first. But Rav Shach deferred,

---

2. Based on *Pirkei Emunah, Maamad Har Sinai*, p. 96.

insisting that Rav Gifter is the resident rosh yeshivah and therefore he should go first. To this, Rav Gifter responded that Rav Shach is the rosh yeshivah of the whole world.

The conversation went back and forth, until finally, Rav Gifter said, "*Genug shoin! Men darf gein* — **tzuzamen**! [Enough already! We must go — **together!**]" And side by side, Rav Shach and Rav Gifter entered the *beis midrash*.

In fact, Rav Gifter was practically allergic to honor. One time, he attended a relative's wedding in Baltimore. It was decided that Rav Gifter would receive the honor of *siddur kiddushin*. However, Rav Gifter took the wine goblet and said, "I, Mordechai Gifter, am *mechabed* the Baltimore rosh yeshivah with *siddur kiddushin*."[3]

Perhaps he excelled in the area of interpersonal relationships because he was so genuine. Often, relationships are so superficial, yet his were so real; he had no airs about him. He thought nothing of himself, while he valued others for who they were. He would often introduce himself as "Gifter," a small example of his humility.

On Simchas Torah, there would be many *kiddushim* in the neighborhood where most of the faculty members of the yeshivah resided. The custom was to go to the various *kiddushim*, stay for a while, and then move on to the next one.

Once, when Rav Gifter walked in unnoticed, he didn't sit at the head of the table. Instead, he sat with the *bachurim*. Only after someone in the crowd saw him was he forced to move up to the front.

Respect

ONCE, A NEWCOMER TO THE YESHIVAH FROM SOUTH AFRICA attended a *shalom zachar* at which Rav Gifter was a participant. This young man's father had been a rebbi in the yeshivah many years earlier, and he was eager to meet the person whom he had heard so much about. He was watching Rav Gifter carefully, amazed that the elderly man had made the lengthy walk to the *shalom zachar*. After spending a few moments in the men's section, Rav Gifter walked into the tiny kitchen and called out, "*Avu iz di mama*? [Where is the mother?]" Immediately, the mother of the child, obviously still

---

3. Rabbi Nosson Scherman.

weak, walked toward Rav Gifter. As the women watched in awe, Rav Gifter said with great feeling and concern, "Mazel tov! How are you feeling?"

The young man from South Africa had just caught his first glimpse into the greatness of Rav Gifter. It had not come in a lecture. It had come in a small eye-opening moment, exemplifying how one should honor others. It was an insight he would never forget.[4]

Rav Gifter always made it a point to greet every worker he saw in the yeshivah. He treated them as human beings, and that is why they mourned him when he passed away.

As a *bachur* in Telz, Lita

The student body of Telz Yeshivah, Lita, 1932

---

4. Rabbi Mutty Suchard.

As a young man, Rav Gifter was already very careful about others' honor. While a student in Yeshivas Rabbeinu Yitzchak Elchanan, at the tender age of 14, he heard that one of the rebbeim did not have enough money to buy food for Pesach. Immediately, he spearheaded a drive to raise money for this rebbi, so that he could celebrate the holiday in an honorable way. What a remarkable achievement for a 14-year-old![5]

One time, when Mordechai was in Telz in Lithuania, many of the older *bachurim* decided that a certain rebbi was not learned enough to handle the particular *shiur* he was given.

The older *bachurim* decided to protest the appointment by telling the younger *bachurim* who were in the new rebbi's class not to attend the *shiur*. In those days, when the *bachurim* protested, it was referred to as a "*hopka*."

Mordechai, a respected older *bachur* who became aware of the plan, mentioned it to his *chavrusa*, Rav Zalman Bloch, who was the spiritual leader (*menahel ruchani*) of the yeshivah (and his future father-in-law). He told Rav Zalman to tell the new rebbi not to come to the *shiur* that day, since no one was planning on showing up. By the following day, Mordechai said, he would have it resolved.

That day, Mordechai chastised the *bachurim* and told them that they had no right not to show up to their rebbi's lecture. Not only that, but the next day, he attended the new rebbi's *shiur* along with them. Thus, the rebbi was spared embarrassment, because if Mordechai, one of the yeshivah's most respected students, could attend his *shiur*, then there was no reason for the younger *bachurim* not to attend.

Mordechai stayed in the rebbi's *shiur* through the winter. By then, the entire yeshivah realized what a great *talmid chacham* the rebbi was.

In one masterful stroke, Mordechai had restored the honor that was due a venerable *talmid chacham*.

---

5. Rav Zalman Gifter.

Rav Gifter with talmidim from the 1970's. In the middle is Rabbi (Yisroel) Indich of Cincinnati.

ON ONE OCCASION IN TELZ YESHIVAH, A NUMBER OF *BACHURIM* were arguing with Rav Gifter about a certain matter. Rav Gifter turned to one of the boys and shared a sentiment that was uttered by the Al-mighty Himself to Moshe when Korach and his horde rose against him, "*Hibadlu mi'toch ha'eidah ha'zos* — Separate yourselves from amid this assembly" (*Bamidbar* 16:21). The message was clear: Stay away from rabble-rousers.

For the Sake of Peace

Once, two *bachurim* in the yeshivah were acting in a competitive manner, to the point of real tension. Rav Gifter called the yeshivah together and warned that there must be unity among his students. If not, he said, "Those *bachurim* should leave the yeshivah right now!" He added, "Humans are like porcupines. If they are too close to each other, they poke [*shtuch*] each other!" Once again, Rav Gifter stressed to his students the importance of peace.

Jews, non-Jews, Torah scholars, laymen, women, children — all were recipients of the wonderful concern and encouragement that Rav Gifter dispensed in his warm, respectful, peaceful, and humble manner.

Chapter 26
Kindness, Appreciation, and Sensitivity

Kindness

ONE TIME, RAV GIFTER AND A *TALMID* WERE WALKING TO the *beis midrash* when a skunk suddenly darted out and nearly ran into them. Shocked, Rav Gifter cried out, "*Oy! Hub shoin rachmanus!* [Have pity!]" The *talmid* commented about the danger of having the skunks running wild on the yeshivah campus. Rav Gifter looked at him in surprise. "About whom do you think I was speaking? It is not a pity on us; it is a pity on the skunks!"

Rav Gifter continued, "This was not always Nutwood Lane; it was Nutwood Farms. The animals were able to roam. But Telz Yeshivah came along and decided that they were going to build a campus. They put a dormitory here, and a dining room there, and a *beis midrash* over there. *Nebach* … the skunks, *zei hubben nit avu tzu loifen!* [they have nowhere to run!]"[1]

---

1. Rabbi Avrohom Alter.

Imagine that reaction; what kind of *neshamah* feels these things? Almost no one has pity on a skunk, but Rav Gifter loved all of Hashem's creatures.

A similarly poignant story is told by Rabbi Zelig Pliskin:

I was a young bachur in Telz Yeshivah and was walking along the road to Rav Gifter's house, when a little frog jumped out on the road. It was drizzling and a car was approaching. Rav Gifter stopped the car. The driver opened the window and asked, "Does the rosh hayeshivah want a ride?" Rav Gifter responded, "No, there's a frog on the road." Then, he bent over and shooed the frog away, explaining that it would have been tzaar baalei chaim [causing suffering to living creatures] to allow the driver to continue. With the frog safely out of the way, he waved the driver on and walked home.

Rav Gifter was always on the lookout for situations in which he could help another person. A *bachur* who traveled standby on the same flight to Cleveland as the Gifters was surprised when the flight attendant brought him a meal; usually when one flies standby there is no kosher meal available. The flight attendant indicated that Rav Gifter had told her to give his meal to the young man. When the *bachur* went over to the Gifters to express his thanks, his rebbi explained, "I am going home, and you are going to the yeshivah — too late to get supper. The rebbetzin and I will find something to eat at home, but what will you eat?" [2]

Appreciation

ONE COULD SENSE FROM RAV GIFTER'S ACTIONS THAT HE TOOK nothing that others did for him for granted. He showed exceptional gratitude, even for the smallest favors.

Rabbi Avrohom Katz (the grandson of Rav Reuven Katz, author of *Degel Reuven*) lives in Eretz Yisrael. He was a *talmid* of Rav Gifter over 40 years ago. Whenever Rav Gifter would visit Eretz Yisrael, Reb Avrohom would drive his rebbi to the airport. Each time, and there were many, Rav Gifter would make sure to "pay" for his ride with a nice Torah thought, a thank-you card, and a warm kiss.

Rav and Rebbetzin Gifter often spent a few weeks of the summer at the home of a *talmid* in Monsey, New York. They would vacation in the small guesthouse that was situated in the back of their host's home. During their stay, the host family's maid cleaned up the Gifters' quarters

---

2. Rabbi Yonah Gewirtz.

Rabbi Hyman Samson

from time to time. When the Gifters left, the maid would receive a tip from Rav Gifter.

Rav Gifter treasured relationships, always making a point to show appreciation, not only to those individuals who had performed acts of kindness to him, but even to the relatives of those individuals.

When Rav Gifter visited Eretz Yisrael, he would make sure to visit the son of Rabbi Hyman Samson, dean of Talmudical Academy in Baltimore, as a sign of appreciation for all that his father had done for Rav Gifter. When young Mordechai Gifter's father had needed some extra reassuring to send him out of town to learn, it was Rabbi Samson who had spoken to him and encouraged Mr. Gifter to let him go.

———◆———

When his son Reb Binyomin had a baby boy and asked him to suggest a name, Rav Gifter said that the baby be named Shimon Yehuda, out of gratitude to Rav Shimon Shkop for the blessing he had given him when he was 8 years old. He added, "Without that *berachah*, what would have become of me?"

When Rav Gifter was still a *bachur* in Telz, one of his older *chavrusos* was Rav Shalom Zundel Kruk, who later became the rav of Shirvint, Lithuania. The two remained close throughout Rav Gifter's tenure in Telz, and Rav Shalom Zundel looked after Mordechai. Tragically, though, they never saw each other again. Rav Zundel, as he was known, was burned alive by the Nazis. He was only 31 years old at the time. About 50 years later, Rav Zundel's younger brother, Reb Yosef Chaim Cook, a businessman from London, came to visit his son — Rabbi Simcha Cook, who is a rebbi in Ner Yisrael and lives on Yeshiva Lane — for Succos. (He had changed his name from Kruk to Cook, since Kruk was not a good name for someone going into business.) Rav Gifter was staying on Yeshiva Lane with his son-in-law and daughter, Rav and Rebbetzin Ephraim Eisenberg, for Yom Tov, as well.

When the *hakafos* began on Simchas Torah in the Ner Yisrael *beis midrash*, Rav Gifter, who was swept up in the dancing, walked over to Reb Yosef Chaim and said, "*Oy, Reb Zundel's bruder! Lomer tantzen tzuzamen.* [Reb Zundel's brother! Let's dance together.]"

And the two of them held onto each other — a renowned rosh hayeshivah honoring an upright layman — and danced together, along with the memory of Rav Zundel.

Sensitivity

RAV GIFTER HELD A SPECIAL PLACE IN HIS HEART FOR THOSE WHO had lost their parents, no matter what the age of the children. He once went to visit a young woman who had just given birth. When asked why he had gone to visit this particular new mother, he explained, "*Zi hut nit kein tatte* — She has no father [to visit her]."

Rav Gifter could often be seen walking with one of Rav Boruch Sorotzkin's young grandchildren, pointing out sights and sounds as they walked. Why did he do this? Because, he'd say, "*Zei hubben nit kein zeide* — They don't have their grandfather [to take them on walks]."

Stories of Rav Gifter's kindness and sensitivity abound from the summers he spent at Camp Agudah. One summer in the early 80's, Rav Gifter and his rebbetzin visited the camp for about two weeks. That summer, Shimon* was the counselor of the staff assistants. Rav Gifter passed by once as Shimon was scolding two Russian boys who'd decided to go AWOL on a camp trip. Prior to cell phones, missing campers or staff members could be very hard on a director's nerves.

At the wedding of Rav Yaakov Reisman to Chasya Gifter. L-r: Rav Gifter, Rav Boruch Sorotzkin (reading the *kesubah*), and Rav Nochum Velvel Dessler

*Name has been changed.

Arriving at Camp Agudah

Suddenly, Rav Gifter's booming voice rang out as he reprimanded Shimon for speaking in such a tone to the boys. Shimon was very embarrassed and resentful. He went to the camp administration and told them what had happened. The members of administration felt that he should meet with the rosh hayeshivah and rebbetzin to explain his side of the story.

Shimon met with Rav Gifter, who was very gracious. He told him about the importance of honoring others, especially the many newly arrived Russian Jews who were working to become observant. Shimon listened and thanked the rosh hayeshivah, but even after he walked away, Shimon still felt insulted.

A few weeks later, the Gifters were leaving Camp Agudah for the summer. Traditionally, the *gedolim* who visit the camp are escorted out as the campers line the camp road singing *"Ki Ve'simchah"* (a song based on a verse in *Yeshayah* that speaks about going out in happiness). Shimon, though, didn't attend. He was still feeling hurt.

All of a sudden, Shimon heard people calling him and telling him that he was wanted outside. In fact, people came to his room and dragged him out. He was brought to the car that carried the rosh hayeshivah, since Rav Gifter himself had summoned him. The car window was open. Rav Gifter smiled at Shimon and said softly, "Please come inside."

Leaving Camp Agudah

Leaving Camp Agudah

Shimon was in shock as he went into the car. He was not sure what to expect. The rosh hayeshivah showered him with blessings, and shared with him all the positive things he had heard about him. Shimon was ashamed and in tears, as he realized that all of this time he had misunderstood Rav Gifter's motives.

As Rav Gifter spoke, Shimon could feel the sensitivity and *ahavas Yisrael* that Rav Gifter carried for each and every being. Nearly 30 years later, this encounter remains etched in this counselor's memory. When he submitted this story to me, he noted, "I hope this story will merit being published in your book. The few people I have told this story to rarely hear the ending, as I usually get choked up in tears…"

Rav Gifter was bothered when affairs did not begin on time or run on schedule, and he did not like to trouble others with speeches at a late hour. One time, he spoke at a *talmid*'s wedding in Chicago. He began his words with a sharp and humorous opening, *"Der sha'ah is shpet, uber ich kum fun Cleveland un der sha'ah is shpetter!* [The hour is late, but I come from Cleveland and the hour is even later!]" (Chicago is one hour behind Cleveland, since it is in the Central Time Zone.)

Rav Itzele Ponovezher

One year, Rav Gifter came, as he often did, to Cleveland Heights to deliver a *shmuess* during the Ten Days of Repentance. He began by apologizing that he was 30 minutes late; in truth, he had been told the wrong time. Nevertheless, he did not blame anyone else. Instead, he acted as though it had been his own fault as he apologized for inconveniencing the audience. Of course, those who were aware of the real reason for his tardiness had already received their first lesson of the night.

Rav Gifter had an uncanny ability to say the right thing in the right way at the right time, to make people comfortable and put them at ease. He once attended a meeting just before Pesach at the home of a Telzer *talmid*. When he walked into the house, it was in a state of pre-Pesach disarray. Apparently, the wife of his *talmid* had not had a chance to clean up before the meeting, and she was highly embarrassed.

Sensing the shame of the woman, Rav Gifter said, "I want you to know, if your house looked like anything *but* this, I would not eat in your home over Pesach!" Immediately, the woman smiled and felt better.

Rav Gifter would often tell a story about Rav Itzele Ponovezher that took place in the 1920's to illustrate the value of treating others with thoughtfulness.

Rav Itzele had appointed someone to be in charge of the finances of the yeshivah. When World War I broke out, the man lost his child in the war, causing him to fall into a deep depression and to ignore his job responsibilities. Although many people, including Rav Itzele, tried to help the poor man, no one was able to get him to snap out of his sadness and get back to his job. Since he had been in charge of the bank accounts, it was he and he alone who could work with the banks, but he was unable to do so. Thus, after a while, the yeshivah's finances were in a desperate state.

It was suggested to Rav Itzele that he take the man to court to force him to do his job. Rav Itzele presented the question to Rav Chaim Soloveitchik, whose response was shocking. He determined that it is better to close up the yeshivah than to risk having the fellow fall into an even deeper depression, at which point he may be at risk of taking his own life.

"The power of Torah study does not override saving a life [*pikuach nefesh*]! And if necessary, it is worthwhile to close the yeshivah so as not to cause another's demise."[3]

This was the level of compassion toward which Rav Gifter strove.

Yet, perhaps the most amazing story of Rav Gifter's sympathy involves a young lady who, as she was about to enter the stage of *shidduchim,* suffered renal failure. Her older sister donated a kidney to her, and she began her long and difficult recovery. At the same time, her father, a Holocaust survivor, was in the hospital undergoing treatments for what she was told was an ulcer. The family was trying to protect her during her recovery and never told her that it was really stomach cancer.

One of the nurses, though, slipped and shared the truth with the young woman. Devastated, she sat by her father's side, begging the Al-mighty to make him better.

Desperate for *chizuk,* she went to see Rav Gifter, crying and sharing her suffering and pain. She knew her father was terminally ill, while she was facing an uphill climb, as well. "Tell me, rosh hayeshivah, when will my salvation come?!"

Rav Gifter listened and then he cried, too.

---

3. Rabbi Nachman Klein.

And cried.

And cried.

The master of words spoke the only language he could to give her *chizuk*: the language of the heart.

Nearly 40 years later, this woman, now a grandmother many times over, recalls that day. "There was almost nothing in the world the rosh hayeshivah could have done or said to give me *chizuk*; there was really only one thing. And indeed, it gave me the *chizuk* I needed."

One *talmid* recalls Rav Gifter's talks in Telz during the Ten Days of Repentance, that illustrate the sensitivity that Rav Gifter instilled into his students:

The days that followed Rosh Hashanah were days of fear and awe of the approaching Yom Kippur. In his Shabbos Shuvah derashah, Rav Gifter would quote from his rebbi, the Telzer Rav, Rav Avraham Yitzchak Bloch, that yeshivah students carry the responsibility of a whole generation. He would add that if there is a breakdown of the law of chalav Yisrael in Telz, it can cause Shabbos desecration in Paris. He emphasized that all Jews have one collective soul. The concept of "Kol Yisrael areivim zeh la'zeh — All of Israel is responsible for one another" unites all of Klal Yisrael into one radiant soul.

On the night of Yom Kippur, he would speak to us before the yeshivah said Tehillim for all Jews who are in distress and captivity. With a tear-filled, choked voice, he would quote to us the famous words of Rav Itzele Volozhiner in his introduction to the Nefesh HaChaim, "… and he would rebuke me for not feeling the pain of another Jew, for this is what man is all about. Man was not created for himself, but was created to do for others in every way possible."

By crying over the tragedies of Klal Yisrael, he taught us how to feel the pain of others: Russian Jewry, our brethren in Eretz Yisrael, or everyone from Klal Yisrael who found themselves in sorrow at the time.

RAV ABBA ZALKA GEWIRTZ, THE EXECUTIVE VICE PRESIDENT OF the yeshivah, recalled the day that Rav Gifter walked into the yeshivah office and began to cry. Reb Abba Zalka asked Rav Gifter what was wrong. He explained, "Reb Abba Zalka, we have not paid the kollel students, and we don't have money to pay them. What will they do for Shabbos?" At that moment,

Strong Emotions

he took a few hundred dollars of his own from his pocket. He gave the money to Reb Abba Zalka to use to help pay the kollel fellows.

One individual who was blessed to know Rav Gifter wrote the following.

Truly, Rav Gifter's every word was an enunciation. Whether a thundering denunciation, a loving word of encouragement, a long-sought decision, or a penetrating shaft of humor, Rav Gifter's every word was an enunciation. His diction was crystal clear. His syntax was perfect. His choice of words, elegant. And his delivery — that incomparable, indescribable delivery — was mesmerizing.

And in writing specifically about his great sense of emotion (*hergesh*):

He had a tremendous depth of soul, that could be moved to great emotion; and he had a tremendous gift of expression, that could communicate his emotions exactly, impeccably. [4]

When the Brisker Rav, Rav Yitzchak Ze'ev Soloveitchik, passed away in 1960, Rav Gifter stood up to speak, began to weep, and wept uncontrollably for two minutes. He then stepped down, without saying a word.

Yet Complete Control

WHEN RAV BORUCH SOROTZKIN PASSED AWAY, RAV GIFTER PAID A *shivah* visit to the family. He shared an enlightening thought on the verse, "*U'machah Hashem Elokim dimah me'al kol panim* — And my L-rd Hashem/Elokim will erase tears from all faces" (*Yeshayah* 25:8).

Rav Gifter said, "It seems that when we ask Hashem to wipe away our tears, we are referring to all tears. But aren't there some tears that we want to continue to cry, such as tears of joy that are shed on happy occasions?"

Rav Gifter explained, in the name of Rav Elya Meir Bloch, that tears come when we are unable to contain our emotions. This occurs during both happy and sad occasions. However, there are many examples of great individuals who control their tears when they receive tragic news

---

4. Rabbi Hillel Goldberg.

on Shabbos. Since their souls are expansive, they are able to fill their souls with more emotions; thus, they do not overflow with tears.

Rav Gifter concluded, "This is what the verse is referring to. We ask the Al-mighty that there come a time when our souls become so expansive that we do not cry anymore, because we are able to handle the emotion."

Rav Gifter was an example of an individual who was in complete control of his emotions.

The day before Pesach 5721 (1961), shortly before *bedikas chametz*, Rav Gifter received the news that a *talmid*, Rabbi Chaim Tzvi Anemer, and two of his children had been killed in a car accident. He walked into his study and sobbed with heartrending cries. His own mother was there at the time and marveled at her son's emotions. However, after crying bitterly, he emerged from the room. It was time to get ready for *bedikas chametz*.

In 1963, Telz Yeshivah suffered a devastating loss when fire swept through the dormitory. The building was completely destroyed. As soon as possible, the administration took a roll call to account for each boy. Two were missing. Everyone hoped that the boys had run from the building and had not yet been found.

On Friday morning, the terrible news reached Rav Gifter; the bodies of the two boys had been found. As can be imagined, he was grief stricken.

On Friday night, though, when Rav Gifter returned from *Maariv* and sat down to the Shabbos meal, he told his family that Shabbos is Shabbos. Thus, there would be no crying or mourning; they would all eat and sing *zemiros*, as usual. However, the moment he finished saying *havdalah*, he broke down sobbing.

Rav Gifter knew that there was a time for everything: for kindness, appreciation, sensitivity, emotions, and controlling emotions, too.

Section 7
Family Life

Chapter 27
Building a Peaceful Home

RAV GIFTER WAS FOND OF TELLING THE FOLLOWING STORY, which illustrates that if one does not behave like a *mentch*, especially with his family, then he is not worthy of respect.

The daughter of Rav Eliyahu Eliezer Grodnanski, the son-in-law of Rav Yisrael Salanter (founder of the *mussar* movement), became engaged to a young man, Rav Chaim Ozer Grodzenski (the future *gadol hador*). Since the *kallah's* grandfather, Rav Yisrael, had not attended the engagement, Rav Eliyahu Eliezer wrote to his father-in-law,[1] informing him of his granddaughter's engagement, and enclosing the *divrei Torah* that the *chassan* had delivered.

Rav Yisrael wrote back, "Mazel tov. I received your letter, and from the *divrei Torah* that you enclosed I can see that the *chassan* is indeed a *talmid chacham*. However, it says in the Torah, '*Es biti nasati la'***ish** *hazeh* — I gave my daughter to this **man**' [*Devarim* 22:16]. *Ve'al ha'***ish** *lo kasavta li me'umah!* [But you wrote nothing about the **man**, i.e., the *mentch*!]."

First and foremost, a husband and father must behave like a *mentch*. When his children got married, Rav Gifter would repeat this verse at

---
1. Later published as part of *She'eilos U'Teshuvos Achiezer* of Rav Chaim Ozer Grodzenski.

each one's *sheva berachos* in order to stress this point.

It is hard to imagine that someone as busy as Rav Gifter would have time for a normal home life. Yet, in the Gifter home, the children grew up in an atmosphere of calm, caring, and unending love from both of their parents. No matter what the issue, Rav Gifter was available to help his children with their needs, both small and large, and taught them by example how to behave as members of Klal Yisrael.

Greeting Rav Shalom Schwadron

Rebbetzin Shoshana Gifter, a refined and aristocratic woman, dedicated her life to her husband's growth in learning. She is the quintessential woman of valor (*eishes chayil*). She did request one thing, though: that his study not be situated in the basement of their home. First of all, she worried about his health, for she knew that the dank and damp basement was not a good place for him to spend his time. In addition, she wanted to see him and hear him learning, because he virtually lived in his study. As she said, "The rosh hayeshivah was always learning."

With the Rebbetzin

At a wedding

330 ☐ RAV GIFTER

HE HAD UNCONDITIONAL LOVE FOR ALL HIS CHILDREN AND THEY felt it deeply. He made a point of complimenting them and making them feel good about themselves. The children remember his generosity, despite the fact that their family was getting by on a rather modest income. They felt that their father never skimped on their needs, and was always available to them.

A Loving Father

When his wife worked late hours, he would leave his study and come to the door as soon as he heard the school bus pull up, so that he could

Enjoying grandchildren

Rav Gifter with his son Binyomin and daughter Shlomis in the late 1940's

Breakfast with a granddaughter

Chapter 27: Building a Peaceful Home ☐ 331

welcome the children with a warm smile and ask about their day. If they had a homework question to ask him, he would look up from his Gemara, answer the question, and go right back to his learning.

The family knew that when their father walked in the door — on Shabbos or during the week — the sense of joy he carried with him pervaded the entire household. His resounding "good morning" made one feel that it really was a good morning. His "*guten Shabbos*" was so distinct that *talmidim* picked up the expression and said it with the same intonation.

Other Family Members

RAV GIFTER'S DEVOTION TO HIS IMMEDIATE FAMILY EXTENDED TO relatives, as well. Rebbetzin Gifter's sister, Naomi, survived the war, but their parents and others did not. Rav Gifter took it upon himself to act as Naomi's father and help find a husband for her. After consulting with many individuals with whom he had close connections, he finally chose Rav Pesach Stein, a prominent student of the Mirrer Yeshivah. Rav Pesach came to Telz and became a very popular rebbi. His *sefarim, Likkutei Shiurim,* are learned all over the world.

Rebbetzin Gifter escorting her sister, Rebbetzin Naomi Stein, to the *chuppah*. At right, holding the candle, is their uncle Rav Chaim Mordechai Katz

Rav Gifter escorting Rav Pesach Stein down the aisle. At left is Rav Zalman Sorotzkin, an uncle of the *kallah*

Even though his own funds were severely limited, Rav Gifter helped pay for her wedding, using the last penny from his savings account. Rebbetzin Naomi Stein once said, "I didn't even feel like an orphan, because my brother-in-law took care of me like I was his own child."

One year at the Seder, a cousin who did not have a father was seated right next to Rav Gifter. As often happens at a crowded table, the child inadvertently spilled his wine onto Rav Gifter's lap. Without saying a

With grandchildren of Rav Pesach and Rebbetzin Naomi Stein

Chapter 27: Building a Peaceful Home ☐ 333

With members of the family

word, Rav Gifter got up and changed his pants. However, the reprieve was short-lived, because soon after, the boy spilled his wine on Rav Gifter yet again! Even though Rav Gifter was left without clean pants for the rest of Yom Tov, he did not react.

RAV AND REBBETZIN GIFTER'S MARITAL HARMONY (*SHALOM bayis*) was exemplary. He treasured her, and she treasured him. As a young woman, she had to make her way across the Lithuanian border in order to get to America. As was common in those days, the guards took her most precious possession, an heirloom jewelry piece that her mother had given her. Rebbetzin Gifter didn't blink when she was forced to give over the jewelry. "I had no *tzaar*," she later told her daughters. "I knew I was going to my true treasure."

Marital Harmony

Her reverence and love for him were evident as she showed me around her apartment (that was built as an addition to their son Reb Zalman's house), stopping to look at family pictures. As she showed me the photos, I was able to sense the

334 ☐ RAV GIFTER

closeness she had with her husband. She laughed at certain pictures, recalling how much the rosh hayeshivah disliked posing for pictures. Most of all, she told me, she enjoys looking at the pictures of him learning.

The following story drives home the depth of the rosh hayeshivah's devotion to his wife. The yeshivah had just concluded the morning session on Erev Yom Kippur. The men hurried home; there was still much to be done before Yom Kippur began. Rav Gifter asked an older *bachur* to give him a ride to take care of an errand. The young man was eager to do whatever he could for Rav Gifter. Just to be extra helpful, he offered to run the errand himself so that the rosh hayeshivah did not have to. But Rav Gifter was adamant that he had to go himself.

Once in the car, Rav Gifter asked him to drive to the flower shop and wait outside for a minute or two. Again, the *talmid* offered to go in, but Rav Gifter was insistent on doing it himself. A moment later, he emerged with a bouquet of beautiful flowers. "We celebrate my rebbetzin's birthday today and I wanted to buy her flowers." Humbled by the incredible sensitivity of his rebbi, the *bachur* realized that he had learned how a husband should treat his wife, even before the holiest day of the year.

One year, the rebbetzin told him that she did not want him troubling himself on Erev Yom Kippur to run and buy flowers for her. He agreed. Then, that year, on Erev Yom Kippur, she saw the empty table where the flowers had always sat, and felt sad, realizing that she really did want those flowers from him! Moments later, Rav Gifter walked in wearing a big smile and holding a bouquet of flowers. She realized that regardless of what she said, he was not going to stop giving her flowers, and she appreciated it.

Chapter 27: Building a Peaceful Home

The last time he was able to purchase the flowers, he was already walking with a walker. In fact, he could not carry the flowers and push the walker at the same time, so his son Reb Zalman carried them. But when he reached the door to the apartment, he asked Reb Zalman to give him the flowers; he wanted to hand them to his wife himself.

Once, a *chassan* asked the rosh hayeshivah if it is worthwhile to read publications that contain guidance about marriage. He responded, "If you're a *mentch,* you have no need for any marriage pamphlets. If you're not a *mentch*, no pamphlet in the world is going to help you!"

A young man once asked Rav Gifter why folding one's *tallis* on Motza'ei Shabbos is considered a *segulah* for *shalom bayis*. "Vacuuming the floors on Erev Shabbos is a much greater *segulah* for *shalom bayis*," was the rosh hayeshivah's reply.

However, he was able to joke about husband-wife relationships, as well. Rabbi Tzodok Suchard, a close *talmid* of Rav Gifter's who hailed from South Africa, got married in Baltimore; that is where he and his wife celebrated their first *sheva berachos*. The rest of the *sheva berachos*, however, were held in Telz.

With the children (l-r): Binyomin, Sroly, and Zalman Gifter, Chasya Reisman, Luba Feuer, and Shlomis Eisenberg

The day after the last *sheva berachos*, Rav Gifter offered Reb Tzadok a position as the ninth-grade rebbi in the yeshivah. Reb Tzadok was overwhelmed by the offer and excitedly went home to tell his wife. But she did not share his enthusiasm. She insisted that she wanted her husband to first learn in kollel, and only after that to become a rebbi.

The next morning, Reb Tzadok went back to Rav Gifter and relayed that his wife did not want him to accept, but that she wanted him to learn in kollel. Rav Gifter did not try to persuade him to take the job. Instead, he quipped, "You are married only a week, and already you're listening to your wife?"

Anyone who ever heard Rav Gifter speak or teach knows that he had a strong voice. Yet Rebbetzin Gifter can attest to the fact that he never raised his voice to her, even though he carried around not only the worries of his family and his yeshivah, but the worries of Klal Yisrael. The rebbetzin would know when something was bothering him, but she also knew that he did not want to involve his wife in these weighty matters, so she didn't ask him.

Chapter 27: Building a Peaceful Home

With the rebbetzin at a grandson's *upsherin*

Once, he returned from a meeting extremely agitated. He waited outside until he calmed down, so that his wife would not see him upset.

When it came to food, Rav Gifter had simple needs, and made sure to compliment his wife on everything that she served.

The rebbetzin once boiled a large pot of water filled with salt to steam up the room for her son, since he was suffering from a cold. She later used the same pot of water to make vegetable soup, forgetting how much salt she had already put into the water. When the rosh hayeshivah was served this salty soup, he complimented the rebbetzin, as always, on how delicious it was, but added that today the soup may have been a bit saltier than usual. It was then that the rebbetzin recalled in shock how much salt the pot actually contained; she could only marvel that her husband was so considerate that he said nothing critical.

Rav Gifter felt that earning a livelihood was his responsibility, and he was very reluctant to allow the rebbetzin to take a job outside of the home. When she informed him that she had found a job, only after convincing him that she truly wanted to teach and that she would greatly enjoy it, did he agree.

One time, a visiting rosh yeshivah stayed with the Gifters over Chanukah. The guest became tense as the time for lighting the menorah came and went, and Rav Gifter did not rise from his learning to light the candles. When the visitor finally asked why they were waiting, Rav Gifter's answer was simple. "I wait until my wife comes home from teaching, and that's when I light." [2]

The rebbetzin's willingness to sacrifice for her husband is legendary. In the late 1950's, shortly after the yeshivah bought its new campus grounds, it began to build homes for the faculty. While his home was being built, Rav Gifter was not living on the yeshivah campus and he would catch a ride to the yeshivah.

Sensing that the commute was hard for him, the rebbetzin offered to move out to an old house on the yeshivah grounds, which some called the "haunted house," to make his life easier. However, for her it was much more difficult. There were many times when she could not find a ride home from Cleveland Heights to Wickliffe (a 30-minute drive)[3] and would have to go home by Greyhound bus. Rav Gifter would walk to the bus stop to meet her.

And, as mentioned earlier, she agreed to move into a tiny dormitory apartment so that her husband could feel the exile when they returned from Telz-Stone, and she never complained.

The rebbetzin was devoted to her husband their entire marriage, and at the end of his life, she became his full-time caregiver. She recalled this challenging time of her life in a beautiful manner. "When I said the words, '*HaNosein la'ya'eif koach* — Who gives strength to the weary' in davening, I asked that Hashem give me the strength to take care of the rosh hayeshivah. And He did."

One of the nurse's aides in the Gifter home for several years was a sweet African-American man named Denzel. Denzel developed a deep

---
2. Rebbetzin Chasya Reisman.
3. This was before she had a driver's license.

love for the Gifters as he cared for Rav Gifter during his illness. As Rav Gifter's health deteriorated and he had to be cared for even more, Denzel took note of how the rebbetzin did not leave his side.

Denzel related to one of the *bachurim* that he had once worked for another elderly couple where the husband was not well. The illness took its toll on the two of them, and the wife, who was the caretaker, would often raise her voice and lose patience with her husband. Hearing this, the young man was curious what Denzel's impression was of the rabbi and his wife.

Denzel's response is telling. "*Not once* did they ever get frustrated or upset with each other! I never saw such a caring couple!"

Their lives and marriage serve as a lesson to all. Sacrifice. Respect. Admiration. All hallmarks of a superlative marriage. The marriage of Rav Gifter and his rebbetzin is a virtual *mussar sefer* in and of itself.

Moreover, he never allowed his stature to serve as an excuse to avoid responsibilities to his family; this is another lesson we can all take to heart.

Perhaps we can never achieve Rav Gifter's greatness in learning, or Rebbetzin Gifter's selflessness in taking care of him, but it is something toward which we can all strive.

Chapter 28
"VeShinantam LeVanecha" You Shall Teach Them Thoroughly to Your Children

RAV GIFTER[1] WOULD OFTEN QUOTE AND EXPLAIN THE *pasuk*, *"Torah tzivah lanu Moshe morashah Kehillas Yaakov — The Torah that Moshe commanded us is the heritage of the Congregation of Yaakov"* (*Devarim* 33:4).

The Torah usually relates to an inheritance by the term *nachalah*. Why does the Torah deviate and use the word *morashah*, heritage?

Let us understand the difference between the two terms. A *nachalah*, inheritance, becomes the property of its heirs, and it is theirs to do with as they wish. However, a *morashah*, heritage, constitutes a "limited ownership," and its inheritors may use it only according to set stipulations.

The Torah is not a *nachalah*, but rather "*morashah Kehillas Yaakov*," the heritage of the Congregation of Yaakov. Although it has been given to us, it is not ours to do with as we wish, and we have no right to change any part of it. It is a heritage that we must guard carefully and transmit to our children in the same manner that we received it.

---
1. *Pirkei Torah, Devarim* 33:4.

With a grandchild

The only other occasion that the Torah uses the term morashah is in Shemos 6:8, where Hashem speaks of Eretz Yisrael, saying, "Ve'heiveisi eschem el ha'aretz...ve'nasati osah lachem morashah, Ani Hashem — I shall bring you to the land...and I shall give it to you as a heritage, I am Hashem." Here, Eretz Yisrael is also not termed a nachalah, but a morashah, for we have been granted Eretz Yisrael only to use in accordance with Torah and to pass it on intact to future generations to do likewise.

Indeed, we bear great responsibility, for only if we preserve the purity of these gifts will we be able to pass them on to our children in a manner that guarantees our nation's continuity.

The education that the Gifter children received in their home exemplified Rav Gifter's outlook on passing on the Jewish tradition to the next generation. Although growing up in the home of a Torah giant brings with it some level of expectation, it also offers incredible life lessons.

Although he never asked it of them, Rav Gifter's children would always stand when he or his rebbetzin came into a room. Their father and their mother were royalty to them.[2] One of Rav Gifter's grandchildren tells that he would never walk out of his grandfather's presence

---

2. Rebbetzin Shlomis Eisenberg.

Rav Gifter and Rebbetzin Gifter with with Rav Gifter's parents, Mr. and Mrs. Israel Gifter

with his back toward Rav Gifter, so as not to show his grandfather any disrespect.

The children and grandchildren learned this kind of respect for our sages from Rav Gifter himself. He held other Torah giants in such esteem that he once remarked that he should really fly to Eretz Yisrael and visit Rav Shach once a month, as that is proper *kvod haTorah*.

When others stood up for him, though, he would show obvious discomfort, motioning that they should immediately sit. Nonetheless, the honor shown to him was endless.

IN THE GIFTER HOME, EVEN WEEKDAY MEALS WERE A LEARNING occasion. Rav Gifter would take the opportunity of sitting around the

Always a Learning Occasion

table with his family to amaze the children with facts about Hashem's wonders — about things as simple as a banana. At other times, he would explain to them what was happening in current events.

RAV GIFTER FREQUENTLY WROTE ARTICLES ABOUT EDUCATING children through example. In a powerful essay written for The Jewish Parent magazine, he writes:

Shabbos

Shabbos is not merely a day of rest. If it were so, the pagan nations who considered the Jew lazy for his Shabbos observance —

Chapter 28: You Shall Teach Them Thoroughly to Your Children ☐ 343

Never wasting a moment

Purim in Telz-Stone

even an intellectual like Seneca taunted the Jew for his Shabbos — would have been right. The menuchah of Shabbos is not rest from work; rather it is to rest for contemplation of the Divine in life — the moment given to man to perceive the neshamah yeseirah — the additional soul of life.

The Torah Jew views with pity his brothers who have lost the Shabbos from their lives. For them, time is a mere monotone, an instrument in their world of material things and affairs. The Torah has taken portions of the Shabbos moment and strewn them into the life of the Jew in the various Yamim Tovim throughout the year, each Yom Tov another opportunity to sanctify time, to save it from being crushed under material things.

Here in this country, it has become customary to say, "Time is money," but the Chofetz Chaim, of sainted memory, used to say, "Money is time." The difference in concept is the difference between day and night, between light and darkness, between spiritual and material, between Shabbos and the Sheishes Yemei HaMaaseh — the Six Days of Creation.

No doubt drawing on his own experiences as a father, Rav Gifter continued:

Parents should take advantage of every facet provided by Shabbos for elevation and inspiration. It should not be allowed to become a day of physical rest from the fatigue of the entire week. The Shabbos meals are part of the Shabbos observance. One of our Tanaaim once explained to a Roman official that the Shabbos delicacies derived their taste from the Shabbos spirit of the Jew. The Shabbos zemiros are another opportunity for inspiration.

Additionally, he stressed that we want to demonstrate to our children just how special Shabbos is, that it is a taste of the World to Come (*me'ein Olam HaBa*).

The Gifter family's Shabbos meals were especially beautiful. With singing and enjoyable conversation, there was a sense of serenity. On Shabbos, the children looked forward to spending time with their parents, not to being tested on the weekly Torah portion. The family loved to hear Rav Gifter sing *zemiros*. Later in life, when his grandson, Ezzy Feuer, lived with him, the two would engage in a little contest, seeing who could hold the last note of the song *Menuchah VeSimchah* the longest.

With his *mechutan* Rav Yisroel Kaplinsky

Yom Tov

THE FOLLOWING EXCERPTS FROM A POWERFUL ESSAY ILLUSTRATE what is important to emphasize to our children at each juncture of Jewish holiday life. Although this essay was written in 1954, its lessons are timeless, its message eternal.

The spring season is heralded into Jewish life with the holiday of Pesach. At this season of the new year, when nature begins to burst forth with new life, the Jew celebrates the birth of Israel as a nation. The soil of humanity, barren and arid of the Divine Word of G-d, became enriched and fructified with a new people, whose very raison d'etre was the permeation of mankind with Divinity — a "mamleches Kohanim ve'goi kadosh — a kingdom of Priests and holy people"[Shemos 19:6].

It is advisable that there be a discussion of the aspects of the Yom Tov between the parent and child prior to the Yom Tov. This not only enhances for the child the importance of the knowledge gained in school, but it serves also to deepen the child's appreciation of the Yom Tov.

Rav Gifter used *bedikas chometz* as an example of "finding G-d in our most mundane affairs." He viewed spring cleaning for the Jew as an act of mitzvah, culminating in the *bedikas chametz* on the evening preceding Pesach.

Kissing a child who is donning *tefilin* for the first time

And here we have a wonderful opportunity for the mother to train and educate her daughter in preparing for the Yom Tov.

In speaking about the Seder itself, Rav Gifter commented:

The Seder service, if properly performed, is beyond doubt one of the most beautiful and inspiring acts of mitzvah in all of Jewish life....[A properly run Seder] infuses pride into the child — pride with being a son of this Chosen People.

Participation in the Seder service with all of its beauty and glory is an experience that leaves an everlasting impression upon the mind and heart of the Jew. There is no theatrical fanfare, but the results achieved are greater than that of any pageantry.

Understanding the importance of focusing on the children at the Sedarim, Rav Gifter did not spend a lot of time speaking above their heads in learning; he kept it simple and straightforward.

Rav Gifter sat at the head of the table like a king, with his family and many guests around him. The Seder epitomized true royalty and made an everlasting impression on his children.

In addressing the importance of counting the Omer, a mitzvah that begins on the second night of Pesach, and how it relates to our children, Rav Gifter writes that this mitzvah is, "Israel's appreciation of the fact that true freedom is not that of the body but rather of the spirit."

Receiving the Torah is of greater significance than freedom from bondage. This mitzvah is an integral part of zman cheiruseinu — the time of our freedom. The parent should see to it that the child be careful in the observance of the mitzvah. He should be impressed with the deep lesson of the mitzvah. A discussion of this lesson at the second Seder would be most proper.

He also chose to utilize the days of *Sefirah* as a time to impart "the great lesson that the loss of the great Torah scholars is a calamity of national magnitude." This article was written in 1954, and thus contains some of his reflections from the events that had transpired in that year:

Since during the past year we have had that great misfortune of losing two giants of the spirit, the saints and sages, the Chazon Ish [Rav Avraham Yeshayah Karelitz] and Rav Isser Zalman Meltzer, it would be fitting for the Jewish parent to impress the child with the national tragedy suffered in their loss. It is well for Jewish children to know that we possessed such great

The Gifters visiting Rav Chaim Shmulevitz in Eretz Yisrael

Visiting Rav Moshe Feinstein at Camp Yeshiva of Staten Island

With Rav Aaron Schechter. Reb Pinchas Yurowitz is in the background

(R-l) Rav Shmuel Brudny, Rav Shneur Kotler, Rav Gifter, Rav Boruch Sorotzkin, Rav Nochum Velvel Dessler, Reb Leibish Rapaport at the wedding of Rav Dessler's daughter to Dovid Simcha Rapaport

men. The story of their lives should be told to the child, and he will appreciate something of the great loss which Israel has suffered in their passing.

Regarding staying up all night on Shavuos, Rav Gifter advises parents to give their sons the opportunity of the thrill of this experience:

Young children cannot stay up for the entire night, but they should be taken to the beis midrash after the Yom Tov meal to spend some time in Torah study. The impression left by this spiritual adventure cannot be overestimated.

But Rav Gifter warns that the night of Shavuos should not be the child's only exposure to Torah learning.

A child must see a continual appreciation by his parents for Torah study…The Jewish home is pervaded with a completely different atmosphere where Torah is studied.

Rav Gifter then offers a solution to many children having problems in school because they are disinterested in their studies.

Little do parents realize how easily this malady could be remedied if they were to set an example for their child through their personal Torah study.

In discussing The Three Weeks, Rav Gifter writes:

There can be no better means of developing a deep love and attachment to Eretz Yisrael than the proper observance of The Three Weeks. If the loss of a true Eretz Yisrael is a cause of deep national mourning, then Eretz Yisrael must be a central factor in the entire framework of Jewish living.

Rav Gifter saw in Succos the chance for:

…the Jew to burst forth with Divine elation, prepared with the spiritual nurture for the New Year…A Yom Tov replete with so many acts of mitzvos should give an opportunity for the child to enjoy its benefits. If possible, the child should have his own lulav and esrog. We can well imagine the sense of pride in the mitzvah this would give him. Have him participate in the Simchas Beis HaSho'eivah. Let him sing and make merry, knowing this is mitzvah, Divine service. Have him study Torah in the succah. What other opportunity is there to actually "breathe" and "inhale" mitzvah into the Jewish soul!

On Simchas Torah, all the elements of joy become united in the one source of all Jewish living, in Torah itself. But what is Torah without Jewish children, our future scholars — gedolei Yisrael? And so, for ages, children have been the yachsanim [important participants] of Simchas Torah. So much so that one of the aliyos has been designated for them, the Kol HaNe'arim.

Rav Gifter taught about the lessons of Chanukah, as well:

The lesson of Chanukah has served to give it the aura of Yom Tov. The meaning of faith, the Al-mighty's guardianship of Israel, is driven home in the story of Chanukah. Israel's feeling that salvation is not man made is conveyed in the Hallel and hoda'ah …"

Rav Gifter encouraged teaching children about the heroism of the Chashmonaim:

They should be impressed with the fact that G-d's holy Priests, the Kohanim, and their religious followers — who died for the Shabbos — had the courage to bear arms and rise in battle against the Greeks. They should become impressed with the fact that the religious Jew, the Torah Jew, is perfectly capable of coping with Israel's national and international problems.

One of the greatest necessities in Jewish education today is the creation of the realization that Torah is all-embracing. Our children must become infused with the feeling that being religious Jews does not place limitations upon them, but rather opens for them the broadest vista upon life and all its problems. The story of Chanukah, if learned through its true perspective, can help greatly in this direction…

At the engagement of Chasya Gifter to Rav Yaakov Reisman. (L-r:) Rabbi and Rebbetzin Gifter, Chasya Gifter, Rav Yaakov Reisman, Mr. and Mrs. Reisman

And finally, Purim.

Rav Gifter discusses the four main components of the Yom Tov of Purim.

The first is pirsumei nisa — a public proclamation of the miracle of Purim — represented in the reading of the megillah be'tzibbur — publicly. The gragger is not a mere noisemaker, and has no similarity to the secular tumult of New Year's Eve...The tumult in the synagogue upon the mention of Haman's name is a reaction against evil and its perpetrators. Here is an opportunity for the Jewish child to be trained into Yiddishkeit in a manner very close to his own heart....

The second is mishteh ve'simchah — the Purim feast. The Purim seudah has always been an occasion for the Purim rhymes and Purim Torah — examples of true Jewish wit and humor, stemming from Torah and the deep wells of Jewish faith. The Purim seudah has many times been the setting of the Purim shpiel where the Jew had occasion to give outlet to his talents for acting in a parody of the galus and his oppressors. The levity of Purim never became a raucous free-for-all. It was always tempered with the knowledge that the levity was a form of mitzvah and as such, part of the Jew's service to G-d. Only the Jew whose simchah is a mitzvah is capable of such forms of unrestrained restraint....this teaches us that even levity can be channeled to the service of G-d.

This author can vividly recall the beautiful spirit of Purim in the home of Rav Gifter. The apartment was packed with *talmidim* and other rebbeim. Some guests sang rhymes (*grammen*); others were beseeching the rosh hayeshivah for blessings. When the feast was over,

Chapter 28: You Shall Teach Them Thoroughly to Your Children □ 351 the entire yeshivah would dance around Rav Gifter, like soldiers surrounding their general.

The third element of Purim is mishloach manos — the sending of food portions. Here again, we are given the opportunity to give the sanctity of a mitzvah to an act quite common in life. The sending of gifts on Purim, therefore, must be raised to the plane and level of sanctity. And when performed as the mitzvah requires, it strikes deep roots in the soil of the Jew. Re'us — bonds of friendship — when bound together with the ties of mitzvos, are more lasting and durable.

With Rav Mottel Katz on Purim

In a very practical piece of advice, Rav Gifter adds that children should be encouraged to perform this mitzvah among their own circle of friends.

In the life of the child, bonds of friendship are one of the great factors in his healthy spiritual development. In mishloach manos, we have a mitzvah which tends to nurture this great factor in the molding of a happy and healthy personality.

And finally, there is the mitzvah of *matanos la'evyonim* — gifts to the poor.

In realizing our common destiny as a people, we begin to feel our responsibility toward those of our brothers who are in need of our aid and our help. We begin to feel that our sphere of interest in others embraces more than our family circle and friends.

An interesting feature of the mitzvah is the need of giving at least two gifts to two evyonim, poor people. The mitzvah thus becomes indicative of the donor's deeper interest in his brother, not merely the mechanical fulfillment of our obligation.

We cannot exaggerate the importance of training the child in this great mitzvah. In developing his personality as a Jew, this mitzvah is of prime importance.

The great lesson that Right conquers Might is taught in the festival of Purim.

These profound thoughts not only gave great guidance to generations of parents in the past, but continue to give encouragement and direction to the parents of the future.

Rav Gifter was a master teacher — in and out of his home.

Section 8
Yamim Noraim

Chapter 29
Preparing for the Days of Awe (Elul)

ALL AROUND THE WORLD, THERE IS A PALPABLE SENSAtion in the Jewish community as soon as Elul begins; there is a feeling of tension, of solemnity, of introspection. This is especially noticeable in a yeshivah environment.

Rav Gifter experienced this awareness when he learned in Telz in Europe. As he explained, even the small children seemed to sense the difference in the atmosphere at the start of Elul.

In the Telzer Yeshivah in Cleveland, too, the transformation came over Rav Gifter slowly, as the month of Elul grew closer. His cries of "Elul!" still ring in the ears of every Telzer *talmid*.

He instilled this feeling into his students. Beginning with Yom Kippur Kattan (a special prayer service conducted on the day before Rosh Chodesh) immediately preceding Elul, there was anticipation in the air. Rav Gifter would don his *tallis* and *tefillin* for the Yom Kippur

A poem written by Rav Gifter in Elul

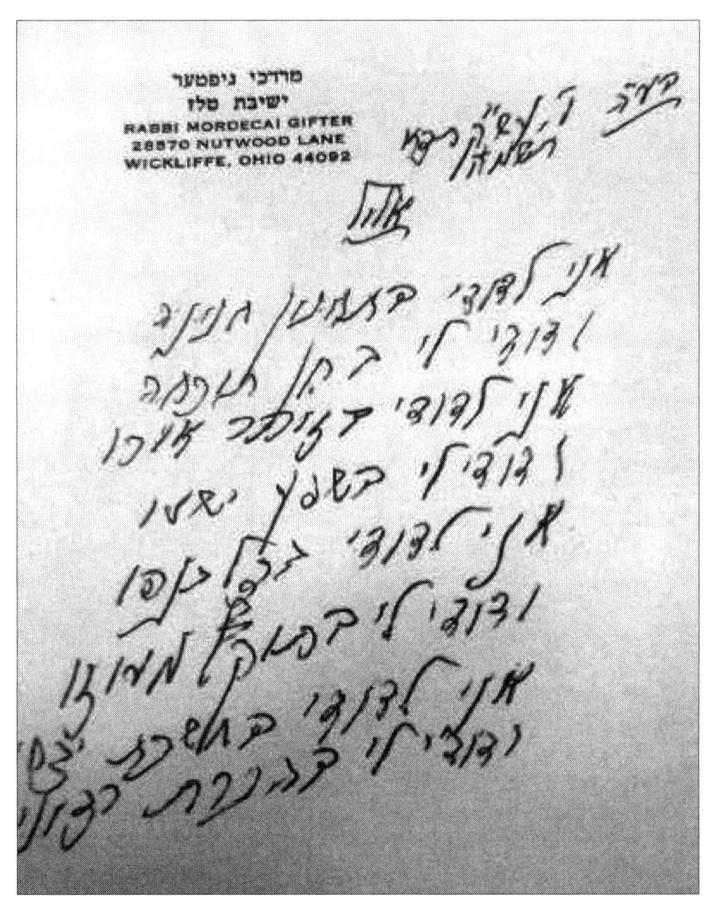

Kattan service. And for the next 40 days, until Yom Kippur was over, the mood in the yeshivah was different.

As is the custom in Telz, every *Shacharis* would conclude with the chapter of *Tehillim* (27) of *LeDavid Hashem Ori VeYishi*. Rav Gifter's inimitable cry of *"LeDavid!"* would be the crowning conclusion to every prayer. The *bachurim* in the yeshivah knew: Elul had arrived.

And the spiritual journey of Elul had begun.

> I can vividly recall my high-school years in the Telzer Yeshivah. Each Elul, we were privileged to hear a special *shmuess* from our rosh hayeshivah, Rav Gifter. It was exclusively for the younger boys, although often some of the older boys would sneak in and listen.
>
> The tone was quite serious. In Telz, everything seemed serious during the month of Elul, most certainly for a young, very impres-

sionable boy. The rosh hayeshivah would usually speak to us on our level, though, recalling his own boyhood in Portsmouth, Virginia, and describing how he became acclimated to the culture of self-sacrifice for learning. But what I remember most from those *shmuessen* is Rav Gifter's battle cry for the month of Elul.

"I am an old man and can no longer do it on my own." We would look around in wonderment and sometimes smile and smirk. After all, he was certainly toying with us. He did not, could not, mean that he was unable to manage on his own. And then he would cry out in a way that only he could, "Carry me on your shoulders!"

Serious minded in Elul

But it was he who carried us. He lifted us to heights we never thought imaginable. He inspired us to dig deeper within ourselves and find the spark that would ignite our souls. This author last experienced Elul in Telz nearly 25 years ago, and Elul has never been the same.

Every evening during *mussar seder*, Rav Gifter would get up in front of the yeshivah and learn *mussar*. Using the classical *mussar* work, *Shaarei Teshuvah*, authored by Rabbeinu Yonah, Rav Gifter's voice thundered through the *beis midrash*. His tone sent shivers up the spine.

ONE *TALMID* VIVIDLY RECALLED THE POWER RAV GIFTER HAD TO penetrate *neshamos*, to awaken a serious attitude toward the Days of Judgment. One of his famous quotes was from *Shabbos* (153). The Gemara quotes the famous words of Rabbi Eliezer: *"Ve'shuv yom echad lifnei misascha* — Repent one day before your death" (*Avos* 2:15).

Always in a State of Teshuvah

Rabbi Eliezer's students asked him, "Does a person know on which day he will die? Certainly not. How can he then fulfill his maximum repentance before death?"

Rabbi Eliezer responded, *"Yashuv hayom shema yamus le'machar* — Let a person repent today for he may die tomorrow. In this way, he will find himself living all his days in a state of *teshuvah*."

The rosh hayeshivah lived with the mantra of *"yashuv hayom shema yamus le'machar."* As he explained, one must set and accomplish goals and reach for heights, for who knows what the next day will bring?

He would tell his students about the famous philanthropist, Reb Meir Amshel Rothschild, who had a casket made for himself well before his death. He would lie down in it every night to remind himself of the day of death.

RAV GIFTER WROTE THE FOLLOWING IN THE SEASONAL ALMANAC of Dos Yiddishe Vort:

The Jewish Heart

The Yamim Noraim season is designated for personal elevation. The preparation days of Elul, the thoughts of repentance, and the soul-searching of repentance days demand a tenderness in the human heart so that hearts of stone can turn to hearts of flesh.

When Rabbi Yitzchak Dinovitzer was the regional director of the Atlantic Seaboard chapter of NCSY, he needed a Torah thought for Elul, one that would reach young people who had not yet tasted the beauty of Torah. A thought from Rav Gifter hit the mark:

It is important to understand the definition of a Jewish heart. King David says, "Lecha amar libi bakshu Fanai — In Your behalf, my heart has

Inspiring the younger generation during a stay in Camp Agudah

said, 'Seek My Presence'"(Psalms 27:8). At first glance, the verse seems to say that the heart is speaking, not G-d. If so, the heart should say, "bakshu Fanav — seek His [G-d's]Presence," meaning that the heart is appealing to us to find ways to better know G-d. The Jewish heart is but an instrument upon which a G-dly melody is played, which calls and summons Man to an awareness of G-d. Only this is a Jewish heart. How aptly our Sages expound upon the verse, "Ani yesheinah ve'libi eir — I am asleep but my heart is awake" (Shir HaShirim 5:2). My heart, this is the Holy One, Blessed is He. "The Heart" of the Jewish people is G-d.

Rabbi Dinovitzer came across this magnificent thought more than 20 years ago and has used it repeatedly, urging thousands of NCSY youth, mostly children who attend public schools, to understand that the Al-mighty is indeed inside of us, whispering, pleading and beckoning us all, "*Bakshu Fanai* — Seek My Presence."

Contemplating Tragedy

EVERY YEAR, RAV GIFTER WOULD GO TO CLEVELAND HEIGHTS TO address the entire community in the Young Israel of Cleveland. One year in the early 1980's, the community endured a number of tragedies; a number of young people had died. The community leaders asked Rav Gifter if he could give his address earlier than usual, prior to

Selichos, instead of waiting until right before Rosh Hashanah. It was an unforgettable lecture. Although we present an excerpt of that address, much of the emotion and impact was the product of Rav Gifter's commanding and thunderous voice, and that is beyond our ability to convey.

The Ramban, in his introduction to Iyov, asks a question: Why do we cry at a moment of death? Why do we shed tears? This is the natural state of things. Men are born. They live. They die. What is there to cry about?

The holy Ramban says that this is not the natural state of things. It's wrong! Men were made to live forever and ever, in the joy and the Countenance of G-d in Gan Eden. Death signifies that things are not working according to the natural course of Creation. It is something unnatural and not ordinary. This is why we are moved to tears. Did we ever give thought of this approach to crying?

The Ramban was also bothered by the natural course of things. Naturally, we should be in Gan Eden, enjoying the proximity, the friendship, the closeness, and the love of Hashem Yisbarach. But why do we seem so far removed? Because sin brought death into this world. This is what brings men to tears.

In one three-minute segment of his talk, Rav Gifter encapsulated the collective cause of the tragedies and the importance of properly utilizing the days of *Selichos* and Rosh Hashanah, which were imminent. Suddenly, everything seemed much clearer.

AS RAV GIFTER EXPRESSED SO ELOQUENTLY:

The Greatness of the Al-Mighty

Man's very essence is directed solely to the goal of recognizing the Creator and consequentially, not only his soul is bound together with the Master of the Universe, but even his body and his entire existence are rooted in the great purpose for which he is intended.

Rav Gifter did not imbue this time period in a negative way, with feelings of dread and fear, but rather with a sense of wonderment and awe. He tried to help us comprehend the greatness of the Al-mighty, and our own smallness in comparison.

On the one hand, the Yamim Noraim are meant to bring us closer to G-d. And yet, the closer we are, the more we realize how very little we understand of his ways. Rav Gifter once wrote, "If man finds his Creator, he has found everything." True. Through *teshuvah,* we return to the Al-mighty and we try to better understand the manner in which we relate to Him, but in terms of understanding Him and how He works, we are so far.

And so, Rav Gifter continued:

But, my friends, I hope you don't mind, but one of the founders of modern science, Albert Einstein, knew the business of science quite well. I'd like to read to you something he once said, and listen carefully:

"Despite all our recent advancements, our knowledge remains rather meager."

Two illustrations:

"First, our increase in knowledge is comparable to that of a man [who is] interested in learning more about the moon[1] *[who]… climbs up on the roof of his house to catch a closer look at it."*

Need I tell you how much more we know about the moon standing on the roof of the World Trade Center in New York or standing at the door downstairs? That's about the difference.

[Einstein] gave another illustration:

"Our minimal knowledge of the universe focuses me on the moment of the completion of my formula of the general theory of relativity."

Just imagine what that moment meant to Einstein and to the world of science.

"At that moment, an ordinary housefly landed on my paper. I reflected that here I had set down all the major universal physical laws as though to say, 'Here's the key to all the secrets of the universe; there is nothing now that man doesn't know…yet I really don't know very much about the nature of that little fly.'"

Need we say any more? From the father of modern science. Yet, we persist in saying we know all and we have conquered all; we are masters of our destiny and we control our fate — that's the way we live.

As we draw closer to Hashem in the days of Elul, we realize more and more how great He is — and how small we are.

Once again, Rav Gifter, in his matchless manner, explained the concept so that his listeners could internalize it.

And all those who heard him speak and watched him prepare for the Days of Awe learned valuable lessons for life.

---

1. This speech was delivered before man landed on the moon in 1969.

Chapter 30
A Deeper Understanding of the Yamim Noraim (LeDavid Hashem)

RAV GIFTER'S INTRODUCTION TO THE DAYS OF *TESHUVAH*, published in the Jewish Parent in 1950, provides us with his overarching approach to the Yamim Noraim, and in explaining the concepts to our children:

On a Child's Level *The need for self-evaluation is the motif of the Yamim Noraim — the Days of Awe — Rosh Hashanah and Yom Kippur. Life must be governed by periods of retrospect in which man is able to examine himself in the light of past experiences and future hopes. Therein lies the secret of that great idea called teshuvah — which connotes much more than the term penitence, usually used as its English equivalent.*

From Hirhurei Teshuvah

Rav Gifter identifies the prayers of the Yamim Noraim as:

... an expression of the recognition of G-d's endless power as Master of the Universe, finding in Judgment the place for compassion and mercy, the source of which lies in Zichronos — in the collective repository of Israel's past, leading ultimately to universal recognition of the Divine Presence of Creation.

Such an intense approach is "too profound for a child's mind and for that matter even for many an adult." But, Rav Gifter encourages:

If the parent begins to feel the approach of the Yamim Noraim, if there begins to live within the parent a fear of the impending Yom HaDin, then the child will unconsciously react to the motif of this specific period in the Jewish year.

Warning against the "chazanic glamorization and commercialization of the Yamim Noraim," Rav Gifter guides parents to realize that it is their responsibility to find and choose a proper shul, so that the child should observe pious *tefillah*, not merely musical incantation.

Although there was a sense of seriousness with the onset of Elul and the Yamim Noraim, Rav Gifter warned that Yamim Noraim are also Yamim Tovim, and therefore, they are:

...not days of backward, despairing spirit. They are days of a renewed spiritual power and struggle...It is a Yom Tov tempered with solemnity but

Chapter 30: A Deeper Understanding of the Yamim Noraim ☐ 365 *it is by no means a day of sorrow and sadness. It is the concept of "Ve'gilu biradah — Be joyous in trembling" (Tehillim 2:11).*

The feeling of personal unworthiness, which is such an integral part of the Yamim Noraim, is a very important factor in controlling the natural instincts of the personal ego, which many times hampers the healthy spiritual development of the child. The Yamim Noraim teach us that Man is greatest when he is on his knees.

IN CAPTURING WHAT MAN'S TRUE REQUESTS ARE, RAV GIFTER writes:

True Desires

He wants a clear understanding, because he cannot gain the light amid confusion. He wants to be cleansed of the sins that impede understanding. He wants health and prosperity only so that he can not be deterred from this recognition. He wants to be freed from the huge impediment of exile, which is the very essence of concealment of G-d's countenance and of much more. An appreciation of G-d's light gives man a sense of what interferes with his recognition of it.

His prayers for personal needs are directed not at the fulfillment of desires related to his animal nature, but to fulfill the higher need, the drive to unite with his Creator.

When a person succeeds in deciphering his heart's primary desire, when he sees within himself the deep desire that encompasses his entire weltanschauung, then he perceives the entire human tragedy: " ki avi ve'imi azavuni — for my father and mother have forsaken me," forlorn and lonely is he in the enormous universe; "va'Hashem yaasfeini — but Hashem will gather me in." Only the light of faith can uplift and strengthen a person.

BUT MAN CANNOT REMAIN WALLOWING IN THE MUCK OF SIN. First, we must elevate ourselves from the darkness. With this thought,

My Light and My Salvation

Rav Gifter would again expound on the paragraph of *LeDavid Hashem Ori VeYishi*. "*Ori*" (my light) refers to Rosh Hashanah. "*Yishi*" (my salvation) refers to Yom Kippur:

When a person considers life earnestly and sees how low his defects have brought him, he is faced with the enormous problem. How does one become better; how does one become different?

One who stands in the dark sees only darkness. The person must raise himself from the dark depths to the brilliant light of G-d's countenance, and then — and only then — can he consider the content of his life. And

then, when he raises himself up to the light, he realizes that "Yesodo me'afar ve'sofo le'afar — A man's origin is from dust and his destiny is back to dust"; he is small and insignificant. And what is the content of this lowly human, who, dwelling in darkness, thinks he has created greatness? He is likened to a broken shard, but even a shard is something tangible. Man looks more deeply, further and further into himself in the perspective of the light of the countenance of G-d and he realizes he is but a dissipating cloud, a blowing wind. More and more, he understands that he is a fleeting dream.

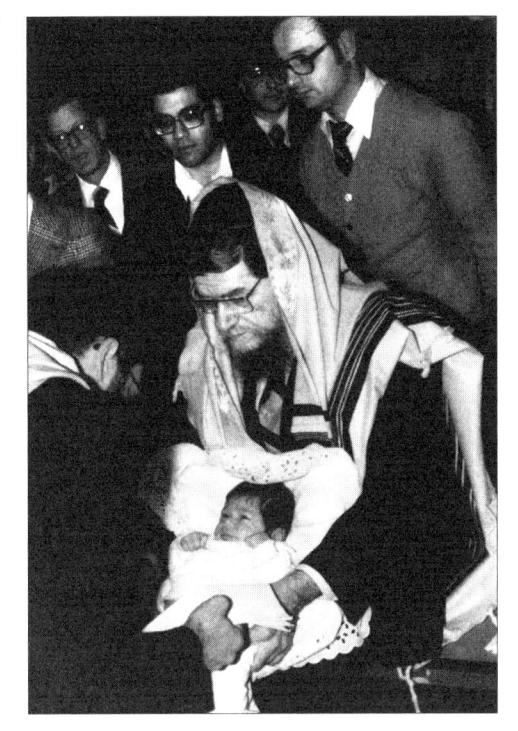

Serving as *sandek* at a *bris*

When man examines his existence in the light of his recognition of G-d, his existence becomes obvious, as a non-existence.

Love of G-d is human exaltation and a terrible thirst for G-d's closeness. To stand in His light is the recognition of the infinity of His G-dliness. And fear of G-d is the recognition of the very same light by realizing that the lowliness and fallenness of the people is the source of all human suffering and tragedy.

In urging man to see his goodness through the light of Rosh Hashanah, Rav Gifter continues:

The light to which Man is privileged on Rosh Hashanah is the light of wisdom, the light of love, of great thirst and yearning for Hashem, Blessed be He. All year long, this is an enormously difficult task. But the Al-mighty did Man the kindness of granting him the period of the Days of Awe, with its flow of Heavenly inspiration. He lowers Himself to humanity so that He can uplift humanity, to cleanse and purify it.

"Ve'yishi, zeh Yom HaKippurim — And my salvation, this is Yom Kippur." When the Jew reaches the ultimate recognition of the illumination offered by G-d's truth — at the climax of the Ten Days of Repentance *that He has designated just for this possibility — and when he has thereby completely perceived and sensed Man's insignificance, and without hesitation set out his path toward the future, at that very moment has Man been privileged to receive G-d's salvation. He has been redeemed from his degradation, from the darkness of human lowliness. Then he has already been vindicated in judgment, and is ready to live through the forthcoming festival of soulful joy, zman simchaseinu — the season of our joy!*

A Time of Closeness

RAV GIFTER ATTEMPTED TO SHOW US HOW LOVED AND CHERISHED we are by the Al-mighty. Thus, a former *talmid* recounted, "His *shiurei daas* in Elul based on the Rambam were awe inspiring. He carried us into the world of *teshuvah* and *kirvas Elokim* [closeness to G-d] as he would quote the Rambam in the seventh *perek*: '*Teshuvah* makes us loved, cherished, close, and a friend to *HaKadosh Baruch Hu*.' He would then lead us into the *kabbalas Malchus* (acceptance of His Kingship) of Rosh Hashanah."

But the love of Hashem, and seeing ourselves in in His Infinite light, must help us to find our own glaring faults. Rav Gifter guides us through this process in a poetic and powerful essay. Rav Gifter writes in the Yamim Noraim almanac for Dos Yiddishe Vort:

It is for man to utilize the potential granted him through the strenuous effort during this period to illuminate his entire inner self and lift it out of the downfall and darkness. And, in direct proportion to how much man merits the illumination of the love of Hashem, he simultaneously merits the trembling of fear, the deep glimpse into man's puniness. And in direct proportion to how profoundly he perceives this puniness, he realizes everything that originates in this smallness is insignificant, without content but an empty dream.

From such recognition, man arrives at deep regret over his past and lifts himself to great undertakings for his future; an undertaking that is unclouded by doubt, clear and direct. Every recognition that emanates from the Light of G-dly truth is clear and without perplexity. At the moment of such an undertaking, man is in a position of such exaltation that G-d — Who alone sees all that is hidden — attests that such a person will not regress to his human foolishness. And if he does so regress, it is only because he has again drawn back from the light of G-dly truth to which he had raised himself, and has returned to the shadow of Divine concealment.

Seeing the inherent goodness in Man, he implores us to be better and to realize how foolish our ways have been. And, in truth, after his profound presentation, it is hard not to see this on our own. But that was the beauty of Rav Gifter's talks and addresses: He brought to life the sayings of our Sages with such clarity that we would wonder that we did not see it all along. How else could these words have been understood? A *shmuess* did not necessarily need many different sources. Quite often, it was merely one quote, brought to life as only Rav Gifter could.

Rav Gifter's tremendous and penetrating insight into human nature, the nature of *teshuvah*, and the nature of our relationship with Hashem provided hundreds of his *talmidim*, and others who heard him, to look at the Yamim Noraim with a completely different, and a much more profound, vision.

Chapter 31
Appreciating Hashem's Beautiful World (Malchiyos and Zichronos)

RAV GIFTER OFTEN DELIVERED A *SHMUESS* IN CLEVELAND Heights during the Ten Days of Repentance.

ONE YEAR, HE BEGAN BY REMINISCING ABOUT HIS GREAT REBBI, Rav Mottel Pogromansky. When Rav Mottel was only 28 years old, the

Through the Light of Torah

Kovno Rav, Rav Yitzchak Elchanan Spector, said that he would have been a *gadol hador* in the times of Rav Akiva Eiger and the Vilna Gaon (great sages from many generations before). Yet he began his Torah study only at the age of 16, after immersing himself in secular studies. (Rav Gifter's life followed a similar path; he had also learned Talmud for only 12 years when he was already recognized as a *gadol b'Yisrael*.)

Yet once Rav Mottel became a Torah sage, he saw everything through the light of Torah.

When Rav Mottel came to visit Rav Zalman Bloch and his rebbetzin, he would speak to the rebbetzin about culture; she had been a student at the University of Charkov. Even so, every word he said was based on a Midrash, but he delivered it in such a way that the rebbetzin compared him to the finest lecturers in the university.

After speaking with her, he would take their 5-year-old child onto his lap and tell him a children's story. He told him deep sayings of our Sages, but in his brilliance, he was able to paint his words as a children's story.

He was a rare and incredible man.

Rav Gifter then shared a thought from Rav Mottel, illustrating how we can all view everything through the light of Torah:

He once told me that if we wish to understand the beauty of this world, we should take an example from a work of art by Rembrandt — the great medieval artist, a painter among painters. If you put his work into a cellar, no one will see anything in it. It's a painting but nothing more; you have to bring it up to the light. However, even that's not sufficient. You have to know how to shed light upon the painting of Rembrandt at the proper angle, a light that will bring forth every line that he painted into it. Connoisseurs of art will understand that; others won't. Although I don't understand art, I was overwhelmed with the example he gave me.

And if people become impressed by a work of art by the great Rembrandt, how impressed should we become when we stand before the greatest work of art, the world as a whole? What is that work of art? Creation itself, the world in which we live. Who is the artist? None other than the Al-mighty Himself, Borei Kol HaOlamos, Creator of all the Worlds. He did not create only this world, that we are able to see with our human eye, but all the worlds: that which is below the sea level and that which is above the heavens; there are worlds upon worlds above the heavens.

All is beautiful, all is overwhelming. But how do we become impressed with it? How are we to see this world?

We must have a light shed upon it, so that we can see all the lines and all the strokes of the Master Painter, Hashem Yisbarach.

Where do we find that light? The light is Torah.

Study Torah and you will become overwhelmed with the light that you shall see, since that light will enable you to take note of every line, of every dot, that's been put into this world of art called Creation. Through the study of Torah, we maintain the existence of the world.

NASA, in all its trials to reach the moon and above, cannot and will not determine the essence of Creation. At best, we will have scientists telling us we've gone above the moon, and as the Russians said at the time, "We have not found any angels there." If we think that human science will conquer Creation, we are fools! We cannot conquer a Creator, so we cannot conquer His Creation. Just as we cannot understand the Al-mighty Himself, we cannot understand His handiwork. Our duty is to study His Torah, the light that sheds a perspective, that shines a light upon all of Creation.

MALCHIYOS AND ZICHRONOS SPEAK OF THE LIMITLESS MEMORY of Hashem Yisbarach. But do not make the mistake of thinking in terms of **Limitless Memory** human memory. We store things in our memory, and then we forget; but our memory store helps us remind ourselves what we put there. However, the memory of Hashem Yisbarach is an eternal memory. There is not a moment that something isn't there, right in front of Him.

And I'm reminded of something I heard from the genius, Rav Meir Simchah HaKohen, the Ohr Same'ach. He was the rav of the misnagdim in Dvinsk, while Rav Yosef Rosen, the Rogatchover Gaon, was the Chassidic

Rogatchover Gaon

Ohr Same'ach

372 ☐ RAV GIFTER

rabbi. Rav Meir Simchah once said, "The whole world says that the Rogatchover is a baki, since he has so much stored in his memory. You are making a terrible mistake. The Rogatchover is not a baki; I have bekiyus, because there is much that I forget and then I remember it. But he has not yet forgotten anything that he ever put into his brain. It's all before him, every moment; not only the Gemara he has studied, but even the works of the Rambam, including the Moreh Nevuchim, are before him in their entirety."

The Zichronos of Hashem Yisbarach are to be understood in that vein. Hashem does not put things in His memory store and forget them, and then later remind Himself. He never forgets. We must realize that all our actions are in the presence of Hashem, the Melech, the Sovereign, and that each of those actions stands before Him, at all times. He overlooks nothing, he forgets nothing: "zocher kol ha'nishkachos — He is the One Who remembers all that is forgotten by us."

This is so important to be aware of during these Days of Penitence.

We would be different individuals if we were actually conscious of the fact that He watches us every moment and knows our every thought, and He forgets nothing. But actually, we don't feel that. We ascribe human characteristics to Him.

Sincerity That Broke Hearts

AS RAV GIFTER PREPARED TO CONCLUDE HIS TALK, AND HE reminded the audience of, "*retzoneinu laasos retzoncha* — Our will is to do Your will," his voice cracked and he began to cry.

Rav Gifter did not necessarily say anything that the audience had not heard before. But the sincerity with which he spoke broke our hearts, and it broke his.

Mashiach's Welcoming Committee

FINALLY, RAV GIFTER BROUGHT HIS DISCOURSE TO A CLOSE WITH A story. During a recent visit to Eretz Yisrael, just before Tishah B'Av, Rav Gifter told Rav Shach, "I feel that Mashiach will soon be here."

Rav Shach replied, "You seem certain about it. Of course, we await his arrival every day. But what's your proof?"

Rav Gifter responded, "Can you imagine the arrival of Mashiach without a welcoming committee? It can't be! Who will head that com-

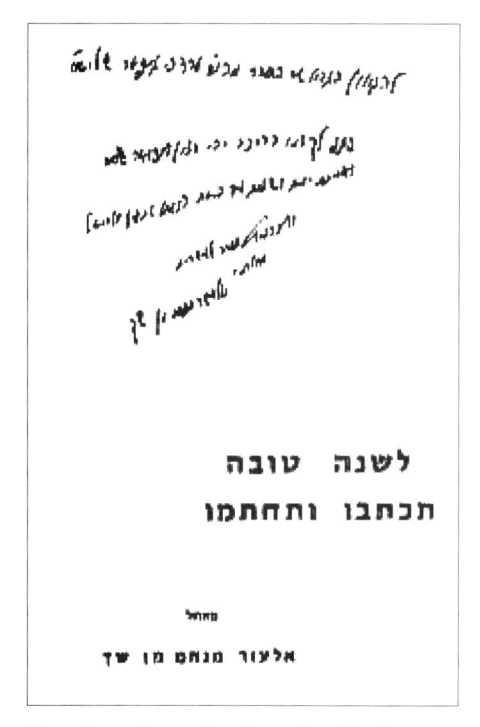

Shanah tovah greeting from Rav Shach

mittee? Who do we have left in our lowly generation — only the rosh yeshivah, Rav Shach — and you do not have too long to wait.[He was already elderly at the time.] So I am certain that he will be here soon." Rav Gifter was not sure if Rav Shach agreed with his assessment, but he seemed happy to hear that Mashiach was on his way. (And Rav Gifter felt that for that alone it was worthwhile.)

He explained that Rav Shach is not only the rabbi of all of Klal Yisrael, but the father of the whole nation, since he is concerned about Jews throughout the world. Rav Gifter ended his conversation with Rav Shach by blessing Rav Shach that he should merit to lead those who greet Mashiach.

(Rabbi Kalman Rubinstein, a close *talmid* of Rav Gifter, once delivered a similar message to Rav Shach from Rav Gifter.

But Rav Shach responded, "Tell Rav Gifter that we are waiting for *him* to lead us to greet Mashiach!")

Although we no longer have Rav Shach or Rav Gifter among us, we can still learn from all the lessons they both taught us. In that merit, we will merit to greet Mashiach.

Chapter 32
Maximizing the Potential of the Days of Awe (Shofros)

Splitting the Heavens

RAV GIFTER WAS A MASTER *BAAL TEFILLAH*; HIS VOICE shook the heavens. The entire congregation appreciated his fervor on the Yamim Noraim, as his rendition of *Nei'lah* penetrated every soul who heard it. As the sun set, Rav Gifter would thunder, "*Shaarei Shamayim, p'sach!* —The Gates of Heaven, open!" One can only imagine what type of impression that made in Heaven. It certainly shook the entire yeshivah *beis midrash*. Many would observe, "How can Hashem not open the Gates of Heaven after Rav Gifter's booming command?"

Rav Gifter was also the one who blew the shofar on Rosh Hashanah. The blasts were crystal clear, powerful, and awe inspiring. Yet the

The older bochurim in the Yeshivah at the time Rav Gifter first arrived; many were in his vaad.

L-r top row: D. Katz (Riga, Latvia), S. Oppenheimer (Seattle, Wash.), Eliyahu Galupkin (Savel, Lithuania), R. Fisher (Cincinnati, OH), H. Hollander (Brooklyn, NY), Yisroel Indich (Brooklyn, NY)

L-r middle row: R. Robinson (Buffalo, N.Y.), W. Altusky (Bronx, N.Y.), M. Epstein (Tavrig), Chaim Tzvi Katz (Canton, O.H.), Mordechai Weinberg (Brooklyn, NY), M. Fink (Taylor, Pa.)

L-r bottom row: Z. Kertzer (Kowel, Poland), Yitzchak Sheinerman (Brooklyn, NY), H. Klein (Detroit, Mich.), Herschel Baron (Tavrig), J. Rennert (Brooklyn, NY)

verses he recited beforehand were, in a sense, more impressive and more extraordinary than the sounds of the shofar itself. In fact, when he felt that he was unable to blow the shofar with the same strength as he always had and therefore stopped blowing, it was requested that he still recite the introductory verses as they inspired such an appropriate sense of awe and trepidation. Many felt that only he could set the tone. What's more, his recitation of the verses and the blessings had the power to split through the Heavens. And those who heard him could not help but feel the awe of the Day of Judgment.

One *talmid* remembers:

Who can ever forget the verses that he said before tekias shofar, as the one who blew the shofar for many years? For example, the cries he uttered when he said the verse of "Arov avdecha le'tov al yaashkuni zeidim — Be Your servant's guarantor for good, do not let the willful sinners exploit me." Or when he enunciated the verse of "Sas anochi al imrasecha — I rejoice over Your word," one could sense his euphoric but tempered feeling of simchah. His earnest request of "Tuv taam va'daas lamdeini ki ve'mitzvosecha he'emanti — Teach me good reasoning and knowledge, for I believe in Your commandments" would remain with the talmidim forever. He formed us into believers as he uttered those words, followed by the awe-inspiring berachos, including, "asher kideshanu be'mitzvosav ve'tzivanu... — Who has sanctified us with His commandments and commanded us..." in which we truly felt the sanctity and reverence of the day, and the acceptance of mitzvos ... at the time of tekias shofar.

This set the tone for the actual blowing of the shofar. The tekios had the power to bring us into the aura of Malchus, a vivid coronation of the King! Finally, the verse of "Ashrei haam yodei seruah Hashem be'or Panecha yehaleichun — Praiseworthy is the people who knows the shofar blast, O Hashem in the light of Your Countenance will they walk," which follows the blowing of the shofar, would be said with such joy and spiritual ecstasy that it lifted us all to the pinnacle of Rosh Hashanah. We felt like we were in another world.

L-r: Rav Moshe Feinstein, Rav Eliezer Silver, Rav Aron Kotler, Rav Gifter

Seated at the heads of the table: Rav Elya Meir Bloch and Rav Boruch Sorotzkin. Amongst those seated in the picture, Rav Moshe Heifan, Rav Nochum Velvel Dessler, Rav Elazar Levi and Rav Shlomo Davis

In a similar vein, a disciple recalls his prayers on Yom Kippur:

For many years, the rosh hayeshivah led the Ne'ilah prayers. It was a Ne'ilah no one would ever forget — from the first words of Kaddish until the final call of "Hashem Hu HaElokim." We felt the rosh hayeshivah carrying us over into other worlds with his unforgettable davening, overcoming all boundaries.

When he reached the words, "Ezkerah Elokim..." in the Thirteen Attributes of Mercy, which speaks about the Destruction, he would break down and cry. At the words that speak about how the gates of tears are never closed, he would cry to the extent that it made us cry.

Within moments after he blew the shofar at the end of Ne'ilah, he would say, "Leshanah haba'ah biYerushalayim [Next year in Jerusalem]," in a clear voice. Then, he would break into dance, which constituted a prayer for the rebuilding of Jerusalem, and a transformation from dread to joy.

IN ONE PARTICULARLY MOVING *SHMUESS*, RAV GIFTER REVEALED the essence and deeper meaning of *teshuvah* and the shofar:

Crying Out to Hashem

The Rambam, in the beginning of the chapter that discusses proclaiming fast days, explains the significance of this mitzvah. He says that it is a positive commandment to cry out to the Al-mighty for every tragic event that takes place in the Jewish community. And this mitzvah is one of the rows and paths to lead a person to think about and return to the Source from which he has wandered.

Repentance does not give the proper connotation of what the term *teshuvah* means in Torah Jewish life. Rather, *teshuvah* means return, because we have wandered from where we should be. One of the ways to arouse ourselves to return is this mitzvah of fasting and of crying out to Hashem when there is a time of sorrow and tragedy in Klal Yisrael. All of us recognize that these events take place because of our evil deeds, as we can see from many different verses. By crying out to Hashem Yisbarach, we can stop these tribulations from occurring.

But if we will not cry out to Hashem, but rather continue living our lives as we usually do, we will view each tragic event as a matter of happenstance — a *mikreh* — and we will say that there is nothing to cry about, nothing to worry about. We will claim that this is the way things run in the world, and sometimes we enjoy happy events, and sometimes we have tragic events.

That is usually the way we react to adversity. In the moment of the tragedy, we shed a tear, but then we wipe it away and life continues the way it was. But the Rambam says that if we react in this manner, "Harei zu derech achzariyus — This is an act of cruelty." This is an act of cruelty against oneself, since one is fighting his emotions and feelings and denying them freedom to come to the fore. This person has a heart of stone. Not because he doesn't react to the emotions of others, but because he doesn't react to his own emotions. He has essentially killed the emotion within himself.

If you will say that tragedy is a natural course of events, then Hashem Yisbarach reacts "ba'chamas keri — with the fury of casualness" [Vayikra 26:28]. The Rambam adds one word, "ba'chamas *oso* keri," through this very event that you term natural. I will let you see where the natural occurrences lead you: to tragedy after tragedy. Why? Because you haven't recognized that the calamity is speaking to you.

It says in Tehillim [90:3], "Tasheiv enosh ad daka — You reduce man to pulp." When G-d brings man to such misfortune, He is telling him something: "Va'tomer shuvu vnei adam — And You say, 'Repent, O sons of man'" [ibid.]. Through the tragedy, Hashem is telling us that something is wrong. We must try to find where we have gone astray, and return to where we should be standing.

We are all living under a general misconception. In the past few years, we have become accustomed to speak about the baal teshuvah movement. A movement of people returning, coming back. In other words, who are the ones talking about the baal teshuvah movement? Those who don't need teshuvah, because they are observant, and they do what they are supposed to be doing.

We forget that all of Jewish life is a baal teshuvah movement. When Adam HaRishon was in Gan Eden, he was on the level upon which man was ordained to be. From the moment that he sinned, all of mankind has been engaged in teshuvah — to try to come back to where Adam once stood. When we stood at the foot of the mountain of Sinai, we rose to the heights of Adam HaRishon in Gan Eden. But soon thereafter, we sank in the morass of the Golden Calf. Even now, we have yet to return. Jewish life, if lived properly, represents a baal teshuvah movement of the highest order. But we are not aware of it. We live a life of happenstance.

As mentioned, Rav Gifter gave a *vaad* that covered topics in current events. He would ask the *bachurim*, "What we can learn from this event? What message is it sending us?" For Rav Gifter, it was like he was learning a *sefer*. He saw the message clearly and taught his *talmidim* to do the same, always emphasizing that tragedies are one of the ways Hashem speaks to us.

Later in that same talk, Rav Gifter punctuated this thought:

"*Ani leDodi veDodi li* — I alone am my Beloved's and my Beloved is mine" [Shir HaShirim 6:3]. *At times, a Jew stands at a period of life when he feels closer to his Creator, and that closeness brings forth an expression of devotion: I belong to my Beloved, to Hashem Yisbarach, and, therefore, I feel He is with me. This is a Jew at this time of year. Under such circumstances, it is easier to feel what the Rambam teaches us and what misfortune means, to realize that tragedies speak to us. For during this time of year, we have an ear attuned to that language.*

And it's a language that isn't besmirched with all the niceties of things that are written in books, newspapers, and articles. The language of misfortune and tragedy is clear, and it calls forth the language of tze'akah, of crying out to Hashem Yisbarach.

The Shofar

A GREAT JEW ONCE SAID: WHAT DOES TEKIAS SHOFAR REPRESENT? It represents exactly what we are speaking about — it's a language without words — tze'akah!

Rav Gifter illustrated his point with a parable:

There was a powerful sovereign who had many lands under his domain. In one of the faraway corners in his dominion, there was a tiny country that found itself in dire need. The countrymen decided to send a delegation to the king to ask for help. However, when the delegation came before the king, they realized that they did not speak his language, nor did he speak their language. Thus, they couldn't understand each other. When the men in the delegation realized the situation, they broke down in tears. When the king saw their tears, he said, "Ich farshtei vos zei meinen — I understand what they mean."

Tze'akah is a language without words. When words fail to express what we feel, tze'akah becomes the language through which we approach Hashem Yisbarach.

This is one of the ideas behind the concept of tekias shofar: "*ois shreien tzum Ribbono Shel Olam* — crying out to the Master of the World!" How do we stand in prayer? What are our interests when we are in front of our Creator? Are we able to completely forget the day-to-day affairs that bother us as individuals — as we stand and speak to Hashem Yisbarach — or do we carry all those affairs into the U'Nesaneh Tokef?

But with tze'akah, if we are able to raise ourselves beyond words, beyond language that we create, into that cry that stems from the depths of the *human soul, then we can speak the language that Hashem Yisbarach is waiting for. Once a Jew cries out, then "Va'taal shavasam — Their outcry went up" [Shemos 2:23]. That prayer reaches to heights where no other prayer can open the doors.*

This is what we are engaged in at this period of the year.

If we take these lessons to heart, we, too, will have the power to split the heavens.

Epilogue
Our Rebbi...Forever

THE HOUR WAS LATE.

I was scheduled to meet with the Munkatcher Rebbe in Boro Park at 10 p.m. Although I had just had a speaking engagement, and still had a three-hour drive to Brooklyn to look forward to, I very much wanted to meet with the rebbe. Since he had been a close *talmid* of Rav Gifter, this was an opportunity not to be missed. However, the rebbe had an emergency, and he would not be able to see me until 11:45. The wait was worth it.

The rebbe said to me, "I'll tell you a story that shows how unique Rav Gifter was. For this alone, a *sefer* should be written about him." As he looked off into the distance, the rebbe recounted, "Although it has been nearly 50 years since I learned in Telz under my rebbi, Rav Gifter, I heard a tape of the final *shiur* that he gave, nearly 20 years ago. It was based on a Tosafos in *Yevamos* 2a. Rav Gifter read the Tosafos and quoted a Rosh. He then asked a question on the Rosh."

At this moment, the rebbe paused and explained, "When my rebbi gave a *shiur*, he never hesitated. His delivery was clear and decisive, penetrating and deep.

"But this time, something was wrong. Rav Gifter tried to tie together the loose ends, but his usual precision and mastery of the subject matter eluded him. He tried once and then again, but tragically, the clarity was lacking."

The rebbe turned to me and asked a piercing question. "What would another person have done in such a situation?" Without waiting for my answer, he continued. "He would have closed his Gemara and justifiably excused himself — but not Rav Gifter. Instead, he looked at the *bachurim* and began to cry. And in his inimitable voice, he thundered, '*Nutz ois yeder minut!* — Make use of every minute! There will come a day when the gifts that the *Ribbono Shel Olam* has given you will be taken away. And the mental capacity you always took for granted will no longer be there …. Nothing lasts forever ….'

"And then he cried once more, '*Nutz ois yeder minut* — Make use of every minute.'"

When the Munkatcher Rebbe concluded the story, he had tears in his eyes. "Do you understand? At the moment that Rav Gifter's most precious gift — the ability to think clearly — was taken away from him, what did he do? He used that moment to teach one final lesson to his *talmidim*. **That is the legacy of Rav Gifter!**"

The rebbe placed his hand in front of his face and said, "It has been nearly 50 years — and this is how I see my great rebbi; he is right here in front of me."

One man who heard this story added a powerful footnote. The Gemara in *Sanhedrin* 103a tells of the four students of Rabbi Eliezer who came to visit him and encourage him when he was sick. The first three told him that he was greater than the sun, rain, and parents, as those three exist only in This World, while he would be their rebbi in the Next World, as well. Rabbi Akiva then declared, "*Chavivin yesurin* — Suffering is dear." Rabbi Eliezer was encouraged by his comment and responded, "*Samchuni* — [Support] elevate me, so that I can hear the words of Akiva, my student."

Rav Gifter asked: Why did Rabbi Akiva's words give so much more *chizuk* to Rabbi Eliezer than the words of his other students? The other students pacified their rebbi by telling him not to worry; he would be their rebbi in the Next World. But Rabbi Akiva placated his rebbi by implying, "Rebbi, you are **still** teaching us; the manner in which you have accepted your suffering has taught us an important lesson. Even in your illness, you are still teaching."

Rav Gifter, you are still our rebbi!

Tiere rebbi, you continue to teach us. Throughout your life, your goal was to be a melamed, a rebbi. The torch you carried from Europe ignited generations of talmidim in America and elsewhere to live with — and through — the fire of Torah. And with this book, your teachings will continue to inspire many generations of talmidim — yes, even and maybe especially, American boys just like you — to dream of becoming great in Torah and yiras Shamayim, to never be satisfied, to always learn more.

Rav Gifter explained the *pasuk*, "*Vegam hanefesh lo simalei* — Yet his wants are never satisfied" (*Koheles* 6:7), to mean that our souls yearn to grow, develop, and expand in This World.

The Gemara employs the term, *nach nafshei* — his (physical) soul rested, to describe death. When one dies, the tireless journey of one's physical component is complete; that part of his *nefesh* can finally rest.

Rav Gifter's life was a relentless journey of growth in Torah, as he strove to be better and closer to his beloved Creator — to bring *nachas ruach* to the Al-mighty.

He did so until his very last breath.

And then, our precious and beloved rebbi finally rested.

Yehi zichro baruch…

Afterword

RAV GIFTER TOUCHED SO MANY LIVES WHILE HE LIVED — and even after he passed away. Recently, when this author traveled to Eretz Yisrael and visited the grave of Rav Gifter, I was given the name of a taxi driver, Momi (a nickname for Shlomo), who would take me to Har Hazeisim. I was told that since Har Hazeisim is a dangerous area, and Momi carries a gun, it would be wise to hire him as my driver.

I was anxious to visit the grave. I had spent the last six months hearing and writing about Rav Gifter, and I very much wanted to pray by his grave. Therefore, I arranged with Momi to pick me up on the first morning of my visit. Momi is a confident Israeli driver who is around my age. I assumed he would wait in the car while I prayed, and then we would be on our way. Shockingly, though, as I began to pray, I saw that Momi was sprawled over the grave. And he was crying. I watched in amazement, wondering what could have possibly connected Momi to Rav Gifter.

After I finished praying, I walked back to the taxi with a red-eyed Momi. As if he were reading my mind, he blurted out, *"Rav Gifter hayah mamash navi*! [Rav Gifter was really a prophet!]" Then, in a broken English, Momi began to share his incredible story. "A short while after Rav Gifter passed away, my wife was expecting a baby. She did not feel well and went to the doctor to see if everything was all right.

"It wasn't.

"After taking the necessary tests, the doctor told my wife that serious complications had arisen and, in all probability, even if the baby lived, she would have little chance at a normal life; the medical issues would simply be too complex to overcome.

"Devastated, my wife called to tell me the news. We were both still crying when the phone rang a little later. It was a customer of mine, Rav Avrohom Chaim Feuer. As soon as I answered the phone, he heard the pain in my voice. As he requested that I pick him up from the airport, he reassured me that we would go straight to his father-in-law's grave. And we would pray there. He then promised me that everything would be all right.

"With all of that on my mind, I went to pick up Rav Feuer and then drive straight to Rav Gifter's grave to pray.

"The next day, my baby daughter was born. Although the hospital had assumed that there would be major complications, miraculously, she was healthy."

Sephardim name their children in honor of those who are living. Thus, as a sign of his appreciation, Momi named his daughter Shoshana, in honor of Rav Gifter's rebbetzin.

When Momi finished his story, he looked at me and repeated, "I'm telling you. *Rav Gifter hayah mamash navi.*"

Who could argue?

Appendix
Family Tree

RABBI ELIEZER GORDON זצ״ל

Chasya ע״ה & Rabbi Yosef Yehudah Leib Bloch זצ״ל

- Rabbi Shmuel Zalman Bloch זצ״ל & Luba Rochel Denis ע״ה (see following pages)
- Rabbi Avraham Yitzchak Bloch זצ״ל & Rassia Denis ע״ה (see following pages)
- Rabbi Eliyohu Meir Bloch זצ״ל & Rivkah Kaplan ע״ה
- Rabbi Eliyohu Meir Bloch זצ״ל & Nechama ע״ה
- Miriam Bloch ע״ה & Rabbi Avner Oklanski זצ״ל
- Perel Leah Bloch ע״ה & Rabbi Chaim Mordechai Katz זצ״ל
- Shoshana Bloch ע״ה & Rabbi Avrohom Vesler זצ״ל

Henna Gordon ע״ה & Rabbi Aizik Hershovitz זצ״ל

- Liba Hershovitz ע״ה & Rabbi Yaakov Pines זצ״ל
- Rabbi Aryeh Leib Hershovitz זצ״ל
- Rabbi Avrohom Shmuel Hershovitz הי״ד
- Rabbi Nachman Hershovitz זצ״ל
- Rabbi Leiber Hershovitz הי״ד

Sarah Miriam Gordon ע״ה & Rabbi Zalman Sorotzkin זצ״ל

- Rabbi Elchonon Sorotzkin זצ״ל & First Wife
- Rabbi Elchonon Sorotzkin זצ״ל & Tzila ע״ה
- Rabbi Eliezer Sorotzkin זצ״ל & Chasya Bloch ע״ה
- Rabbi Eliezer Sorotzkin זצ״ל & Tzipporah
- Tamar Sorotzkin ע״ה & R' Zeidman ע״ה
- Rabbi Boruch Sorotzkin זצ״ל & Rochel Bloch
- Rabbi Bentzion Sorotzkin זצ״ל & Chana ע״ה
- Rabbi Bentzion Sorotzkin זצ״ל & Bella Friedman-Brodt
- Rabbi Yisroel Sorotzkin זצ״ל & Chasidah ע״ה

Rabbi Shmuel Gordon הי״ד

R' Mordechai Gordon הי״ד

Esther Gordon ע״ה & Yaakov Shapiro הי״ד

- Eliezer Shapiro ע״ה
- Tamar Shapiro ע״ה

RABBI SHMUEL ZALMAN BLOCH ז״ל & LUBA ROCHEL DENIS ד״ה

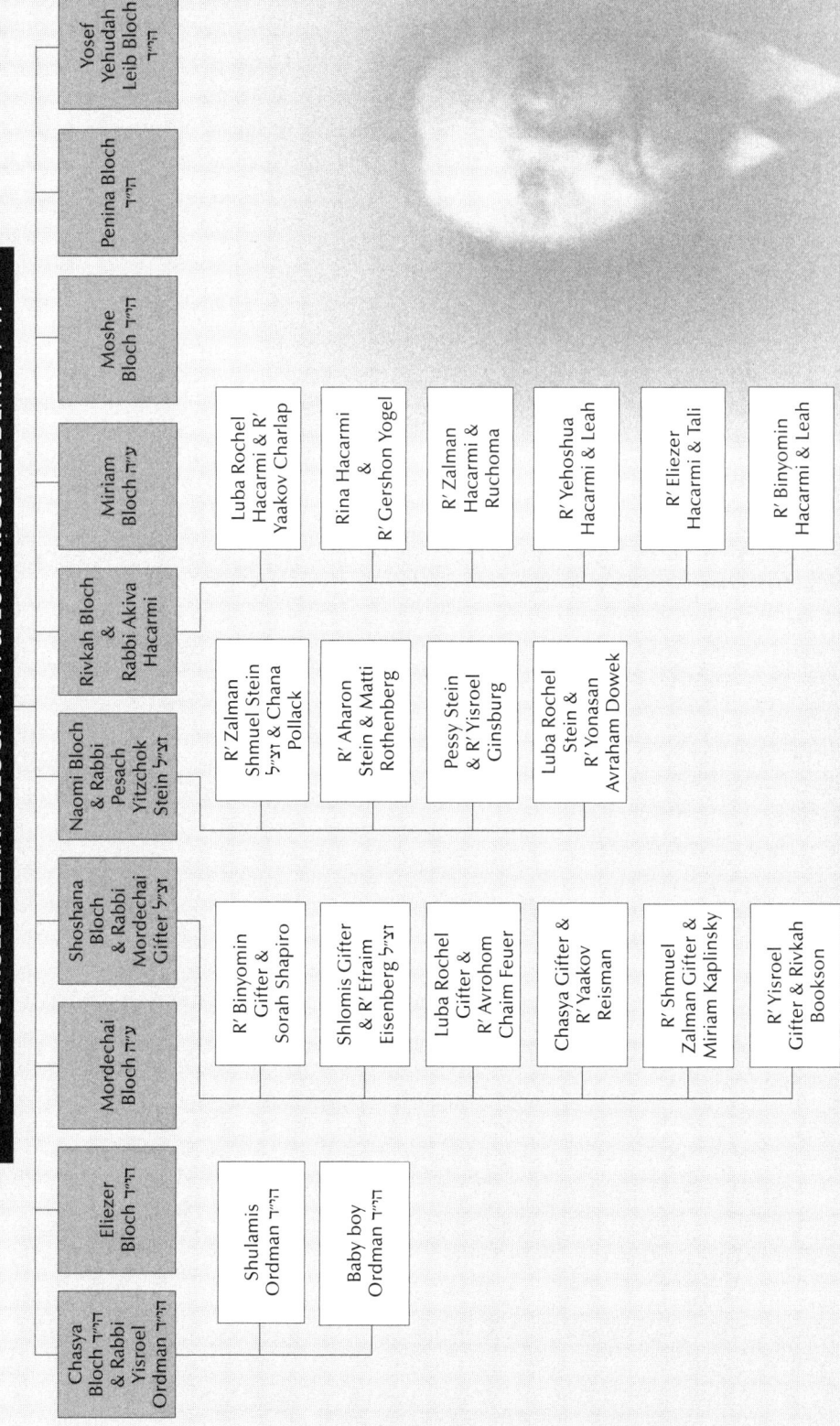

- Chasya Bloch ד״ה & Rabbi Yisroel Ordman ד״ה
  - Shulamis Ordman ד״ה
  - Baby boy Ordman ד״ה
- Eliezer Bloch ד״ה
- Mordechai Bloch ע״ה
- Shoshana Bloch & Rabbi Mordechai Gifter ז״ל
  - R' Binyomin Gifter & Sorah Shapiro
  - Shlomis Gifter & R' Efraim Eisenberg ז״ל
  - Luba Rochel Gifter & R' Avrohom Chaim Feuer
  - Chasya Gifter & R' Yaakov Reisman
  - R' Shmuel Zalman Gifter & Miriam Kaplinsky
  - R' Yisroel Gifter & Rivkah Bookson
- Naomi Bloch & Rabbi Pesach Yitzchok Stein ז״ל
  - R' Zalman Shmuel Stein ז״ל & Chana Pollack
  - R' Aharon Stein & Matti Rothenberg
  - Pessy Stein & R' Yisroel Ginsburg
  - Luba Rochel Stein & R' Yonasan Avraham Dowek
- Rivkah Bloch & Rabbi Akiva Hacarmi
  - Luba Rochel Hacarmi & R' Yaakov Charlap
  - Rina Hacarmi & R' Gershon Yogel
  - R' Zalman Hacarmi & Ruchoma
  - R' Yehoshua Hacarmi & Leah
  - R' Eliezer Hacarmi & Tali
  - R' Binyomin Hacarmi & Leah
- Miriam Bloch ת״ח
- Moshe Bloch ד״ה
- Penina Bloch ד״ה
- Yosef Yehudah Leib Bloch ד״ה

RABBI AVRAHAM YITZCHAK BLOCH ז"הי & RASSIA DENIS ה"יד

Rochel Bloch & Rabbi Boruch Sorotzkin זצ"ל

- R' Binyomin Sorotzkin & Feigie
- R' Yitzchok Sorotzkin & Kreindy Grubner
- Rassia Leah Sorotzkin ה"ע & R' Yaakov Bussel
- Cheyenne Sorotzkin & R' Aryei Shulman
- R' Eliyohu Meir Sorotzkin & Goldie Berenbaum
- Shani Sorotzkin & R' Nosson Hertzka
- Chassy Sorotzkin & R' Yisroel Brog

Chasya Bloch ד"הי

Chaya Bloch & Rabbi Aizik Ausband

- R' Avraham Ausband & Rivkah Zeilberger
- R' Eliyohu Ausband & Gila Brody
- Rivka Ausband & R' Dovid Goldberg
- Rassia Ausband & R' Moshe Bressler
- Leah Ausband & R' Eli Bursztyn
- R' Eliezer Ausband & Chana
- Sorah Ausband & R' Yitzchok Finkel
- R' Chaim Mordechai Ausband & Malkie
- Rochel Ausband & R' Binyomin Shapiro

Eliezer Bloch ד"הי

Miriam Bloch & Rabbi Yosef Kleiner ז"ע

- R' Chaim Kleiner & Chana
- Rassia Kleiner & R' Yaakov Borenstein
- Shula Kleiner & R' Naftali Sternbuch
- Yitzchok Kleiner & wife
- R' Yaakov Kleiner & Tzila

Perel Bloch ד"הי

Yosef Yehudah Leib Bloch ד"הי

Glossary

Acharonim — authoritative commentators on the Talmud, 16th century to the present

Aggadah, Aggadata — the homiletical, non-halachic teachings of the Sages

agunah — a woman unable to remarry because she has neither a divorce nor evidence of her missing husband's death

ahavas haTorah — love of Torah

ahavas Yisrael — love of Jews

al cheit — "For the sin …"; confessional recited on Yom Kippur and before death

al kiddush Hashem — for the sanctification of G-d's Name

al pi seichel — according to logic

aliyah, pl. *aliyos* — growth, in a spiritual sense

am Hashem — the nation of Hashem

ameilus, amal haTorah — toiling in the study of Torah

amen — "So be it"; the word recited after hearing a blessing or Kaddish, which expresses agreement with the message

Amerikaner (Yid.) — an American

Amoraim — Sages cited in the Gemara

amud — one folio of the Talmud; podium or lectern

Ani Maamin — "I believe"; one of the Rambam's 13 principles of faith

anivus — humility

av beis din — chief judge of a rabbinical court

Avinu — our father, usually used in reference to the Patriarchs

avira de'ara — the atmosphere of Eretz Yisrael

avodas Hashem — the service of Hashem

baal hamesorah — one who transmits the Torah heritage

baal tefillah — leader of the prayer service

baal teshuvah, pl. *baalei teshuvah* — a returnee to Jewish life, observance, and study *baal tokea* — one who blows the shofar on Rosh Hashanah

baalebas, pl. *baalebatim* (Yid.) — householder

bachur, pl. *bachurim* — unmarried young man

baki — learned or proficient in Torah; having a wide range of knowledge

bar mitzvah — the occasion at which, at 13 years of age, a boy becomes responsible for observing the commandments of the Torah

batlan — someone naïve in worldly matters

bechinah, pl. *bechinos* — test

be'eimah — with trepidation

bein adam lachaveiro — between man and his fellow

bein hazmanim — vacation time between semesters in a yeshivah

beis din — rabbinic court

beis haknesses — synagogue

Beis HaMikdash — the Holy Temple

beis midrash — study hall

bekiyus — expertise; proficiency; erudition; wide-ranging knowledge in a given subject

ben Torah, pl. *bnei Torah* — one who studies and observes the teachings of the Torah

ben yeshivah, pl. *bnei hayeshivah* — yeshivah student

berachah, pl. *berachos* — blessing

be'simchah — with happiness

be'tzibbur — with a congregation or a *minyan*

bimah — table or platform in the synagogue from which the Torah scroll is read

Bircas HaChamah — blessing on the sun, recited every 28 years

bitachon — trust in G-d

blatt — folio page (of Talmud)

bnei aliyah — people aspiring to spiritual elevation

Borei Kol HaOlamos — Creator of all Worlds; i.e., G-d

brillen (Yid.) — eyeglasses

bris, bris milah — circumcision

bris achim — a pact among brothers (or friends)

chaburah, pl. *chaburos* — group learning together

Chachamim — Sages; wise men

chalukah — stipend given to needy students

chalav Yisrael — milk produced under Jewish supervision

chanukas habayis — celebration of the dedication of a building (or home)

chareidi, pl. *chareidim* — one who is strictly observant of Jewish law

chas ve'shalom — Heaven forbid

chashuv — important

chassan — bridegroom

Chassid, pl. Chassidim — followers of the Chassidic movement founded by Rabbi Yisrael Baal Shem Tov

chatzi taanis — a partial fast

chaveirim — friends

chavrusa — learning partner

Chazal — Our Sages, of blessed memory

cheilek — portion

cherev — sword

chesed — lovingkindness; acts of beneficence

chiddushei Torah — original Torah insights

chillul Hashem — a desecration of G-d's Name

chinuch — education

chiyus — energy; life

chiyuv Talmud Torah — the obligation to learn Torah

chizuk — encouragement

Chol HaMoed — the intermediate

days of Pesach and Succos
Chumash — the Five Books of Moses
chumros — stringencies
chuppah — canopy under which the marriage ceremony takes place
churban — destruction
chutz laAretz — outside of the land of Israel
chutzpah — nerve; gall; brazenness
daas Torah — Torah outlook or perspective; a determination made by Torah sages
daf — page
Daf Yomi — Talmud study project in which one folio is learned every day
daven, davening — pray(ing)
derech eretz — proper conduct; respect; politness
derech halimud — an approach to learning; study plan
deveikus — the state of cleaving to G-d
din — law; justice
dochek — stress, poverty
d'var Hashem — the word of G-d
d'var Torah, pl. *divrei Torah* — a Torah thought
eisek — occupation; preoccupation
eishes chayil — woman of valor
Eliyahu HaNavi — the prophet Elijah
emes — truth
emunah — faith
Eretz Yisrael — the land of Israel
erev — the eve of
esrog — citron; one of the Four Species taken on Succos
ever min hachai — a limb removed from a live animal
evyonim — paupers
falsh (Yid.) — false
frum (Yid.) — religious; Torah observant

gabbai — synagogue sexton; attendant of a tzaddik
gadlus — greatness
gadol, pl. *gedolim* — outstanding Torah scholar
gadol hador, pl. *gedolei hador* — leaders of the generation
galus — exile; Diaspora
Gan Eden — the Garden of Eden
gaon, geonim baTorah — brilliant Torah scholars
gashmiyus — materialism
gedolei Torah — Torah giants
gedolei Yisrael — leaders of Israel
Gehinnom — purgatory; the place where, after death, souls are purified through suffering
gemach — fund providing interest-free loans or services
Gemara — loosely, the Talmud as a whole
geshmak (Yid.) — enjoyment, gusto
get — a bill of divorce
geulah — future redemption
gevaldig (Yid.) — outstanding; wonderful
girsa de'yankusa — knowledge acquired during one's youth
gragger — noisemaker, used on Purim
grammen — rhymes, usually clever and humorous
guf — body
gut Shabbos (Yid.) — "have a good Shabbos"
gut yahr (Yid.) — "have a good year"
gut Yom Tov (Yid.) — "have a good holiday"
haftarah — portion of Prophets read following the Torah reading
hakadosh — the holy
HaKadosh Baruch Hu — the Holy One, Blessed is He
hakafos — the ceremony on Simchas Torah marking the completion of

the reading of the Torah
halachah — Jewish law
halachic — pertaining to Jewish law
Hallel — Psalms 113-118, recited on Rosh Chodesh or festivals
Har Sinai — Mount Sinai
HaRav — title of esteem for a rabbi
Hashem yinkom damo — may G-d avenge his blood
Hashem Yisbarach — G-d, may He be blessed
hashkafah — outlook; ideology; worldview
hasmadah — diligence in learning
havdalah — ceremony marking the conclusion of the Sabbath and holidays
heilig (Yid.) — holy
hisbatlus — self-negation
hishtadlus — effort
hoda'ah — thanks
iluy — genius
Imeinu — our mother, usually used in reference to the Matriarchs
ish emes — a man of truth
kabbalah, pl. *kabbalos* — an obligation taken upon oneself
kabbalas Malchus Shamayim — accepting the Yoke of Heaven
kallah — a bride
kanai, kana'us — zealot; zealousness
kapota (Yid.) — black frock coat; rabbinic frock
kashrus — Jewish dietary laws
kavanah — concentration or intent in prayer and religious observance
kavod — honor
kavod ha'medumeh — imaginary or false honor
kelev she'beyam — sea lion
Kever Rachel — the burial place of the matriarch Rachel
kever Yisrael — burial according to Jewish ritual

kiddush — blessing expressing the sanctity of Shabbos or festivals; festive gathering at which kiddush is recited
kiddush Hashem — sanctification of G-d's Name
kiddush Shem Shamayim — sanctification of the Name of Heaven
kirvas Elokim — closeness to G-d
kivshan ha'eish — a fiery furnace
Klal Yisrael — the community of Israel
kleine masechtala (Yid.) — a small tractate (of Talmud)
koach hasbarah — the ability to explain clearly
Kohen, pl. Kohanim — members of the Priestly family of the tribe of Levi
Kol HaNe'arim — ceremony conducted on Simchas Torah in which all the boys stand under a tallis
kol haTorah — the sound of Torah learning
kollel — academy of higher Jewish study, whose students are usually married men
korban Pesach — the paschal lamb
Kosel HaMaaravi — the Western Wall, remnant of the Holy Temple
krechtz (Yid.) — a sigh; to sigh
krias haTorah — the reading of the Torah
kuntrus — a pamphlet
kushya — a question on a Torah topic
kvod habriyos — respect for people
kvod haTorah — honor or respect for the Torah
kvod Shamayim — honor due to heaven, i.e., G-d
lamdan, pl. *lamdanim* — Talmudic scholar
lashon hakodesh — the holy tongue; i.e., Hebrew

lashon hara — gossip; slanderous talk

le'havdil — to differentiate between (generally used for holy and secular items)

limud haTorah — learning of Torah

Lita — Lithuania

lomdus — erudition; method of Talmud study

lulav — palm branch; one of the Four Species taken on Succos

Maariv — the evening prayer

maaseh Satan — an act (or provocation) of the Satan (yetzer hara)

machshavah — thought; philosophy

madreigah — level

maggid shiur — teacher of Torah to students on an advanced level

malach — angel; Divine messenger

malach Elokim — an angel of G-d

Malchiyos — section of the Mussaf prayers on Rosh Hashanah dealing with G-d's Kingship

mama lashon (Yid.) — mother tongue; native language

Maran — "our master"; respectful form of address

marbitz Torah — one who disseminates Torah

masechta — a tractate of Talmud

mashgiach — spiritual guide in a yeshivah

Mashiach — the Messiah

maskanah — conclusion

maskil — adherent of the Haskalah movement

masmid — an exceptionally diligent student

matanah — present

matanos la'evyonim — gifts to the poor, distributed on Purim

me'ein Olam HaBa — a taste (or semblance) of the World to Come

mechabed — to honor

megillah — scroll; term commonly applied to the Book of Esther

melamed — a teacher, esp. of young children

Melaveh Malkah — meal eaten after Shabbos in honor of the departed Sabbath

melech — king

menachem avel — comforting a mourner

menahel — supervisor; principal

menahel ruchani — spiritual guide

mentch (Yid.) — a decent human being

menuchah — rest

mesader kiddushin — one who conducts the marriage ceremony

mesirus nefesh — self-sacrifice

mesorah — heritage

mevakshei hachochmah — those who seek wisdom

mezuzos — parchment scrolls affixed to the doorpost

midbar — desert

Midrash — the Sages' homiletical teachings

mikreh — a happening

mikvaos — ritual baths

Minchah — the afternoon prayer

minyan — quorum of 10 men necessary for conducting a prayer service

Mishkan — the Temple used by the Jews during their sojourn in the wilderness

mishloach manos — gifts of food sent on Purim

Mishnah, *mishnah* — teachings of the Tannaim that form the basis of the Talmud

mishteh ve'simchah — feasting and happiness

mitzvah, pl. *mitzvos* — Torah commandment; good deed

Modeh Ani — prayer recited upon awakening in the morning, expressing gratitude for life
moed — festival
mohel — one who performs a circumcision
Motza'ei Shabbos — Saturday night, after nightfall
Mussaf — additional prayers recited on Shabbos and festivals
mussar — ethical teachings, aimed at self-refinement
Mussar movement — a movement founded by R' Yisrael of Salant that encourages the study of mussar and the pursuit of self-refinement
mussar shmuess — a lecture on self-improvement
nachalah — portion
navi — prophet
nebach (Yid.) — what a pity!
nefesh — soul
negios — personal prejudices or interests
Ne'ilah — the concluding prayer of Yom Kippur
neshamah, pl. *neshamos* — soul
neshamah yeseirah — "extra" soul given to us on Shabbos
Nevi'im Rishonim — the early prophets
niflaos haBorei — the wonders of the Creator
niggun — tune, melody
nishmas chaim — a soul of life
ohel hameis — the tent of the dead
omek hap'shat — the depth of the meaning or explanation
Omer — refers to the 49-day period between Pesach and Shavuos
oneg, oneg Yom Tov — the pleasure of Yom Tov
parashah — weekly Torah portion

pashtus — simplicity
pashut — obvious; plain or simple meaning
pasken — to issue a halachic directive
pasuk, pl. *pesukim* — verse
payos — sidecurls
pera'us — wildness, savagery
perek — chapter
pikuach nefesh — danger to life
pilpul, pilpul chaveirim — analytical method of Talmud study
pirsumei nisa — publicizing the miracle
poskim — halachic authorities
p'shat — basic explanation
p'tcha — Shabbos delicacy
Rabbeinu — our teacher
rachamim — compassion
rachmanus — mercy
rakefet — flower indigenous to Eretz Yisrael
rav, pl. rabbanim — rabbi
rebbi, pl. rebbeim — teacher
re'us — friendship
Ribbono Shel Olam — Master of the World
ris'cha de'Oraissa — the fire of Torah learning
Rishon, pl. *Rishonim* — early commentator(s) on the Talmud (11th-15th centuries)
rosh yeshivah — dean of a Torah institution; senior lecturer in a yeshivah
ruach — spirit, enthusiasm
ruach memalela — a "talking spirit"; i.e., man
ruchniyus — spirituality
sar ve'gadol — i.e., a great person
Satan — refers to the evil inclination
schmooze (Yid.) — chat
seder (as in learning) — study session
Seder, pl. Sedarim (Pesach) — traditional festive meal commemorat-

ing the Exodus from Egypt
sefer, pl. *sefarim* — book
Sefer Torah — Torah Scroll
Sefirah — period between Pesach and Shavuos during which certain mourning customs are observed
segulah — spiritual remedy
seichel — intellect, rational faculty, good sense
Selichos — penitential prayers recited before and after Rosh Hashanah
semichah — term used for the ordination of rabbis
Sephardi, pl. Sephardim — Jew of Spanish, Oriental, or Middle Eastern ancestry
seudah — meal, esp. a festive meal
sevarah — theory, reasoning
Shacharis — the morning prayer service
shailah, pl. *shailos* — question on Jewish law
Shalom Aleichem — traditional greeting; "peace be on you"
shalom bayis — harmony in the home; peaceful relationship between husband and wife
shalom zachar — Friday-night gathering in honor of the birth of a son
shalosh seudos — the third meal of the Sabbath
Shamayim — Heaven
Shas — the Talmud as a whole
Shechinah — Divine Presence
Sheishes Yemei HaMaaseh — the six days of work, activity
sheker — falsehood
Shemittah — the Sabbatical year when agricultural work is forbidden in the land of Israel
Shemoneh Esrei — the prayer of 18 blessings that forms the central core of each weekday prayer service

sheva berachos — festive meals honoring the bride and groom during the week after their wedding
shidduch — marriage match
shiur, pl. *shiurim* — lecture
shiur daas, pl. *shiurei daas* — a lecture of Telzer mussar thought
shiur klali — a lecture given to the entire student body in a yeshivah
shivah — seven-day period of mourning
shmuessen — lectures on Torah topics
shochet — ritual slaughterer
shofar — ram's horn, blown on Rosh Hashanah
shtuch (Yid.) — to stab; refers to a putdown
shuckel (Yid.) — to sway back and forth, as when praying
Shulchan Aruch — Code of Jewish Law
sichah — lecture
siddur, pl. *siddurim* — prayer book
sifrei mussar — books on mussar topics
sifrei Tanach — 24 Books of the Bible
simchah — joy, happiness
Simchas Beis HaSho'eivah — "celebration of the water drawing"; takes place on Succos
siyum, pl. *siyumim* — completion of a portion of Torah or Talmud
siyum haShas — completion of the entire Talmud
succah — booth in which Jews dwell during Succos
sugya, pl. *sugyos* — conceptual unit in Talmud study; topic in Talmud
taam — taste; rationale
tallis, pl. *talleisim* — prayer shawl
talmid chacham, pl. *talmidei chachamim* — Torah scholar
talmid, pl. *talmidim* — student

talmidah — (female) student
Tanach — acronym for Torah, Neviim, Kesuvim; the Written Torah
Tannaim — Sages of the Mishnah
tante (Yid.) — aunt
tatte (Yid.) — father
tefillah — prayer
tefillin — phylacteries
Tehillim — Psalms
teirutz — explanation; answer; excuse
tekias shofar, pl. *tekios* — blowing of the shofar
teshuvah — answer; repentance
Tosafos — explanatory notes on the Talmud by scholars of the 12th-14th centuries
treife — term used to describe anything not kosher
tzaar — pain, trouble
tzaar baalei chaim — cruelty to animals
tzaddik, pl. *tzaddikim* — righteous person
tze'akah — a scream
tzibbur — congregation
Tzion — Jerusalem
tzitzis — four-cornered garment containing fringes, worn by Jewish men and boys
tzorchei tzibbur — needs of the community
vaad, pl. *vaadim* — committee
Vaad HaChinuch — committee in charge of education
Viduy — the confession recited on Yom Kippur and before death
vort (Yid.) — a Torah thought; celebration of an engagement
yachsanim — those of distinguished lineage

yahrtzeit (Yid.) — anniversary of the death of a person
Yamim Noraim — the high holy days
yashrus — integrity, honesty
Yerushalayim — Jerusalem
yeshivah — a school where Torah is studied
yeshivish — pertaining to the yeshivah way of life
yetzer hara — evil inclination; connotes desire to violate the Torah
Yid — Jew
Yiddishkeit — the Jewish way of life
Yiddishe mama (Yid.) — Jewish mother
yiras Shamayim — fear of Heaven
Yom HaDin — the "Day of Judgment"; i.e., Rosh Hashanah
Yom Kippur Kattan — the day before Rosh Chodesh, traditionally a day of repentance, a miniature Yom Kippur
Yom Tov, pl. Yamim Tovim — holidays, festivals
yosheiv rosh — chairman; head of a committee
yungerman (Yid.) — young man
zakus hanefesh — purity of soul
zechus — merit; privilege
zechus avos — merit of the forefathers
zeidy (Yid.) — grandfather
zekeinim — elders
zemiros — songs sung at Sabbath and festive meals
Zichronos — Remembrance; a section of the Mussaf prayers on Rosh Hashanah
zman cheiruseinu — "the time of our freedom"; i.e., Pesach
zman, pl. *zmanim* — semester, time

Index

A

Abraham, Reb Chaim 117 (fn)
Abu Ghoush 91
Acharonim 112
Achashveirosh 21
Adam HaRishon 380
address to school children, acquired sweet taste of Torah 135
advice given with warmth and wisdom 212
Agudas Yisrael of Long Island 135
Agudath Yisrael of America 85, 149
Aharon 260
Aish HaTorah, Jerusalem 154
Alter from Kelm (Rav Simcha Zissel) 113
Alter of Kelm 113
Alter, Rabbi Avrohom 316 (fn)
Altschuler, Rav Ezra (*Takanas Ezra*) 53, 272, 309
Altusky, W. 376
Am HaTorah (journal) 222
Amudei Shmuel (sefer) 40
Amudei Yehonasan (sefer) 39
Anemer, Rabbi Chaim Tzvi 202, 326
article written by Rav Gifter
 A Word to Jewish Parents 119
 Chesed, a gift from Hashem to share with others 297
 Emerging from darkness to merit the light of Hashem's love 368
 Eretz Yisrael: Focal point of world issues 189
 Guf is fleeting, *Neshamah* is eternal 157
 power of the Torah scholar 110
 preparatory days of Elul 360
 self-evaluation is the motif of the Days of Awe 364ff
 Shabbos rest: a model for children, 343
 Torah is infinite and unbounded 124
 Torah is our very life 137
 Torah study, prerequisite to mitzvah observance 121
 Torah to the exclusion of all else 137
ArtScroll 281
 letter of encouragement to 166 (illus.)
Auerbach, Aharon Meir 181
Auerbach, Rav Shlomo Zalman 77
Ausband, Rav Aizik 61 (illus.), 245 (illus.), 264
Ausband, Rav Avrohom 83 (fn), 207, 231 (fn), 245 (illus.), 262 (illus.), 263 (illus.), 264
Ausband, Reb Chaim Mordechai 98 (illus.), 245 (illus.), 310 (illus.)
Ausband, Rebbetzin Chaya 71
Avnei Miluim (sefer) 255
Avodas Yisrael 242
Avraham Avinu 260

B

Baal HaLeshem (Rav Shlomo Elyashiv) 261
Baal HaTanya 242
Baal teshuvah, everyone must be a 380
Baalas teshuvah, the nurturing of a 245ff
Bak, R' Binyamin 46 (illus.)
Baltimore, Maryland 33, 72
 Yeshiva Lane 121, 318
Bamberger, Rabbi Moshe 245 (fn)
Barkin, Rav Dovid 103 (illus.), 219, 221, 224, 258, 259 (illus.)
Baron, Baruch 52 (illus.)
Baron, Herschel 376
Bayit VeGan 244
Beis HaMikdash 92
Ben Torah, behavior befitting a 172

Index ☐ 403

Bensinger, Rav Yeruchem   19
Berditchev, Rav Levi Yitzchak of   185
Beren, Adolph   84
Berger, Reb Leibel   133 (*fn*), 215 (*fn*)
Berlin, Germany   110, 236
Bilaam   309
Bircas Shmuel (*sefer*)   96
Birnbaum, Nathan   183
Bloch, Moishele   67 (*illus.*)
    final moments   67
Bloch, Rav Avraham Yitzchak   43, 44, 45 (*illus.*), 60 (*illus.*), 61 (*illus.*), 66, 67, 69, 70, 84, 101, 110, 115, 163, 170, 171, 172, 187, 192, 208, 218, 230 (*illus.*), 232, 261, 277, 324
    with talmidim   70 (*illus.*)
Bloch, Rav Eliyahu (Elya) Meir   16, 60 (*illus.*), 61 (*illus.*), 65, 65 (*illus.*), 70, 80, 82, 126, 127, 127 (*illus.*), 163, 178, 210, 226, 261, 325
Bloch, Rav Yosef Leib   43, 44 (*illus.*), 64, 65, 178, 180, 230 (*illus.*), 232, 261, 277, 286
Bloch, Rav Zalman   40, 44, 45 (*illus.*), 53, 58, 58 (*illus.*), 61 (*illus.*), 66, 68 (*illus.*) 70, 101, 163, 208, 226 (*illus.*), 227 (*illus.*), 232, 261, 262, 313, 371
    and family   54 (*illus.*)
    with talmidim   70 (*illus.*)
Bloch, Rebbetzin   247
Bloch, Rebbetzin Luba   67, 68 (*illus.*), 371
Bloch, Rebbetzin Rassia   60 (*illus.*)
Bloch, Rebbetzin Rivka   60 (*illus.*)
Bloch, Shoshana   *see* Gifter, Rebbetzin Shoshana
Bogart, Rabbi Yaakov   99 (*fn*)
Borchardt, Rabbi   248
Bressler, Rav and Rebbetzin   99 (*fn*)
Bressler, Yehoshua   99
Breuer, Rav   278
Bris Achim   93 (*illus.*)
Brisk   64
Brisker, Rav Chaim   76, 117, 149, 207, 235, 76
Brisker Rav   *see* Soloveitchik, Rav Yitzchak Ze'ev
Brodie, Rabbi Aharon   83 (*fn*), 124 (*fn*)
Brothers, Pact of   93 (*illus.*), 94
Broyde, Rav Simcha Zissel   113
Brudny, Rav Shmuel   349 (*illus.*)
Bunim, Rabbi Amos   162 (*illus.*)
Burnham, Rabbi Aryeh   78 (*fn*), 210, 211 (*fn*)

C

Camp Agudah   168, 188, 319 (*illus.*), 320, 320 (*illus.*), 361
Camp Kol Rinah   275
Camp Kol Torah   102
Camp Yeshivah Staten Island   348
Carlebach, Rabbi Daniel   88 (*fn*)
Case Western Reserve University, Cleveland, Ohio   173
Chacham Tzvi, 96
challenge, to draw near to Hashem   177
Chanukah   350
chanukas habayis, Telz Yeshivah, Rav Gifter speaking   85 (*illus.*)
character, becomes obvious under challenge   192
Charan   260
Chasam Sofer   109, 227
Chashmonaim   21, 350
Chaveirim, unique study group   231
Chavel, Lithuania   33
Chazon Ish (Rav Avraham Yeshayah Karelitz)   22, 235, 347
Chiddushei HaRim (*sefer*)   132
Chiddushei Reb Reuven (*sefer*)   96
Chillul Hashem, when one does not do one's best   243
Chizkiyahu HaMelech, what we learn from   140
Chofetz Chaim   149, 235, 344
Churban, what we have lost   236
Cleveland Clinic   296
Cleveland Jewish News   286
Cleveland, Ohio   78, 80*ff*, 92*ff*, 95*ff*
Clevelander Rebbe of Ranaana   306
Compton, Reb Zev   307 (*fn*)
Cook, Rabbi Simcha   318
Cook, Reb Yosef Chaim   318
Correspondence
    with family member   57
    with Rav Poleyeff   56
    with Rav Yehoshua Klavan   56, 76, 81
    with Rav Yehudah Leib Forer   76
    with Steipler Gaon   56, 199
    with students and strangers   202, 257
    with young boy   283
Cracow, Poland   236, 237 (*illus.*)
current events as a tool for *emunah*   189
Current events: the language of misfortune calls forth the language of *tze'akah*   381

D

Daas Soferim   86 (*illus.*)
Daas Torah   146
David, Rabbi Avishai   122
Davis, Rav Yehudah   39, 150, 152
Day of Judgment   22, 189, 376
Days of Awe   *see Yamim Noraim*
death, weeping at moment of   362
death, of a gadol leaves the world a lesser place   22

Degel Reuven (sefer)   317
Denis, Leah   69 (*illus.*)
Denis, Reb Binyomin Beinush   69 (*illus.*)
Denis, Malkiel   67 (*illus.*)
Denver, Colorado   215
Dessler, Rav Eliyahu Eliezer   47
Dessler, Rav Nachum (Zev) Velvel   47, 52 (*illus.*), 65, 65 (*illus.*), 161, 161 (*illus.*), 162 (*illus.*), 162 (*fn*), 204 (*illus.*), 319 (*illus.*), 349 (*illus.*)
Detroit, Michigan   243
Dicker, Estie   281
Dinovitzer, Rabbi Yitzchak   360
Divrei Yehoshua (sefer)   76
Dolinger, Rav Shaul   224
Dos Vort (newspaper)   164
Dos Yiddishe Vort, seasonal almanac of   360
dream, Rav Gifter appears in a   208, 241
Dvinsk, Latvia   372

E

Eiger, Rav Akiva   112, 132, 273, 370
Eisenberg, Rav Ephraim and Rebbetzin   121, 318
Eisenberg, Rav Ephraim   130 (*illus.*), 131
Eisenberg, Rebbetzin Shlomis (Gifter)   49 (*fn*), 131, 331 (*illus.*), 337 (*illus.*), 341
Eisenstadt, Reb Hershel   109
Elbaum, Rabbi Shlomo   303 (*illus.*)
Eliyahu HaNavi   306, 307
Elul   97, 138, 148, 234, 357ff, 365, 368
Elyashiv, Rav Shlomo (Baal HaLeshem)   261
Elyashiv, Rav Yosef Shalom   261
Emden, Rav Yaakov   96
emotions, need to control   325
Epstein, M.   376
essay, written by Rav Gifter
    Torah is not another subject; it must be *Toras Moshe*   156
    Utilizing Yom Tov as a tool for *chinuch* on application of Torah and Eretz Yisroel   345
Eulogy on Rav Gifter
    article by Rabbi Hillel Goldberg   81, 216, 275
    by Rav Avrohom Ausband   207
    by Rav Yaakov Reisman   101
    by Tzvi Feuer   99
    by Rabbi Azriel Goldfein   27, 212
    by Rav Moshe Shapiro   51
euthanasia   175
excellence, the gold standard to strive for   206

F

Far Rockaway, New York   101
Fear, only of G-d   160
Feinstein, Rav Moshe 22, 78, 129, 348 (*illus.*), 377 (*illus.*)
Feitman, Rabbi Yaakov   303
Feldman, Moshe Yosef   283
Feldman, Reb Shlomo   283
Feuer, Rav Avrohom Chaim   36, 114, 116, 218 (*illus.*), 261,262 (*fn*), 276 (*illus.*), 277
Feuer, Rabbi Eliezer (Ezzy)   38 (*fn*), 113, 180, 234, 234 (*illus.*), 345
Feuer, Rebbetzin Luba   337 (*illus.*)
Feuer, Tzvi(ki)   99, 124, 137, 223
final lesson, make use of every minute   384
Fink, M.   376
Finkel, Rav Nosson Tzvi   103 (*illus.*), 276 (*illus.*)
Fischer, R.   376
Fishman, Rabbi Avrohom   303 (*illus.*)
Fishman, Eli   172
Forer, Rav Yehudah Leib   76, 77, 77 (*illus.*), 101,
Frankfurt, Germany   236
Fried, Rebbetzin Breiny Helfan   304, 305 (*illus.*)
Fried, Rabbi Getzel and Breiny, wedding of   202 (*illus.*)
Friedman, Rabbi Eli   254 (*fn*), 272
funeral in Eretz Yisrael   103 (*illus.*), 104 (*illus.*)

G

Galupkin, Eliyahu   376
Gan Eden   380
Gateshead, England   247
Gemara   96, 21, 373, 384
    Schottenstein Edition of the Talmud   167
Gerson, Rabbi Reuvein   153 (*fn*)
Gertzovitz, Reb Leib (Minsker)   59
Gewirtz, Rav Abba Zalka   23, 73ff, 74 (*illus.*), 142, 210, 224,307, 324
Gewirtz, Danny (Doniel)   224
Gewirtz, Reb Dovid   75, 78, 307
Gewirtz, Rabbi Yonah   74 (*illus.*), 74 (*fn*), 75, 224, 307, 317 (*fn*)
Gifter, Reb Binyomin   47 (*fn*), 257, 285, 318, 331 (*illus.*), 337 (*illus.*)
Gifter, Israel (Yisrael)   19, 33ff, 34 (*illus.*) 343 (*illus.*)
Gifter, Jeanne and Joseph   18
Gifter, Joe   34
Gifter, May (Matla)   33ff,34 (*illus.*) 343 (*illus.*)
"Gifter moment"; indelible impact of   15
    Gifter Mordecai, grandfather of Rav Gifter   33

Gifter, Rav Mordechai
   a committed correspondent   257
   a man who embodied the truth   23
   able to concede when he was in error   39
   accustoming oneself to self-sacrifice for learning   359
   adjusting to Telz   46
   after-school religious program   34
   anguish due to forgetfulness   99 ff
   appointed rabbi of Nusach Ari Shul   72
   appreciating the value of *mussar*   172
   appreciation for his wife and all she does for him   339
   articles   *see* article written by Rav Gifter
   as *maggid shiur*   84
   as Rosh Yeshivah   84ff
   asked for his insights   40
   asked to speak in shul   39
   assuming the anguish of others — physically and emotionally   293ff
   becomes force to be reckoned with   38
   begins Jewish education   34
   begins to influence others   52
   bein hazemanim spent learning   53
   beneficiary of blessing from Rav Shimon Shkop   35
   born in Portsmouth Virginia   33
   carrying tradition to a new front   230
   challenging a student to achieve greatness   224
   close relationship with his rebbe, Rav Poleyeff   37
   close ties to Rav Azriel Rabinowitz   49
   completely immersed in yeshivah in Lita   217
   conveyed thoughts to be comprehensible to all   228
   corresponds with his rebbi, Rav Poleyeff   37
   defines a *baal hamesorah*   229
   defines a religious Jew   152
   delivers a *shiur* in language the students understand   223
   demands stellar performance in learning and behavior   243
   deriving pleasure from learning   111
   develops an appreciation for *mussar*   170
   eager to attend yeshivah   36
   empathizing and taking action   299
   encouraged to learn in Telz, Lithuania   42

Gifter, Rav Mordechai *continued*
   engagement to Shoshana Bloch   53
   enjoying grandchildren   331
   enters Riets   36
   essays   *see* essays written by Rav Gifter
   establishes his yeshivah and community in Telz-Stone   87
   every thought and action guided by Torah   178
   expending considerable effort for a Jew in need   296
   father of ArtScroll series   167
   father sells life insurance to fund his learning   45
   feeling the pain of others   323ff
   fierce desire to learn   36
   final years   95ff
   first *blatt* of Gemara   36
   focused solely on fulfilling the will of Hashem   161
   Friday night *oneg* with the *bachurim*   89
   gives *shiur* on the majesty of Telz   58
   giving *chaburos* in Ner Yisrael   72
   giving respect to all — great and small   310
   graduation from high school   42, 38 *(illus.)*
   has profound influence on those not yet *frum*   245
   heeding *daas Torah*   92
   high expectations of himself and of his students   39
   higher secular studies have a detrimental impact   155
   his "letter of purpose"   57
   his ability to teach was his greatest pride   17
   his actions speak even louder than his words   271
   his entire being was permeated with Torah   19
   his passing   101
   his response to Zionism   148
   his ultimate mission   102
   hospitalization, regrets lack of time to learn   48
   humble even in death   197
   immediately available to all who needed him   254
   impact of the eulogies at his funeral   101
   impending engagement   40
   importance of not wasting a moment   138

Gifter, Rav Mordechai *continued*
   indication of his wry sense of humor 224
   influenced by local *shochet* 35
   infused with the joy of Torah 114
   instilling the value of even a small sum of money 283
   involvement in issues of the day 86
   joins Telz, Cleveland 81*ff*
   joy in learning in Telz 47
   kept detailed record of his lessons and accomplishments 39
   kindles the spark of love 211
   knowing when to heed his wife 335
   knowledge of Tanach 36
   known as Max 34
   known for his sharp mind 41
   lasting legacy 94
   learns despite adversity 38
   learns from his mistakes 165
   learns the benefits of guarding one's health 57
   leaves for New York at age 13 36
   legacy to all generations 99
   lengthy preparation to give *shiur* 88
   lessons gleaned from the wonders of the Creator 90
   letter
      accepting Rav Gifter as rabbi of the Waterbury Hebrew Institute 74 (*illus.*)
      accepting the position to visit the Waterbury Hebrew Institute 73 (*illus.*)
   living Torah, not just learning it 108
   love for Torah remains fresh 118
   makes a *Kiddush Hashem* by standing up for Torah 164
   making his family a top priority 329
   marriage to Shoshana Bloch 72
   mashgiach in Telz 82
   meeting notable Torah scholars 53
   mesmerized by Rav Mottel Pogromansky 49
   mollifying hurt feelings 320
   motivating students through praise 258
   moves to Baltimore 33
   need for parents to sacrifice to create *gedolim* 120
   need to strive for greatness 119
   no downtime in learning 115
   no effort to great for a student 210
   not hurting anyone was primary 163
   not intimidated by power or influence 160

Gifter, Rav Mordechai *continued*
   not wasting money 158
   obtains visas for *roshei yeshivah* and married students 64
   offers wise counsel 215
   one with the Torah 107*ff*
   only desired to teach Torah 199
   only faith can uplift or strengthen 366
   our livelihood is in Hashem's hands 209
   outstanding self-control and patience 238
   parental fear of Yom HaDin impacts the children 365
   parents of 33, 343 (*illus.*)
   parting from his parents 44*ff*
   passion in learning 83
   plea to yeshivah *bachurim* to learn more quickly 95
   praise from the Steipler Gaon 199
   prepares for learning in Telz 45
   profoundly influenced by Rav Avraham Yitzchak Bloch 44
   promoting Agudas Yisrael policies 149
   propensity for study and deep thought evident early in life 34
   pursuit of the truth 39
   quick thinking averts a massacre 48
   "Quintessential Orator" 186
   rallying cry to *teshuvah* 359
   rapid advancement in learning and *avodas Hashem* 41
   refutes need for secular higher studies 124
   relishing learning 262
   relocates to Eretz Yisrael 87*ff*
      to Waterbury 73*ff*
   resolves to succeed 36
   respect, accorded to all 310
   returns to America 64, 92
   root of our *neshamah* is humility 157
   saving his future wife 65
   shmuess see *shmuess* delivered by Rav Gifter
   sefarim by 222
   sets all else aside for his students 205
   shiur, difficulty in following 218
   solemn awareness of significance of Elul 357
   sounds of learning kept him awake 131
   speech see speech delivered by Rav Gifter
   spokesman for Torah Jewry 84

Index   ☐ 407

Gifter, Rav Mordechai *continued*
　sticks to his principles　162
　student in public school　34
　study partner with a student　212
　studying with a French *bachur* in Telz, Lita　48 (*illus.*)
　sublimated his actions to the will of Hashem　165
　takes a stand for truth　285
　taking leave of Telz-Stone　93
　taste of Torah is the best thing in the world　136
　tears for Torah　212
　the ultimate pedogogue　200
　The World That Was: Lithuania　71 (*fn*)
　toiling in Torah　129
　　transforms a person　155
　Torah determines both right from wrong and life and death　156
　Torah giants decipher Hashem's messages　146
　Torah giants *see* the world through Torah lenses　146
　Torah Judaism is the only (true) Judaism　152
　Torah novellae　40 (*illus.*)
　total involvement as inspiration　123
　travels to Telz　45
　treasured every word of Torah　56
　trusted by Rav Shach　167
　turning hearts of stone to hearts of flesh　360
　unforgiving in his search for truth　218
　unparalleled oratorical skils　84*ff*
　vacations in Polongin　60 (*illus.*)
　views everything as a means to draw closer to Hashem　177
　walking with his rebbi　110
　walks out in middle of speaking　232
　warns of dangers of outside knowledge　58
　weeping with emotion　91
　with Binyamin Bak in Telz　46 (*illus.*)
　words as inspiration　361
　writes "Pact of Brothers"　94
　writing enabled him to develop his ideas　38
　wrote down everything for posterity　38
　yearns for Mashiach　91
　yearns to learn in Telz　43
Gifter, Rose　34
Gifter, Shimon Yehuda　318
Gifter, Rebbetzin Shoshana (Bloch)　15, 40, 49 (*fn*), 53, 54 (*illus.*), 64, 65, 69, 72, 72 (*illus.*), 74 (*fn*), 129 (*fn*), 165, 180, 234 (*illus.*), 248, 253 (*illus.*), 282, 294, 295, 308, 317, 330, 330 (*illus.*), 332 (*illus.*), 334, 338 (*illus.*), 343 (*illus.*), 351 (*illus.*)
　grandparents of　69 (*illus.*)
Gifter, Rabbi Yisroel (Sroly)　98 (*illus.*), 99, 113, 337 (*illus.*)
Gifter, Rav Zalman　313 (*fn*), 336, 337 (*illus.*)
Ginsberg, Rav Gavriel　260
Goldberg, Rabbi Hillel　84, 215, 216 (*fn*), 275, 325 (*fn*)
Goldberg, Rabbi Moshe　129 (*fn*)
Golden Calf　380
Goldfein, Rabbi Azriel　51 (*fn*), 112 (*fn*), 125, 212, 213 (*illus.*), 219, 237 (*fn*), 252 (*fn*), 273
Goldhaber, Rabbi Shlomo　126 (*fn*)
Gordon, Rav Eliezer (Leizer)　42, 43, 44 (*illus.*), 264
Granofsky, Rav Yosef　241
gratitude for even the smallest favor　318*ff*
greatness
　a dream that is achievable　17
　striving for　235
Greenwald, Mrs. Toby (Klein)　175
Greenwald, Rabbi Dr. Yaakov　275
Grodnanski, Rav Eliyahu Eliezer　329
Grodno, Lithuania　35
Grodzenski, Rav Chaim Ozer　149, 329, 329 (*fn*)
Groz, Moshe　46

H
Hadarom (journal)　222
Hapardes (journal)　222
Har Sinai　228, 309
Hashem lowers Himself to humanity to uplift, cleanse, and purify it　367
Hebrew Academy of Cleveland　161, 298
Helberg, Mr.　210
Helfan, Reb Eliyahu Chaim　63, 63 (*illus.*)
Helfan, Rav Moshe　62 (*illus.*), 63, 202 (*illus.*)
Helfan, Rav Pinchas, and family　228 (*illus.*)
Heller, Rav Aryeh Leib HaCohen　132
Hellman, Moshe　39 (*fn*)
Hershovitz, Rav Yitzchak Isaac　63
Hertz, Rabbi Yitzchak　52
Herzl, Theodore　183
Hirsch, Dr. Marcus　210
Hirsch, Michael　85 (*fn*), 173
Hirsch, Naftali　210
Hirsch, Shimon　83, 210
Hirschfeld, Rabbi Boruch　184, 203, 234 (*fn*)
Histadrus HaRabbanim　287 (*illus.*), 288
Hollander, H.　376
Holocaust　44, 186*ff*, 323

aftermath of 229*ff*
education regarding 188
Holyoke, Massachusetts 76
honesty in all matters above all else 281*ff*
humility, cause of elevation and glorification 309
Hutner, Rav Yitzchak 184

I

Ibn Tibon 111
Iglei Tal 111 (*fn*)
Igra, Rav Meshulem 227
illness, statistics are irrelevant — Hashem is the Ultimate Healer 306
Indich, Y. 314, 376
Intermountain Jewish News 215
Isbee, Avrohom Mordechai 131

J

Jewish education cornerstone of Jewish existence 161
Jewish People, one collective soul 324

K

Kahan, Rabbi Chaim 257
Kahaneman, Rav Yosef Shlomo 181
Kamenetzky, Rav Binyamin 135
Kamenetsky, Rav Yaakov 22, 135 (*illus.*)
Kanievsky, Rav Yaakov Yisroel *see* (Steipler Gaon)
Kant, Emmanuel 110
Kaplan, Rav Aryeh Moshe 70
Kaplan, Mr. Isidore 210
Kaplinsky, Rav Yisroel 345 (*illus.*)
Karelitz, Rav Avraham Yeshayah Karelitz *see* (Chazon Ish)
Katz, Rabbi Avrohom 317
Katz, Rav Chaim Mordechai (Mottel) 16, 60 (*illus.*), 65, 65 (*illus.*), 80, 82, 82 (*illus.*), 84, 124, 130 (*illus.*), 178, 179 (*illus.*), 266, 332 (*illus.*), 352 (*illus.*)
Katz, Rabbi Chaim Tzvi 171 (*illus.*), 202, 376
Katz, Rebbetzin Chaya 60 (*illus.*)
Katz, D. 376
Katz, Rebbetzin Esther 179
Katz, Mrs. Moshe (Anemer) 202 (*fn*)
Katz, Rav Reuven 317
Kaufman, Rabbi Aharon 78
Kaufman, Rabbi Shmuel 243
Keller, Rav Chaim Dov 262 (*illus.*), 266
Kertzer, Z. 376
Ketzos HaChoshen (*sefer*) 38, 112, 126, 132
Kever Rachel 71
Kfar Chassidim 51
Kiddush Hashem, making a 174
King David 90, 360
Klavan, Rav Yehoshua 56, 76, 81
Klein, H. 376
Klein, Nachman 323 (fn)
Kleiner, Rebbetzin 67
Kohn, Rabbi Shloimie 104 (*illus.*)
Kol Torah (yeshivah) 244
Korach, 315
Kosel HaMaaravi 71
Kotler, Rav Aharon 377 (*illus.*)
Kotler, Rav Shneur 349 (*illus.*)
Kovno, American Consul in 48
Kovno Kollel 150
Kovno, Lithuania 53
Kovno Rav 370
Kozhnitzer Maggid 242
Kramer, Michoel 83
Kravitz, Rabbi Mordechai 39*(fn)*, 159
Kruk, Rav Shalom Zundel 318

L

Lapidus, Yisroel 83
Law Journal of Western Reserve University 173 (*illus.*)
learn from everything one experiences and from everyone one encounters 261
learning Torah 241
creating lifelong bonds 213
Leff, Rabbi Baruch 241 (*fn*)
Leff, Rav Zev 214, 217, 259 (*illus.*), 260
Lefkovitz, Rabbi Yehuda 254 (*fn*)
Leibowitz, Rav Dovid 73
Leibowitz, Rav Henoch 73
Lemberg, Poland 236
Leshem Shevo VeAchlamah (Kabbalah *sefer*) 49
letter of purpose; pursue knowledge only to discern the will of Hashem 57
letter
accepting Rav Gifter as rabbi of the Waterbury Hebrew Institute 74 (*illus.*)
accepting the invitation to visit the Waterbury Hebrew Institute 73 (*illus.*)
discusses his *avodas Hashem* 41
from Rav Gifter's uncle Dr. Shmuel Sar congratulating the Waterbury community 76 (*illus.*)
need to recruit full-time learners 150
reveals his rapid advancement 41
to a *talmid* 300 (*illus.*)
to Histadrus HaRabbanim 287 (*illus.*)
wonders of Telz and utilizing every moment wisely 148
Levi, Rav Elazar, Rosh Mechinah 179 (*illus.*)

Levin, Rabbi Avrohom Chaim   264, 266
Levin, Rabbi Dovid   240 (*fn*)
Lieff, Rabbi Moshe Tuvia   239 (*illus.*)
life, every moment is precious   252
Likkutei Shiurim   332
Lipins, Dovid   201 (*illus.*)
Lisa, Poland   227
Lithuania   244
Livelihood   209
Lopian, Rav Elyah   51
Lorberbaum, Rav Yaakov   227
Lutzker Rav   140
Luzzatto, Rav Moshe Chaim (*Ramchal*)   142

M

Maharal   260
Maharsha   108
Mandel, Rabbi Shlomo   285
Mannes, Rabbi Hillel   125, 243
Maran, Bob   77
Marcovich, Yossi   207
Marcus, Rav Yosef Yaakov   35
marriage, hallmark of a superlative   340
Mashiach   91, 373
    eagerly awaiting   185
Meidessar, Rav Shmuel Yaakov   39
Meiri   96
Meisels, Reb Yaakov Dovid   62
Meltzer, Rav Isser Zalman   37, 77, 347
Menachos   21
mentch, need to be a   173
Mesillas Yesharim   142
method of learning   272
Miami, Florida   114
Michtav MeEliyahu (*sefer*)   47
Midrash Tanchuma (*sefer*)   309
Midrash, learning Torah directly from the king   109
Mili DeIgros (Volume I)   76
Mili DeIgros (Volume II)   37
Miller, Rav Avigdor   39, 150, 152
Minneapolis, Minnesota   212
Minsker, Reb Leib (Gertzovitz)   59
Mirrer Yeshivah   332
    in Yerushalayim   89, 99
Mishkan Yisrael shul   35
Mishneh Torah (*sefer*)   228
Mission, to fulfill Hashem's will   102
Moetzes Gedolei HaTorah   175
Mordechai HaYehudi   21
Moreh Nevuchim (journal)   373
Moriah   222
Mosdos Ohr HaTorah   303 (*illus.*)
    girls' division   304
Moshav Mattisyahu   214, 217

Moshe Rabbeinu   46, 78, 228, 229, 260, 309, 315
Movshovitz, Rav Daniel, of Kelm   110
Munkatcher Rebbe   242, 242 (*fn*), 383
Mussar
    appreciation of   170
    in Telz   244
    precious if one knows its value   171
    sharp, to the point and effective   207
Myers, Mr. and Mrs.   226 (*illus.*)

N

NCSY, National Council of Synagogue Youth   360
Neilah   115
Nefesh HaChaim   324
Ner Yisrael   318
Nesivos HaMishpat   23, 227, 260
Nesivos Mordechai   218 (*illus.*), 220 (*illus.*), 221 (*illus.*), 222
Nesivos Olam   260
Neuberger, Rabbi Boruch   18
Nevis, Reb Zelig   131 (*fn*)
Noach HaTzaddik   307
Novominsker Rebbe   103 (*illus.*)
Nussbaum, Rav Chaim   15, 38 (*fn*), 87(*fn*), 94 (*fn*), 125, 125 (*illus.*), 156, 163 (*fn*), 178 (*fn*), 232 (*illus.*), 277, 278 (*illus.*), 301 (*fn*)
    children of   108 (*illus.*)
Nutwood Farms   16

O

Oelbaum, Reb Eli   182 (*fn*)
Ohr Elchanan   19
Ohr Same'ach [Rav Meir Simchah HaKohen of Dvinsk]   46, 235, 372, 372 (*illus.*)
Ohr Zarua   192
Oklansky, Rav Avner   60 (*illus.*), 227 (*illus.*)
Oklansky, Rebbetzin Miriam   60 (*illus.*)
Oppenheimer, S.   376
Orach Meisharim   37
Ordman, Chasia (Bloch)   232 (*illus.*)
Ordman, Rav Yisroel   232 (*illus.*)

P

Paperman, Rabbi Aharon   46, 151, 307 (*illus.*)
Partzovitz, Rav Nachum   89
Pe'er Mordechai (Torah publication)   260
Perl, Rabbi Moshe Yaakov   45 (*fn*), 201 (*illus.*)
Pesach seder   345, 346
Pirkei Emunah   23, 222
Pirkei Emunah, Maamad Har Sinai   310 (*fn*)
Pirkei Iyun (sefer)   222
Pirkei Moed (sefer)   222
Pirkei Torah (sefer)   221 (*illus.*)

Pirkei Torah, Devarim 341
Pirkei Torah, Vayikra 278
Pitei Minchah (sefer) 220 (*illus.*), 222
Pliskin, Rabbi Zelig 154, 278, 304, 317,
Pogromansky, Rav Mordechai
  (Mottel) 49ff, 50, 64, 108, 145, 370, 371
Poleyeff, Rav Moshe Aharon 37, 37 (*illus.*),
  40, 56, 101, 208
Poliakoff, Mendel (Manuel) 61 (*illus.*), 151
Ponovezher, Rav Itzele 322
Portnoy, Samuel 71
Portsmouth, Virginia 17, 33, 36, 359
potential, how to maximize 263
praise, as a motivational tool 258ff
Pressburg Czechoslovakia 109, 227, 236
Pri Eitz Chaim (journal) 222
prophecy, essence of 309
Purim 351
  in Telz-Stone 344 (*illus.*)

R

Rabban Yochanan ben Zakkai 228
Rabbeinu Avraham Min HaHar 111
Rabbeinu Gershom Me'or HaGolah 229
Rabbeinu Yonah 360
Rabbi Akiva 115, 214, 229, 272, 384
Rabbi Eliezer 360, 384
Rabbi Yehudah HaNasi 229
Rabinovich, Rav Moshe Leib 242
Rabinowitz, Rav Azriel 49, 208
Rabinowitz, Rabbi Chaim Dov, letter to 86
  (*illus.*)
Rabinowitz, Rav Chaim (Telzer) 49, 49
  (*illus.*), 63
Rabinsky, Mr. Asher 296
Rachel, wife of Rabbi Akiva 115
rainbow, Heavenly sign that we have
  sinned 192
Rakefet 90, 91 (*illus.*)
Rambam 111, 177, 228, 258, 275, 309, 368,
  373, 379, 380, 391,
Ramban 362
Ran 97, 110
Rapaport, Dovid Simcha, wedding of 349
  (*illus.*)
Rapaport, Reb Leibish 349 (*illus.*)
Rashba 97, 108, 112, 137
Rashbam 97
Rashi 96. 112, 229
Ratzkofsky, Reb Itzele 181
Rav Abba bar Kahana 229
Rav Ashi 228
Rav Berachiah 229
Rav Meir Simchah HaKohen [Ohr
  Same'ach] 46, 235, 372, 372 (*illus.*)
Rav Tzadok HaKohen of Lublin 192

Rayan, Latvia 66
Reisman, Mr. & Mrs., 351 (illus.)
Reisman, Rebbetzin Chasya (Gifter) 319
  (*illus.*), 337 (*illus.*), 339 (*fn*), 351 (*illus.*)
Reisman, Rav Yaakov 101, 134 (*fn*), 135,
  189, 222 (*fn*), 262 (*illus.*), 264, 277, 319
  (*illus.*), 351 (*illus.*)
Rennert, J. 376
Riets, see Yeshivas Rabbeinu Yitzchak
  Elchanan
Rishonim 112
Rivash 96
Riverdale, New York 263
Rivkah Imeinu 229
Robinson, R. 376
Rosen, Rav Yosef (Rogatchover Gaon) 53,
  372, 372 (*illus.*)
Rosenberg, Moshe 298
Rosenbaum, Reb Yankel 294 (*fn*)
Rosh Hashanah 20, 139ff, 180, 189, 236,
  246, 247, 251, 281, 302, 307, 324, 362, 364,
  366, 367, 368, 375, 377
Rosh 97, 383
Rothschild, Reb Meir Amshel 360
Rozovsky, Rav Shmuel 97
Rubinstein, Rabbi Kalman 90 (*fn*), 91, 374
Ruderman, Rav Yaakov Yitzchok 112
  (*illus.*), 130 (*illus.*), 258, 277 (*illus.*)

S

Salanter, Rav Yisrael 274, 329
Samson, Rabbi Hyman 318, 318 (*illus.*)
Sanhedrin 384
Sapirman, Reb Aharon 78 (*fn*)
Sar, Dr. Shmuel 42, 42 (*illus.*)
  letter to the Waterbury community
  76 (*illus.*)
Sarah Imeinu 229, 260
Schechter, Rav Aaron 348 (*illus.*)
Scheinerman, Moshe 91
Scherman, Rabbi Nosson 36 (*fn*), 101 (*fn*),
  166, 167 (*fn*), 211 (*fn*), 311 (*fn*)
Schmeltzer, Rav Chaim 264 (*illus.*), 266
Schneider, Rabbi Yisroel 114, 218 (*fn*), 219
Schreiber, Rav Moshe 227
Schuster, Rabbi Harold 77
Schwab, Rav Shimon 254 (*illus.*)
Schwadron, Rav Shalom 330 (*illus.*)
Schwartz, Rabbi Avrohom Nachman 39
Schwartz, Rabbi Yitzchak 216 (*fn*)
science, proof that a Greater Force is at the
  helm 184
secular studies 155
Seder Hayom of Telz Yeshivah, Lita
  1928 90 (*illus.*)
sefarim, written by Rav Gifter 222

Index ☐ 411

Sefer HaChinuch 85
Sefirah 347
Shaarei Teshuvah (sefer) 360
Shach, Rav Elazar Menachem Mann 76, 97, 98 (*illus.*), 101, 147 (*illus.*), 167, 245, 245 (*illus.*), 310 (*illus.*), 310, 343, 373
   letter from 310 (*illus.*)
      shanah tovah greeting from 374 (*illus.*)
Shadav 164
shalom bayis, first and foremost 329
Shapiro, Rav Aharon Yeshaya 88 (*illus.*)
Shapiro, Rav Moshe 51, 113
Shapiro, Rav Shalom 218
Shavuos 349
She'eilos U'Teshuvos Achiezer 329 (*fn*)
Sheim MiShmuel (sefer) 242
Sheinerman, Yitzchak 376
Sheinfeld, Aharon Yosef 181
Shemonah Perakim (Rambam) 111
Sher, Rav Issac 53
Sherer, Rabbi Moshe 86
Shimon HaAmsoni 271, 272
Shkop, Rav Shimon 35, 35 (*illus.*), 274, 318
shmuess delivered by Rav Gifter
   Essence of *teshuvah* and *shofar* 379
   Our duty is to study His Torah 370*ff*
Shmulevitz, Rav Chaim 348 (*illus.*)
shofar-blowing 375
Shomer Shabbos and Khal Yereim shuls 298
Shoshanah, Rabbi Avrohom 233 (*fn*)
Shulman, Rabbi Eli 94 (*fn*)
Siegel, Mr. Morris (Yosef Moshe HaLevi) 147
Siegel, Pesach 229 (*illus.*)
Silver, Rav Eliezer 130 (*illus.*), 377 (*illus.*)
Simchas Torah 116, 350
Sinai 380
Shirvint, Lithuania 318
Six-Day War 279
Slabodka, Lithuania 53, 150, 152
Slonim, Reb Shlomo 85 (*fn*), 112 (*fn*), 122 (*fn*), 133 (*fn*), 226 (*fn*), 254 (*fn*), 295 (*fn*)
Slutzk, Belarus 37
Sofer, Rav Moshe 109
Soloveitchik, Rav Chaim 323
Soloveitchik, Rav Moshe 41 (*illus.*), 42, 101
Soloveitchik, Rav Yitzchak Ze'ev (Brisker Rav) 22, 41 (*illus.*), 64, 325
Soloveitchik, Rav Yosef Dov 122, 211
Sorotzkin, Rav Baruch 16, 84, 92, 125, 130 (*illus.*),247, 249, 274 (*illus.*), 319, 319 (*illus.*), 325, 349 (*illus.*)
Sorotzkin, Rav Leizer (Eliezer) 204, 280 (*illus.*)

Sorotzkin, Reb Yosef 280 (*illus.*)
Sorotzkin, Rav Zalman 140, 333 (*illus.*)
Sova, Reb Yudi 310
Spector, Rav Yitzchak Elchanan 39, 370
speech, delivered by Rav Gifter
   body vs. soul 157
   Churban Holocaust *Beis HaMikdash* 186*ff*
   drawing close to Hashem 362*ff*
   final days in Telz, Lithuania 69
   Hashem punishes like a father 188
   learning, one must amass knowledge, then understanding 96*ff*
   love of Torah means no time off 115
   on the majesty of Telz 59
   on Tishah B'Av; exile of the Holocaust 187
   striving for success by maximizing potential 235
   time, a moment wasted is a moment lost 139
   time, every wasted moment is life-threatening 138
   to make total immersion is primary 96*ff*
   Torah law is unique 174
   Torah, cure for all the ills of society 154
   wonders of Creation 182 *ff*
Spero, Dr. Abba 82 (*fn*)
Spero, Rabbi Aryeh 199 (*fn*)
Spero, Chaim Isaac (Herbert I.) 16, 82, 82 (*fn*)
Spero, Yehudah 16
Stein, Aron 171 (*illus.*)
Stein, Rav Chaim 61 (*illus.*), 114 (*illus.*), 141 (*illus.*), 179 (*illus.*), 224, 258
Stein, Rebbetzen Naomi 332, 332 (*illus.*), 333
Stein, Rav Pesach 62 (*illus.*), 122, 130 (*illus.*), 276, 276 (*illus.*), 332, 333
Stein, Rav Pesach and Rebbetzin Naomi, grandchildren of 333
Steipler Gaon 56, 56 (*illus.*),92, 101, 258
   funeral of 147 (*illus.*)
Stern, Rav Yosef Zecharyah (Zecher Yehoyasaf) 33
Stone, Mr. Irving 87, 204 (*illus.*)
stringencies, self-imposed 277
Succos 116, 350
Suchard, Rabbi Mutty 256, 256 (*illus.*), 312 (*fn*)
Suchard, Rabbi Tzodok 279, 280 (*illus.*), 336, 337
Sutton, Nechemia 203
Svei, Rav Elya 102 (*illus.*)

T

Takanas Ezra (Rav Ezra Altschuler)   53
Talmidim, early 1950's   314 (*illus.*)
Talmudical Academy in Baltimore   39, 318
Talpios (journal)   222
Tarshish, Reb Peretz   17, 34
Taz   128
teaching
    deep bond, anchor in Torah, rooted in *mesorah*   17
    focus on the students   200
teaching Torah, in time of adversity   193
tefillah   365
Tehillim   90, 380
    as an expression of gratitude   184
    in tears and in gratitude   294
Telshe Yeshiva, Chicago   264ff, 266
Telz, Lithuania   59 (*illus.*), 236
    legacy of   71
Telz Yeshivah, Cleveland   78, 80
    chanukas habayis, Rav Gifter speaking   85 (*illus.*)
    student body   312 (*illus.*)
Telz Yeshivah, Lithuania   42, 43ff, 52 (*illus.*) 313
    final days in   66ff
    Seder HaYom of   90 (*illus.*)
Telzer, Rav Leizer   149
Telz-Stone   87, 122, 204 (*illus.*), 310
Ten Days of Repentance   *see Yamim Noraim*
Terumas HaMelech (sefer)   53
teshuvah   362, 364
Three Weeks   349
time, each new moment is an opportunity   179
    sanctified by Shabbos and Yom Tov   344
Tishah B'Av   373
Torah Journals, in which R' Gifter's articles appeared   222
Torah leaders, troubled by desecration of   146
Torah learning as a zechus for recovery   296
Torah novella teen-age Mordechai Gifter   40 (*illus.*)
Torah U'Tefillah shul   298
Torah Umesorah   85
Torah
    all-encompassing   155
    his primary interest   107
    incorporating in all our actions   236
    more precious than diamonds   116
    must be evident in all one's actions   20

    need for total immersion to succeed in   132
    need to toil in learning   132
    Rav Gifter was the embodiment of   19
    recovery in merit of intense learning   125
    sharing with others   239
    surpasses all logic   127
    understanding the truth   271
    viewed through Torah spectacles   146
Tosafos   21, 96, 99, 108, 383
tragedy, not the natural course of events   380
truth
    a standard to be upheld   271ff
    always seeking   273
    in every word Rav Gifter spoke   16
    taking a stand for   285ff
Turk, Moshe   182
Tze'akah, a language without words   381

U

Uganda, Africa   183

V

Vaad Hatzalah of Agudas HaRabbanim   188
Varsha [Warsaw], Poland   236, 237 (*illus.*)
Veinuter Rav   272, 309
Veitzner Rav   262 (*illus.*)
Vessler, Rav Avrohom   58 (*illus.*), 60 (*illus.*)
Vessler, Rebbetzin Shoshana   60 (*illus.*)
Vilkomir, Lithuania   53
Vilna Gaon   110, 112, 139, 370
Vilna, Lithuania   110
Virbaln, Lithuania   63
Volozhiner, Rav Itzele   324

W

Waldman, Aron   98 (*illus.*), 229 (*illus.*)
Washington, D.C.   76
Wasserman, Rav Elchanan   19
Waterbury, Connecticut   38, 73, 112, 288, 307
    house   77 (*illus.*)
    planting seeds of Torah   78
    R' Gifter lasting impact on   75
    taking leave of   81
Waterbury Hebrew Institute   73 (*illus.*), 74 (*illus.*), 75
Weinberg, Rav Chaim Aharon   117, 222 (fn)
Weinberg, Mordechai   376
Weiss, Tommy   243
Weissmandl, Rav Michoel Ber   188
Westwood, New Jersey   264
will of Hashem   178

Index   ☐   413

Wise, Stephen   288
world events are Hashem's message to us   190

Y

YABI (*Yeshivath Adath B'nai Israel*)   174
Yale University   112
Yamim Noraim   21, 324, 360, 362, 364*ff*, 375
   solemnity not sorrow   366
Yavneh   305 (*illus.*)
Yehoshua   229
Yelen, Rabbi Eli   90 (*fn*), 159, 185 (*fn*)
Yeshiva Ateres Shmuel of Waterbury   77
Yeshiva Darchei Torah   101
Yeshiva Lane, Baltimore   121, 318
Yeshiva of the Telshe Alumni   263, 264*ff*
Yeshiva Ohr David   241
Yeshiva University   244
Yeshivah Rabbi Chaim Berlin   184
Yeshivah Torah Ve'eumah Parochial School   39
Yeshivah Toras Chaim of South Shore   135
Yeshivas Bais Yehuda, Detroit   243
Yeshivas Chofetz Chaim   73
Yeshivas Ner Yisrael   18, 72
Yeshivas Ohr Samayach   305
Yeshivas Rabbeinu Yitzchak Elchanan (Riets)   36, 37, 79, 122, 313
Yeshivat Ateret Torah   117
Yeshivat Porat Yosef   296
Yeshivath Adath B'nai Israel   174
Yesodei HaTorah   309
yetzer hara, need to fight against   181
Yevamos   383
Yiddish, importance of   167
Yom Kippur   66, 115, 247, 258, 324, 335, 364, 366, 367, 379
Yom Kippur Katan   357
Yom Kippur War   189*ff*
Young Israel of Cleveland   81, 85, 303, 361
Yurowitz, Reb Pinchas   348 (*illus.*)

Z

zealousness   164*ff*, 165
Zecher Yehoyasaf (Stern, Rav Yosef Zecharyah)   33
zemiros, an opportunity for inspiration   344
zerizus (alacrity)   235
Zlotowitz, Rabbi Meir   166, 281, 281 (*illus.*)
Zusmanowitz, Rav Yosef   53, 151
Zwiebel, Reb Chaim Dovid   86
   letter   176 (*illus.*)